I0606143

THE RULING FAMILIES OF RUS

DYNASTIES

A series of substantial narrative histories that look at the genesis of dynasties, their dynamics and the derivation of power, demonstrating that history can be seen and reflected through the dynastic process and who or what ruling dynasties believed themselves to be. It seeks to put dynasties under discussion and reflection.

Already published:

Ashoka and the Maurya Dynasty: The History and Legacy of Ancient India's Greatest Empire
COLLEEN TAYLOR SEN

The Braganzas: The Rise and Fall of the Ruling Dynasties of Portugal and Brazil, 1640–1910
MALYN NEWITT

The Ruling Families of Rus: Clan, Family and Kingdom
CHRISTIAN RAFFENSPERGER AND DONALD OSTROWSKI

THE RULING FAMILIES OF RUS

Clan, Family and Kingdom

CHRISTIAN RAFFENSPERGER
AND DONALD OSTROWSKI

REAKTION BOOKS

Published by
Reaktion Books Ltd
Unit 32, Waterside
44–48 Wharf Road
London N1 7UX, UK

www.reaktionbooks.co.uk

First published 2023

Printed and bound in India by Replika Press Pvt. Ltd

A catalogue record for this book is available from the British Library

ISBN 978 1 78914 715 5

Contents

1 Rus and Europe, *c.* 1100.

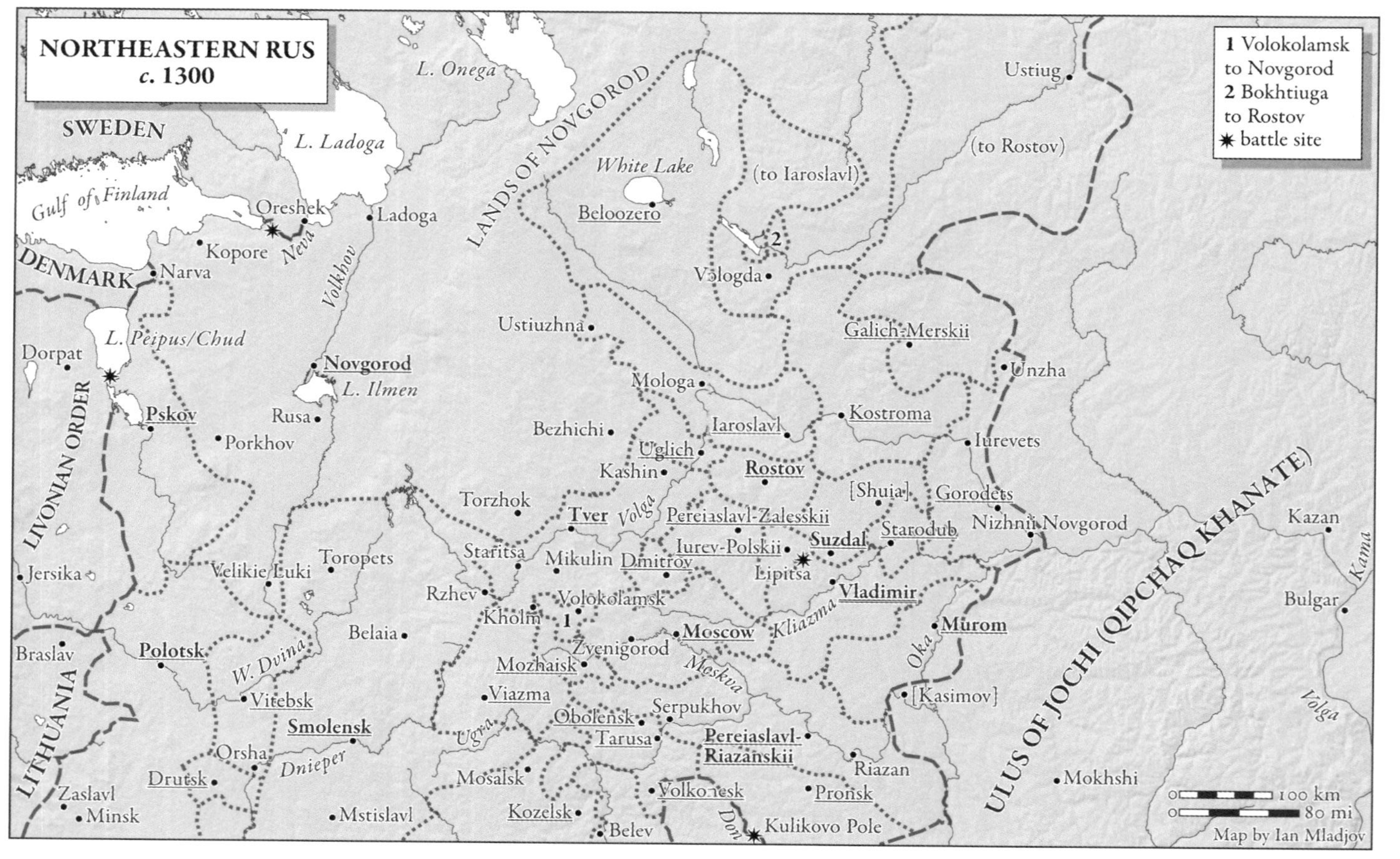

2 Northeastern Rus, *c.* 1300.

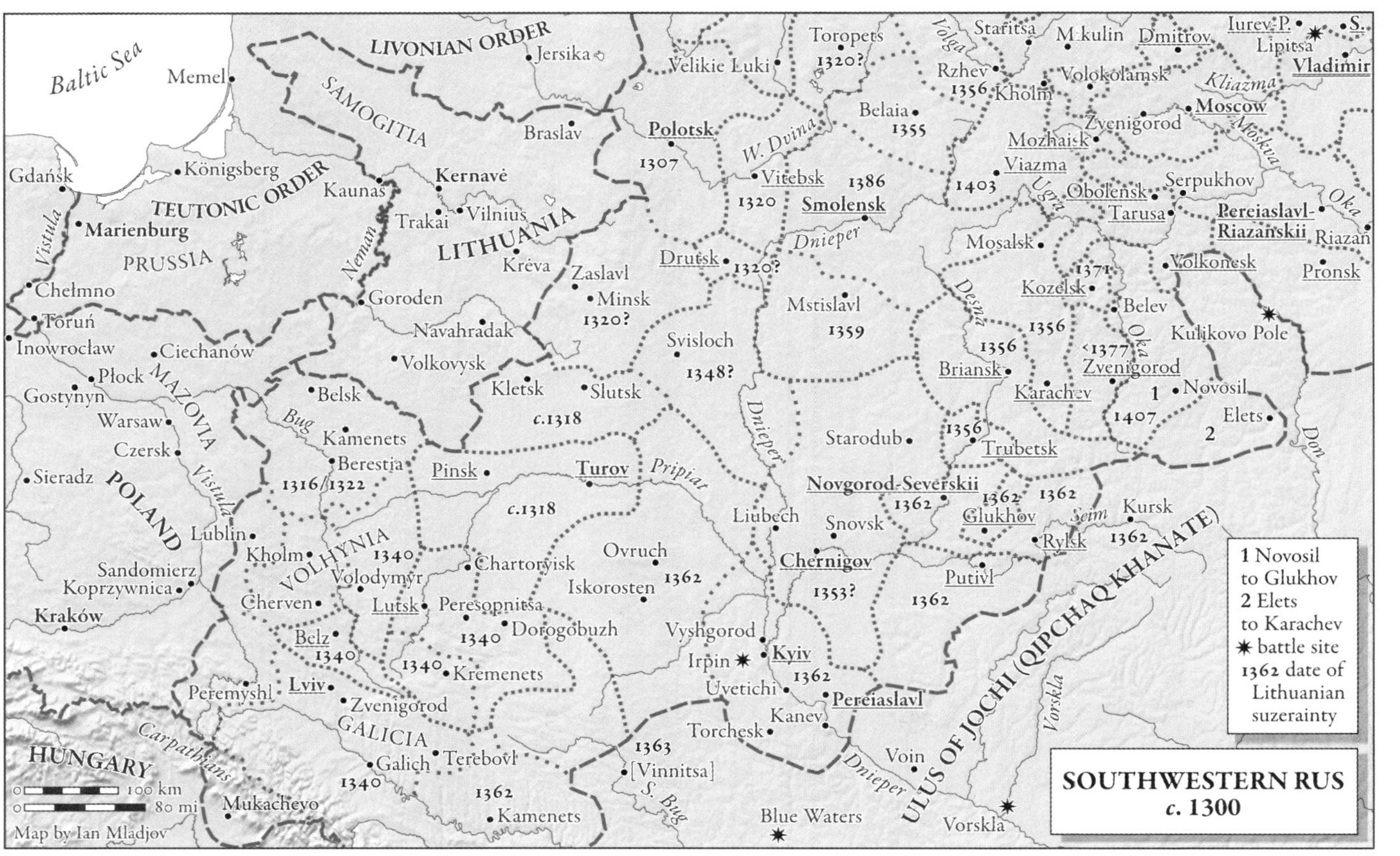

3 Southwestern Rus, *c.* 1300.

Introduction: The Problem with Dynasty

A typical dictionary definition of the word *dynasty* is 'a line of hereditary rulers of a country'.[1] This rather innocuous definition conceals a historiographical problem. Apropos of this problem, the Polish historian Natalia Nowakowska, in her study of the Jagiellonian dynasty (*c.* 1385–1572), concluded that a change in the definition of the term occurred with the publication of the fifth volume of the French *Encylopédie* in 1755, which changed the meaning from any 'government' or 'regime' in general to the specific definition 'a hereditary line of princes'.[2] Yet, according to the *Oxford English Dictionary*, the usage of the term 'dynasty' to mean 'a succession of rulers of the same line or family; a line of kings or princes' pre-dates the other meaning of 'lordship, sovereignty, power, regime', which it now considers obsolete.[3] For the history of Rus, the term 'dynasty' is woefully inadequate in relation to the dictionary definition and is misleading in relation to the source evidence. Historians have indeed focused on those who ruled, presenting them as part of a hereditary line, as the typical genealogical table of Rus rulers indicates. However, doing so overlooks half of our evidence; knowing who was married to each ruler and to those in line to rule, as well as who their parents and children were, is an essential part of understanding the context of our sources. If we ignore their familial ties, we not only risk presenting, but indeed do present only part of the story they have to tell, ignoring the rest.

But there is an even larger problem, that of anachronism. By using the concept of 'dynasty', we are imposing on the rulers of particular towns in Rus a mindset for which we have no evidence. Did Iaroslav the Wise consider himself a 'Riurikid' and a member of the 'Riurikid dynasty'? Did Vsevolod 'Big Nest' Iurevich, or Alexander Nevsky?[4]

There is no evidence that they did. One might respond that, surely, they must have positioned themselves as part of the Riurikid dynasty as a way to legitimize their claim to rule and increase their charisma, much as contemporary leaders do. Well, no. The evidence tells us, instead, that until the second half of the fifteenth century, rulers in Rus legitimized their claim to rule a particular town by asserting that their father (and later, their father and grandfather, or some variation of father and brother, or father and uncle) ruled it.[5] We find no connection to Riurik or any assertion that they are part of a dynasty. We do not see the invocation of 'a line of hereditary rulers' going back to Riurik until the end of the fifteenth and the beginning of the sixteenth centuries, when such tales as the *Story about Vladimir Kniazi* began to appear (see Chapter Twelve). If one wants to use the assertion of 'my father ruled' or 'my father and grandfather ruled' as the basis for a dynastic claim in terms of our dictionary definition of 'a line of hereditary rulers', then this assertion can only be used to support the claim that Iaroslav saw himself as a member of the Volodimer 'dynasty'. Vsevolod saw himself as a member of the Iurevich 'dynasty' or, at most, of another Volodimer line, that of Volodimer Monomakh (his grandfather); Alexander Nevsky saw himself as a member of the Iaroslavich 'dynasty' or, at most, of the Vsevolodovich 'dynasty' (Vsevolod being his grandfather). In other words, any particular right to rule belonged to the immediate family, as evidenced by the invoking of 'father' along with 'grandfather', 'brother' and/or 'uncle', not to a larger dynastic entity. The point of this book is to explore the concept of the family rule of local towns and how that morphed through the centuries into the concept of the Riurikid dynasty, to which scholars are so fond of ascribing the first six hundred years of Rus history.

Another problem with imposing such a dynastic construct on pre-1500 Rus history is its lending an air of inevitability to the eventual outcome of the competition for the title of ruling family, which is exactly what the winning family wanted to achieve. The Daniilovich clan (the rulers of Moscow), a sub-branch of the Aleksandrovichi of Pereiaslavl who were, in turn, a sub-branch of the Iaroslavichi of Vladimir, won out in the person of Ivan III. Why did that clan rule and not the Iaroslavichi of Tver, or the Daniilovichi of Galicia and Volhynia, or even the Olgierdovichi of Lithuania? These other clans were all excellent candidates to become the inheritors of Rus. However, the dynastic rhetoric of texts such as the *Stepennaia kniga*, from the second half of the sixteenth century, presented the generational steps or degrees from Volodimer I to Ivan IV as being divinely guided. In highlighting that apparently providential intervention, such works diminished the significance of competitors and historical alternatives. Those historians who are in 'read–write' mode tend to repeat such Muscovite rhetoric uncritically, much as the White House correspondents of today sometimes merely repeat verbatim the press briefings that they are handed.

Such panegyrical histories also diminish the role of wives, mothers and daughters in the process. The structure of Rus politics was defined by the rulers (*kniazi*), but the relationships among the ruling families were defined by the wives, mothers and daughters of the rulers, both through alliances formed by marriage and, more directly, through the influence of particularly well-placed, politically astute women like Iuliana Alexandrovna of Tver, the wife of Algirdas of Lithuania, and Sofia Vitovtna, who served as regent for her son Vasilii II during his minority.

By focusing on various ruling families rather than on the dynastic construct of the one family that finally won the right to rule, we hope to show the contingencies of history and the paths not taken. As the historian David McCullough wrote: 'Because the outcome of great events becomes so well established in our minds, there is a tendency to think things had to go as they did. But there is nothing inevitable about history.'[26] For us, at least, the lack of inevitability makes the history of Rus richer and much more interesting.

✢

WE WILL ATTEMPT to keep the focus throughout this book on the members of the Volodimerovich clan and their descendants and, by doing so, demonstrate the multiplicity of identities inherent within that clan. We have chosen this technique as one that will help us to avoid problematic national or nationalistic terminology (which is anachronistic anyway) and will allow us to look at individual people and how they shaped their families, clans, and the growth of their own areas and polities. What follows is a brief overview and plan of the chapters to help orient the reader.

Chapter One lays out the background behind the kingdom of Rus itself, with a focus on the foundation of Rus by the Scandinavians, the kingdom's early contacts with neighbouring powers and the

Christianization of Volodimer Sviatoslavich. It also discusses the historiographical complications inherent in writing about the kingdom of Rus – all of which create a foundation for the following chapters.

Chapter Two discusses a few key principles that will be used to further build a base for the rest of the book. The first part presents the argument for focusing on the Volodimerovich clan, rather than the more common Riurikid dynasty. The second part will discuss why the book is orientated around family ties – a particular focus on a married couple and their children provides a way to better understand what is going on with the larger clan, the kingdom and, most importantly, the individuals who make up those other entities. The final part will deal with the issues of collateral succession and inheritance in Rus. The collateral system of succession was a mutually agreed-upon grammar of 'rules'. It had three major component parts: (1) eligibility (whether someone's father had ruled, but only down to the fourth son); (2) self-regulation (whether the other members of the ruling family or clan recognized that person's authority); and (3) external regulation (whether the townspeople accepted that person as the ruler of their town). The system had a certain flexibility built into it.

Chapter Three focuses on one of the most famous rulers of eleventh-century medieval Europe, the son of Volodimer the Christianizer of Rus. Iaroslav married a Swedish princess, Ingigerd; together, they hosted multiple foreign rulers who spent time in Rus, and they married their children to royalty from Anglo-Saxon England, Norway, France, Poland, Hungary and Byzantium. This was not just a Rusian or a Volodimerovich family, but a family that intermeshed with all of medieval Europe.

Chapter Four deals with a ruler who had many names. In fact, many Rusian rulers had two names, a Christian one and a Rusian one; for Mstislav, these were Fëdor (Theodore) and Mstislav. Like his father, however, Mstislav also had a third name, indicative of his mother's family – Harald; this was for his maternal grandfather, the last Anglo-Saxon ruler of England, Harold Godwinson. Mstislav/Harald himself married first a Scandinavian princess, Kristín Ingesdottir of Sweden, and subsequently the daughter of the mayor of Novgorod, one of the few non-royal marriages for which we have sources. This family, like Iaroslav's, was deeply interconnected with other medieval European families; however, Mstislav also solidified his own family's hold on power in Kyiv, at the expense of other members of his clan.

Chapter Five focuses upon the ruler of Vladimir-Suzdal, an area of Rus between the Volga and Oka rivers, northeast of the Dnieper River valley and Kyiv. This area was one of new development and burgeoning wealth, and Vsevolod, following his father, Iurii Dolgorukii ('Long-Arm'), and his brother, Andrei Bogoliubskii ('God-Lover'),[7] was keen to make the region a new centre of Rus. Vsevolod's own marriages, entirely internal to Rus, demonstrate the changing focus away from the rest of medieval Europe, which would become one of the hallmarks of the family, while, at the same time, his and his family's architectural and economic interests were still enmeshed with medieval Europe in general. This family of Volodimerovichi is typically viewed from the modern Russian historical perspective as foreshadowing the growth of Muscovy, although they are presented here in the context of the wider clan at the time.

Chapter Six deals with a contemporary and sometime rival of Vsevolod 'Big Nest' Iurevich, Roman Mstislavich. Roman is acknowledged to be the founder of Galicia-Volhynia (often considered a predecessor of western Ukraine) in the southwest of Rus. Roman's world was a wide one, involving negotiations with other members of the Volodimerovichi to devise a system of succession for Kyiv, as well as intervention in Polish conflicts, attacks against the Polovtsy (who were steppe nomads), negotiations with the Hungarian king, the sending of emissaries to the Byzantine emperor and much more. He and his family stand in, then, not just for an interesting period in Volodimerovichi history, but as a break from the typical 'Russian-centric' narrative of progression from Kyiv to Moscow.

Chapter Seven deals with the famous ruler of Novgorod who fought the Teutonic Crusaders and conceded to the Mongols. Qagan Güyük granted the rulership of Kyiv first to Alexander's father and then to Alexander himself; while to Alexander's younger brother, Andrei, he granted rulership over Vladimir-on-the-Kliazma during their sojourn in Qaraqorum in 1248. Andrei fled Rus in 1252, when Khan Batu sent an army against Andrei in conjunction with an army against Andrei's father-in-law, Daniil of Galicia, most likely because he saw them as involved in a papal anti-Mongol conspiracy. Batu gave the rulership of Vladimir to Alexander, while allowing him to remain the ruler of Kyiv. Alexander's reign, his relations with the Mongols and Catholic Europe, and the story of his children involves international political intrigue from Rome to Qaraqorum.

Chapter Eight concerns the grandson of Alexander Nevsky, Iurii Daniilovich, who was one of the first notable rulers of Moscow. In 1315, Iurii went to the Mongol capital of Sarai, gained the favour of Khan Uzbeg and married the khan's daughter, Konchaka. As a result, he was the first ruler of Moscow to gain the patent (*iarlyk*) from the Mongols that gave him the right to collect taxes, and even negotiated for Mongol assistance in his own struggle against his Volodimerovich brethren in the city of Tver. Moreover, his son Ivan, later nicknamed 'Moneybags' (*Kalita*), cemented Moscow's power through his continuing tax collection for the Mongols, using the metropolitanate authority to enhance both his own power (as well as vice versa) and ultimately his claim to being the ruler of Vladimir.

Chapter Nine shifts the focus away from the Volga–Oka River region back to the areas southwest of Kyiv. Here Iurii and his father Lev were rulers in Galicia–Volhynia in the fourteenth century, after the family line of Roman Mstislavich (discussed in Chapter Six) had died out. Like Roman, their rule engaged the various players who bordered on this region, such as the Tatars, Hungarians, Poles (including Iurii's spouse), Byzantines (which entailed the creation of a new metropolitanate) and Lithuanians, new arrivals with whom Iurii contended. Within the kingdom, Iurii and his father shifted the power base of the region to the city of Volodymyr; Iurii took the city's emblem of a mounted knight for his own on his seals, on which he named himself 'King of Rus, Prince of Volodymyr'.

Chapter Ten is the only one of the chapters to focus explicitly upon a specific woman as the centre of the family. Uliana was the daughter of the ruler of Tver, in the northeast region of Rus. She was the granddaughter of Iurii Lvovich from the southwest of Rus and, in her person, combined those two families. Furthermore, she was married to the powerful ruler of Lithuania, Algirdas. Uliana was a pivotal figure in the history of eastern Europe. It was her son, Jogaila, who inherited the right to rule in Lithuania, eventually taking Poland as well; she was the dowager involved in all the marital arrangements and political manoeuvring during the conflicts in Lithuania and Poland at that time. According to traditional dynastic language, her family would be treated as Algirdas's family – but within the concept of families discussed in this book, we can see that Uliana is a powerful woman, the matriarch of a family and a member of the Volodimerovich clan as well.

Chapter Eleven focuses on the son of the famed ruler of Moscow, Dmitri Donskoi. Early in Vasilii's reign, he fastened his power and ties to those of the Mongols through his submission to Khan Toqtamish, in exchange for a patent of rule, eventually gaining additional territories. However, Vasilii also benefitted from discord among the Mongols, which led him to build his own ties with the Lithuanians, including marrying Sofia, the daughter of Vytautas of Lithuania – although this did not mean peace between the two sides. This was a time of rising prosperity in Moscow, which saw artistic and technological advances via its connections with the rest of Europe, along with a return to a royal Byzantine marriage when Vasilii and Sophia's daughter, Anna, married the Byzantine emperor, John VIII Palaiologos.

Chapter Twelve deals with the aftermath of an internal clan conflict between Vasilii II Vasilevich and his uncle Iurii Dmitrievich, as well as with his two sons, Vasilii Kosoi and Dmitrii Shemiaka. When Vasilii II eventually won out in 1453, he appointed his own son, Ivan, as co-ruler and ended the receiving of patents (*iarlyki*) by local Rusian rulers from the khan of the Orda, declaring that they now had to receive such patents from him. Ivan himself undertook a number of changes in the organizational structure of Muscovy and brought in Italian engineers and architects, who gave the Moscow Kremlin the look it has today. Ivan used the title of *tsar* sparingly and judiciously to grant safe passage to merchants and diplomats through his realm (a function that the khan of the Orda used to exercise). It was during his reign and that of his son that the construct of the Moscow rulers being descended from Riurik came into existence (making them the scions of the Riurikid dynasty), thus giving their particular family line precedence over other Volodomirovich family lines.

The Epilogue marks the end of this book but not of the family lines; the story of the Volodimerovichi certainly does not end with the last of the families discussed herein. There are still members of the family today who bear the title of *kniaz* and claim descent from Volodimer Sviatoslavich the Christianizer. This chapter will take us to the end of the clan's tenure as rulers of Moscow in the late sixteenth century and follow the continuing importance of the clan in Romanov Russia.

As a whole, one can see that *The Ruling Families of Rus* really is about families and individuals, rather than focusing upon any one dynastic progression from male heir to male heir. We have attempted to define the place of Rus in the medieval world, as well as highlight the important role that women played in these families and clans. We have tried not to be bound by any national structure of history writing – situating these Rusian families both within Rus and in the wider world, rather than binding them in any modern historical narrative that is read back in time. These efforts should make for a historical representation that is as true to the time as we can make it and should provide a thorough introduction to the Volodimerovich clan and its component parts, as well as the territories over which they ruled.

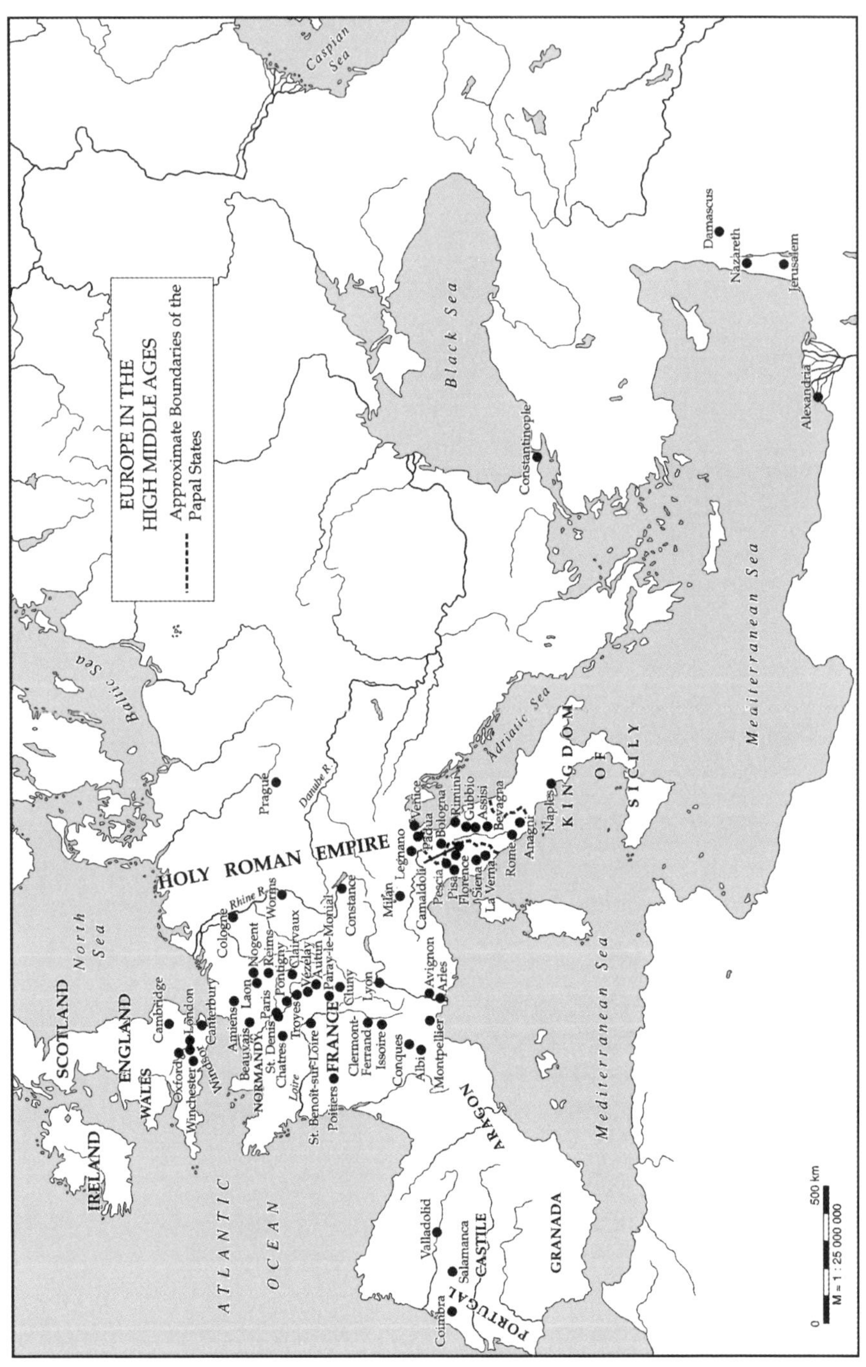

4 Europe in the High Middle Ages (after Cook and Herzman, *The Medieval World View* (1983)).

1

What Is the Kingdom of Rus?

THE RULING FAMILIES OF RUS is about Rus; but what is, or rather was, Rus? Why use this descriptor? This chapter will be bookended by historiography, beginning with a brief discussion of what this polity has been called and ending with a discussion of how it has been represented in some of the scholarship published in the last hundred years. In the middle, we present a narrative developing the early centuries of Rus, from its foundation to the rule of Volodimer Sviatoslavich, the Christianizer of Rus. In this way, we hope to provide a background for subsequent chapters, which discuss the families that ruled this early polity and their many successors throughout the next five hundred years.

You would only rarely find the Kingdom of Rus on an early map if you were to go looking for it. Most representations of medieval Europe do not include much of eastern Europe; although Rus was a large polity by the eleventh century, stretching from the Gulf of Finland in the north and nearly down to the Black Sea in the south, it simply does not appear in them. Take, for example, the map opposite, which is based upon an image from a popular textbook of medieval European history (illus. 4).

As one can see, there is no eastern Europe shown and certainly no Rus, as a kingdom or anything else. Other maps, such as those produced by John Haywood, do show the polity, but simply refer to it as 'Russia', which raises another issue.[1] Russia is a modern state and has incorporated the territories ruled by Rus since roughly the eighteenth century, but before that time, there was a variety of polities that exercised control over the territory that the medieval peoples knew as Rus. These included the Lithuanian, Polish, Ottoman and other polities.

Similarly, in the recent past of the nineteenth and twentieth centuries, the modern state of Ukraine occupied much of the territory formerly ruled by Rus, on the Dnieper River. As one might imagine, the issue of what to call this area has been quite contentious and politically fraught over the years. At the end of the nineteenth and into the early twentieth century, Mykhailo Hrushevsky (who served as the first president of the Central Rada of Ukraine, following the collapse of the Russian Empire, and who was a well-known historian) wrote a multi-volume *History of Ukraine-Rus'*, in which he traced the history of the territory of his modern-day Ukraine back to its beginnings in the first millennium CE. This was part of the process of creating a national background and a claim to power for Ukraine, although he also produced some excellent history in the process.[2] Russian historians similarly claimed the territory of Rus for themselves and for their national history in seminal works such as V. O. Kliuchevskii's multi-volume *History of Russia*, which was written at the same time as Hrushevsky's work.[3] Even in the very recent past, the Russian president, Vladimir Putin, has claimed Rus for Russia as part of his justification of the invasion and annexation of Crimea and for the ongoing war against Ukraine by saying that 'Kiev is the mother of all Russian cities.'[4] Given the politically loaded terminology of calling Rus either Russia or Ukraine, we have followed the policy (common in our own work) of using Rus, the name that was used by the denizens of the time, both internally and externally, to designate this territory. Further, we have continued to use this term when discussing events after the *terminus post quem*, or earliest possible date for, the kingdom of Rus, as each of the successor territories was still identifiable by this description and its rulers utilized the term for their titles.

The Beginnings of Rus

The story of the beginning of Rus is told in the *Povest vremennykh let* (PVL), often translated as 'The Tale of Bygone Years', the main Rusian source for much of the polity's early history. The PVL was written and compiled at the end of the eleventh and the beginning of the twelfth centuries, and so the truth behind the information that it conveys about the foundation period in the ninth century would have already been lost by then to the dim mists of history, surviving instead via received wisdom that was recorded orally, if at all. Nevertheless, for the PVL, the story begins in the year 858/9, where it notes that 'the Varangians [an eastern European name for Vikings] from beyond the sea imposed tribute upon' multiple groups in the eastern European river systems.[5] This was the first indication in the PVL of a Scandinavian presence in eastern Europe. However, if we look beyond this later Rusian source, there is a story in the *Annales Bertiniani*, a Frankish source from the ninth century, that tells of a group of 'Rhos' who were travelling from Byzantium through the Frankish territories to return home. They met with Louis the Pious, who decided that they were Sueones (Swedes, in the English translation) and denied them the ability to continue on their trip northwards.[6] Further, there is plentiful archaeological evidence that Scandinavians had been visiting the eastern shore of the Baltic for many centuries before that time.[7] Typically, the evidence for the Scandinavian origins of the Rus is from finds of Scandinavian materials, such as weapons and glass beads, in the eastern Baltic, along with finds in Scandinavia that were transmitted from and through eastern Europe. Over the course of the eighth and ninth centuries, there was a rise in the transmission of Islamic and Byzantine coins to Scandinavia. The Islamic coins were minted in the Abbasid Caliphate, the capital of which was Baghdad; they were carried north via the Caucasus and the Caspian Sea, and up the Volga to the Bulgars, eventually making their way to Scandinavia. These dirhams (the name for the Islamic coins) have been found in abundant coin hoards in both northern Rus and in Scandinavia, particularly on the island of Birka (illus. 5). The Byzantine coins were minted in Constantinople and followed various routes to northern Rus and Scandinavia. For instance, Byzantine coins and seals from the time of Emperor Theophilos (r. 829–42) have been

5 Silver dirham from the 9th century.

found in Hedeby, Tissø, Birka, Ribe, Gnëzdovo, Spillings, Gorodishche and Styrnäs.[8]

The explorations of these Scandinavian travellers seemed eventually to turn to conquest or, at least, tribute-taking, as recorded by the PVL. However, only a few years later, the PVL says that: 'The tributaries of the Varangians drove them back beyond the sea and, refusing them further tribute, set out to govern themselves.'[9] This expulsion of the tribute-taking Scandinavians is the real beginning of the creation story of Rus; while they were expelled by the local population, the locals proved to be unable to rule themselves and, thus, the 'Varangian Rus' were invited back to rule over them: 'Our land is great and rich, but there is no order in it. Come to rule and reign over us.' Thus, the author of the much later PVL account, writing at the behest of the descendants of these same Rus, or at least for people claiming descent from them, had now created a proper origin story – not one of conquest and bloodshed, but one where their ancestors were invited in as saviours and peacekeepers by a local population who were unable to take care of themselves.

The PVL tells of three brothers who came to eastern Europe and established a territory for themselves. The myth of three brothers as founders is quite a common one, found everywhere from medieval to early modern sources; the myth typically progresses with only one brother surviving and ruling all the territory.[10] The eldest, and surviving, brother in this story was named Riurik; he has sometimes been identified with a ruler named Roric of Jutland, who was known from German sources in the earlier ninth century, although he is likely no relation. The Riurik who is mentioned in this story occupied territory and began taking tribute in what would become northern Rus, near Lake Ladoga and Lake Ilmen. The original settlements seem to have been at Staraia (old) Ladoga and Riurikovo Gorodishche, which have been excavated numerous times, and today are in the Novgorod region of Russia (illus. 6).[11]

These communities in the north would eventually be superseded by the region of Novgorod, which became the second city of Rus after Kyiv. Riurik died, according to the PVL, in 879, after which there began a complicated sequence in Rusian history, in which Riurik passed the right to rule to Oleg, who is listed as a kinsman, and 'entrusted to Oleg's hands his son Igor, for he was very young'.[12] The complication here arises from the fact that Oleg is not the child of Riurik, but he does rule

6 Ruins of a medieval church on the site of Riurikovo Gorodishche.

after him for 33 years (d. 912), ostensibly while raising Riurik's young son, Igor. Igor then rules in place of Oleg until his own death in 945, a rule that lasted 32 years and a lifespan, if he was just one year old at the time of Riurik's death, of some 66 years. This state of affairs is possible, of course, but is widely seen to be unlikely, especially since he remained subordinate to Oleg for the 33 years of Oleg's rule. The narrative of Riurik-Oleg-Igor creates problems for the idea of a dynastic line founded by Riurik, which itself has other problems (as discussed in the Introduction), especially since Oleg's rule was incredibly important in creating a Rusian polity, one that was based in Kyiv and engaged with the Byzantine Empire.

In 882, Oleg mustered his forces and began moving south along the river systems, taking Smolensk and Liubech, eventually arriving at Kyiv. Kyiv at the time was ruled by two different Scandinavian rulers – Askold and Dir.[13] Oleg's taking of Kyiv offers multiple interesting lessons regarding contemporary attitudes to both rulers and the land, as well as how the encounter has been interpreted by modern observers. Using deception, he garnered a meeting with the two rulers and said to them, 'You are not *kniazia* [rulers] nor from the family of rulers, but I am from the family of rulers.'[14] While one must acknowledge that this text was written down approximately two hundred years later, this is still a fascinating statement, in which Oleg clearly states that there was a ruling family and that he was a part of it, while Askold and Dir were not. This appears to be in contrast to the idea expressed earlier that while Oleg was of Riurik's kin, he was ruling only in Igor's stead. However, immediately following this line of the story in the PVL, there is another odd moment when, after stating his own qualifications for ruling, Oleg then produced Igor and proclaimed him to be the son of Riurik.[15] Subsequently, Askold and Dir were killed, and Oleg declared himself the ruler of Kyiv. Again, Oleg is the actor who is making all of this happen and who is a ruler from a ruling family, yet Igor and Igor's connection to Riurik is still mentioned, even if in a seemingly offhand way. One possibility is that the eleventh-century chronicler had access to the various pieces of information about Oleg's rule, Igor and the story of Riurik; he was attempting to knit them into one complete story and this was how he chose to achieve that, treating Oleg's long rule as a sort of extended regency for Igor. Once Oleg was established in Kyiv, he was quoted as saying that it would become the 'mother of Rusian cities',[16] which has, in modern times, been translated as the 'mother of all Russian cities' and is, thus, the basis for the statement that Vladimir Putin made regarding the annexation of Crimea and the war on Ukraine (as mentioned earlier). However, this modern claim of national rule does not seem to have been the intent of the early chronicler, who immediately followed that sentence with one saying that 'the Varangians and Slavs and others who followed him [Oleg] were called Rusians [Rusiu].'[17] With this additional context, it seems clear that the intent of the chronicler was to note that Kyiv was to be the centre of the cities which were ruled by the Rusians, those who followed Oleg, whether they were Scandinavians, Slavs or others.

Unlike Riurik, scholars are quite sure that Oleg is a genuine historical figure, as he appears in multiple sources. One of the most interesting incidents in his life and in the development of Rus is his raid on, and subsequent treaty with, Byzantium. There are three treaties recorded in the PVL; the first is dated immediately following Oleg's raid in 907, while the second is recorded under the year (*sub anno*) 912 and begins with the phrase, 'This is the copy of the treaty.'[18] This second, much more formulaic, treaty conforms to the style established by the Byzantines and others around this same time; thus, it is believed by Frank Edward Wozniak Jr to be copied into the PVL from a then-extant original or copy.[19] The treaty has multiple signatories; on the side of the

Byzantines are the emperors Leo and Alexander, while for the Rusians there are numerous individuals, the majority of whom bear Scandinavian names, such as Karl, Ingolf, Farulf and Vermund. The treaty reads much as one might expect of a modern treaty, in that there are mutual obligations covering punishments, theft and such similar affairs. Interestingly, the treaty appears in many ways to demonstrate the equality of the two sides; for instance, many of the clauses begin with stipulations that penalties or benefits apply to both Rusians and Byzantines ('Christians', as they are called in the text). As a final note to certify the importance and validity of the treaty, it was noted that 'we have caused the present treaty to be transcribed in vermilion script upon parchment in duplicate', so that both sides could possess a copy. This was Oleg's last accomplishment; with the conquest of Smolensk, Liubech and Kyiv, he had created the polity of Rus, from Lake Ladoga in the north through to Kyiv in the south, and had established peaceful relations with the most powerful Christian empire in Eurasia – Byzantium.

Upon Oleg's death in 911, Igor finally assumed rule over Rus. In 903, according to the PVL, Igor married a woman named Olga from Pskov.[20] Although these are the Slavic variants of their names, both are originally Scandinavian – Helga for Olga, and Ingvar for Igor. Their marriage in 903 and the birth of their son Sviatoslav, who was a minor at the time of Igor's own death in 945, represent another problem in the line of succession of early rulers. If Olga was fourteen at the time of her marriage, a reasonable conjecture based upon marital age during this period, she would have been 55 in 945.[21] Sviatoslav does not seem to have taken up ruling on his own until 964.[22] If he had been a minor waiting to come of age, as the PVL suggests, this would be perhaps at sixteen years of age; thus, he would have been born in 948, after Igor had already died. All these issues present a fatal problem for a continuous line of descent from Riurik to Sviatoslav.

Igor, like Oleg before him, raided Constantinople and established a treaty with the Byzantines. However, unlike Oleg's, Igor's raid was an unmitigated disaster, with the Rusian ships being burned by Greek fire, a toxic combination of ingredients known only to the Byzantines that they used to protect Constantinople.[23] Greek fire, most likely made from naphtha and quicklime (calcium oxide), was pumped through pipes and would burn even on the surface of water, making it an excellent weapon to stop naval attacks on the city – only sand and vinegar would quench the fire. Though Igor was defeated, the PVL immediately records a second attack three years later in which Igor is successful and the Byzantines surrendered and negotiated a new treaty. This second attack is possibly a face-saving device by the chronicler, who did not want Igor to be perceived as a failure in his conflict with Byzantium. When we look at the resulting treaty, Igor's defeat can be seen in its less favourable terms, whereby the Rusians receive fewer privileges than they did in the earlier treaty that Oleg negotiated. Despite that shortcoming, the treaty is another formal document, copied into the PVL and attested by both the Byzantine and Rusian signatories. In this instance, the Rusians are not uniformly non-Christian, as they seem to have been in the first treaty, which is evidence of the slow progress of Christianity in Rus. The Rusian signatories also represent another very interesting element of this treaty as there are, once again, many of them; the majority of the named individuals are sent as personal representatives of the Rusian elites. Igor's envoy, Ivar, is the first to be named, as one would expect, but he is followed by a representative of Sviatoslav, Igor's son; one is named for Olga, who is here given the title *kniaginia* (queen); a representative of Igor's nephew and many others, including other representatives present on behalf of women.[24] The presence of all of these representatives confirms the power structure of Rus, with Igor and Olga at the top but with many other key participants, both male and female. Furthermore, the document states that there was a chancellery, an office producing sealed documents, in Kyiv, as merchants from Rus were required to bring sealed documents as proof of their peaceful intent when trading with Byzantium. However, given the status of this treaty as a document copied into the chronicle, not merely a recollection by the chronicler, we can suggest that its provisions are accurate and thus the governance of Rus was developed and documented from an early pre-Christian period. Even though Igor was unsuccessful in his attack on Constantinople, the presence of this important treaty with Byzantium in the PVL tells us much about Rus in the tenth century.

Igor's death immediately following the record of his treaty with Byzantium in 945 gives us further important information about the power structure of Rus. His warband, the personal entourage of warriors that a ruler of whatever rank kept with them and was responsible for, was discontented because other warbands seemed to have been treated better – in a nutshell, they wanted more of the loot. To get them more money, Igor decided to enforce a second tribute upon one of the groups subordinate to him, a group that the PVL termed the Derevlians.

For all concerned, this ended up being a bad decision, in part because Igor had already taken tribute from the Derevlians that year; it seems that this was a regular process when a new ruler took power in Kyiv. The first thing that Igor did was to move out and resubjugate the tribute-paying groups that had been subordinate to his predecessor. The loyalty of those groups, largely based on fear and intimidation, one imagines, was directed towards an individual, not towards any idea of a larger political entity such as we might see in the Byzantine Empire of the period. This tribute-taking was an annual affair, we believe; Igor's attempt to take a second tribute from the Derevlians was an affront both to them and to this process – thus, they refused to pay and fighting ensued. Igor was killed, his warband did not get their pay increase, and the Derevlians felt empowered by their defeat of Igor, leading to their ruler proposing to marry Igor's widow – Olga.

Olga was in charge of Rus following Igor's death, largely due to the fact that their only known son, Sviatoslav, was a minor. Mal, the ruler of the Derevlians, thought to marry Olga and thus take over Rus, perhaps telling us something about Olga's status and that of Rus as a whole. However, this story has become conflated with folk tales that demonstrate Olga's position as a 'wise woman', as the PVL calls her. Over a series of four linked tales, she buries, burns and murders Mal's envoys in increasingly clever ways, and eventually even burns down the Derevlian town with a manoeuvre also attributed to others in such folk tales, including Harald Hardrada. As a condition of making peace with the town, she asked for birds from each house as tribute. Once she had received this tribute, her soldiers tied burning brands to the birds' feet and released them to return to their homes, setting the entire town ablaze, thus completing her revenge on the Derevlians for killing her husband.

This was not Olga's only recorded action as the ruler of Rus. She too is a historical character as she appears in multiple primary sources from Rus, Byzantium and the German Empire. Olga is the first ruler of Rus to visit Byzantium with a peaceful purpose, although what that purpose was is debated. In the PVL's telling of the story, Olga goes to Constantinople to convert to Christianity.[25] Much as with the tales of her revenge against her husband's killers, she is portrayed as a clever woman who is able to outwit her foes. In this situation, Olga does not use her wisdom to find a way to kill her opponent, the Byzantine emperor, but instead demonstrates her superior knowledge of Christianity to trick him. Following the plot of the story, the emperor was smitten with

Olga and desired to marry her, but she was not yet a Christian. She declared that she would convert to Christianity only if he would baptize her and stand as godfather, a requirement for baptism in the medieval church. Olga is baptized, the emperor proposes, and Olga displays her knowledge of the law, noting that because the emperor stood as godfather to her, under Christian law, it would be unlawful for them to marry; at which point the emperor says simply, 'Olga, you have outwitted me!' While the story is largely taken up with conversion and a Christian history lesson in the voice of the Patriarch of Constantinople, the PVL entry concludes the story on an odd note; after her return to Kyiv, the emperor sends for the agreed-upon trade goods (slaves, wax and furs) and soldiers to aid him in battle. Olga refuses to send them, however, noting that she would only do so if the emperor came to Kyiv and remained there for as long a period as she had spent in Constantinople. Given the tone of the earlier part of the story, this is a strange ending, a rebuke to the Byzantine emperor. A partial explanation for this shift in tone might be found in the other sources regarding Olga.

The main Byzantine source that records Olga's visit to Constantinople is called the *Book of Ceremonies* – it is exactly what it sounds like, a prescriptive book on how to complete various ceremonies in Constantinople, recorded using actual examples of embassies, receptions and dinners, to make it clear where people should sit, how much money they should receive, what hymns should be sung and so on. It records Olga's visit as an example of the visit of a ruler of Rus. It is quite a positive reception in that Olga is treated very well. She sits near the emperor and empress and both she and her party are given gifts at the various stages of the visit.[26] In this account, though, there is absolutely no mention of baptism. In fact, while the PVL account says that Olga took the Christian name 'Helena', after the fourth-century emperor Constantine's mother, the *Book of Ceremonies* only refers to her as Olga, not Helena.[27] Interestingly, it does record a priest in her entourage, by the name of Gregory, although there is no indication of who he was or where he came from. The majority of her entourage was made up of representatives of the rulers of Rus, much as in Igor's treaty, and then merchants, who accounted for well over half of the people involved. The 43 merchants who were included, twice the number mentioned in the treaty of 945, might well suggest that the purpose of the visit was for trade, rather than religion; this perhaps provides an insight into why trade goods were mentioned at the end of the PVL's entry regarding Olga's visit to

Constantinople. Given the differing purposes and times of composition of the two sources, it is much easier to take the *Book of Ceremonies* as a record of what actually happened (as it is a source uninterested in aggrandizing Olga, or Rus), as opposed to the PVL, whose folkloric-type tales about Olga seem aimed at depicting her cleverness.

However, other sources do note her baptism, such as John Skylitzes, who records quite briefly that Olga 'came to Constantinople after her husband died. She was baptized and she demonstrated fervent devotion, then she went back home.'[28] It is obviously a much terser account than those in either the PVL or the *Book of Ceremonies*, as it does not provide details of almost any kind, but it does record her baptism in Constantinople. Similarly, a source from the German Empire corresponds with that, saying that Olga requested a bishop and priests from the Ottonian emperor Otto I.[29] Given the religious politics of the time, the potential to convert a non-Christian ruler and their polity would be a major coup, and thus Otto responded positively, ordaining Adalbert, later Archbishop of Magdeburg, and sending him to Rus with an entourage.[30] Adding a further wrinkle to this story, this source does refer to Olga as 'Helena', the baptismal name recorded in the PVL for her, but this is not present in either of the Byzantine sources, as we discussed earlier. Regardless, Adalbert's mission to Rus was not successful; he returned to the German Empire in 962, citing pagan opposition to his missionary activities.[31] This pagan opposition may have coincided with the ascent to power of Olga's son, Sviatoslav, as he was a confirmed non-Christian. Thus, while Olga has gone down in history as a Christian, and even as a saint, in the PVL and later Eastern Orthodox traditions, her conversion is still surrounded by a bit of mystery.[32] As for the political aspects, Olga seems to have been well aware of the importance of conversion, beyond mere religion; although she approached Byzantium

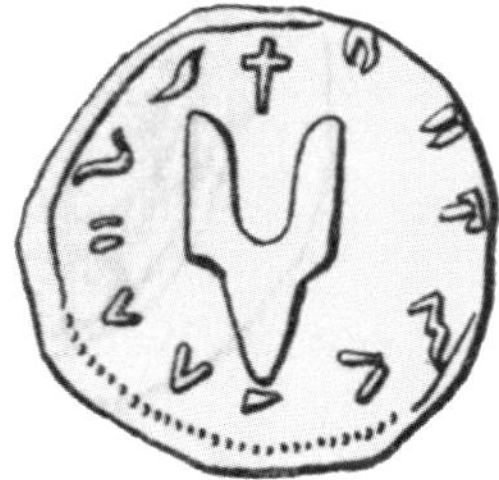

7 Seal of Sviatoslav, son of Igor and Olga, from *Aktovye pechati drevnei rusi* X –XV *vv. tom* I *of* III*: Pechati* X*–nachala* XIII *v.*, ed. V. L. Ianin (1970), table 1, no. 1.

for her personal conversion, she reached out to the German Empire for a bishop to help spread Christianity in Rus, keeping her polity independent from any one set of imperial influences.

Sviatoslav, Igor and Olga's son, maintained an eventful rule over the Rusian polity. He was active on multiple fronts. One of his military actions was to attack the Khazar khanate, a semi-nomadic polity located on the lower Volga River, controlling the steppes to the south and east of Rus. The Khazars had long been rivals with Rus for dominance over the region and were recorded in the same PVL entry with Riurik taking tribute from a different set of groups. Sviatoslav attacked the Khazars and defeated them, taking their city of Sarkel (Bela Vezha) in 965.[33] At the same time, he also attacked and defeated the Iasians, Kasogians and Viatichians, which George Vernadsky has suggested was part of a broader effort to move eastward and take control of territory towards the Volga, inclusive of the northern Caucasus.[34] However, before he could continue that campaign, Sviatoslav was distracted by affairs to the southwest of Rus, in the Balkans. The Byzantines, using their typical strategy of arranging for one neighbour to attack another, recruited Sviatoslav to attack the Bulgars, who had become problematic neighbours.[35] Sviatoslav enjoyed his campaign on the Danube so much that he decided to move his capital there, describing it as the place 'where all the riches come; gold, brocaded silk, wine, and various fruits from the Greeks, from the Bohemians and Hungarians, silver and horses, from Rus', furs, wax, honey, and slaves'.[36] Sviatoslav's desire to be on the Danube permanently presented a major difficulty for the Byzantines, who were happy to have him fight the Bulgars, but not to take their place and become a threat to their empire. Thus, Emperor John Tzimiskes marched out to fight Sviatoslav's army, which ultimately resulted in a peace treaty in which Sviatoslav would return to Rus, but would be well looked after. However, on his trip home to Kyiv, Sviatoslav was killed by the Pechenegs, a nomadic group from the steppe, and his skull was made into a drinking cup for their leader. It is suspected by scholars that the Byzantines were behind this assassination of the Rusian leader, but there is, of course, no evidence.[37]

Sviatoslav did not leave a legacy of shifting the Rusian polity to the Danube, but he did leave an important mark on the internal politics of Rus. When he decided to go to the Danube, he appointed his sons as his subordinate rulers within Rus, each of them to a major town: Iaropolk in Kyiv, Oleg in Dereva and the youngest, Volodimer, in

Novgorod with his maternal uncle, Dobrynia, as his regent.[38] This process wherein the ruler of Rus assigning his sons as subordinate rulers had not previously been recorded, but this was to become the normative model for rule within Rus. The ruler of Kyiv, typically, was the *paterfamilias*; he used his sons as his regional governors. There was no handbook, such as the *Book of Ceremonies*, recording who was assigned where or how such assignments were decided; thus, we are only left with the information recorded in the PVL and other chronicles if we wish to piece together whether this was a system, or a more *ad hoc* arrangement of rule. For instance, was every son given a city to rule? Possibly, but in addition, we do not necessarily know all the names of the children of the rulers of Rus. Were women able to rule? Again, possibly, but we have only a couple of examples of women who ruled cities, and they are the widows of the male rulers. Regardless of all that we do not know, this process of assigning cities to sons and male relatives would come to be normative in Rus after this time.

Volodimer and the Christianization of Rus

Volodimer took power in 980 and ruled for 35 years, transforming Rus in many ways and becoming the touchstone for future rulers. Although Volodimer lived an active life, we will focus largely here on one series of events related to his religious decisions, through which we can see a variety of changes in both internal and external affairs. At the beginning of Volodimer's reign in Kyiv, he decided to change the worship practices within Rus.[39] The Christian chronicler was not pleased by the erection of 'idols' but he did at least provide the names of the gods and goddesses – Perun, Khors, Dazhbog, Stribog, Simargl and Mokosh.[40] It is incredibly important that we know the names of these deities, as they represent a blending of different non-Christian religious traditions from Slavic, Scandinavian, Baltic and Iranian backgrounds.[41] Modern historians have assumed that Volodimer's intent was to create a united pantheon from elements of the various religious traditions that were worshipped within Rus, in an attempt to create a unified religious structure without wholesale conversion to a single monotheistic religion, as had taken place around him with the conversion of the Poles to Christianity, the Volga Bulgars to Islam and the Khazars to Judaism. The end goal would then be creating a religious structure that would unite his population. If that was the case, Volodimer's bold attempt to

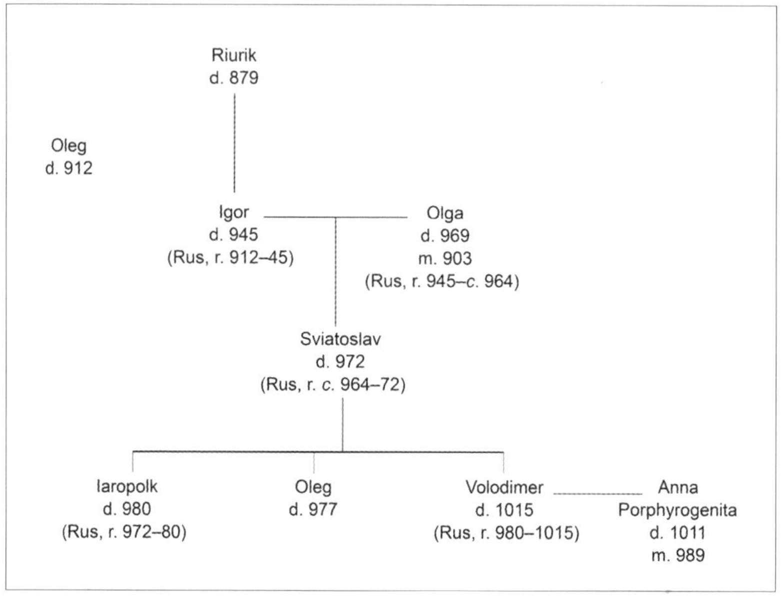

8 Genealogical table depicting the major figures discussed in this chapter.

create a new religious tradition failed and, in just a few years, he was seeking out conversion opportunities among the various monotheistic religions.

The conversion of Volodimer, and of Rus, is a process, but the story of the conversion is also a process. There is evidence that the Rusians converted to Christianity before Volodimer. The most authoritative source for the early Christianization of Rus is an encyclical letter of Patriarch Photius, which has been dated to 867. Citing the Rusian siege of Constantinople of 860, Photius informed the patriarchs and bishops that after the Bulgarians turned to Christ in 863, the Rus followed suit. As was the case with the Bulgarians, the Patriarch found it prudent to send a bishop from Constantinople. With some modifications, the story is repeated by Constantine VII in *De administrando imperio*, followed by mentions from several generations of Byzantine historians, including John Skylitzes and Joannes Zonaras. That the imperial court and patriarchate regarded the tenth-century Rusians as Christians is evident from the fact that the bishopric of Rus was enumerated in the lists of Christian sees, which were compiled during the reigns of Leo the Wise and Constantine VII. There is also an *argumentum ex silentio* (absence of evidence to the contrary): no Greek source recorded what would have been the second baptism of the Rus in 988.

The PVL chronicler records none of these things. Instead, he combines four different stories of the conversion occurring in the late 980s: (1) missionaries arrive at the court of Volodimer in Kyiv, uninvited; (2) Volodimer sends out ten good men to investigate other religions; (3) Volodimer demands marriage to Anna, the sister of the Byzantine emperors Basil and Constantine, if his plan to capture Cherson works; and (4) Anna tells him that he will regain his eyesight if he is baptized.[42] To these four stories we will add a fifth, which summarizes and elucidates additional information from other sources, to try and present a wider picture of the Rusian conversion. We will begin with the arrival of the missionaries, which is recorded in the PVL as happening in the year 985/6.[43] This entry of the PVL details the visits of four groups of representatives to Volodimer: Muslims from Bulgar, Germans as 'emissaries of the pope', Jewish Khazars and then the Byzantines, whom the Rus called Greeks. Each presented their way of life and their faith to Volodimer. In response to the first three, Volodimer ends the recitation with a pithy comeback. For the Muslims, he tells them that he cannot convert to Islam, where one does not drink alcohol, because 'drinking is the joy of the Rusians.' For the German Christians, he is unimpressed with the idea that all one eats or drinks is to the glory of God, for 'our fathers did not accept that principle.' To the Jewish Khazars, when pressed on their lack of a homeland (since they had been dispersed from Jerusalem), Volodimer says, 'Do you expect us to accept that fate too?' It is the fourth presentation, that of the Byzantine Christians, that offers a faith to which Volodimer will eventually convert; it is also with these representatives that Volodimer has the most recorded interaction. Their dialogue covers approximately twelve pages in the English-language translation of the PVL, which is perhaps indicative of the sympathies of the chronicler. But even with that final interaction, the entry for 986 ends with no resolution.

The PVL entry for 986/7 begins with Volodimer calling together his advisors and questioning them about the religions that they had heard about. The possibility of Judaism disappears here and only the Muslim Bulgars, German Christians and Byzantine Christians remain.[44] On the basis of the advice of his boyars and the city elders, Volodimer chose ten 'good and wise men' to go and visit each of the places to see how they worship, as that would tell them a great deal more than mere words about their religious practice. The emissaries set out and visited each place in turn; they described their finding that among the Muslim

Bulgars, 'there is no happiness . . . but instead only sorrow and a great stink,'[45] a common Christian critique of Muslims (and everyone else) in medieval European writing; the Germans were simply described as without 'glory'; and yet, among the Byzantine Christians, once they entered the church, which was presumed to be Hagia Sophia in Constantinople, 'they knew not whether [they] were on earth or in heaven.' However, this entry also ends with no decision being made, although it is noted that Byzantine Christianity was good enough for Volodimer's grandmother, Olga.

The entry for the year 988 brings the most elaborate of the four stories, in which Volodimer, without any mention of a prompt or *casus belli*, besieges the Byzantine city of Cherson on the north shore of the Black Sea.[46] The siege was eventually broken when a man inside the city, Anastasius by name, shot an arrow out with information on how to cut the water supply to the city, allowing Volodimer to take Cherson. At that time, Volodimer sent a message to the Byzantine emperors Basil and Constantine, demanding the hand of their sister, Anna, in marriage. After some deliberation and discussion, Volodimer agreed to convert to Christianity as a way to gain the princess's hand in marriage. She was sent to Cherson, but Volodimer still did not convert. Then he was struck down by blindness. Anna told him that the way to regain his eyesight was to be baptized. Volodimer was baptized by the bishop of Cherson and the priests who had accompanied Anna, and the two were married. After the wedding and his conversion, Volodimer returned the city of Cherson to the Byzantines as a wedding present. He and Anna proceeded back to Kyiv, where he threw the city's idols into the Dnieper River and then herded the people of Kyiv into the water, to be baptized by the priests from Cherson and those in Anna's entourage. In addition to founding other churches, assigning priests throughout the cities and inviting people to accept baptism in all the cities and towns, as well as taking the children of the best families and sending them for instruction in book-learning, the PVL tells us that Volodimer founded a church in Kyiv (apparently the Tithe Church (*desiatinna*)) in the next year, of which he appointed the liberator (or betrayer, depending on one's point of view) of Cherson, Anastasius, as caretaker.[47]

What do we make of this combination of four conversion stories, any one of which should have been sufficient to convert a ruler? The chronicler of the PVL seems to have been attempting to share the multiple stories that he knew of the conversion in the later eleventh or early twelfth century; rather than choosing one over another, he included all of them in the chronicle, serially. He does choose, however, to accept that Volodimer was baptized in the Church of St Basil in Cherson, rather than in Kyiv, Vasilev or other places mentioned by 'those who do not know the truth'.[48]

There are elements in each of those stories that we can include in our historical narrative, but it begins elsewhere. At that time, the Byzantine Empire was ruled by Basil II and Constantine VIII, two brothers, and their sister Anna Porphyrogenita (so-called because she was born in the purple room of the imperial palace, while her father was still emperor), who was of great interest as a potential alliance for multiple possible dynastic marriage partners around Europe. For instance, both the king of France and the German emperor wrote to Basil II, seeking to marry their respective sons to Anna Porphyrogenita. Basil II, however, had a more serious problem in the late 980s: a revolt from first one and then two of his own generals.[49] A rebellion by his own generals meant that Basil II was short of soldiers; thus, he turned to Volodimer of Rus as someone who could assist him, both with his own additional forces and as a contractor who could procure mercenary forces from Scandinavia. Volodimer agreed, and we have a record of 6,000 soldiers being sent to assist Basil II.[50] We can suggest that Volodimer's price was marriage with Anna Porphyrogenita, a marriage that would not only connect him to the Byzantine empire but increase his legitimacy as well, via his recognition by one of the most powerful and important empires of his day. However, to continue our conjecture, once Basil II won his victory, he did not send Anna to marry Volodimer; in response, Volodimer besieged and took Cherson. We know that the latter event happened and, given that Anna was then dispatched to marry Volodimer, we can suggest that taking a Byzantine city was the leverage required to force Basil II to hand over his sister. Christianization was a *sine qua non* for marriage. This, then, is our historical reconstruction of Volodimer's conversion, a power play that had as much to do with politics as it did with religion; one that also allowed Volodimer to be in control of his own marriage and conversion, rather than subordinating himself to anyone else's rule, even his brothers-in-law, the Byzantine emperors.

Volodimer and Anna did not have children together, but Volodimer had already sired a great many children from his relationships before he was Christianized. The PVL records that he had twelve sons and at least four daughters by four wives – one named Rogneda, and three women identified only by region (two Czechs and a Bulgar) – as well as by his brother's wife, a Greek. The PVL also claimed that he had '300 concubines at Vyshgorod, 300 at Belgorod, and 200 at Berestovo'.[51] While these figures may be a self-conscious reference to Solomon, who is mentioned in this same entry, even the contemporary German chronicler referred to Volodimer as a '*fornicatur immensus*'![52] Volodimer followed his father's method of delegating power, and assigned his sons as rulers in various towns around Rus: 'Vysheslav in Novgorod, Iziaslav in Polotsk, Sviatopolk in Turov and Iaroslav in Rostov'.[53] This list was amended as his various sons died, but it is clear that he was placing his sons in positions of power under him and that not all of his twelve sons received a town of their own to rule. This system of subordinate rulers, all chosen from the Volodimerovichi (sons of Volodimer), would set the tone for the future placement of members of the wider Volodimerovichi clan. As the clan grew over the decades and centuries, it spawned not just multiple families within it but new clans as well, often centred on particular towns, or regions, as hubs of power. However, none of this would have been possible without Volodimer acting as *paterfamilias*.

Historiography of Rus

As noted at the beginning of this chapter in relation to the name of this polity, there have been numerous works published on Rus over the years, from multiple different perspectives. Briefly here we would like to orient the reader in terms of a few of those debates and highlight what we are doing and why, in relation to these theories. Modern studies on Rus often take place within the framework of Slavic studies or, more specifically, Russian studies. This kind of framework can certainly be useful, but it is important to acknowledge that it is a vertical (or silo) framework of history. That is to say that the framework takes a later starting point, modern Russia for instance, and then looks at the history of the area that Russia today occupies as a way to help us understand what Russia was and why it came to be. Such a perspective causes problems for interpretation because there is a built-in explanatory framework of the end result – Russia. This kind of work is conducted by excellent scholars; for example, one recent publication, *Russia's Empires*, is an attempt to analyse 'how and why Russia expanded to become the largest country on the globe and how it repeatedly fell under the sway of strong, authoritarian leaders'.[54] Rus is included in the book as the preliminary to everything else, with the authors pointing out that Rus was not Russia and did not have the centralization necessary to be Russia. Although only a single example, this is a clear demonstration of the problem with this kind of work – Rus was not Russia; it was its own polity and should be analysed on its own terms, not as a means by which to explain later history.

Other scholars have attempted a horizontal approach to situating Rus in a larger world. The classic example of this approach is the work of the Eurasian school of historical study. The Eurasian school was founded in Sofia, Bulgaria, in 1921 by Russian émigrés escaping the Bolshevik Revolution. It was an amorphous movement, the proponents of which held widely differing views. Among the core ideas that can be said to have been shared by the adherents and those influenced by the movement was an assumption that 'Eurasia' encompassed the area of the former imperial Russia. It is a different use of the term from that used by world historians, who consider 'Eurasia' to mean all of Europe and Asia combined. Another core idea of the Eurasianists was a conceptualization of the culture of that area as being a blend of European and Asian elements (thus being neither wholly European nor wholly Asian), as well as a generally positive evaluation of all things Asian in that mix. In contrast, they advanced a negative critique of Eurocentrism and imperialist colonialism (including that of the Russian Empire) and gave priority to Russian Orthodoxy as the religious-cultural identifier of 'Eurasia'. Among the scholars who could be considered part of this Eurasian movement were Nikolai Trubetskoi, George Vernadsky and Lev Gumilev.[55]

A few present-day scholars, such as David Christian, John LeDonne and Donald Ostrowski, have views that are similar in certain ways to some of these core ideas, but they eschew the religious priority of Orthodoxy and they base the area of focus on the geographer Halford Mackinder's concept of the Heartland, calling it 'inner Eurasia'.[56] Doing so keeps the term 'Eurasia' reserved for use in the way that world historians employ it.

A similar horizontal view was taken in the early twentieth century by scholars such as Samuel Hazzard Cross, who discussed Rusian affairs in relation to what was going on at the time in Scandinavia and, to a lesser extent, in medieval Europe.[57] This idea of situating Rus within medieval Europe has become much more prominent in the twenty-first century, with a string of books and articles by Christian Raffensperger, Yulia Mikhailova and Talia Zajac, to name just a few.[58] These scholars are attempting to take Rus out of any vertical silo and instead view it as part of the medieval European world, comparing its experiences to what was going on not just in Scandinavia or Byzantium (areas that have been examined before), but in regard to England, the German Empire, Iberia, Poland, Hungary and much else. They suggest that this is the proper framework for viewing Rus, as Rus considered itself to be part of this medieval European world through dynastic marriages, religious interaction and much more.

Our framing for *The Ruling Families of Rus* attempts to be horizontally expansive, following the connections wherever they lead at the time. We have not created either a Russian history or a Ukrainian history book; instead, we have focused on the clan founded by Volodimer Sviatoslavich and, subsequently, the various individuals and families that made up that clan over the next five hundred years. Since individuals like Iaroslav Volodimerovich married off their children into important families throughout Europe in the eleventh century, those alliances will be discussed. Similarly, we will follow the Mongol interactions of the thirteenth and fourteenth centuries and include the Mongol capitals of Sarai and Qaraqorum in our narrative. Since members of the wider Volodimerovich clan ended up ruled by Lithuania, we will include Lithuania in our broader picture, focusing on Uliana Alexandrovna. In this way, our goal is to keep the focus of this book on individuals, working within the framework of the ruling clans and families of Rus, rather than on any particular horizontal or vertical agenda. Thus, we present to the reader the ruling families of Rus, charted from the eleventh to the sixteenth centuries.

2

Rule and Succession among the Volodimerovich Clan

The goal of this chapter is to address a series of 'why' questions that underlie the structure of this book. Why do the authors follow the Volodimerovichi as the ruling clan, when following the family line of Riurikid (Rurikid, Ryurikid and so on) is so much more common? Why is a book in a series on dynasties centred around families? Perhaps, even, the question: what is a family versus a clan? In answering these questions, the framework for both our thinking and our understanding of medieval Rus will be fleshed out and explained. In the pursuit of understanding medieval Rusian royalty as well, this chapter also takes on the much-contested topic of succession among the Volodimerovich clan, and its consequences within individual families, in an attempt to create a foundation on which the following chapters may be built.

Why the Volodimerovichi?

Open any book on Rus (or medieval Russia or Ukraine, for that matter) and the ruling family will be described as the Riurikids, who will usually be referred to as a dynasty. The examples are too numerous to list, as this is, de facto, the normal usage for this description. However, if one digs into the primary sources in an attempt to understand how the medieval people of Rus thought about themselves and their forefathers, specifically, the elites who commissioned the written works that are now extant and who were their subjects, one will find that the term *Riurikid*, and the concept behind it, is entirely absent.

The idea of a Riurikid dynasty appears in sixteenth-century Muscovy and has a particular political purpose – to legitimize the Muscovite rulers and to connect them with some sense of antiquity.[1]

In the PVL, and even in other early chronicles, such as the Novgorod Chronicle or Kyivan Chronicle, there is no sense of a dynastic link that can be traced back to Riurik. Riurik appears in the earliest pages of the PVL as the Scandinavian leader who was invited to rule over the disparate groups in the eastern European north and who had a tenuous connection to Oleg, along with an unlikely relationship with Igor. Beyond that entry, he is not the subject of further discussion in the PVL or elsewhere. Instead, when rulers claim authority for themselves as the ruler of Kyiv, in particular, they cite their father's rule of the city and sometimes their brother, uncle, or maybe their grandfather. However, they do not go further back in time to trace their authority to a more distant ancestor.

By the early sixteenth century, Muscovite churchmen were constructing longer and longer genealogies for their patrons, with the ultimate goal of connecting them to Volodimer Sviatoslavich, the Christianizer of Rus. However, it is important to note that they did not initially go the three generations further back to connect their patrons to Riurik. This system worked for a brief time, but the rulers still seemed to lack the proper connection to antiquity that would create in their subjects the sense of authority that could only be derived from connection to the Roman Empire or to the ancient Greek world. The British ruling class, according to many historians, decided that they were descended from Brutus, a Trojan descended from Aeneas, who came to the shores of their island and became its first ruler.[2] This connection with antiquity was already established in the medieval world and was repeated multiple times throughout the period. Brutus was related to 'Bruti', the name that Isidore of Seville applied to the inhabitants of that island, thus creating not only an ancestor with ties to antiquity but an eponymous founder as well.[3] Other medieval kingdoms had already settled for merely eponymous founders, such as those described in Saxo Grammaticus' *Gesta danorum*, which begins with Dan, the founder of the Danes, and his brother Angul who goes on to found Anglia.[4] Despite their not having a connection to antiquity, Saxo's dedicatory preface sums up the situation we are discussing quite nicely, when he begins: 'Because other nations are in the habit of vaunting the fame of their achievements, and joy in recollecting their ancestors . . .'[5] This was the purpose of the author of the *Historia Brittonum*, who was the first to write down the idea that Brutus was the founder of Britain, as much as it was that of the Lithuanian churchmen, who added to their descent myths Palemon (perhaps Polemon II of Pontus?), a relative of the emperor Nero who led five hundred noble families from Rome to the Baltic. The myth of the Roman origins of the Lithuanian rulers first appeared in the mid-fifteenth century as a way of counteracting the claims of the Polish nobility that they had civilized the Lithuanians.[6] By the early sixteenth century, the version in the Lithuanian chronicles now tells of a Roman patrician named Palemon, a kinsman of the Roman emperor Nero, who flees with five hundred families to Samogitia. The Gedyminids are described as descendants of these Palemonids.[7] Novgorod and the Muscovite churchmen, in turn, initially extended the genealogy of Muscovite rulers back to Volodimer as a way to justify the claim that Muscovite rulers were the legitimate rulers of all Rus. Then, they extended the genealogy, which they felt they could do, based on the PVL, to Riurik in order to add on a connection with Prus, after whom Prussia was named and who was a relative of Augustus Caesar. These descent myths were a way to create a connection tracing the ruling classes back to antiquity, to bolster the claim that their countries had a dynasty with ancient Roman origins.[8]

Thus, we find no mention of a Riurikid dynasty in any of the Rusian territories before the early sixteenth century. The creation of a dynastic link to Riurik all the way back to Prus, a relative of Augustus, was an attempt by the Muscovite churchmen to bolster the legitimacy and authority of their Muscovite patrons, who were becoming tsars, aspiring to be caesars, in imitation or appropriation of their ancient, as well as medieval, Roman connections. It is a testament to the success of those churchmen that the idea of a Riurikid dynasty has persisted this long and has become so firmly embedded in modern historiography. It is also another example of one of the problems with the historical record that this book is attempting to challenge – namely, our reliance on the works written by the scholars before us. This sounds like an odd thing for a historian to label as a problem, but if we cite other scholars without critical thinking, or without wondering why and in what context something was written, we risk perpetuating ideas that we may, in fact, not know to be correct. Returning to the primary sources and evaluating them in their own milieu is a safe and reliable way to check our historiographical resources; in this way, we make sure that we are representing the evidence as accurately as possible and presenting the best explanation we can find for how that story came to be.

Why Families, not Dynasties?

Dynasties are one of the main ways that we understand and structure our historical narratives. For instance, the lead-up to the First World War is often discussed through the lens of the Hohenzollerns, the Romanovs and the Habsburgs, their actions and interactions. While this can be a useful tool for understanding relationships, it can also be deceptive, as it elides personal agency, family loyalty (which is separate from, but within the structure of, dynasty) and especially the important role that women play in history. All of this is particularly true for the medieval period where, generally, dynasties are post-facto constructs by either later rulers and their agents or by historians themselves. Early modern rulers, with the aid of chroniclers, historians and other writers, created a grand patrilineal descent for themselves from the Middle Ages or antiquity as a way to reinforce their own rule, validate their power and lend historical legitimacy to their cause – as we will see, for example, with the creation of the Gediminovichi by the Lithuanian churchmen and the Riurikids by the Muscovite churchmen.

If dynasties are difficult to apply to the medieval world, where then does this leave us? The answer is with families. Families are the building blocks of dynasties, and it is through studying families – fathers, mothers, sons, daughters and the spouses of both – that we are able to understand better the human face of our sources. Families, in turn, are part of more extended kin entities that we call clans, which themselves can be composed of multiple families that may, or may not, share the same overarching objectives (the specifics of which terms are discussed below). In fact, it can be the case that families within clans vie with one another and make alliances with families within other clans to advance their own interests. Viewing history through the lenses of state, nation, kingdom or dynasty (that is, macro-concepts) can and often does obscure the complexity of these arrangements, whereas studying families and clans (that is, micro-concepts) can be more informative.

This book has at its core the ruling families of the kingdom of Rus. Many of the members of these families were all from one larger clan, which was designated as the Riurikids from the beginning of the Early Modern period. The individuals in those families, however, come from a variety of families, clans and kingdoms. Iaroslav the Wise, king of Rus, was a member of the Volodimerovichi, being a son of Volodimer himself. Iaroslav's wife, Ingigerd, was the daughter of the king of Sweden, and thus hailed from a different clan, family and kingdom. Utilizing the traditional construction of dynasties, Ingigerd's identity is subsumed due to her marriage; her children are thus of the Volodimerovichi. But what happens, then, when these children marry? Iaroslav and Ingigerd's sons married princesses from Byzantium and Poland, while their daughters married the rulers of Hungary, France and Norway. Are the males all considered Volodimerovichi but the females are not? What, then, happens in that next generation? Dynasty, especially within the traditional patrilineal construction, elides all this complexity, while the concept of family accepts and acknowledges this network of relationships – all the children of Ingigerd and Iaroslav (male and female), for example, are part of their family. Likewise, Iurii Dolgorukii married the daughter (whose name is not given) of the Polovtsian chieftain, Aepa, in 1108. Historians might mention this marriage, if they acknowledge it at all, in relation to their son, Andrei Bogoliubskii, but often neglect to mention its diplomatic importance, such as its contribution to the formation of an alliance network that stretched from the western Eurasian steppes to central Europe, with the Suzdal branch of the Monomakhovichi being a crucial connecting link. A third example is the struggle between the Mikhailovichi of Tver and the Daniilovichi of Moscow for the khan's favour, with the Daniilovichi winning out. Political considerations of the time were messy, open-ended and had multiple possible outcomes, whereas dynastic constructs make the events appear neat, tidy and teleological (they have only one possible outcome).

What are Families and Clans?

There is an immense corpus of scholarly literature on familial and social groupings. This habit began among anthropologists and was adopted by historians in an attempt to apply those discussions of less-developed societies to the world of the Middle Ages.[9] For medieval Europe, the discussion has centred around Germanic kinship models, used by Karl Schmid and spread widely by Georges Duby.[10] The basic idea that they articulated was that prior to the year 1000, the Germanic kinship structure was organized around both male and female connections (*Sippe*) but that after the year 1000 it changed to a patrilineal model of descent (*Geschlecht*). This idea was challenged by Constance Bouchard, who argued that it was overly simplistic and that the year 1000 was not a definitive marker; she pointed out instances of both models (*Sippe* and

Geschlecht) on either side of this divide.[11] Furthermore, she suggested that our modern term 'family' did not have a precise medieval equivalent; the group of people that a person gathered around themselves did not always include every member of their natal and marital kin or of their maternal and paternal kin. Similarly, Alexander Murray suggested further complexity, including the idea that the Franks operated by way of a bilateral kindred system, using both male and female kin, and incorporated relations out to their second and third cousins.[12] Thus, in these debates, a 'family' could be everything from a modern 'nuclear family' to an 'extended family'.[13]

For the purposes of this book, we are defining family and clan according to the arrangement shown in illustration 9. 'Clan' is used as a term for a group that shares common descent from a single ancestor. This could be a mythical or semi-mythical ancestor, such as Riurik, Árpád or Piast, or it could be a historical figure, such as Volodimer Sviatoslavich. 'Family' will be used for a slightly expanded nuclear family: to put it simply, a husband and wife, with their children and their children's spouses, sometimes extending to the grandchildren of the original husband and wife. Thus, in the table below, Iziaslav (at top left) is the son of Iaroslav, so he is considered part of the Iaroslavichi, Iaroslav's family; however, he is also the progenitor of his own family, the Iziaslavichi. We recognize that this definition of family is open to the problem of overlap, but we are using it nonetheless, with the intention that the reader will understand and follow the discussion. It is also worth noting that while all the members of the clan depicted in the illustration are Volodimerovichi, it is also possible for a family to become a clan. This

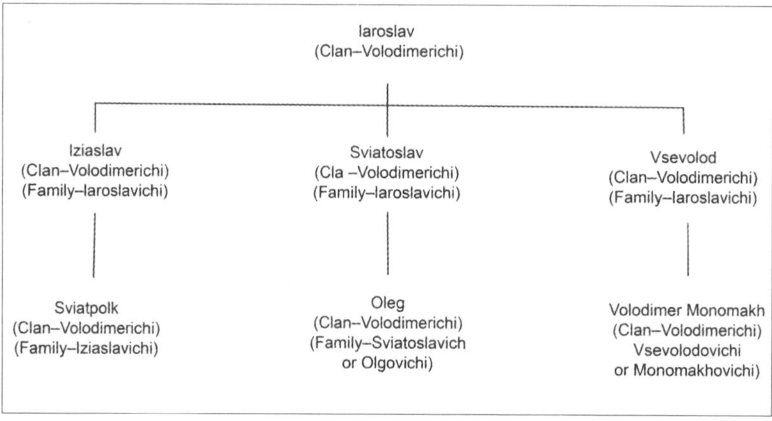

9 Table depicting the relationships between 'family' and 'clan', as discussed in the text.

could be said to have happened among the children of Volodimer Monomakh (bottom right). He had a large family that identified themselves as his kin (Monomakhovichi); however, that family also fractured into multiple independent families (Mstislavichi and Iurevichi, for instance) that still claimed descent from Volodimer Monomakh for the purposes of gaining and holding power. These instances can also generate overlap, but this will be noted in the text when such an overlap appears.

Succession Among the Volodimerovichi

Succession in Rus lands was collateral. That is, when a ruler (let us call him A-1) died, the priority to succeed him went to his eldest living brother (A-2), and so on down to the fourth brother (A-4). When the fourth brother died, then the eldest son (A-1a) of the eldest brother (A-1) had priority, followed by the next eldest brother (A-1b) down to the fourth brother (A-1d), after which the eldest son (A-2a) of the second brother (A-2) of the previous generation had priority. Bifurcation of the brother-to-brother succession thus passes to cousins, since A-2a is a cousin of A-1d. That is where the succession turns from lateral (from brother to brother) to collateral (from cousin to cousin). Such a system works best in societies where the death rate is high, as the result of wars and/or disease. However, when rulers have large families and many of their offspring survive to adulthood, this system can get complicated.

In addition, in Rus, there was a certain flexibility built into the system because, for a person to ascend to the rulership of a town, he had to fulfil three criteria. One of these criteria was that his father had ruled in that town. However, on occasion, this criterion could be overridden by one or both of the other two criteria – namely, approval by the other rulers and acceptance by the townsmen. As a result, numerous historians have thrown up their hands in despair, declaring that there was no system or that it was too complex to figure out. We see it differently; there was a system that was clearly understood by the participants, that it was rational, and that it had exceptions, with processes built into it for those exceptions to take place.

In the early chronicles – the PVL, the Kyivan Chronicle and the Novgorod First Chronicle – one finds a formula for describing what happens when someone becomes a ruler: 'sit on the throne of his father' or some variant, such as 'sit on the throne of his father and brother' or 'sit on the throne of his father and grandfather' and so forth. The persistent references to a ruler occupying the throne of his father and grandfather (and/or brother or uncle) are not merely empty phraseology, but a legitimizing formula. It indicates the individual's eligibility to rule a town and is one of the three criteria that we can glean from the sources regarding the legitimizing of a ruler. The other two criteria are aristocratic self-regulation and external regulation, that is, whether the other rulers approved and whether the townsmen accepted him.[14] If an individual's father did not rule in a particular town, then that individual was not eligible to rule there. That lost eligibility also extended to all his descendants, as well. The one exception was that a council (*snem*) of *kniazi* could override that criterion and appoint someone as the *kniaz* of a town, even though that person's father had not ruled there; if the townsmen approved, that individual could rule in that town. However, we see that this override occurs only rarely.

Notably, in these chronicles' descriptions of succession, one finds no mention of Riurik as the founder of a dynasty. Nor is someone's being a Riurikid ever invoked as a justification for that person's eligibility to rule. For example, the *Sermon on Law and Grace* (*Slovo o zakone i blagodati*), thought to have been written in the 1050s by Metropolitan Ilarion, refers only to Volodimer Sviatoslavich's father and grandfather: 'the great kagan of our land Volodimer, the grandson of old Igor [and] the son of blessed Sviatoslav'.[15] *The Memorial and Encomium for Prince Volodimer of Rus* by the monk Iakov also refers only to Volodimer's father and grandfather: 'the Rus King Volodimer, son of Sviatoslav and grandson of Igor'.[16]

The Kyivan Chronicle does have two five-generation genealogical lists, but neither one is used to justify the legitimacy of succession. The first is for Iurii Dolgorukii when he first became ruler in Kyiv *s.a.* 6657 (1148/9): '[The] son of Volodimer Monomakh, grandson of Vsevolod, great-grandson of Iaroslav, and great-great-grandson of Volodimer the Great, who Christianized all the Rus land'.[17]

The second list is for Riurik Rostislavich, *s.a.* 6707 (1198/9), when he laid the foundation for a stone wall below the church of St Michael at the Vydubitsii Monastery, the church that his great-great-grandfather had built 111 years earlier:

> This Godwise Kniaz Riurik was the fifth [generation] from that [Kniaz Vsevolod], as it is written about the righteous Job [who was the fifth generation] from Abraham: for Vsevolod begat Volodimir,

Volodimir begat Mstislav, Mstislav begat Rostislav, and Rostislav begat Riurik and his brothers.[18]

The chronicler draws an explicit parallel with the five generations between Abraham and Job. Two points are significant for our discussion here. First, the chronicler makes no reference to Riurik, who supposedly founded the dynasty. This absence is even more telling because the *kniaz* whom he is extolling has the same name. Second, although the five-generation list associated with Iurii Dolgorukii reaches back to Volodimer Sviatoslavich, there does not seem to be any deliberate intent to include him, other than the fact that he happened to be the great-great-grandfather of Iurii. The chronicler provides the reason for a list of five generations when making his list associated with Riurik Rostislavich.

While a connection with Riurik could be made with the addition of just one more generational antecedent, no attempt is made to do so before the late fifteenth century. Even later, when one would expect the chroniclers to be predominantly concerned with the Volodimerovichi (that is, the descendants of Volodimer Sviatoslaich, who converted the Rus to Christianity), one finds few attempts at establishing dynastic connections through genealogy that go beyond the father and, sometimes, the brother or the grandfather.[19]

From the point of view of the Rus rulers themselves, all that mattered was the immediate familial connection, going back no further than two generations. That is how they identified themselves as members of the ruling elite. It was not any connection with Riurik or even with Volodimer Sviatoslavich that told them who they were; it was whether their father ruled in a town that made each of them a *kniaz* – whether eligible or not. In other words, they did not see themselves as either Riurikovichi or Volodimerovichi; they each saw themselves as the sons of their fathers, and that perception provided the glue that held the system together.

So when do the constructs of Riurikid and Volodimerovich begin?

At the beginning of the Hypatian Codex, which dates to 1425, is a list of the rulers of Kyiv until its capture by Batu in 1240. This list precedes the Hypatian copy of the PVL. It begins with 'Dir and Askold' and moves immediately on to first Oleg and then Igor.[20] The list-maker does not attempt to connect the rulers to each other using genealogy. The absence of Riurik can be explained by the fact that Riurik is not recorded as ever having ruled in Kyiv. Nonetheless, this list provides a sharp contrast to those lists that began to appear about 25 years later.

At the beginning of the Archaeographic Commission's copy of the Novgorod First Chronicle, which dates to the middle of the fifteenth century, two genealogies and a chronological list of Rus rulers appear. All three of them begin with Riurik.[21] These lists seem to be the earliest record that we have of attempts to create a genealogy of Rus rulers, based on the narrative account in either the Novgorod First Chronicle or the PVL. There is no mention, however, that the rulers are Riurikids, although one might see that indication as implicit in the lists. *The Life of the Blessed Volodimer*, the earliest copy of which dates to the late fifteenth century, does refer to Volodimer as 'the grandson of Igor and the descendant of Riurik',[22] but the latter part of that description can be seen to be a later interpolation dating to the time at which that particular copy was made.

By the early sixteenth century, when Moscow was expanding and consolidating its control over the other Rus principalities, churchmen constructed long genealogies for the Muscovite grand princes, going back to Volodimer Sviatoslaich. For example, in the year *s.a.* 6897 (1388/9), we find in the Nikonian Chronicle of the early sixteenth century the following eleven-generation lineage for Grand Prince Dmitrii Ivanovich (r. 1363–89), upon his passing away:

> [The] grandson of Ivan, great-grandson of Daniil, great-great-grandson of Aleksandr, great-great-great-grandson of Iaroslav, great-great-great-great-grandson of Vsevolod, great-great-great-great-great-grandson of Iurii, great-great-great-great-great-great-grandson of Volodimir, [who was the] son of Vsevolod, the son of Iaroslav, the son of Volodimir, the great new Constantine who baptized the Rus' land.[23]

Even here, the chroniclers do not go three generations further back to connect Volodimer with Riurik.

The only texts that do make the connection explicit between Riurik and Volodimer and, thus, with the Muscovite rulers are two early sixteenth-century works, *The Tale About the Vladimer Kniazi* and the *Letter of Spiridon-Savva*. The *Letter* created a fictive genealogy for Riurik as being descended through fourteen generations from Prus, a 'kinsman' (*srodnik*) of Augustus Caesar, the first Roman emperor.[24] The *Tale* adds that Prus ruled 'to the banks of the Vistula River to the city of Malbork, and Torun, and Chvoini, and glorious Gdansk, and to many other cities along the river, called the Neman and flowing into the sea', and that that is why the land was called Prussia. The *Tale* then tells of a ninth-century mayor of Novgorod, Gostomysl, who told the townsmen to go to Prussia to find a ruler. They went and found Riurik, who came to Novgorod with his two brothers, Truvor and Sineus, and succeeded Gostomysl as mayor of Novgorod.[25] Sigismund von Herberstein, an ambassador from the Holy Roman Empire who visited Muscovy in 1517 and 1526, appeared to be alluding to the Prus story when he reported: 'The Russians boast that these brothers [Riurik, Sineus and Truvor] derived their origin from the Romans, from whom even the present prince of Russia asserts that he is sprung.'[26]

The *Tale* next goes on to tell a story about the Rus ruler, Volodimer Vsevolodovich, having fought a war against Byzantium. The war went badly for the Greeks and so the Byzantine emperor Constantine Monomachos sent Volodimer some gifts: a crucifix made from the wood of the true cross of Christ, his own crown, a carnelian cup from which Augustus Caesar drank, a necklace from his own shoulders and 'a chain forged of Arabian gold', as well as many other gifts. From this point on, Volodimer Vsevolodovich was known as Volodimer Monomakh. There is an anachronistic problem with this story, in that the conflict with Byzantium occurred before Volodimer was born, while Emperor Constantine died in 1055 when Volodimer was a little over a year and a half old. So not only is the chronology wrong but the story is entirely fictitious. For example, the crown of the Moscow rulers, which they called the crown of Monomakh, was of Tatar origin.[27] Nonetheless, the Muscovites had a walnut and linden wood throne that was made for Ivan IV in the middle of the sixteenth century, with twelve carved panels depicting the fictitious story of the Byzantine emperor sending his regalia to Volodimer Vsevolodovich, as related in the *Tale*.[28]

Along with most manuscript copies of the *Tale* is a *Genealogy (Rodoslovie) of the Lithuanian Kniazi*. In contrast to the Lithuanian attempt to connect the Gediminovichi with ancient Rome through Palemon, the Muscovite version claims that Gedimin was a *rab* or servant of the Smolensk ruler, who married his widow when the ruler died. The intent of the author was to contrast the high-born genealogy of the Moscow rulers with the low-born genealogy of the Lithuanian rulers. Presumably, the authors of the *Tale* and the *Genealogy* were aware of the claims that the Lithuanian rulers were descended from the ruling elite of ancient Rome and wanted to counteract that claim to show that the Moscow rulers were better suited to rule Rus than the Lithuanian rulers were.

In his book *Historians' Fallacies*, David Hackett Fischer discussed a particular type of fallacy called, aptly enough, 'the historians' fallacy', which can be defined as 'the error of assuming that a man who has a given historical experience knows it, when he has it, to be all that a historian would know it to be, with the advantage of historical perspective'.[29] This type of fallacy is closely related to another type of fallacy called 'presentism', in which one views past events through the lens of the present and judges an event's significance based on whether it led to the present or not. In other words, as Fischer states it, this represents 'a complex anachronism, in which the antecedent in a narrative series is falsified by being defined or interpreted in terms of the consequent'. The historians' fallacy here, in what may be a classic example, judges the relevance of events in early Rus in terms of their leading to the creation of the Russian dynastic state, from the end of the fifteenth until the beginning of the sixteenth century. However, there is another chronological dimension that will lead eventually to the present-day state of Russia. In this respect, according to Fischer, what has been created is 'the mistaken idea that the proper way to do history is to prune away the dead branches of the past and to preserve the green buds and twigs which have grown into the dark forest of our contemporary world'.[30] The various branches of the history tree that do not lead to the present are chopped off as irrelevant. What we have tried to do in this book is to study early Rus until the sixteenth century from the point of view of the people who lived it, what they knew and what they didn't know at the time. Our evidence tells us that, among other things, they did not know that they were part of a dynasty. They did, however, know that they were part of a family.

3

Iaroslav the Wise, Ingigerd and Their Family

Iaroslav grew up as the son of Volodimer Sviatoslavich, the first Christian king of Rus, and his partner Rogneda (historians are unsure of their marital status, as this was before Volodimer converted to Christianity). Iaroslav was not the only son of Volodimer, nor even the only son of Volodimer and Rogneda. The contemporary German chronicler Thietmar of Merseburg referred to Volodimer as a '*fornicatur immensus*', a Latin expression that needs no translation, even to modern English-speaking readers.[1] Volodimer had sixteen children (for whom we have names) with at least five different pagan women; in fact, with his one Christian wife – Anna Porphyrogenita, the sister of emperors Basil II and Constantine VIII of Byzantium – he had no known children whatsoever.[2] Undoubtedly, this made for a complicated household situation, which resulted in a struggle over inheritance after Volodimer died in 1015.[3] We do not, unfortunately, have an original source to reveal Iaroslav's life before his entry onto the political scene. Thus, any reconstruction of his life before then is, at best, speculative, given the few details that we do have.

While Volodimer lived and ruled in Kyiv, he assigned his sons to rule the major cities and towns of Rus under him. This had been a tradition in Rus since the time of Volodimer's father, Sviatoslav, and had resulted in Volodimer ruling the northern city of Novgorod from the time he was a boy until he took over the rule of Kyiv, by force, from his brother in 980. Iaroslav, like his father before him, was granted the rule of Novgorod in approximately 988, at roughly the time of Volodimer's Christianization and the subsequent Christianization of Rus. Novgorod was an important city in Rus since it acted as the northern outlet for trade and contact with the Baltic world. It had also been one of the first cities over which the larger clan ruled, dating back to its earliest foundations in the ninth century. The ruler of Novgorod had to negotiate with the many traders coming from Scandinavia who were looking for local goods, such as furs, amber, slaves and honey; they also travelled through Rus via the Volga or Dnieper rivers to source silver from the Bulgars or a host of products, including prized silks, from the Byzantine Empire. Thus, Novgorod was an essential entrepôt for Rus as a whole, and its ruler was, in many ways, one of the key visible faces of the ruling family. We know a great deal about Novgorod, not only through its foreign connections but because of a trove of documents written on native birch bark (illus. 10, 11) that record a host of information about daily life, beginning in the eleventh century. Novgorod's important position within the kingdom of Rus allows us to speculate that Iaroslav was, himself, important to Volodimer since he was assigned to rule this essential outpost.

This position of importance may have gone to Iaroslav's head, however, as he reappears in the sources when he disobeys his father, King Volodimer. One of the things that Volodimer, as the ruler of Rus, demanded from his subordinate rulers (all of whom were his sons) was a tax levy that was designed to help support the central government of Rus, located in Kyiv. In 1014, Iaroslav decided to withhold the tribute that was due from Novgorod for his father in Kyiv. This was a *casus belli* (cause for war), and both Iaroslav and Volodimer treated it as such. The PVL records that: 'Volodimer declared, "Repair roads and build bridges," for he proposed to attack his son Iaroslav.'[4] Iaroslav, for his part, prepared for conflict by recruiting troops from Scandinavia, to buttress his own Novgorodian troops. The connections he had made while he was the ruler of Novgorod over the previous decade clearly came in useful here, as he was able to gather a good number of Scandinavians to aid his attempt to resist his father. Rather than being helpful, it seems that the presence of the Varangians in Novgorod ended up causing conflict with the local population; the disturbances resulting from this introduction sparked the creation of the first legal code for Rus – the *Russkaia Pravda* – as a way for Iaroslav to let both the Novgorodians and the Varangians know that they would be treated equitably.[5] Before Volodimer and Iaroslav could come to battle, Volodimer died in 1015 and he was succeeded in Kyiv by Sviatopolk.[6] The PVL, written much later and possibly at the behest of Iaroslav's (not Sviatopolk's) branch of the Volodimerovichi clan, refers to Sviatopolk as 'the Accursed',

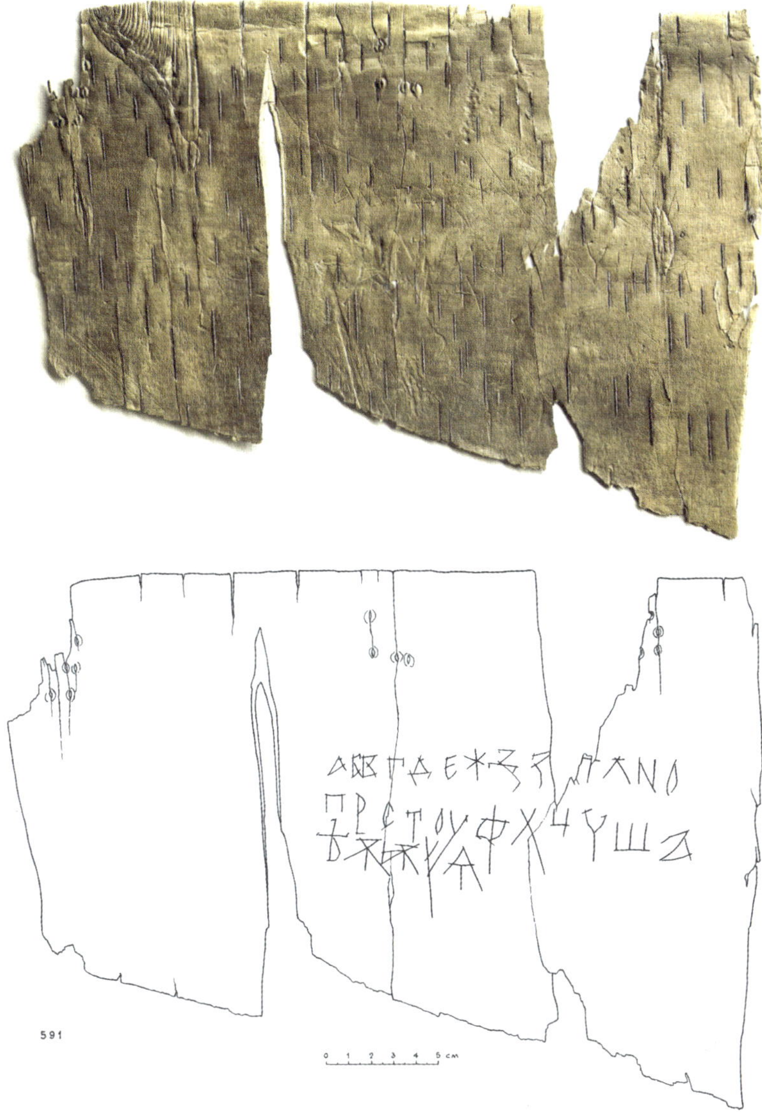

10, 11 Novgorod birch bark letter, no. 591, mid-11th century.

indicating, with no small amount of foreshadowing, his future role in the history of Rus.

Sviatopolk's position as ruler did not go unchallenged. To solidify his position, he ordered the killing of numerous sons of Volodimer, before Iaroslav and his army of Varangians drove him out of Kyiv in 1016.[7] Sviatopolk fled to his father-in-law, Bolesław Chrobry (the Brave), the ruler of Poland.[8] Bolesław, eager to aid his son-in-law and gain influence in Rus, ceased his war with the German Empire, recruited more soldiers (including ones from the German Empire and Hungary) and marched on Kyiv. The story of Bolesław's battles with Iaroslav are interesting, although the accounts vary in the German, Polish and Rusian sources that record them – which is, perhaps, as one might expect. One of the most illuminating accounts comes from the German chronicler Thietmar of Merseburg. He records that Bolesław sent emissaries from Kyiv to both the German and the Byzantine emperors. To the German emperor he sent presents and thanks for his support during the war and, presumably, implicit thanks for not invading Poland while Bolesław was otherwise occupied. To the Byzantine emperor he sent a notification that he had claimed power in Rus and asked for friendship between the two of them – with an explicit threat of violence if that friendship was not accepted.[9] Although it seems that Bolesław intended to settle down, this was not to be. For reasons that differ among the sources, it seems probable that Sviatopolk drove him out; Bolesław returned to Poland and a union between the two polities did not come to pass.[10] Without Bolesław to support Sviatopolk, Iaroslav was able to return from his earlier flight north to Novgorod with an army of Novgorodians and Varangians and had reclaimed Kyiv for himself by 1019.[11]

However, this was not the end of Iaroslav's struggles to claim sole rule over Rus. In fact, his rule in Kyiv did not last long before it was challenged. His challenger, this time, was another kinsman – his brother Mstislav. Mstislav was the ruler of Tmutorokan, a city in the southernmost part of Rus near the Black Sea. In 1023, Mstislav challenged Iaroslav for the right to rule Rus as a whole, and the two fought to a stalemate over the course of the next several years. This conflict between the two brothers resulted in the division of Rus. The dividing line was the Dnieper River; Mstislav held the parts to the east, and Iaroslav the parts to the west.[12] Although the realm was split in an east–west fashion, the divide between the rulers was really more about north and south. When the two battled, Iaroslav was supported by the Kyivans, but the army was typically composed of Novgorodians and Scandinavians (Varangians, in the Rusian sources); Mstislav was supported by his own forces from Tmutorokan and groups from the south, like the Kasogians. One could quite plausibly suggest that this was a pivotal moment in Rusian history. Should both brothers continue to live and rule for decades, the kingdom of Rus would thenceforth be divided into two. Should Iaroslav die and Mstislav claim all the territory for himself, then the orientation of Rus might be towards the south and east. In fact, what happened was that Mstislav died in 1036 with no heir, and Iaroslav assumed the role of ruler over all of Rus, solidifying its orientation towards the north and west (as will be seen with the various marriages of his children) for the foreseeable future.

Iaroslav's travails when becoming the sole ruler of Rus demonstrate a key purpose of our narrative in this volume – the succession and politics among the larger Volodimerovich clan do not always operate according to a clear-cut system, much as we might like them to. There are numerous individuals who vie for power with one another; there are also families who vie with other families within the larger clan, attempting to enhance their power compared to their cousins. Thus, while the Volodimerovichi can be called a clan since they share a common ancestor and are descended from a historical figure – Volodimer – they do not always fit our modern definition of a dynasty. Rather, it seems more appropriate for us to discuss them as families within this overarching area and period, sometimes cooperating, sometimes conflicting, but always related.

Marriage to Ingigerd

Sadly, we do not have specific details from Rusian sources about the wedding of Iaroslav and Ingigerd. However, we do have material finds from Rus of headdress pendants that were worn by elite women and that may have decorated the headdress of Ingigerd, or one of her daughters, in the eleventh century. The couple's marriage arrangements are recorded more fully in the Scandinavian sources, whence we also learn that although Ingigerd ultimately married Iaroslav, he was not her first betrothed.

Before Iaroslav, Ingigerd was betrothed to King Olaf of Norway. Although that engagement was broken, Olaf did end up marrying Ingigerd's sister, creating a lasting alliance between the Swedish and Norwegian rulers that would also have an effect on Ingigerd and Rus. The Scandinavian sources provide us with a rare glimpse into how such marriages were arranged; we see Iaroslav sending envoys to Ingigerd's father, King Olof Skötkonnung. The sources also reveal that Ingigerd had to be consulted about the marriage and her own consent given. Additionally, we see that there were negotiations for lands and resources as part of the marriage agreement. As was noted in the sources, Iaroslav needed Scandinavian troops to assist him in his struggles against other members of his clan to achieve complete control of Rus. The Scandinavian *Heimskringla* records that it was Ingigerd who demanded the city of Ladoga, a smaller trading city near Novgorod, as her own and that her follower, Jarl Ragnvald Ulfsson, should rule it.[13] Not mentioned in the account, but surely present in a group of people who were leaving their own country for a completely new one, were the other women who travelled with them, Jarl Ragnvald's wife in particular – Ingebjörg, the sister of the earlier Norwegian king, Olaf Tryggvasson. This gave Ingigerd a familiar coterie of Scandinavians around and near her, even while she was moving to a foreign land. Furthermore, the presence of Jarl Ragnvald and his troops would provide Iaroslav with the assistance he needed to gain, and keep, the throne of Kyiv.

This was not the end of Ingigerd's connection to Scandinavia, however. The *Heimskringla*, a thirteenth-century source of information on Norway's kings, tells a more involved tale, which begins in 1029 when Ingigerd's former betrothed and current brother-in-law, Olaf of Norway, was defeated by Knud of Denmark and fled to Rus, along

12 Temple pendant with two sirens flanking a Tree of Life, 11th–12th century, cloisonné (enamel and gold), Kiev.

with his son, Magnus. Iaroslav and Ingigerd welcomed the exiles into their home and court at Novgorod. When Björn the Marshal came from Norway later that year to bid Olaf back home to rule, the Rusian royal couple bade them stay. The *Heimskringla* even reports that they encouraged Olaf to conquer the Bulgars on the Volga and rule there.[14] In what was ultimately a fateful decision, Olaf decided to go home, where he would be killed at the Battle of Stiklestad in 1030, beginning his path to becoming St Olaf. Magnus, however, was entrusted into the care of Iaroslav and Ingigerd; he stayed in Rus as their ward for several years, before he too was summoned home to rule – successfully, in his case – in 1035.

Overlapping Magnus's stay at the court of Iaroslav and Ingigerd was another Scandinavian exile, the eventually famous Harald Hardrada. Harald was the half-brother of St Olaf; he fled to Rus after Olaf's defeat at Stiklestad. The accretion of legends around Harald is quite enormous and difficult to disentangle, but it is clear that he stayed in Iaroslav's court during the time that Magnus was there. He served Iaroslav in some military capacity; the *Heimskringla* reports that he was captain of Iaroslav's guard, which seems unlikely. Eventually, around 1034, he made his way further south to Constantinople, to begin a career in the vaunted Varangian Guard that served the Byzantine emperor. This, though, was not the end of Harald's involvement with Rus, as he returned from Constantinople a decade later and married Elisabeth, the daughter of Iaroslav and Ingigerd, and travelled with her to Norway. There, thanks to Elisabeth's connections (on her mother's side), Harald was able to claim friendship with the new Danish ruler, Knut Estridsson, and seize a portion of the authority to rule Norway from his kinsman Magnus, with whom he had spent time at the Rusian royal court.[15]

Thus, it is safe to say that Iaroslav's marriage to Ingigerd achieved very much more than merely providing a mother for his future children. Their marriage alliance created ties with Scandinavia that affected multiple ruling clans, including not only the Volodimerovichi but others well beyond their realm.

The Golden Age of Rus

The rule of Iaroslav and Ingigerd, both of whom were referred to in the literature as wise, the latter by medieval sources and the former by early modern and modern ones, was a period of rebuilding for Kyiv and Rus; this has typically been referred to as a Golden Age for the kingdom.[16] This was a time of new construction and expansion, religious developments as well as scholarly ones, and the growing integration of Rus into the community of the Christian kingdoms of Europe.[17]

Although Volodimer theoretically Christianized Rus in 988/9, and Thietmar of Merseburg declared that, circa 1018, Kyiv had four hundred churches, it was under the rule of Iaroslav and Ingigerd that Christianity developed more robustly.[18] For the year 1037, the PVL records: 'During [Iaroslav's] reign, the Christian faith was fruitful and multiplied.'[19] One of the signs of that multiplication is the creation of the first monastic foundations in Rus – the monasteries of SS. George and Irene. Neither of these monasteries is still extant, but the PVL lists their construction as taking place in 1037. They were dedicated (as was common, but not required) to the patron saints of their founders – Iaroslav (St George) (illus. 13) and Ingigerd (St Irene).

The so-called Golden Age of Rus saw the fortification and growth of the city of Kyiv. Kyiv, which was most likely founded in the ninth century, was built upon the hills above the shores of the Dnieper River. Volodimer built and expanded the city, and one district of it was named after him. This was where his first church, the Tithe Church, was built, and where the royal palace complex was located. Iaroslav expanded the city further over the hills, tripling its size, and created a district named after himself. The walls concomitantly expanded; there were gates facing the various roads that extended out from Kyiv to connect to the wider world. The most famous of those gates was the Golden Gate – which has been reconstructed in modern times and can be seen in illustration 14, with the pre-reconstructed version shown in illustration 15.

As one may be able to tell from the image, the gate itself was not of gold; rather, the name referenced the similarly named gate in Constantinople – one of many appropriations of names, titles, saints and so forth that were common throughout medieval Europe, as new kingdoms and powers sought to create authority for themselves via a connection with Byzantium – the medieval equivalent of the Roman Empire.

One of the other gates was known as the Jewish Gate, which testified to the large role that Jewish traders played in transporting goods throughout medieval Europe and into Central Asia.[20] These trade routes may also have been influential in the conversion of the semi-nomadic Khazars, based at Itil on the Volga (near where it flows into the Caspian Sea), to Judaism. Until the arrival of the Scandinavians, it is most likely that it was the Khazars who controlled Kyiv or, at least, were in a position to regularly tax it and its trade.[21]

Although the majority of the elite lived on the hills above the Dnieper River, the bulk of the river trade happened in a riverside region beneath the hills, known as the Podol. The Podol contained a marketplace, houses with courtyards, workshops and much more. It also seems to have had wooden streets from the eleventh century, which is perhaps a testament to the increasing construction encouraged by Iaroslav and Ingigerd and the changes that they were making within Rus.

The Golden Gate was not the only appropriation of Byzantine imagery in Iaroslav's new and growing Kyiv. Iaroslav commissioned a new church, the Holy Sophia church, to be built in Kyiv near the Golden Gate, in homage to the Church of Hagia Sophia (both of which mean holy wisdom) in Constantinople. The church was designed by Byzantine craftsmen and was certainly decorated by them. This was a time in which Byzantine craftsmen were some of the most sought-after in all medieval Europe; they created mosaics in both the Italian peninsula and Rus at the same time, during the early eleventh century. The church was filled with icons of the Virgin Mary as the Mother of God, St George (a later St George icon can be seen overleaf) and many others. It also had images of the Hippodrome, the imperial racetrack in Constantinople, painted on a special staircase area that was reserved for the sole use of the royal family – enhancing their connection with the Byzantine emperors.[22] The Holy Sophia church was created as the metropolitan church for Rus; in fact, quarters for the metropolitan were built next to it. It also became the model for churches throughout Rus, and a similar Holy Sophia church was erected in Novgorod (perhaps even by the same artisans) for Iaroslav's son, Volodimer.

The metropolitan of Constantinople was the highest churchman in the realm and was traditionally appointed by the patriarch in Constantinople. Metropolitans began appearing regularly in the Rusian sources from the time of Iaroslav's rule and were uniformly Greek in this period, with only one exception. That exception was a native Rusian priest named Ilarion, who was appointed by Iaroslav in 1051.[23] This appointment most likely coincided with the disjunction in the Rusian relationship with the Byzantines created by the 1043 attack on Constantinople, which was resolved by the eventual marriage of Vsevolod Iaroslavich to a Byzantine princess. Ilarion is famous not only for being the first native Rusian metropolitan but because we have some of his

13 Icon of St George and the dragon from Novgorod, 1400–1450, wood, gesso and gold.

14 Reconstruction of the Golden Gate of Kiev.

writing still extant, including his 'Sermon on Law and Grace'.[24] Much as Iaroslav was working to create a political realm integrated into medieval Europe, Ilarion used his 'Sermon on Law and Grace' to integrate Rus into biblical history, situating Rus, Volodimer and Iaroslav himself as agents of Christian devotion and the expansion of God's Law.

Another of the ways by which Iaroslav attempted to enhance the power of the Volodimerovich clan was to create a cult of a martyred ruler. Such cults were increasingly popular in medieval Europe, especially for newly Christianized polities.[25] St Oláf in Norway, St Wenceslas in Bohemia, St Edmund in England: all were rulers who were killed while ruling and who then became saints, enhancing not only their sanctity but that of their ruling line as a whole. Iaroslav, working with one of the first known metropolitans, Ioann, helped to create and spread the cult of ss. Boris and Gleb. Boris and Gleb had been two of Iaroslav's brothers who were, supposedly, killed by Sviatopolk's men during his ascent to power after Volodimer's death in 1015. According to the *Life of Boris and Gleb*, the brothers did not resist their fate, much like Jesus Christ in the Garden of Gethsemane, and thus became 'passion-sufferers'.[26] The creation of a cult of ruler saints was a way to enhance the legitimacy of the Volodimerovichi as a whole; this aim was furthered by labelling the brothers' murderer as Sviatopolk 'the Accursed' in the PVL. It thus seems to be a common theme of Iaroslav's reign that he was trying to build a powerful Rus for himself using all the available channels.

One claim of the PVL that modern scholars have found difficult to substantiate is Iaroslav's drive to promote writing and perhaps even literacy. The PVL records that Iaroslav 'applied himself to books and read them continually day and night. He assembled many scribes and translated from Greek into Slavic. He wrote and collected many books, through which true believers are instructed and enjoy religious education.'[27] Thus, one part of Iaroslav's Golden Age was a continuing Christianization through books. The difficulty for modern scholars is that there is so little writing from Rus extant from this, or any, period prior to the Mongol invasions of the mid-thirteenth century. Simon Franklin, who has studied this topic extensively, notes that there are only 23 manuscript books or fragments from the eleventh century; that number only goes up to 83 for the twelfth century.[28] Thus, it seems inappropriate to talk at length about a written culture – and yet, the PVL quite clearly states that Iaroslav himself wrote and encouraged writing in others. Furthermore, in a tenth-century treaty with Byzantium (recorded in the PVL), there are stipulations that the ruler of Rus will send written and sealed certificates with merchants travelling to Constantinople, detailing how many ships have been dispatched and

15 Early 20th-century photograph of the Golden Gate before its reconstruction.

what goods they carry.[29] Elsewhere, in the *Russkaia Pravda*, the law code of Rus, there are examples of tables for the payment for workers, the provisioning of bloodwite collectors (bloodwite being the money that a wrongdoer had to pay to their victim or the victim's family after bloodshed (with a cut paid to the ruler, too)) and even interest and debt payment schedules – all of which were written down in that document and could very well have been written down elsewhere.[30] Further writing is continually being excavated in the form of birch-bark documents. While these are often from Novgorod in the north, they have appeared in numerous excavations and represent a window onto the medieval world, showing small transactions and lending, complaints against husbands and wives, love letters and even children's drawings.[31] All of these suggest a larger world of writing for which we have good evidence in the twenty-first century, 1,000 years after the fact. Thus, it is possible to suggest that while Iaroslav and Ingigerd's 'Golden Age' may not be as well documented today as we might like, they did their best at the time to record their accomplishments and those of many others.

The Children of Iaroslav and Ingigerd

One of the defining features of medieval politics was its focus on the family; thus, when families made arrangements with one another, it was often in the form of a marriage that helped to seal the arrangement and provide both parties with a tie to one another. A key part of such a marriage was, of course, the woman involved. She travelled from her natal family to her marital family; this has historically been seen as her leaving her birthplace and birth family to become a member of her new family. However, it is much more accurate to consider her to be an ambassador, when seeing these marriages as political acts. She was an agent of her natal family who went to serve them in a foreign locale, advocating for them throughout her life; as we saw with Ingigerd earlier, she was accompanied by a coterie of officials and others from her homeland.[32]

As we have already seen, during the reign of Iaroslav and Ingigerd, Rus was a resting place for exiles who had been deprived of their position as a ruler or, at least, their families had been. Iaroslav and Ingigerd seem to have made a concerted effort to turn this situation to their advantage, as they proceeded to arrange for many of their children, especially their daughters, to be wedded to exiled royals from elsewhere

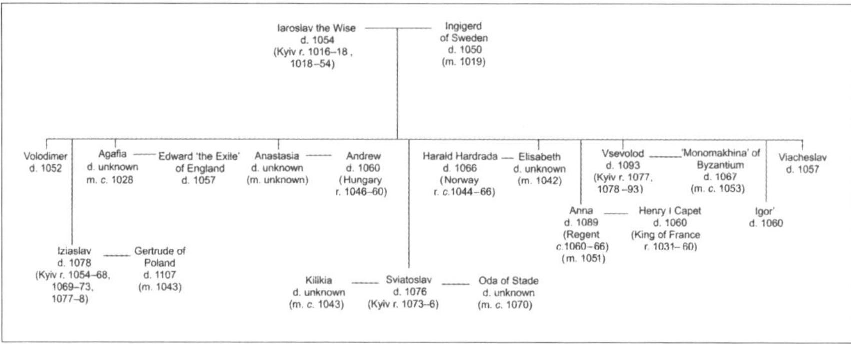

16 Iaroslav, Ingigerd and their children.

in Europe, such as Harald Hardrada. These were not the only marital ties that were arranged, however; we shall see several examples that elucidate how the royal family tied itself into the larger medieval European world by means of a web of dynastic marriages. Of the ten children that the couple had, six were male and four were female, and we know about the marriages of seven of them. This is a good amount of evidence, given the state of our written sources for Rus in the eleventh century; this is explained in large part because these children married into the ruling families of Europe and the details are preserved in a variety of sources from elsewhere in medieval Europe. Of those seven marriages, we will examine one of the daughters' and two of the sons' marriages to try to demonstrate the broader picture of such marriages and the lives of these Iaroslavichi – the children of Iaroslav.

The most well known of all the children of Iaroslav was Anna. Iaroslav first attempted to arrange a marriage for Anna with one of the rulers of the German Empire in the 1040s. That overture was declined but was noted by the ruler of France, Henry Capet.[33] Henry was much older and had been married before, but none of his children had lived to adulthood and he was currently without a wife. The base of the source material for medieval France is greater than that for Rus; thus we know that in 1049, Henry sent two French bishops, Gauthier of Meaux and Gauzlin of Chauny, to Kyiv as the leaders of his embassy to negotiate a marriage agreement with Iaroslav. Unfortunately for our purposes, we do not have any record of the embassy in Rus and so we can but guess at what was discussed, although we can certainly conclude that the embassy was successful; when the bishops returned to France (and to the French literary sources) in 1050, they returned not only with many gifts but with Anna herself.

Anna and Henry were married in 1051, in a grand affair in Paris. This daughter of Iaroslav and Ingigerd, a member of the Volodimerovichi clan from the easternmost Christian kingdom in Europe, was now the queen of France. In 1052, she fulfilled one of her most important royal duties when she gave birth to a son – Philip – the heir to the French throne.[34] The birth of the heir to the throne was, of course, a matter of immense import, but the naming of the heir was also incredibly important. In the Capetian royal line, there were largely only two choices: Hugh and Robert. King Henry, for instance, became ruler only after the elder Hugh had died; before Henry, the Capetian rulers had been either Hugh or Robert for one hundred years. In fact, Anna's second and third sons were named Robert and Hugh. But then, where did the name Philip come from? It has been widely suggested, and by now is accepted, that this was Anna's choice of name and that this was a way in which she could exercise her power, both in the royal family and as an agent of Rus.

This name was not Anna's only influence on France during her time there. Henry died in 1060 and, after his death, Anna ruled as part of a regency council on behalf of her son, Philip. She travelled the country with him; the French ruler, as in the case of most medieval rulers, was often itinerant and Anna signed documents alongside her young son. One of the most well-known examples of this is a charter from Chartres, in which both Anna and Philip are jointly referred to as 'king'.[35] Additionally, there is even a document in which Anna has signed her own name as 'Anna Regina'; however, she uses the Cyrillic alphabet rather than the Latin.[36] This small inscription gives us a remarkable insight into the potential literacy of a female member of the Volodimerovichi, as well as her activities as a ruler in France.

Iziaslav was the second oldest son of Iaroslav and Ingigerd; because his elder brother, Volodimer, predeceased Iaroslav, it was Iziaslav who ended up ruling Rus after Iaroslav's death. All of that was still in the future, however, when Iziaslav made an important marriage in 1043, forming an alliance with the ruling family of the closest neighbour of Rus – Poland.[37] This was not the first royal marriage with Poland, as we saw earlier; Sviatopolk, with whom Iaroslav had vied for the throne of Rus, was married to a Polish princess, the daughter of Bolesław I. After the death of Bolesław I, Poland began to experience internal conflicts; by the third decade of the eleventh century, it was disunified and subject to warring factions. Into this breach came Casimir, subsequently known as 'the Restorer' for his restoration of a united Poland. To accomplish that feat, though, Casimir would first need allies; while he could call on help from the German Empire via his mother's connection to the ruling family there, he also needed help from Rus. Thus, in 1043 Casimir married his sister Gertrude to Iziaslav, son of Iaroslav and Ingigerd, as a way to connect their two families together. Like many royal marriages, this too served to cement a political agreement. Casimir needed assistance in regaining and reuniting Poland, but he also needed a peaceful border with his powerful eastern neighbour. In this marriage, he got both: Iaroslav's Rus did not attempt to take any of the Polish lands and, in fact, Iaroslav dispatched military forces to assist Casimir in seizing the territory of Mazovia. Iaroslav even went so far as to hand over the captured ruler of Mazovia, Miecław, to Casimir rather than using that position of power himself. Such a powerful tie with Rus was not created with just one relationship, however. Casimir married a Rusian princess, a sister of Iaroslav named Dobronega, who was also called Maria.[38] Thus, there were two ties that bound the Piast and Volodimerovich families together and created the basis for an alliance to rebuild Poland.

The marriage of Gertrude and Iziaslav may have been created with a particular purpose in mind (the rebuilding of Poland), but it was a lifelong relationship and one that would have additional consequences for both ruling families. In 1068, Iziaslav was removed from the throne of Kyiv and he fled to Poland as a refugee. His flight was similar to that of Sviatopolk, as seen earlier during his conflict with Iaroslav; once again, it resulted in Polish assistance. In this instance, Bolesław II (who was Casimir and Dobronega's son, as well as Iziaslav and Gertrude's nephew) assisted Iziaslav in regaining his throne in 1069, demonstrating the value of these ties between ruling families beyond their original purpose of marriage. Unfortunately for Iziaslav, this assistance was not the last time that he would need to take advantage of such ties. In 1073, his throne was usurped by his own brothers, Sviatoslav and Vsevolod. Once again, Iziaslav fled to Poland, although this time he was more prepared and took not only Gertrude with him, as well as one of their children, but the Kyivan treasury.[39] Bolesław II, however, was less amenable to assisting him a second time and expelled his aunt, uncle and cousin from his realm, although he kept the treasury for himself. This expulsion left Iziaslav and Gertrude to try alternate tactics; they utilized both their connections in the German Empire, via Gertrude's extended family, and their religious ties, sending their son Iaropolk and his German bride Cunigunda to the papacy, in a second attempt to regain their throne. Ultimately, it was again Bolesław II who helped with that endeavour, after being pressured (and crowned as king) by Pope Gregory VII; Iziaslav and Gertrude were returned to rule in Kyiv in 1077. Iziaslav's travels and travails would not have ended as successfully were it not for the presence and intervention of Gertrude, demonstrating once more the importance of marital alliances and women in medieval politics.

The youngest of the sons of Iaroslav and Ingigerd to marry was Vsevolod, who would himself become king of Rus in 1078. Vsevolod's marriage requires a bit of backstory, as it is related to the last Rusian raid on Constantinople, which occurred in 1043.[40] In that year, Rusian forces, under the command of Iaroslav's eldest son Volodimer (who later predeceased Iaroslav), attacked the city of Constantinople in retribution for the death of a Rusian merchant in the city. It is widely suggested that this attack led to peace talks and that those talks were confirmed via a marriage between the ruling families of Rus and Byzantium. Unfortunately for us, the only record of this marriage comes from the PVL, where it says merely that Vsevolod fathered a son with a '*tsesaritsa Gr'kyna*' (Greek princess).[41]

The medieval Rusian chroniclers were churchmen and were typically monks. As such, they often worked in monasteries that were supervised by or related to the Byzantine ecclesiastical establishment. Thus, we find a trend in the early Rusian chronicle sources of noting ties with Byzantium more fully than ties with other nations, as can be seen from our earlier discussion. This is significant in the case of Vsevolod's marriage because the identity of Vsevolod's wife, beyond the fact of her being a Byzantine royal, is never revealed by the Rusian chroniclers – and, quite oddly, the copious eleventh-century Byzantine sources do not mention this marriage at all. We are left to puzzle out the identity of this woman from little evidence. One piece of evidence that has given us a large clue is the nickname of her first-born son with Vsevolod, who was named Volodimer but nicknamed Monomakh. This name, which occurs in the chronicle sources as well as in the material culture (illus. 17), is a Rusian version of a Byzantine family name and accords with the family name of the contemporary ruler of the Byzantine empire – Constantine IX Monomachos.[42]

As a result, it has been assumed that the Greek princess who married Vsevolod was a member of the Byzantine imperial family.

17 Seal of Volodimer Monomakh. *Aktovye pechati drevnei rusi* X-XV *vv.*, table 3, no. 25.

Moreover, the continued use of his mother's family name – Monomachos – by Volodimer indicates her importance and that of her family to her son and his self-conception. It is a slightly different situation from what we saw with Volodimer's sister Anna naming her firstborn son Philip, but it is very similar in terms of female influence, this time within Rus.[43]

INGIGERD DIED IN 1050 and Iaroslav died in 1054, thus ending what was one of the longest and most productive ruling partnerships in the history of Rus. Iaroslav and Ingigerd had multiple children and although their eldest, Volodimer, predeceased Iaroslav, there were still numerous sons who were ready to take over the throne (illus. 16). The PVL records what has often been called 'Iaroslav's Testament' – a recording of the last will from a father to his sons: 'My sons, I am about to quit this world. Love one another, since ye are brothers by one father and mother . . . remain rather at peace, brother heeding brother.'[44] Iaroslav continues, naming Iziaslav as the heir to the throne of Kyiv and bidding his other sons to 'heed him as ye have heeded me, that he may take my place among you'.[45] He further went on to assign territories for each of his other sons to rule, and 'laid upon Iziaslav the injunction to aid the party wronged, in case one brother should attack another'.[46] It seems quite clear, according to the PVL, that Iaroslav wished to pass on his kingdom intact to Iziaslav, with all of his sons ruling under Iziaslav, who would act as the new father figure. As we have already seen, however, that does not happen, and brother does indeed rise up against brother; however, even after being twice usurped (once by his brothers), Iziaslav does go to the aid of his wronged brother at the last, causing his own death. Many scholars have suggested that this internecine warfare among the sons of Iaroslav brought about the end of the Golden Age of Rus. We would suggest otherwise, since, as can be seen from the subsequent chapters, the families of Rus continued to both build and expand, as well as make alliances and vie for power in the subsequent decades.

4

Mstislav/Harald Volodimerich and His Family

Mstislav or Harald 'Feodor' Volodimerich was born in 1076.[1] He was the son of Volodimer Vsevolodovich, who was also called Monomakh after his mother's family, and Gyða, the daughter of Harold Godwinson, the last Anglo-Saxon king of England. After Harold's defeat at the Battle of Hastings in 1066, his family fled in various directions, with some of his sons going to Ireland to seek assistance and other children going to Denmark.[2] Via her Scandinavian family connections, Gyða ended up in Rus, where she married Volodimer.[3] Mstislav, much like his own father, had multiple names. A Slavic name that was given to him at birth – Mstislav; a Christian name that was bestowed upon him at his baptism – Feodor,[4] and a nickname that indicated the importance of his ties to his maternal family – Harald. Mstislav's nickname of Harald was not used (or at least recorded in extant sources) in Rus but was applied to him regularly in the Scandinavian sources. The *Heimskringla* refers to Mstislav as 'King Harald of Garthar in the east. He was the son of Valdamar Jarizleifsson.'[5] Although the author gets the name of Mstislav/Harald's grandfather wrong, mistaking him for his great-grandfather Iaroslav, the rest of the information is correct. This gives us an interesting introduction to our story of Mstislav and his family, including the importance of his maternal family in terms of his connections in Scandinavia, which he would develop throughout his life.

As is typical for this period, not much is known of Mstislav's early life. We see him enter more fully into the literature when he is older and begins to rule in his own right. In 1095, the Novgorodians (as they are described in the *Povest' vremennykh let*, though we cannot assume it was all of them) rose up to change their current ruler.[6] David, the son of Sviatoslav Iaroslavich, had been ruling in Novgorod but he shifted his power base at that time, first to Smolensk and then, only a year later, to the main seat of the Sviatoslavich family – Chernigov.[7] With David gone, the Novgorodians sought out Mstislav to make him their ruler. This is an odd, but interesting choice that deserves a bit of discussion. In Chapter Three, we saw that Novgorod had been treated as the second city of Rus and numerous rulers placed their heirs there to gain experience. This habit seems to have fallen out of favour when Iaroslav the Wise's eldest son, Volodimer, predeceased him. In 1095, the ruler in Kyiv was Sviatopolk, the son of Iziaslav Iaroslavich, who had himself been the ruler of Novgorod from 1077 to 1088 after his own father's death. Sviatopolk did have sons who could have ruled in Novgorod, and yet the Novgorodians chose Mstislav, the son of Volodimer Monomakh, the ruler of Pereiaslavl. While it is true that Volodimer Monomakh was a powerful figure in Rus, it would have been more likely that a son of the ruler of Kyiv would be chosen. Why one of his sons was not chosen is entirely conjectural, given our lack of sources, but that same lack of sources is relevant to this question. The existing sources that we do have were written on behalf of the family of Mstislav/Harald himself and were designed to glorify his family line.[8] Thus, it is possible to suggest (although this is only a possibility) that there was more going on at the time than is recorded in the chronicles, and that the Novgorodians' choice of Mstislav in 1095 was simply the first step in his grand life plan that happened to be highlighted in that record. For

18 Rus finger ring from Kiev, 12th century, silver and niello.

whatever reason, once Mstislav was ruling in Novgorod in 1095, he became part of the chronicle record and we thereby learn more of him and of his family.

While Mstislav was ruling happily in Novgorod, busily engaging in marital arrangements, both his own and those of his family, the political landscape was changing apace in Rus. In 1113, King Sviatopolk died in Kyiv.[9] A succession is always a difficult time, and the situation was no different in Rus. Succession in Rus was collateral; after Sviatopolk's death, the throne should have passed to his next oldest brother. Given that he did not have one, the right to rule should have passed to the eldest member of the next family in line, the Sviatoslavichi. Instead, although there were multiple Sviatoslavich members of the family available to rule, the kingship bypassed the Sviatoslavich family entirely and went to the third (and last) family, the Vsevolodovichi, in the person of their eldest member, Volodimer Monomakh, the son of Vsevolod. There has been a great deal of discussion regarding why this happened, but one of the most persuasive reasons is that because of Sviatoslav, the patriarch of the Sviatoslavichi family, usurping the throne of his brother Iziaslav, his family was ineligible to rule in Kyiv. Regardless of the rationale, this was a shift in the succession process and set a precedent that would act as a potential trigger for further changes to be made.[10]

Volodimer Monomakh was already sixty years old by the time he inherited the throne of Kyiv. While a collateral succession system worked well when most people had short life expectancies, at a time when individuals were long-lived, this could be one of its perils. Just imagine: if a member of the Sviatoslavichi had taken the throne, Volodimer would likely not have lived long enough to rule. Sixty years old in early twelfth-century Rus was a respectable old age and Volodimer had lived a difficult life of battle and travel, yet he ruled firmly for several years. It was only in 1117 that a shift in the power structure began to be seen. In that year, Volodimer called Mstislav back from Novgorod and gave him the town of Belgorod.[11] Belgorod was a city only a few hours' ride from Kyiv, and not one that had heretofore had its own ruler. Situating Mstislav in Belgorod seems to have been a strategic placement by Volodimer of his eldest son close to Kyiv, both so that his son could assist Volodimer Monomakh in ruling Rus and to ready Mstislav for his own succession to the throne. To maintain the family's ties with Novgorod, Mstislav placed his own son, also named Volodimer, on the throne of Novgorod.[12]

Volodimer Monomakh maintained an active lifestyle as the ruler of Rus, including engaging in conflicts against rival families such as the Iziaslavichi and the Vseslavichi, but Mstislav seemed comfortable to stay at home in Belgorod, or at least is not mentioned as travelling widely with his father, reinforcing the idea of his placement there being related to a possible succession.

Volodimer Monomakh died in 1125, and Mstislav was immediately enthroned as king of Rus in Kyiv.[13] Mstislav's succession of his father was another break in the system of collateral succession that had previously been followed in Rus. Given the existing system and its method of functioning, after Volodimer Monomakh's death, the succession should have gone to the children of Sviatopolk Iziaslavich; some of them were still alive, despite Volodimer's persistent attacks upon the Iziaslavichi family during his rule in Kyiv. Instead, collateral succession became lineal succession, at least insofar as the succession stayed within Volodimer Monomakh's line until 1139. The chronicle sources note that Mstislav took over the throne as the eldest son of Volodimer Monomakh, which was potentially something that both Volodimer and Mstislav had been preparing for since his move to Belgorod, nearly a decade before.[14] Thus, it is from 1125 that we can begin to discuss a Rus ruled by Mstislav, the culmination of three decades of political development that was designed to bring him to the throne as the king of Rus.

The Marriages of Mstislav

Rus, as we saw under Iaroslav and Ingigerd, was a home for refugees and runaway royals, many of whom the royal couple took in and aided, and even helped to provide marriages for. This tradition continued through the end of the eleventh century, even if it happened less often, and is most likely responsible for the marriage of Mstislav and Kristín.[15] Kristín was the daughter of King Inge Steinkelsson of Sweden, but Inge was not always the ruler; before that, he was an outcast. Between 1075 and 1080, Inge was forced to flee Sweden; instead, he went to Rus, where Vsevolod, the grandfather of Mstislav, was ruling in Kyiv. Like the other exiles before him, he made his home there but kept an eye out for the chance to return. That return happened sometime after 1080. None of the sources specifies the date when the Swedish nobles appeared in Rus to call him home to rule.[16] Inge's connection to Rus continued; sometime around 1095, when Mstislav was enthroned as ruler of Novgorod, he married Inge's daughter, Kristín. Unfortunately, due to the paucity of source material, we do not know the rationale behind the marriage. We do know that Inge was at war with the Norwegian king over territory; therefore, perhaps the marriage was to secure aid or resources, or simply to ensure peace on his eastern border, while Inge engaged in conflict to the west and south. Regardless of the rationale, the marriage of Mstislav and Kristín set up a major link between Rus and Sweden – one that would be acknowledged numerous times in the genealogies of later rulers.[17]

Due to the dearth of Rusian sources, we do not know much about Kristín's life after her marriage to Mstislav. We know that her sister Margaret inherited lands in Sweden, as a daughter of King Inge. Margaret was able to pass that land on to whomever she chose, and so we can speculate that Kristín also had lands and the ability to pass those on, although we have no evidence for it, nor for what she may have done with that ability. Instead, we are only able to talk about her children (below) and about her own death, which occurred in 1122.[18] She lived and ruled in Rus for nearly thirty years, but we are unable to speak with much authority about her life there.

The same chronicle entry that gave us the information about Kristín's death informs us of Mstislav's remarriage. His second wife was a daughter of Dmitri Zavidich, a former *posadnik* of Novgorod. This marriage, internal to Rus, represents another puzzle for historians, as we not only have few sources for it but because it is one of the very few marriages that we know about wherein a member of the Volodimerovichi does not marry another royal.[19] The *posadnik* was chosen by the people of Novgorod to be the city's administrator. Novgorod, as has been seen here and elsewhere, was quite an important city for Rus and, in addition to keeping

19 Seal of Kristín, from *Aktovye pechati drevnei rusi* X-XV *vv.*, table 3, no. 39.

their own chronicle, we see Novgorodians appearing in a variety of situations elsewhere in Rus. This is particularly true for Kyiv, where Novgorodians often show up, either of their own volition or because their attendance is requested and required by the king, to play a role in ensuring successions or when choosing Volodimerovich rulers for Novgorod – for instance, as happened when Mstislav was requested to be the ruler of Novgorod in 1095.

Part of the rationale for this process is the existence in Novgorod of an assembly known as the *veche*. There has been much debate about what the *veche* was and was not, both in this period and later. In later periods, the existence of the *veche* led to the claim that Novgorod was a republic, ruled by the people to a certain extent.[20] The gathering of the Novgorod populace, which came to be known as the *veche*, was instigated by the ringing of the *veche* bell, a sound to which all within earshot could respond. The importance of the *veche* bell was such that when Ivan III of Moscow conquered the city, centuries after this period, he took the bell with him and had it melted down to signal the end of Novgorod's self-governance.[21] While the *veche* and its elite backers, such as the *posadniki* (plural of *posadnik*), *tysiatskii* (the local military leader), and the archbishop, helped to administer the city, there was still always a ruler from the Volodimerovich clan ruling in Novgorod. In fact, one of the signal moments demonstrating the *veche*'s ability to choose their own ruler comes with Mstislav's family, in the person of his son Vsevolod, whom the Novgorodians imprisoned and rejected as ruler in 1136.

A marriage between a member of the nobility of Novgorod and the heir to the throne of Rus was certainly an oddity but, as one can see from the information about the internal political structure of Novgorod, it does make sense that they should have wished to reinforce the Mstislavich family's connection with the local political structure, especially with a family who were among the elite of that hierarchy. Although this noblewoman's father, the former *posadnik* Dmitri Zavidich, was already deceased at the time of her marriage, her brother would later go on to hold the position of *posadnik*, like his father – which is indicative of the continuing power and influence of the family in the city. While Mstislav's first marriage was about strengthening foreign ties for himself and for Rus, his second marriage seems to have been to create a stronger tie to the second city of the kingdom, making sure that its people were represented and perhaps even felt heard at the royal court in Kyiv.

Rus under Mstislav

Mstislav/Harald ruled as king of Rus for only seven years, dying in 1132. We can, however, present a picture of what life was like in Rus, as well as the major events of the time that occurred during and around the time of his reign.[22] One of the most iconic of those events was related to his assumption of the throne of Rus from his father, Volodimer Monomakh. Apart from the circumstances that we have already discussed, Volodimer also left his children something unique, a written testament telling of his life and providing them with information about his rule, to create a model for how to be a king.[23] This document is unique in the history of Rus; some have suggested that it has parallels with an Anglo-Saxon tradition, which Volodimer Monomakh may have known about through his wife, Gyða Haroldsdottir.[24] However, others have included it in the medieval tradition of 'mirrors of princes', in which the author typically writes a manual on how to be an ideal Christian ruler.[25] Though Volodimer begins by declaiming his own misery before God, suggesting that his readers praise and fear God, and quoting Psalms liberally in the opening, the document is not primarily focused on the Christian duties of rulers. Instead, Volodimer suggests that his sons 'not be disposed to laziness, but labour zealously' and then goes on to relate how he did just that, largely by discussing his many military campaigns and hunting experiences.[26] He does provide practical advice to his sons, including taking responsibility for their own affairs, rather than leaving this task to their subordinates, and not allowing their men to commit violence against the local population while travelling.[27] Volodimer Monomakh also gives us a fascinating glimpse into the standard of education in medieval Rus. He encouraged learning in his sons by providing the example of his own father (Vsevolod Iaroslavich), who 'understood five languages'.[28] Which five languages he understood is a mystery, unfortunately, but one that has kept students and scholars guessing for numerous years. All in all, the Testament, as it is called, is a fascinating glimpse into Monomakh's life, presented in a format otherwise unseen for this period.

It is also during this period that we believe the *Povest vremennykh let* was compiled, which begins with the biblical Flood and extends to 1117.[29] The PVL is a combination of earlier Rus annals, accounts and eyewitness reports that also incorporated material from other sources, such as the *Chronicle of Georgios Hamartolos*, including treaties between the

Greeks and the Rusians; the Pannonian *Life of Methodius, Archbishop of Moravia*; *The Revelations of Pseudo-Methodios of Patara*; the Rus *Paleia*; the Psalter and other books of the Bible, accounts of the seven ecumenical councils and so forth. Some scholars include the account of the Tower of Babel from the *Chronographia of John Malalas* as a source, and the *Testament of Volodimer Monomakh* is also often considered part of the PVL. There is also a question as to whether other narrative subunits, such as the 'Philosopher's Discourse' (986) and the 'Testament of Iaroslav' (1054) were existing standalone compositions that were incorporated into the text or if they were compositions written by one of the chroniclers specifically for the PVL, as with the 'Tale of the Founding of the Caves Monastery' (1051), which was most likely written by the final author/redactor of the PVL, Vasilii.

In terms of its composition, the question is whether the PVL should be considered a homogenous text, written from beginning to end by a single author who incorporated and at times modified other sources or the PVL, or if it should be considered the result of a final redactor who merely edited an already existing earlier work or works, as is seen in the 'Beginning Compilation' (*Nachalnyi svod*), the redaction of the monk Nestor or the redaction of Hegumen Silvestr. In other words, who was the author of the words that appear at any particular point in the text? It is presumed that the author or authors of the PVL did not write the text of the treaties, but uncertainty remains as to what extent the author modified the sources that are incorporated, and whether such modifications were made by the final author/redactor or by the compiler of an earlier compilation (*svod*) that was subsequently incorporated into the text of the PVL. One can discern two narratives in the PVL – one from the beginning through *s.a.* 6545 (1037); the other from *s.a.* 6562 (1054) to the end. The most likely author of the second narrative is a monk of the Kyiv Caves Monastery named Vasilii, who identified himself through his own eyewitness accounts.[30] The author of the first narrative (through 1037) also identifies himself as a monk of the Caves Monastery, but he does not give his name. In the opening lines of the PVL, the author proposed to explain 'from where came the Rus' land and who first began to rule in it, and from where the Rus' land began'. Between the end of the first narrative (1037) and the beginning of the second narrative (1054) are a series of yearly entries, possibly written by the Caves Monastery monk Nikon as part of his Compilation of 1073. Despite the complicated history of the production of this document, it remains one of our most vital sources for the study of the history of Rus.

In Chapter Three we discussed the Rusian outpost of Tmutorokan on the Black Sea. By the early twelfth century, this city was lost to Rus; the rolling grasslands that made up the steppe north of the Black Sea were increasingly inhospitable, due to the presence of the Polovtsy. The Polovtsy had arrived in the second half of the eleventh century and made themselves felt as both raiders and traders, especially in the southernmost cities and towns of Rus during that period and throughout the twelfth century. These were not the first nomads to occupy that steppe, nor would they be the last, but they were one of the most persistent, being both a thorn in the side of the Volodimerovich clan as a whole and an irritant to internal stability. In particular, the chronicle sources record that the Polovtsy were particularly friendly with Oleg, the son of Sviatoslav Iaroslavich, and his descendants.[31] Their relationship with the Sviatoslavichi (or Oleg's own branch of that family – the Olgovichi) would do lasting harm to that family's image over time, for they have been pictured in the historiography as breaking the peace both within Rus and within the clan.[32] The very presence of the

20 Rus armlet from Kiev, 12th century, silver and niello.

Polovtsy also complicated the trade routes to the south with Byzantium; alternatively, we see the growth of avenues of trade during the twelfth century, as in the case of the southwest.

Galicia and Volhynia, which were crucial territories in the southwest region of Rus, became increasingly important during the rule of Mstislav/Harald. His father, Volodimer Monomakh, acted multiple times against Iaroslav, son of Sviatopolk Iziaslavich, the ruler of the western town of Volodymyr. Iaroslav, like much of the wider Iziaslavichi family, had ties with the Polish ruling family, including marrying a daughter of Władysław Herman (r. 1079–1102). However, demonstrating the breadth of his ties in eastern Europe, Iaroslav had also married a daughter of the Hungarian prince, Ladislaus, before that – all of which built up his connections with his western neighbours and presented a threat to the rule of Monomakh and his family. The one attempt to bridge that gap was circa 1112, when Iaroslav's third, and final, marriage was arranged with a daughter of Mstislav/Harald.[33] Unfortunately for peace among the larger clan, Iaroslav repudiated her in 1118, and ended up dying the same year while in conflict with Mstislav and his father.

Iaroslav was not the only ruler, nor was he even the most famous, to make a career in the southwest. Shortly after the death of Mstislav, we see the rise of Volodimerko, son of Volodar Rostislavich, who became the first prominent ruler of Galich, circa 1140.[34] Volodimerko, who was not from one of the main or most important families within the Volodimerovich clan, nevertheless made a name for himself, first by supporting the outsider king in Kyiv, Vsevolod Olgovich, and then by turning against him.[35] Vsevolod Olgovich ended up requiring assistance from both the Hungarian and Polish ruling clans to gather enough forces to defeat Volodimerko. Volodimerko's policies, while potentially destructive, actually enabled him to create a space for himself within the larger clan hierarchy. The end result was a powerful Galician territory, which would end up growing into the nucleus of a later centre of power in a divided Rus (see Chapter Six).

Iaroslav the Wise created the *Russkaia Pravda*, the law code for medieval Rus. This law code was expanded by the sons of Iaroslav, and the final expansion was made by Volodimer Monomakh. The opening section of his addition to the code presents us with a fascinating scenario that does not appear in any of the chronicle sources; briefly, Volodimer called together a group of councillors that included the military leaders (*tysiatskie*) of Kyiv, Belgorod and Pereiaslavl, as well as several other individuals, including a representative of Oleg Sviatoslavich, the current patriarch of the Sviatoslavich family of the Volodimerovichi.[36] This opening section provides us with much interesting information, even before the contents of the legal changes are considered. Volodimer Monomakh, as king of Rus and ruler of Kyiv, was able to change the law code, like his predecessors; however, in the execution of that process, he called on support from the military leaders of multiple cities over which he and his own family (the Vsevolodovichi) had control. The position of *tysiatskii* is typically only noted in relation to Novgorod, but its inclusion in the *Russkaia Pravda* informs us that the position was, in fact, much more widespread, telling us a great deal about governance in Rus. In addition to these military retainers, he also included a representative of one of the other major families of the royal clan. Given that at this time, Volodimer Monomakh actively moved against the Iziaslavichi, the other major family line within the clan, it is not surprising that he did not include them in his legal changes. All this, combined in just a few lines of the addition to the law code, gives us a wider view of the consultative governance process in Rus than is typically portrayed in the chronicle narratives.

As for the additions and changes to the law code under the rule of Volodimer, many of them are about debt, indentured servitude and slavery. It was certainly possible in twelfth-century Rus to get into debt with both foreign and local lenders. Even members of the ruling clan could act as lenders, according to the law codes. This kind of reading of legal history is often described as descriptive, describing what was going on in practice, as opposed to a prescriptive reading, which would describe what the authors of the laws wanted to happen. Debt in Rus could lead to indentured servitude, but these servants were very clearly not considered slaves under the law. They could gain their freedom and they did have rights, including the right to flee from their lord and seek justice at the ruler's court.[37] Slaves, on the other hand, had far fewer rights, but these were still included in the laws.[38] They could not be killed out of hand, but nor could they serve as witnesses. Slaves could engage in trade, and their owners were the ones to incur debts on their behalf, even if the slaves ran away or stole goods.

There are many more provisions in this expansion to the code that tell us much about Rusian society. We can see the importance of beehives and how they were a source of economic prosperity for their honey as well as for their wax; the former was used for sweetening and mead production, the latter for candles.[39] In a similar vein, hunting and grain were prized and were protected against theft.[40] Some of the most interesting articles give us information about the life of women in medieval Rus, whether intentionally or otherwise. For instance, women were worth half that of a man in terms of bloodwite.[41] The daughters of the elite could inherit from their family, but only if there were no sons left, and wives were due a portion of their husband's property after his death.[42] In one of the most interesting, and telling, legal provisions, the *Russkaia Pravda* notes that the mother may give her own wealth to any of her sons, but: 'If all her sons are wicked, she may give her portion to her daughter who feeds her.'[43] These additions to the law code provide us with a fascinating glimpse into many elements of Rusian society that were not recorded by the chronicle writers.

The Children of Mstislav and Kristín

One of the oddities of attempting to discuss the various marriages and kinship ties within Rus is the lack of good source material. Simon Franklin notes that there are only 83 extant documents from the twelfth century, most of which are ecclesiastical.[44] This is one of the reasons why any analysis of royal marriages needs to be inclusive of sources from other parts of Europe, not only because that is where the marriages occurred but because there are additional sources in those areas.[45] However, while the children of Iaroslav and Ingigerd largely married out of Rus in alliances with other royal and noble families, by the time of the twelfth century, the Volodimerovich clan was robust enough in numbers and in generations to avoid consanguineous marriages, so that more and more marriages within the clan could occur.[46] One final factor is important to note in regard to these marriages; that is, the different roles played by men and women in royal marriages. Typically, women would marry outside of the family, clan and kingdom; thus we see them moving to Norway, England and France in the examples from Chapter Three. Men, on the other hand, would stay within their kingdom and marry women who were local or from other kingdoms. The combination of the three mentioned factors (a lack of good information sources for Rus, an increase in internal marriages and the differing roles of men and women) means that in terms of the family of Mstislav and Kristín, we can identify with some confidence most of the men that their daughters married, as they almost all married outside of Rus,

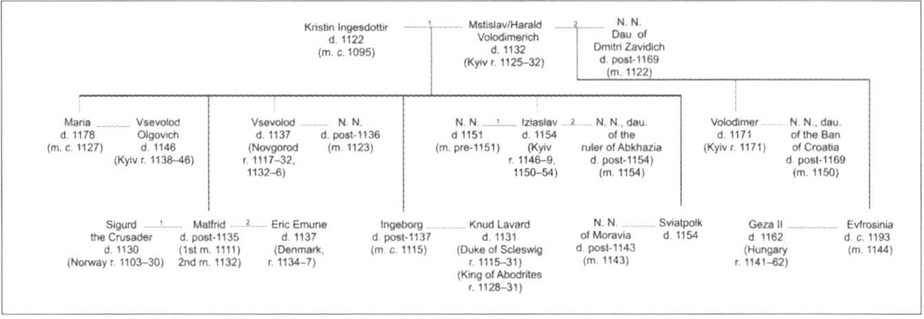

21 Mstislav, his wives and children.

whereas we cannot tell you the names of most of the women that their sons married, as they largely married within Rus.

For instance, Vsevolod was the eldest male child of Mstislav and Kristín, and as such was placed in Novgorod to be the ruler there in 1117, when Mstislav began assisting his own father to rule. Given the importance of the eldest male and the idea that he might inherit, it would seem important to know to whom he was married and to make that marriage an important one. Instead, what we have is a note in the Novgorod Chronicle from 1123 that Vsevolod was married.[47] There is no information other than that – no who, where or why recorded. The Novgorod Chronicle records that Vsevolod was still married a few years later in 1136 when he, along with his wife and children, was imprisoned in a church in Novgorod for two months before being forced out of the town.[48] Here again, although there is no mention of who this woman was, we do have children to be added to the narrative. This lack of information is the case for the majority of the male children of Mstislav and Kristín.

In two instances, however, we do have a bit more information. Iziaslav, who would later end up ruling in Kyiv multiple times in the twelfth century, had a completely unknown first wife, but in the case of his second wife, we are at least told that she was the daughter of the ruler of Abkhazia.[49] Abkhazia, a polity on the Black Sea near the Caucasus, is often identified with modern Georgia, but is separate from it. This is one of the few marriages in this period of Rusian history wherein we see a connection not with areas to the west of the kingdom, but with areas to the south. Perhaps it is indicative of an interest in expanding the kingdom in that direction, or in making peace, but it is difficult to know; the problem is made more difficult by the fact that Iziaslav died later that same year. The second example is Mstislav's son, Sviatopolk, who married a woman 'from Moravia'.[50] We do not know who the woman was, and although many people have attempted educated guesses, there is no evidence (in either the Rusian or the Bohemian sources) to confirm or deny any of those theories. Thus, her identity, as well as the purpose behind the marriage, is still a mystery.

Apart from the mysterious male marriages, we actually know quite a bit about some of the daughters of Mstislav and Kristín, including whom they married and why. This section will explore three of those women and their marriages, discussing not only the royal marriage policies of Rus in the twelfth century but what we know about Rusian women and the roles they played in marriage, family and politics. The three women in question are three of their oldest daughters, one of whom stayed within Rus and married (Maria) and two who would marry into Scandinavian royal families (Malfrid and Ingeborg).

One of the most important marriages in twelfth-century Rus is also one of the marriages about which little is known. Although it involves one of the daughters of Mstislav and Kristín, she is largely absent from the sources – as is not uncommon with women in the Rusian chronicles. The story of her marriage must, therefore, begin with her husband, Vsevolod, who was the son of Oleg Sviatoslavich.[51] The Sviatoslavich family had been problematic members of the larger clan since the time of their patriarch's (Sviatoslav) usurpation of his brother Iziaslav's throne. This tradition of difficulty was extended to Vsevolod, when he usurped his own uncle who was ruling at the time in Chernigov – a major city in Rus that had come to be the Sviatoslavich seat of power. This usurpation in 1127/8 was Vsevolod's first major political move within Rus, and it resulted in Mstislav Volodimerich mobilizing troops and resources to march against him. However, the end result was simply that Vsevolod Olgovich maintained his rule in Chernigov and his uncle, the prior occupant, was moved elsewhere. This event provides the most likely context for the marriage of a daughter of Mstislav to Vsevolod – as a way to seal an agreement between these two members of the larger Volodimerovich clan that kept the peace within Rus.

However, Maria's marriage to Vsevolod would become increasingly important over time as several years later, following the death of Maria's uncle Iaropolk in 1139, Vsevolod was able to seize the throne of Kyiv for himself. Judging by prior practice, this was most likely another usurpation of the Kyivan throne, but it is possible that Vsevolod's marriage to Maria offered a way to justify his claim to rule in Kyiv. Vsevolod was one of the last to rule a unified Rus – before the polity became increasingly pulled in the direction of its different regions later in the twelfth century – and Maria Mstislavna played a major part in ensuring that continuity.

The marriages of Malfrid and Ingeborg are interlinked and thus must be treated as one piece of the puzzle, although an attempt will be made to divide them up chronologically.[52] Both sisters are unknown in the Rusian sources, and we are reliant on the Scandinavian sources in which they appear for all the knowledge we have of them. Scandinavian connections were not uncommon for the Volodimerovichi. We have already seen the origin of the family, Iaroslav's ties with the region and, more recently, Mstislav's own marriage to a Swedish princess. While he ruled in Novgorod with Kristín, they engaged in creating further ties across the Baltic that shaped these marriages.

King Sigurd of Norway was known as the Crusader, because of his trip to the eastern Mediterranean from roughly 1107 to 1110. On his return trip to Scandinavia, Sigurd travelled from Constantinople through Rus and it is most likely there that he met with Mstislav and Kristín, and his marriage to Malfrid was arranged.[53] Malfrid and Sigurd returned to Norway and lived together for nearly twenty years before Sigurd's death. During that time, Malfrid bore a daughter, Christina, and a mistress of Sigurd's bore a son, Magnus, who would be the heir to the throne. Unlike many women in dynastic marriages, but in a move that seems common for Rusian women, Malfrid stayed in Norway after her husband's death and continued to play a role at court during the reign of her stepson, Magnus.

The marriage of Ingeborg also took place for the purpose of cementing Scandinavian ties, though it had an additional element as well in that it put pressure on Poland, the perennial ally of the Iziaslavich family. Ingeborg married Knud Lavard, the son of the deceased Danish king Eric Ejegod. Knud's uncle Niels ruled in Denmark and was married to a sister of Kristín's; Saxo Grammaticus (a thirteenth-century source for Danish history) suggests that the marriage was arranged by Kristín and Margaret, her sister, to advance Margaret's son's claim to the throne.[54] Knud himself did not stay in Denmark, due to hostility between him and his uncle, and he was taken in by Lothar, the Duke of Saxony, who appointed him as the Duke of Schleswig – an important border territory with the Danes. Later, Knud seized the territory of the Abodrite Slavs for himself and took the title 'King of the Slavs', along with the right to rule over their Baltic shore. His increasing power was seen as a threat to Niels and most especially to the succession of Niels and Margaret's son, Magnus; therefore, plans were made to eliminate him. Under the auspices of a peace meeting with Magnus and Niels in 1131, Knud was killed by his cousin. Ingeborg, reportedly, had told her husband not to go, as she had been warned in a dream that it would mean his death.

Eight days later, Ingeborg gave birth to the couple's fourth child and their first son. She named him Valdemar, a vowel-shifted version of her grandfather's name, Volodimer.[55]

This is already a fascinating story of two Rusian princesses, sisters who married into the Scandinavian royal family, but after the murder of Knud Lavard, their lives became even more entangled as they attempted to assist one another. Soon after the murder, King Magnus of Norway reached out to Knud's brother Eric, who had taken on a self-appointed role as both the avenger of Knud's death and the protector of his family. Magnus of Norway wanted to marry Kristín, Knud and Ingeborg's eldest daughter.[56] The marriage was agreed, with one addendum: that Malfrid (King Sigurd's widow) would marry Eric as well. This double connection would help tie the families together to protect Ingeborg and her children, as well as avenge Knud's death. The marriage ties were needed as soon as possible; already, in 1132, Eric and his army had been defeated by King Niels of Denmark and his son Magnus, and Eric, Malfrid and Ingeborg were forced to flee to Norway and the court of King Magnus. There, the familial rather than marital ties soon came in handy; after his defeat of Eric, King Niels of Denmark reached out to Norway and paid King Magnus to turn the runaways over to him. Magnus agreed; he needed this wealth to assist in his own kingdom's conflicts. However, King Magnus's wife, Kristín (the daughter of Ingeborg and niece of Malfrid), told the runaways about the plan and helped them to escape. Kristín's protection of her own natal kin over the interests of her marital kin cost her her marriage (she was

22 Bead bracelet from Gotland, 11th–12th century.

quickly repudiated by Magnus) but this demonstrates the importance of those family ties.[57]

Although Malfrid passes out of the story soon after, Eric does eventually become king of Denmark. Ingeborg appears once again in the Danish sources upon his death, when (as we are told by the Danish sources) the great and the good of Denmark wanted to make her son, Valdemar, the ruler of Denmark. She refused on his behalf, as he was only eight at the time, but Valdemar would eventually still end up ruling Denmark and would found one of the most powerful dynasties of the late twelfth and thirteenth centuries. All of this only happened because of the marriages of two Rusian princesses, sisters who aided one another during their marriages elsewhere in medieval Europe.

While these marriages present us with a fascinating picture of Mstislav and Kristín's family and their ties both within and outside of Rus, if we extend our reach to Mstislav's second wife and their children, we can note two more interesting connections. Both Volodimer and Evfrosinia formed alliances to help regulate political relations with southwest Rus. Evfrosinia married Géza II of Hungary (r. 1141–62), creating a massively important tie that would subsequently be used multiple times to seek aid and assistance for members of the Mstislavichi family.[58] Volodimer, her brother, was married to a daughter of the Ban of Croatia, a subordinate of the Hungarian crown but one with unique powers, as the ban himself was a particularly powerful player within Hungary. This is also the only known marriage of a member of the Volodimerovich clan with the South Slavs, a group who, we are told, had a good deal of ecclesiastical influence on the development of the Rusian Church, but with whom there were few political relations. All in all, we can see that under the rule of Mstislav and his wives, the family played a robust role in organizing their marriage alliances in terms of future political endeavours, as well as engaging in spreading their influence and connections through both Scandinavia and parts of eastern Europe. While the geographic reach was not as broad as that seen under Iaroslav and Ingigerd, there is still a significant amount of engagement with a wider medieval Europe.

✠

MSTISLAV/HARALD 'Feodor' Volodimerich died in 1132, and his immediate succession to the throne of his father, Volodimer Monomakh, was not in line with the collateral succession that had previously been dominant in Rus. Largely, with only a few exceptions, the next rulers of Kyiv would be from the line of Volodimer Monomakh, and in the main contest for power his sons, Mstislav/Harald or Iurii 'Dolgorukii' ('Long-Arm'), would prevail. Thus the Monomakhovichi (the family of Volodimer Monomakh) splintered into two oppositional groups, the Mstislavichi (the family of Mstislav) and the Iurevichi (the family of Iurii). Iurii Dolgorukii held the throne of Kyiv from 1149 to 1150 and from 1155 to 1157, but he was ousted from the throne both times. Three of Mstislav's own children ended up succeeding him as ruler of Kyiv during the twelfth century, setting up a strong claim for Kyiv being reserved for the Mstislavichi.

The twelfth century is typically portrayed as a time of great fragmentation in Rus, when central control from Kyiv began to lag and the various Rusian regions went their separate ways. However, this is not entirely the case, as we see Kyiv maintaining its importance as the centre of Rus throughout the century, even if control of that centre is being contested among multiple claimants for the throne, who may have had their own power bases in Pereiaslavl, Smolensk, Vladimir on the Kliazma, or Galicia–Volhynia. By the end of the century, those shifting power bases laid the groundwork for future changes in what Rus was and would become, which will be examined more in chapters Five and Six, as we deal with the development of northeastern and southwestern Rus, respectively.

23 Statue of Iurii Dolgorukii in Moscow.

5

Vsevolod 'Big Nest' Iurevich and His Family

Chapters Three and Four (much like Rus itself during the period) were centred on Kyiv and the Dnieper River region. Chapter Five begins our shift to cover the expanding territory of Rus and the proliferation of the ruling families that inhabited it. The territory that we focus on in this chapter is in the northeast of Rus and is located between the Volga and the Oka rivers, a region that would come to be known as Vladimir-Suzdal. The main figure in the establishment of this region, and certainly the architect of its rise in importance, was the youngest brother of Mstislav/Harald Volodimerich – Iurii, who was subsequently known as 'Dolgorukii' (Long-Arm), either because of his reach covering the northeast of Rus or for his reaching out from the northeast towards Kyiv, depending on one's perspective.

Iurii and his sons and successors founded numerous towns in the northeast, including Moscow, Iurev-Polski (named after Iurii), Tver and Kostroma. Historically, there has been some debate about the foundation of the region.[1] The Russian argument has been that the people for these new towns came from the Dnieper region of Rus, migrating in a mass movement away from the Dnieper valley, creating their own, new centre of Rus from the nothingness of the forest region. However, the PVL notes the city of Rostov in this region is already established in the first early tenth-century agreements between Oleg and the Byzantine emperors, while the city of Suzdal appears in the record in 1024 as an existing settlement when magicians appeared there.[2] The archaeological evidence demonstrates that both settlements were also active in the tenth century. All of this throws doubt on the creation of the region *ex nihilo* by Iurii and his family. It does not, however, undermine the important role that they played in shaping its future. Although he was assigned this area, being the youngest son of Mstislav/Harald, Iurii subsequently developed it, and played an important role in the larger world of Volodimerovich clan politics. He contended with Novgorod, placing his children on the throne there at careful intervals, and he even took the throne of Kyiv twice, the first time in 1149–50 and then again from 1154 to 1157, at which point he was killed, supposedly poisoned by those who disapproved of his rule. Vladimir-Suzdal would go on to become one of the new centres of Rus under the rule of his children.

Iurii Dolgorukii had two wives and multiple children, which was quite common in Rus, as we have seen. His legacy was carried on first by his son Andrei, who was eventually given the nickname 'Bogoliubskii' (God-Lover), because of his piety. Andrei shifted his residence from Suzdal to the town of Vladimir and began to build it up to rival the pre-eminence of Kyiv. This Vladimir was known as Vladimir on the Kliazma to differentiate it from Volodymyr in Volhynia, which is in the southwest region of Rus. Below, we will discuss his construction of the Assumption Cathedral (Uspenskii sobor) and the translation of the icon of the Mother of God; he also had a copy of the Golden Gate constructed in Vladimir. The Golden Gate of Vladimir was meant to emulate the Golden Gate of Kyiv, which itself was meant to emulate the Golden Gate of Constantinople. All this construction was part of Andrei's attempt to appropriate history, grandeur and legitimacy from Kyiv and Constantinople and bring it to the town of Vladimir.

However, the events of 1162, as recorded in the Hypatian Chronicle, demonstrate another interesting shift in dealing with the plethora of potential heirs to the throne.[3] In that year, we are told that Andrei Bogoliubskii exiled his brothers, Mstislav, Vasilko and Vsevolod, their mother and Bishop Leon. Bishop Leon begged for forgiveness and was allowed to return, but Mstislav, Vasilko and Vsevolod, who is noted as being quite young at the time, along with their mother all ended up in Constantinople. Why they went there and whether it was of their own volition is unclear – although an argument can be made about the family ties between the Suzdalian line and the Byzantines. The rationale for this exile, according to the Hypatian Chronicle, was that Andrei wanted to act as the 'sole ruler' in the region.[4] Multiple historians have suggested that the later idea of Russian autocracy had its roots in Andrei's desire for sole rule (*samovlastets*), being so close to the autocracy (*samoderzhets*) seen in later periods. While one could make this argument, this requires eliding multiple data points across time and it seems rather anachronistic to do so. Instead, we might suggest that this was Andrei's way of handling the multiplicity of possible heirs to the throne of Vladimir and limiting the pool, thereby allowing his own children to succeed him more directly. If this is indeed the case, the end goal of lineal, rather than collateral, succession mirrors the behaviour that we saw in Andrei's own grandfather, Volodimer Monomakh, and what he tried to do for his own sons – a situation that possibly contributed to the feeling of disenfranchisement felt by Andrei's own father, Iurii, who was the youngest of the family. Exile was not unprofitable for the younger Iurevichi. It is possible that the choice of Byzantium was deliberate, as the Byzantine emperor assigned territories for the older brothers, Mstislav and Vasilko, to rule, making them part of the Byzantine ruling hierarchy and demonstrating a typical Byzantine policy of absorbing nobles from other places.[5] Vsevolod, one imagines because of his youth, was not given a place to rule, but he would eventually return to Rus, become the ruler of Vladimir and, consequently, the protagonist of this chapter.

Andrei Bogoliubskii's shift in focus can also be seen in 1169, when he ordered an attack on Kyiv. He did not take part in the attack, assigning that task to his generals and other members of his family; instead, he stayed in Vladimir-Suzdal. Once Kyiv was taken, it was sacked in what was considered a major event at the time. Unlike any of the previous members of the Volodimerovich clan who had taken Kyiv, he chose not to rule there himself, leaving a subordinate, his brother Gleb, to rule in his stead.

Making the choice not to rule Kyiv himself represented a major shift in the history of the Volodimerovichi and, as such, has generated much discussion and disagreement about Andrei's rationale. The first of the two main perspectives is that Andrei, as *paterfamilias* of the clan, by choosing to stay in Vladimir was signalling that the focus of Rus had moved to the northeast. The other is that Andrei felt safer in the town of Vladimir but wanted to claim Kyiv for the older generation, not wanting to let it slip into the hands of the generationally younger members of the clan and thus lose its importance as a major centre.[6] While we cannot know Andrei's thoughts, we can see his actions; after Gleb's death in 1171, Andrei continued to place other subordinate rulers in Kyiv and required them to act according to his will.[7] For example, after the death of Gleb and of Volodimer (Andrei's second ruler in Kyiv), Andrei sent a message to the Rostislavichi family, saying, 'You have called me your father and I want good for you; I give Kyiv to your brother Roman.'[8] Traditionally, the ruler of Kyiv had been the *paterfamilias* of the Volodimerovich clan but, here, Andrei was clearly making the statement that while he was the *paterfamilias*, he would rule from wherever he wished and, thus, could assign rulers as he wished – even for the city of Kyiv.

Not long after the assignment of Kyiv to Roman, the Rostislavichi incurred Andrei's wrath and he ordered them to leave the city, giving it instead to his brother, Mikhalko. Mikhalko refused to accept the command; instead, Vsevolod, who by now had returned from Byzantium, began to rule there.[9] Their expulsion from Kyiv was the last straw for the Rostislavichi; they ousted Vsevolod from Kyiv and told Andrei that they would no longer call him 'father', indicating their independence from his authority and from his control. Andrei, who was enraged, ordered the gathering of a massive army, which the Hypatian Chronicle says numbered 50,000 men (although this is clearly a typical exaggeration), and marched against the Rostislavichi and their allies, only to lose to them because 'they had come in pride', according to the chronicle.[10]

It was perhaps this conflict over Kyiv, and Andrei's behaviour, that helped lead to his murder in 1174. The proximate cause, according to the Hypatian Chronicle, was Andrei's order that one of his servants should be put to death for a crime the servant had committed. The servant's friends and family, the Kuchkovichi, rallied together and attacked Andrei in his bedchamber at night, ultimately killing him.[11] The story, as told in the Hypatian Chronicle, is a long one and portrays Andrei as a *strastoterpets* (passion-sufferer), one who imitates Jesus Christ in the Garden of Gethsemane, waiting, knowing his fate, and staying anyway to suffer it. This saintly portrayal of Andrei is much in line with that of St Boris; in fact, Boris is mentioned numerous times in this account, even to the point of Andrei owning, but not possessing, St Boris's sword at the crucial moment of his murder. This connection to a sainted member of the Volodimerovichi clan is an important tie not only to the past but to Christian religiosity for the new power centre of Vladimir-Suzdal.

Andrei's death opened the way for a new ruler in the town of Vladimir; the subsequent struggle included the sons of Andrei as well as his remaining brothers. This contest was eventually won in 1177 by his youngest brother, Vsevolod, who then began to consolidate his power in Vladimir-Suzdal. In part, that meant moving Andrei's sons out of positions of power. It also meant attempting to gain recognition using Novgorod, the powerful northern trading centre that actively chose its

24 The murder of Andrei Bogoliubskii, as portrayed in the Radziwiłł Chronicle. *Radzivilovskaia Letopis'*, 15th-century copy of 13th-century original, f. 215.

own rulers. After Andrei's murder, the Novgorodians had moved away from Vladimir-Suzdalian rulers, and Vsevolod had to work hard to regain the lost influence there. Similarly, he worked to hold and retain influence in closer areas such as Riazan, which had been subordinate to the Olgovichi of Chernigov. Riazan's civic leaders had attempted to steer a path between the Olgovichi and the Iurevichi, a path perhaps modelled on Novgorod's ability to choose its way, but Vsevolod put an end to that in 1208/9 when he depopulated the city, moving the majority of people into Vladimir-Suzdal lands as unwilling colonists. He subsequently razed Riazan and the surrounding area to the ground, to dissuade people from returning.[12] Even more so than his older brother Andrei, Vsevolod displayed no interest in Kyiv, and despite arranging marital ties with Kyivan rulers, he never contested for Kyivan rule. The creation of Vladimir-Suzdal as a Rusian polity that was not dependent upon Kyiv was complete.

Vsevolod Iurevich and His Wives

Vsevolod 'Bolshoe Gnezdo' ('Big Nest') Iurevich most likely derived his nickname from the number of children that he fathered over the course of his life. According to the genealogical account of Nicolas de

Baumgarten, he had twelve living children, although some historians have put the number as high as eighteen in total.[13] Vsevolod's first wife, who rarely appears in the sources, was named Maria, but very little is actually known about her. She first appears in the sources, completely obliquely, in 1176, when the chronicle notes that 'Sviatoslav sent Mikhalko and Vsevolod's wives . . . to Moscow.'[14] We are not told her identity, or when they were married, but the event occurred before 1176. The most common assumption, following the account of Baumgarten, is that she was an Ossetian princess, which would not be unlikely given the family connections that the Iurevichi had established with the Caucasus. For instance, Iurii, the son of Andrei Bogoliubskii, had briefly been the ruler of Novgorod from before his father's death until he was expelled and fled to the Caucasus, where he became a political player.[15] In 1185, Iurii became involved in a political cabal to check the power of the reigning queen, Tamar I, granddaughter of King Demetrius I. At that time, a daughter of Demetrius, Rusudan, allied herself with the Catholicos (the head of the Georgian Church) to arrange the marriage of Iurii to Tamar.[16] Although Tamar had been crowned by her father, Georgius III, as *mepe* or ruler, their marriage meant that Iurii was *mepe* as well and shifted Tamar's title to 'king of kings and queen of queens'.[17] Apart from Iurii's aggressive start to his reign, which began with a military campaign against the Sultanate of Rūm, he was also reported to have been abusive to Tamar. The marriage was annulled by 1188 and Iurii was then exiled to Constantinople. This was not the end of Iurii's involvement in Georgia, however, as he returned twice more to attempt to take over the kingdom and dethrone Tamar, failing both times.

Unfortunately, although the Ossetian hypothesis is an interesting one, there is no positive evidence to support it. The identification of Maria hinges on her patronymic, Shvarnovna, which would make her father's name Shvarn. Fjodor Uspenskij and Anna Litvina have conducted exhaustive research, attempting to decode the origins of Shvarn, and they excluded both the Ossetian possibility as well as the idea that she was Bohemian (an older hypothesis). Instead, they theorize that she was of Novgorodian birth.[18] While this hypothesis is fascinating, it too cannot be corroborated. An internal marriage, however, does fit into what seems to be the larger marital policy of Vsevolod and his family.

Vsevolod's second marriage came near the end of his life; we know nearly as little about this woman as we do about his first wife. The

Nikonian Chronicle, a comparatively late chronicle written in the sixteenth century, is the only chronicle to record the marriage and it does so laconically – Vsevolod 'took another wife for himself, the daughter of Vasilko, the ruler of Vitebsk'.[19] While the other chronicles, particularly the Hypatian Chronicle, consistently reported the births of Vsevolod's children (for instance, they were a regular occurrence in the 1190s), there are no children recorded after his marriage to this Vasilkovna. Vasilii Tatishchev gives more detail about this marriage, including a name for the woman, in his *Istoriia Rossiskaia* (History of Russia), but this is an even later source that is often viewed as inaccurate, if not made up.[20] Thus, we know very little about Vsevolod's second wife, and it is most likely that they did not have any children. It is clear, though, from the little information preserved that this was another marriage internal to the Rusian ruling clan, in keeping with the larger practice in the wider Iurevichi of not engaging in European-wide dynastic marriages.

Vladimir-Suzdal (and Rus) under Vsevolod and His Family

One of the difficulties in studying the medieval past of any area is dealing with preservation issues. We have mentioned source preservation multiple times in this book, in terms of which written sources have survived and what we can, and cannot, know about these people (and Rus) because of that. The same is true of material culture. Some of the grandest objects of material culture are churches; because of their size and their position in the culture, they tend to be preserved and, if destroyed, rebuilt. We often have a picture of the Middle Ages as highly religious because of the preservation of so many churches and monasteries. Understanding source preservation, that what has been saved is privileged, is an important corrective to our assumptions about what we can still see of the medieval world around us.

That being said, we do have multiple extant churches from the period of Iurii Dolgorukii and of his sons Andrei Bogoliubskii and Vsevolod 'Big Nest'. Churches in the Dnieper area were largely constructed out of brick because of the lack of availability of large stones, but this was not the case in Vladimir-Suzdal. The Kama, a tributary of the Volga, was the source of a white limestone that became the standard construction material for churches throughout the region. One example that we will discuss here is the Vladimir Uspenskii sobor, which can be translated into English as the Cathedral of the Dormition of the Virgin or the Cathedral of the Assumption. Andrei Bogoliubskii ordered the construction of this church, beginning in 1158.[21] It was built to serve as the main seat of the bishop for Vladimir-Suzdal; eventually it would become an important ecclesiastical centre for all of Rus. The construction brought together craftspeople from a wide variety of areas, including central and western Europe, as well as Byzantium.[22] Unfortunately, a fire destroyed the church, as well as much of the town of Vladimir, in 1183. Fire was an omnipresent threat in Rus, as it was throughout the medieval world, and such blazes were a regular feature of life. Nevertheless, Vsevolod began the reconstruction of the church during his rule. He had the church expanded, adding an arcade on three sides and four corner cupolas.[23] The finished church was reconsecrated in 1189 and became the centrepiece of Vladimir-Suzdal (illus. 25).

Maria, Vsevolod's wife, also contributed to the growth of the ecclesiastical complex in northeastern Rus. In the year 1200, Maria founded a monastery dedicated to the Mother of God (*Theotokos*) – the aspect

25 Uspenskii sobor, Vladimir, from Samuel Hazzard Cross, *Medieval Russian Churches*, ed. Kenneth John Conant (1949).

of the Virgin Mary as the mother of Jesus, most commonly venerated in Rus, Byzantium, and Orthodox polities generally.[24] This monastery was founded with great fanfare and would come to be well known in Vladimir-Suzdal, as well as being closely associated with Vsevolod and Maria's family. For instance, only a year after it was founded, Evgenia, a sister of Maria, was buried there; in 1205, Vsevolod and Maria's daughter Elena was buried in the monastery as well. Maria herself took holy orders, becoming a nun in 1206 and remaining in her own monastery. Sadly, she did not live out the year and was interred there with her sister and daughter.[25] This was only the beginning of the tradition of burying female members of the Vsevolodovichi family in Maria's monastery, which was eventually known as the monastery of the Kniagini, or 'Queen's monastery'.

In the same vein of religious preservation, one of the most famous icons from Rus dates to this period. Icons were simply images, depictions of saints, Jesus, Mary and the angels, created for the purpose of directing the devotion of their worshippers. Icons also told stories to a largely preliterate audience, helping them to familiarize themselves with the cast of Christian characters that they heard about from the priests. This familiarization is one reason that the images shown on icons remained relatively unchanged through time and were consistent from place to place so as to provide a basic understanding of who each saint was, no matter who painted the image on the icon. One of the most famous icon types was the icon of the Mother of God (*Bogoroditsa*). This type of icon showed Mary holding the baby Jesus, in one of several poses. In the middle of the twelfth century, an icon of the Mother of God was made in Byzantium and was sent to Iurii Dologorukii while he was in Kyiv. This icon was then taken by Andrei Iurevich to Vladimir-Suzdal, although, as the story goes, it did not quite make it to the city itself at first: divine intervention caused the procession to halt in a particular spot, where Andrei felt moved to found the town of Bogoliubovo ('the one loved by God'). Eventually, the icon found a home in the Uspenskii sobor in Vladimir, and its move from Byzantium to Kyiv to Vladimir later came to symbolize the transition of ecclesiastical power and sanctity to the city of Vladimir. However, at the time when Andrei Bogoliubskii was attempting to create a separate metropolitanate for Vladimir-Suzdal, the patriarch of Constantinople, Loukas Chrysoberges, rejected the request and the then current metropolitan of Kyiv even mutilated Andrei's candidate, Feodorets.[26]

It was during the reign of Vsevolod Iurevich that an incredibly momentous event in medieval European history took place – the Fourth Crusade's sacking of Constantinople in 1204. This crusade was a logical expansion of the crusading movement, beginning in 1095 with Pope Urban II's call for the capture of Jerusalem by Christian forces. The crusading movement first focused upon Muslims, but by the time of the sacking of Jerusalem in 1099, Jews had also been killed in large numbers, both in Jerusalem and by the crusaders while on their way there. The preaching of Bernard of Clairvaux in the twelfth century energized and spread the crusading movement, expanding the 'armies of the Devil' to include pagans. By the early thirteenth century, all those who were not the right kind of Christian (the right kind being Latin Christians who were subordinate to Rome) also became the target of crusaders – thus the sack of Constantinople, the capital of the Byzantine Empire and a major centre of Orthodox Christianity. Interestingly, the attack on Constantinople is recorded in the Novgorod Chronicle for 1204 in some detail, without a great deal of bias against the attacking crusaders.[27] It would take a couple of decades before the break between Latin and Orthodox Christianity would truly be felt in Rus.

The repercussions of the attack in 1204 were reinforced in 1222 when Pope Honorius III declared that all Orthodox churches should be closed in Latin lands, reinforcing the idea that there was only one correct form of Christianity. In 1224, this provision came closer to home for Rus with the Latin crusaders' attack on, and conquest of, the city of Dorpat (Rusian Iurev, modern Estonian Tartu) in the Baltic. Dorpat was closely connected to Novgorod and there were Rusian churches there, which were closed under Pope Honorius's edict. Moreover, a papal legate, William of Sabina, was on hand to encourage the proselytization of not just the local pagan peoples but the Orthodox Rusians across Lake Chud. This was incredibly frustrating for Iaroslav Vsevolodovich, the ruler of Novgorod, especially when multiple subordinate towns and rulers attempted to use the provocation of the papal legate as a lever to resist Novgorodian control. Iaroslav took matters into his own hands when, in 1234, he led a major attack on Dorpat, ravaging the area and sacking the city as a way to counter the '*Nemtsy*' (foreigners, but particularly Germans) who were agitating against the Rusians and Orthodoxy.[28] However, this attack would merely inflame the conflict and encourage Legate William to call for a wider crusade

26 Unknown artist, Our Lady of Vladimir icon, 12th century, tempera on panel.

directed solely at Rus – something that Iaroslav's son, Alexander, would have to deal with.

Concurrent with the attacks of the Latins, resulting from William of Sabina's eventual success in his call for a crusade, was the arrival of the Mongols in Rus. The Mongols captured the Rusian city of Riazan in 1237/8, an event memorialized in a later text, 'The Tale of the Destruction of Riazan', which (while fictionalized) carries a certain drama relevant to the moment.

> The accursed Batu began the conquest of the land of Riazan . . . On the dawn of the sixth day the pagan warriors began to storm the city . . . and they took the city of Riazan on the 21st day of December. They cut to pieces the Great Princess Agripina, her daughters-in-law, and other princesses. They burned to death the bishops and the priests and put the torch to the holy church. And the Tatars cut down many people, including women and children . . . and they burned this holy city with all its beauty and wealth.[29]

The tale is a dramatic one, intended to evoke sympathy for the Rusians killed, especially by highlighting the Mongols' killing of royals, priests, women and children. At the same time, the text demonizes the Mongols (called Tatars in the text) and refers to Batu as 'accursed'. This kind of rhetoric is in contrast to the cooperation that we will see taking place between later Rusian rulers and the Mongol khans. Following on from the taking of Riazan, the Rusian rulers, led by Vsevolod's son, Iurii, who was then the ruler of Vladimir, gathered together to fight against the Mongols at the Battle of the Sit River. This battle resulted in the death of Iurii himself, as well as the deaths of three of his sons and two of his nephews.[30] This was just the beginning of the death toll of Rusian rulers who opposed the Mongols, as will be seen in the next several chapters.

In addition to fighting the Mongols, the Rusian rulers also made peace with them. Vsevolod's son Iaroslav, Iurii's successor on the throne of Vladimir, went to the court of Khan Batu at Sarai to have his rule confirmed. On his journey to Sarai in 1243, he was awarded the titles of '*Velikii kniaz*' of Vladimir, as well as '*Velikii kniaz*' of Kyiv.[31] This designation is interesting for two reasons. One is that Iaroslav was already the ruler of Vladimir, due to his inheritance of the throne from his brother; the Mongol khan only confirmed this position. However, that confirmation was to become essential in the struggles between Iaroslav's descendants. The second reason is that Iaroslav had never claimed the title of ruler of Kyiv for himself, but after the sacking of Kyiv by the Mongol forces in 1241, the Mongols felt that they could also assign this title; giving it to a ruler who visited them and, most likely, gave them gifts would have seemed a good choice. For Iaroslav, a journey to Sarai on the Volga was comparatively easy, especially when beginning from Vladimir-Suzdal, but in 1246, Iaroslav was obliged to journey to the Great Khan's capital at Qaraqorum, in modern-day Mongolia. This was a much longer journey; while later Rusian rulers would accomplish it successfully, Iaroslav did not survive. His death and subsequent succession by his remaining brother, Sviatoslav, helped to set in motion a series of events that tied together the Mongols, the crusaders and internal Rusian politics.

Vsevolod Iurevich and Maria's Children

It is likely that all the children of Vsevolod Iurevich that are discussed here were borne by his first wife, Maria, rather than by his second wife. We can make this assumption based on the dates that we have for those children. These are rarely a date of birth, although sometimes those existed, but are more often marriage dates, especially for women, and regnal dates for men. For instance, we see a series of entries in the 1190s in which 'a son was born to Vsevolod'.[32] The mother, as is commonplace, is not mentioned, but this birth occurred during the period of his marriage to Maria, before she retired to her monastery and subsequently died in 1206. There are no such entries after 1209.

One of the major trends that demonstrates the differences between northeastern Rus and elsewhere in Rus, apart from events in the Dnieper region or in Galicia-Volhynia, is that the majority of the marriages made were internal to Rus and were largely within the wider Volodimerovich clan. In chapters Three and Four we saw marital alliances with Hungary, Norway, France and Byzantium, but in the many marriages of Vsevolod and Maria's children discussed in this chapter, we will see only marriages that are internal to Rus. Illustration 27 shows the marriages of the Vsevolodovichi. Six of the seven children who are shown married into other families from the Volodimerovich clan; these internal marriages are by far the majority. The one who does not do so is Iaroslav, who marries a Polovtsian princess, although she was most likely already Christianized. The prevalence of marriages internal to Rus is quite important when looking from the perspective of the political relations of Vladimir-Suzdal. At this point, there were no longer pan-European connections being made, maritally speaking, at the very least; instead, the family is focused on consolidating power within the larger Volodimerovich clan. This shift in focus is also important for our understanding of later history, when Muscovy (the territory ruled by the members of Vsevolod and Maria's line) will be seen as separate from the rest of medieval Europe rather than an integral part of it, as demonstrated by Vsevolod's own forebears.

The eldest son of Vsevolod and Maria was Konstantin, who was born in 1186.[33] In 1195, Konstantin married the daughter of Mstislav of Smolensk.[34] This marriage was part of a larger union with the Rostislavichi family to foster an alliance against the Olgovichi (all of whom were members of the wider Volodimerovich clan). The inter-familial, but intra-clan, politics of Rus were becoming increasingly complicated by the end of the twelfth century; Vsevolod Iurevich was the eldest member of the clan, generationally speaking, even if he did not rule in Kyiv.[35] Thus, as we will see with those of Konstantin, his sister Verkhuslava and their brother Iurii, each the marriages tied Vsevolod's family into other ruling families of Rus and advanced the interests of Vsevolod and his line.

Although he was the eldest son, Konstantin did not immediately inherit after his father Vsevolod's death in 1212. The chronicles tell us that Vsevolod had disinherited Konstantin, because when Vsevolod lay dying, he had asked his son three times to come to him, and Konstantin had refused each request. Vsevolod bequeathed the throne of Vladimir to Iurii instead.[36] Quite understandably, this was not to Konstantin's liking, and he set about gathering allies to contest his disinheritance. It took several years before he could mount a challenge for his throne, but in 1216, with the help of Mstislav Mstislavich (a member of the rival

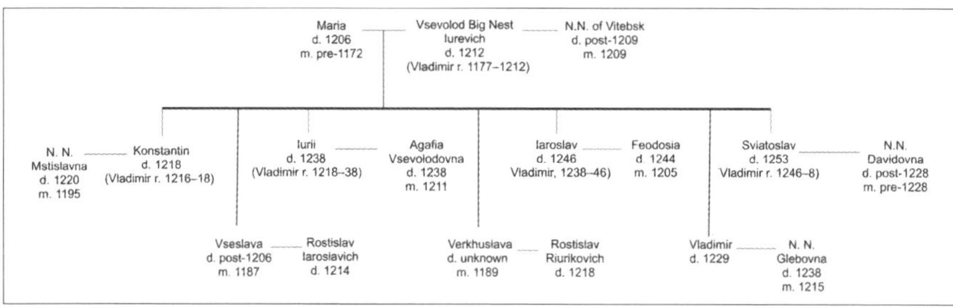

27 Vsevolod Iurevich, his wives and selected children.

Rostislavich clan), he went to war with his brother Iurii for the throne of Vladimir. This battle, known as the Battle of the Lipitsa River, pitted Konstantin and Mstislav Mstislavich against Konstantin's brothers – Iurii, the ruler of Vladimir, assisted by their younger brother Iaroslav. Konstantin and Mstislav were successful, and Konstantin took the throne of Vladimir, the throne of his father and grandfather. Konstantin only lived another two years, however, dying in 1218, but he did manage to retain his father's throne as the ruler of Vladimir, albeit briefly.

We know much more about the sons of Vsevolod and Maria than we do about the daughters, as is common in our source material. However, there is one daughter whose marriage is of particular interest. In 1189, Verkhuslava Vsevolodovna married Rostislav Riurikovich, the son of the ruler of Kyiv.[37] This might have been the typical laconic entry of a marriage in the Rusian records, but fortunately we have a wealth of information provided in the Hypatian Chronicle about the marriage itself. The story of the marriage begins with a procession in which Riurik, Rostislav's father and the ruler of Kyiv, sent his brother-in-law Gleb, along with Gleb's wife (sadly unnamed), as well as multiple boyars and their wives to Suzdal to meet Verkhuslava and bring her to her new husband, Rostislav. Upon their arrival in Vladimir-Suzdal, Vsevolod greeted them and then gave his daughter to them to escort her away. But first, he bestowed upon her numerous gifts, including a great deal of gold and silver, and also granted gifts to Riurik's party. Perhaps the most touching part of this story is the human element: 'He [Vsevolod] followed his dear daughter as far as three days' march [from home]. And the father and mother wept for her, because she was dear to them and young, being eight years old.'[38] It is fascinating for the historian to know that he gave his daughter gifts, her own gold and silver, for her marriage. However, in terms of her relationship with her parents, it is an astonishing detail to hear that both Vsevolod and Maria followed the departing train of people for three days because they loved their young daughter and would miss her a great deal. Such details are not often recorded in medieval sources, especially in Rus, and so they are especially valuable when we do have them to provide a truly human element to our history.

Verkhuslava's story does not end with her departure from Suzdal, however; the chronicle notes her arrival in Belgorod and her marriage on 8 May in the Church of the Holy Apostles.[39] The chronicle tells us that this was the greatest wedding that had been held in Rus up to that time and that there were twenty *kniazia* in attendance – itself a fantastic number, highlighting not just the importance of such a marriage between the families of Vsevolod and Riurik but the plethora of rulers within Rus. After the wedding, Riurik bestowed on his new daughter-in-law many gifts and the city of Bragin, which is further evidence of women being able to own and possess goods, even towns, in Rus. Riurik also sent messengers to Vsevolod to tell him of the wedding's success and to give him gifts, just as Vsevolod had given gifts to Riurik's party. This elaborate story of an equally elaborate wedding is a rarity in the chronicle sources, making it a fascinating gem for historians. We can learn about not just the marriage itself but the fact that an entourage was sent to escort the bride, along with details about gift exchanges, property rights, the age of marriage, travel times and even that the parents loved their children. The last seems obvious to us, but it was a much-debated subject until relatively recently.[40]

In the same year that Verkhuslava married Rostislav Riurikovich, the Laurentian Chronicle also recorded the birth of another son to Vsevolod, who was christened Iurii.[41] A brief discussion of Iurii's marriage is relevant as a framework for the political context for the marriage of Verkhuslava, as discussed above. Verkhuslava's father-in-law, Riurik, was dispossessed of Kyiv by Vsevolod Sviatoslavich, who was also called 'Chermnyy', of the Olgovich family of the Volodimerovich clan in 1208; subsequently, Riurik died. Vsevolod Chermnyy and Vsevolod Iurevich were not on good terms over numerous issues. However, in 1210, Vsevolod Chermnyy sent Metropolitan Matvei to Vladimir to negotiate a peace treaty between the two sides.[42] This negotiation was successful. The two sides redivided the territory between the two families; to seal the agreement, Iurii, the son of Vsevolod Iurevich, was betrothed to Agafia, the daughter of Vsevolod Chermnyy. The two were married the next year in the Uspenskii sobor in Vladimir, in a grand ceremony.[43] Much like the dynastic marriages discussed in earlier chapters, this was also a marriage arranged to ratify an agreement between two parties. Unlike those earlier marriages, this one (like the others made by Vsevolod's children) was internal to the Volodimerovich clan; however, this did not make any of them less political, as the clan was large enough to have multiple families, each with their own identity and agenda within Rus.

After the death of his older brother Konstantin, Iurii took over once more as the ruler of Vladimir in 1218, as we saw in the discussion of Konstantin above.[44] Iurii's second reign was brief but important, in that it set up the future success of the town of Vladimir. In 1221, he campaigned against the Volga Bulgars, taking territory from them that he used to found a new city – Nizhnii Novgorod (Lower Novgorod). This city, which is at the confluence of the Volga and Oka rivers, would become a major trading hub and would play an important role in the future growth of the region. In that same year, Iurii was able to place his own ruler in Novgorod, setting up a series of Vladimir-Suzdalian rulers in that city, thus extending the power of Vladimir-Suzdal from the Volga-Oka in the northeast to the Baltic in the northwest.

Iurii's death came at the hands of the Mongols, a new participant in the politics of the western steppe. They had made an exploratory raid into wider Rusian and steppe territory in 1223, culminating in a battle on the Kalka River in which many Rusian and Polovtsian rulers were killed. One of the Polovtsian rulers killed by the Mongols was actually the son of Konchak (also named Iurii), who was himself the father of the bride of Iaroslav Vsevolodovich.[45] At the time of the 1223 battle, there was little expectation among the Rusians that the Mongols would return, but a decade and a half later they did so. After their attack on Riazan in the winter of 1237–8, they penetrated further into the territory of Vladimir-Suzdal and Iurii led his troops to meet them, dying himself at the Battle of the Sit River on 4 March 1238.[46]

The next youngest son of Vsevolod and Maria was Iaroslav, whose birth was recorded *s.a* 1190 in the Laurentian Chronicle, just one year after the birth of his elder brother, Iurii.[47] The Hypatian Chronicle, which does not record Iaroslav's birth, contains an interesting entry for 1192, which says, 'Vsevolod set his son Iaroslav on a horse and it was a happy day.'[48] This fascinating anecdote, continuing the chronicle's seeming interest in the human side of Vsevolod Iurevich and his family, most likely indicates a possible rite of passage in which the young boy was able to ride a horse for the first time. It is a charming insight into the youth of someone who would become a major figure in Rusian history.

There is some controversy over Iaroslav's marriage or marriages. His first and potentially only marriage was definitely to the daughter of Iurii Konchakovich. This Polovtsian princess is not given a name in the chronicle sources, as is so often the case, but the *vita* of Alexander Nevsky (Iaroslav's son) notes his mother's name as Feodosia.[49] This woman's father (Iurii Konchakovich) is clearly named in the entry for

1205 in multiple chronicles.[50] It has been speculated that Iurii was a Nestorian by faith, which would have made the marriage more palatable to the Orthodox Church leaders. Reports of marriages between members of the Rus elite and the daughters of Polovtsian rulers occur less frequently in the sources than reports of royal marriages to Europeans, perhaps because of the religious issue, or it may simply be because of a lack of frequency. Nonetheless, when such marriages did occur, they were undertaken for the same political reasons – the confirmation of an alliance. We have no record of when the marriage to Iurii's daughter ended, or if it did end before Iaroslav's own death.

The controversy about the second marriage comes from a comment related to the Battle of the Lipitsa River, as discussed above, stating that Iaroslav was the *ziat'* (son-in-law or brother-in-law) of Mstislav Mstislavich of the Rostislavich clan.[51] No marriage is ever explicitly recorded between Iaroslav and a Mstislavna, by whatever name, but multiple attempts have been made to find evidence, or at least to reconstruct such a marriage.[52] Part of the problem has to do with the parentage of Alexander Nevsky. We will address Alexander Nevsky more fully in Chapter Seven but, given his status as a hero of Rus and its defender against the Latin Christian crusaders, it is possible that it was considered unseemly for him to have been born of a Polovtsian, and possibly non-Orthodox, woman; thus, the search was on by scholars in the modern period for a potential Rusian Orthodox bride for Iaroslav to be the mother of St Alexander Nevsky. Nevertheless, given the lack of any evidence of a second marriage in the chronicles, which cover the lives of Vsevolod, Iaroslav and Andrei in some detail, we have suggested here (see illus. 27) that there was just the one marriage for Iaroslav.

During Iurii's rule in Vladimir, Iaroslav had served as the ruler of Novgorod and, briefly, as the ruler of Kyiv. These positions allowed the Vsevolodovichi to extend their reach well beyond Vladimir-Suzdal, even if they did not hold the positions for long, as in the case of Kyiv. The Novgorod First Chronicle records that in 1236, Iaroslav left his son Alexander in charge of Novgorod and, taking 'the best men of Novgorod' as well as '100 men from Novitorg', he went to Kyiv and 'took his seat upon the throne'.[53] He did so during a time of great instability in Kyiv, when, in the words of the historian John Fennell, 'between 1235 and 1240, Kyiv changed hands no less than seven times: three times it was held by Rostislavichi, twice by Ol'govichi, once by Iaroslav, and once by Daniil of Galicia.'[54] Clearly, this was not to be a long-term rule, but the presence of a member of the Vsevolodovichi on the throne of Kyiv demonstrates both the continuing importance of that capital city and also the growing importance of their family within the larger Volodimerovich clan.

Iaroslav succeeded his brother Iurii in Vladimir in 1238.[55] He was the third son of Vsevolod and Maria to take the throne as the ruler of Vladimir. Much as we saw the throne passed down laterally in Iurii Dolgorukii's family, eventually culminating in Vsevolod's rule as the youngest son, we see the same thing happening among Vsevolod's children. Iaroslav's rule in Vladimir was in the context of the Mongol invasion of Rus and, as such, Iaroslav had to be aware of the Mongols and their impact on every facet of life in his territory. As we saw above, Iaroslav himself had to travel twice to the khan's capital at Sarai on the Volga to have his rule endorsed by Khan Batu; once, he was required to travel as far as Qaraqorum, a trip from which he did not return. Iaroslav left behind him multiple sons, whose activities will populate Chapter Seven.

When Iaroslav died, his youngest (and last) brother, Sviatoslav, took over the throne of Vladimir. Apart from the brief issue with Konstantin's inheritance, this period showed collateral succession working well as each of the living sons of Vsevolod inherited his throne, one after another. Some of this was due to the elimination of multiple candidates by the Mongols, but this is an important note to make, as the succession after this period will become complicated once more. The complications arose soon after Sviatoslav began his rule; in fact, when he allots territory to his many nephews, as is his right as the new *paterfamilias*, the sons of Iaroslav take exception.

✠

ALTHOUGH THE FOCUS of this chapter is on Vsevolod Iurevich and his family, the wider context is the rise of the region of Vladimir-Suzdal in the northeast of Rus in the twelfth and early thirteenth centuries. In the early days of Iurii, this region, which was founded through the work of Iurii Dolgorukii and his sons, particularly Andrei and Vsevolod, was peripheral to the focus of Rus in the Dnieper River valley. However, by the time of the death of Vsevolod, it was the centre of a thriving region and was easily a challenger to the might of Kyiv, not to mention the power centres established by the rival clans (the Olgovichi, Iziaslavichi and Rostislavichi). This challenge would only grow after the arrival of the Mongols in the middle of the thirteenth century. Vladimir-Suzdal also formed the basis for the growth of a small town called Moscow, which over the course of the thirteenth and fourteenth centuries would become quite a big town, eventually being the centre of its own polity of Muscovy and ultimately of Russia. One of the most popular ways to tell the history of Rus is as a prelude to the history of Russia. In that style of narration, Kyiv (spelled Kiev, typically, in those cases), passes its light and power to Vladimir, which passes it to Moscow; fundamentally speaking, the rest of Rus fades away until it is retaken by a triumphant Muscovy many centuries later. This book narrates a different story of Rus; in Chapter Six, we will see a different branch of the Volodimerovich clan rise to prominence, this time in the southwest region of Rus.

6

Roman Mstislavich and His Family

Chapter Six, like Chapter Five, shifts our focus from the Dnieper River valley to other regions elsewhere in Rus. The events in both chapters occur largely concurrently (from the end of the twelfth into the early thirteenth centuries), and both the geographic shift and the chronological overlap demonstrate that this period in Rusian history was one of divergent trends. In Chapter Five, we saw the rise of Vladimir-Suzdal in the northeast of Rus and of its powerful ruling family. Here, we will see the development of Galicia-Volhynia, a region to the west of Kyiv, from its roots in the eleventh century to the height of its power in the early thirteenth century. One of the main differences between the two regions is the degree of foreign interaction that each of these areas had. Because of its location on the western border of Rus, Galicia-Volhynia had extensive relations, both marital and martial, with Hungary and Poland, as well as with the Polovtsy and Byzantium. These interactions, as well as the relationship of Galicia-Volhynia with the rest of Rus, will be examined in the following pages.

Although often conflated into a single region, Galicia and Volhynia were two separate territories in Rus. Volhynia, through its capital city Volodymyr, appears first in the records regarding Volodimer's division of his lands, where it is given to his son Vsevolod; it appears again in Iaroslav Volodimerich's division of lands upon his death, where it is assigned to his son Igor, although it was only a few years later that Igor moved to Smolensk.[1] Volodymyr-in-Volhynia, as it came to be called, was then part of the territory of Iziaslav Iaroslavich and his family for some time. Galicia was not a single territory, or at least under a single ruler, in the eleventh century.[2] Its component cities were ruled by Volodar and Vasilko Rostislavich, the grandsons of Volodimer Iaroslavich, who had predeceased his own father, Iaroslav the Wise. Both regions underwent something of a renaissance in the middle of the twelfth century when Volodimerko, the son of Volodar Rostislavich, began to rule over the entirety of Galicia, while Iziaslav Mstislavich, the grandson of Volodimer Monomakh, ruled over Volhynia and made it his patrimony.[3] Even at that time, in the 1140s, there was the possibility of a union between the two territories, although not a peaceful one, as Volodimerko Volodarich invaded Volhynia but was repulsed by a union between several Rusian rulers, with the assistance of kinship relations from the Polish ruling family.[4] Volodimerko was economically powerful and had trading relationships with the Danube region, south to Byzantium, as well as a familial connection with the Hungarian ruling family, but even he could not stand against multiple Rusian rulers and their allies.

Iziaslav Mstislavich of Volhynia succeeded to the throne of Kyiv after the death of Vsevolod Olgovich in 1146; his throne in Volhynia eventually passed to his son, Mstislav Iziaslavich.[5] Similarly, after Volodimerko's death in Galicia, his throne passed to his son, Iaroslav. Iaroslav had a curious nickname – Osmomysl. It is typically translated as 'Eight-minded' and is thought to mean that he was clever, although there is no precise confirmation of that thinking. The two rulers, Iaroslav Osmomysl and Mstislav Iziaslavich, worked cooperatively in 1158 to put Rostislav Mstislavich, Mstislav's uncle, on the throne of Kyiv. After 1160, some accounts suggest that Mstislav Iziaslavich acted as a co-ruler with his uncle.[6] When Rostislav died in 1167, Iaroslav Osmomysl supported the candidacy of Mstislav Iziaslavich for the Kyivan throne.[7] This was a momentous episode that helps to tie the events in Galicia-Volhynia not only to those in the Dnieper River valley but to the ones discussed in Chapter Five, relating to Vladimir-Suzdal. Just a few years before, the Rostislavichi of Smolensk and the Iziaslavichi of Volhynia (both of the line of Mstislav/Harald Volodimerich) had been allies in taking Kyiv; however, at this point, they were in opposition. The Rostislavichi of Smolensk sought out Andrei Bogoliubskii of Vladimir-Suzdal, as well as the Olgovichi of Chernigov, as their allies. Mstislav Iziaslavich had fewer and less powerful allies, but one important source of support for his claim to the throne of Kyiv was the city of Novgorod. The Novgorodians cast out Sviatoslav Rostislavich (of the Smolensk Rostislavichi) and put Mstislav Iziaslavich's son, Roman, in his place. Mstislav was able to rule Kyiv for only a couple of years before the combined forces of the opposition, led by Andrei Bogoliubskii, pushed him from the

28 Illumination of St Luke in the Ostromir Gospel, 11th century.

throne and sacked the city of Kyiv in 1169 (as discussed in Chapter Five).[8] Roman Mstislavich fared slightly better in Novgorod, where he had strong support. Andrei Bogoliubskii moved against him as well, first by attempting to cut off the city's food supply (a tactic used successfully numerous times in the city's history), then by attempting to stop Novgorodian tax collectors from gathering wealth; finally, they used an outright assault, which Roman Mstislavich and his forces repelled. Unfortunately for Roman, however, it was the lack of food that eventually undermined his support among the Novgorodians, and he was ousted in 1170, first in favour of a member of the Rostislavichi, and then for a son of Andrei Bogoliubskii.[9] Mstislav Iziaslavich did not survive the experience; the Laurentian Chronicle records that he died back in his city of Volodymyr in August of 1170, and was buried in the Church of the Holy Mother of God, which he had built.[10] Roman, returning home from Novgorod, succeeded his father in Volodymyr, and began his rule at that time.[11]

Roman Mstislavich's Wives

The age of medieval individuals at the time of their first marriage is a subject that has received a good deal of discussion. Typically, among elites, men needed to be fourteen to sixteen and women twelve to fourteen. The idea was that the marriage had to be consummated; thus, the woman had to have reached the age of menarche, though this concept was not always followed rigorously. Given this information, Roman Mstislavich's first marriage is quite late. He was born circa 1155, ruled first in Novgorod and then in Volodymyr, and did not marry until he was approximately thirty. Why? Unfortunately, we do not know, since we are only able to work with the material that we have. It is one of the many unanswered questions we have about medieval life, even among the most elite.

Roman's first marriage occurred between 1182 and 1184, but even that date is a product of much scholarly deduction. Who he married is well known, however; his bride was Predslava, the daughter of Riurik Rostislavich, of the Smolensk Rostislavichi. Riurik Rostislavich, at the time, was the co-ruler of Kyiv, along with Vsevolod Olgovich of the Chernigov Olgovichi.[12] The two rulers had agreed on a power-sharing arrangement in which Vsevolod Olgovich was accepted as the senior ruler, with Riurik as his junior, allowing both of the families a key role in the governance of Rus and the key territory of Kyiv. Despite Riurik's prominent place in the history of Rus, there is no mention of this marriage at the time in any of the chronicle sources (thus the need for guesswork about the date of their marriage). The uncertainty of the years 1182–4 is owing to the marital date of their first, and only, child – Feodora, who (as we will see below) was married in 1188. She would have been only four to six years of age, thus undermining the whole discussion of marital age with which this section began. Problems like these demonstrate the speculation inherent in filling in the gaps in medieval history, as well as the problems with propounding overarching theories of how things were generally done.

We know little more about the end of the marriage of Predslava and Roman than we do about the beginning. Though initially allied with Riurik Rostislavich, Roman broke that alliance numerous times, beginning in the 1190s. Thus, Dąbrowski suggests that at some point in the second half of that decade, Roman repudiated Predslava and sent her home to her family.[13] Given that the conflict between the two sides began to increase in 1200, it is a likely conclusion that he was no longer married to Predslava Riurikovna.

After repudiating his first wife, Roman married again, but exactly to whom has also been a matter of some debate. Dąbrowski lists her as Maria of Byzantium, with extensive discussions of who she might be.[14] Márta Font also discussed the possible identity of this woman, noting that she was referred to in primary sources as a relation of the Hungarian king Andrew II.[15] Such a relationship with Andrew II does not rule out a Byzantine connection, however, as the king himself also had kinship ties with Byzantium; for instance, his sister Margaret was married to the Byzantine emperor, Isaac II Angelos. Much as with the marriages from the eleventh century discussed in earlier chapters, the lack of details regarding women in the primary sources leaves historians in the dark when trying to determine who they were and why the marriages happened. Once again, we are left using the children's birth dates as a means of determining an approximate date for the marriage. The first child of this marriage was Elena, who married Mikhail of Chernigov. Because of the circumstances of that marriage, Dąbrowski has concluded that she was born around 1200; thus, the marriage of Roman and Maria most likely took place not long before then.

We know more about Maria's life after Roman's death than before it, oddly enough. After Roman died in 1205, Maria attempted to rule on behalf of her two young sons, Daniil and Vasilko.[16] Her attempt to rule as regent for her sons was not successful; instead, factions of nobles, as well as the Polish and Hungarian rulers, moved into Galicia and Volhynia to cement their own control. In fact, it is possible that Leszek the White of Poland and Andrew II of Hungary agreed to divide the territory between them in 1206.[17] Leszek would control Volhynia, Andrew II would control Galicia and Daniil would be held at the Hungarian court as a ward, theoretically until he came of age. This agreement did not work well or for very long. Andrew II attempted to use Daniil to maintain control in Galicia, while Leszek used Maria and her second son Vasilko to attempt to control Volhynia. By 1211 we see that Maria was with Daniil, initially in Galicia and then fleeing to Hungary to gain support to maintain their rule. By 1213, both Daniil and Vasilko were back in Volhynia.[18] The peripatetic life of Maria and her sons is an interesting one and speaks to the itinerancy of medieval rulers, as well as to the portability of rule. Neither Galicia nor Volhynia 'belonged' to either Daniil or Vasilko. Both sons had to stake their claims on the territories against many other individuals (only a few of whom are mentioned here) who were also contending for the thrones, and some of these rivals were much more successful than the sons of Roman Mstislavich. For the purposes of our discussion of marriage, however, we see that Maria, whatever her natal identity, was an active participant in the fate of her sons and in both helping them to rule and gaining support for their rule.

Galicia-Volhynia under Roman Mstislavich

One of the most momentous events in the rule of Roman Mstislavich was his conquest of Galicia. However, this action, which is sometimes portrayed as a unification, was not completed in one fell swoop; in fact, it involved not just internal Rusian politics but the politics of a large sector of medieval central Europe. In 1187, Iaroslav Osmomysl died and passed Galicia to Oleg, his son by a mistress, while giving his other son Volodimer (borne by his wife) the land of Peremyshl to rule.[19] Although Oleg and his mother were both Iaroslav's favourites, the nobles of Galicia preferred Volodimer; therefore, they ousted Oleg and put Volodimer on the throne. Oleg fled to the court of Riurik Rostislavich (of the Smolensk Rostislavichi), who, alongside Sviatoslav Vsevolodovich (of the Chernigov Olgovichi), was ruling in Kyiv. The Hypatian Chronicle records that Volodimer was a drunkard and took a priest's wife as his own, not to mention assaulting any woman he chose; it also notes that 'he did not like to confer with his men,' casting a different kind of opprobrium on him.[20] This behaviour angered his nobles and they sought to oust him, despite his connection to the powerful Vsevolod 'Big Nest' (who was his maternal uncle, and who had protected him earlier in another matter). At this point, Roman Mstislavich of Volodymyr-in-Volhynia incited the nobles against Volodimer. He had recently married his daughter off to Volodimer's son and he had been actively involved in the affairs of Galicia. Thus, in 1188, Roman formally ceded control of Volodymyr-in-Volhynia to his brother Vsevolod and marched in to occupy Galicia.[21] The nobles returned his daughter to him and reported that Volodimer had fled to the Hungarians.

In Hungary, Volodimer met with King Béla III and asked for his assistance in regaining the throne of Galicia. Béla III acquiesced, mobilized his army and moved into Galicia. Once Roman heard that the Hungarian king was coming, he fled with his Galician supporters and took the treasury with him, returning to Volodymyr. However, his brother Vsevolod would not let him enter the city, as Roman had previously ceded it to him. Thus, Roman sent his wife and some of the Galician women to safety elsewhere, while he himself went to the Poles for assistance. Finding no help was forthcoming, he ended up seeking aid from his father-in-law, Riurik Rostislavich, who offered assistance and support, but whose military campaigns alongside Roman were unsuccessful.[22] Ultimately, however, Riurik was somehow able to force Vsevolod to give up Volodymyr and return control of the city to his brother, Roman. Back in Galicia, Béla III had no intention of turning power over to Volodimer. Instead, he placed his son Andrew (later King Andrew II of Hungary) in charge of Galicia and went back to Hungary with his armies, taking Volodimer with him as a captive.[23] Thus, Roman's first attempt to take Galicia ended in failure; he was left at certain times during the year as a ruler without a home before eventually retreating back to Volodymyr.

Though the remainder of this story does not involve Roman, we should finish the account of the Hungarian rule of Galicia. In 1189, Béla III, perhaps playing on the rivalries between the Olgovichi of Chernigov and the Rostislavichi of Smolensk, sent an envoy to Sviatoslav Vsevolodovich in Kyiv, asking him to send a son to rule in Galicia.[24] Sviatoslav, flattered by the offer, sent his son Gleb but did not inform his co-ruler, Riurik Rostislavich, who nevertheless found out about it and condemned Sviatoslav for attempting to take territory that did not belong to him. The two ultimately made peace, aided by the proclamation of the metropolitan of Kyiv that they should unite to oust the foreigners from Galicia.[25] Despite a subsequent military campaign, they had no success and Andrew continued to rule in Galicia. The next year, in 1190, Volodimer escaped from his imprisonment in Hungary and fled to the German Empire, where he was able to meet with the Holy Roman emperor, Frederick Barbarossa.[26] Barbarossa's support of Volodimer hinged on the latter's relations with Vsevolod 'Big Nest' of Vladimir-Suzdal; he offered to support Volodimer via his ally, Casimir of Poland, in exchange for a yearly payment. Once back on the throne in Galicia, Volodimer sought assistance from Vsevolod 'Big Nest', who subsequently sent a message to all of the Rusian leaders and the leaders of the Poles that Volodimer was not to be touched.[27]

Given Volodimer's successful return, how, then, does Roman Mstislavich come to control Galicia as well as Volhynia? There is no better way to put it than in the words of the eminent historian Mykhailo Hrushevsky, who wrote: 'The details of this event are a complete mystery to us because at this point there is a seven-year break in Ukrainian chronicle-writing, from 1198 until the death of Roman Mstyslavych in 1205.'[28] Unbelievably, this incredibly important event does not appear in the chronicle record and we have reference to it only in retrospect.[29] Even the death of Volodimer Iaroslavich, the ruler of Galicia, is not mentioned; Hrushevsky theorized that it occurred in 1199.[30] We include this important event, despite the unknowns surrounding it, to highlight that very point – our writing of history is based upon the preserved records that are written at the time, or shortly thereafter. We can only know the information that is recorded by those sources; if the chroniclers chose to turn a blind eye to something, or if a particular source is destroyed, we are left with a black hole in the literature, a lacuna, in scholarly terminology, that we can only fill with conjecture. Thus, while we know that Roman Mstislavich became the ruler of both Volhynia and Galicia, we do not know how or exactly when that happened.

In roughly 1200, Roman Mstislavich, backed by the might of Galicia and Volhynia, and with the assistance of the Olgovichi of Chernigov, marched against his father-in-law Riurik Rostislavich in Kyiv. He was successful in this campaign, as the Laurentian Chronicle records that the people of Kyiv opened the gates and welcomed him in.[31] Roman, however, did not want to rule personally in Kyiv, much as we saw Andrei Bogoliubskii and Vsevolod 'Big Nest' making the same choice. Instead, Roman installed a subordinate ruler in Kyiv, his cousin Ingvar, the ruler of Lutsk. As we discussed in Chapter Five, this was quite the comedown for Kyiv, which had for centuries been the central point of Rus but had now been claimed by rulers from both Vladimir-Suzdal and Galicia-Volhynia, who chose not to occupy it. In addition, similarly to Andrei Bogoliubskii, the Hypatian Chronicle calls Roman Mstislavich the 'samoderzhets' (autocrat/sole ruler) during the period of his rule in Kyiv.[32] This attribution is an important one as, when it was applied to Andrei Bogoliubskii, historians have taken it to be the beginning of Russian autocracy; however, nothing similar has occurred in the case of Roman Mstislavich.

29 Church of St Panteleimon in Galicia, *c.* 12th century.

Vasilii Tatishchev records in his *History* that Roman conceived of a grand plan to rotate the rule of Kyiv among the major families, even suggesting that this was how things were done 'in other well-ordered states'.[33] Roman was said to have suggested that the main six rulers within Rus, controlling the areas of Suzdal, Chernigov, Riazan, Polotsk, Galicia and Smolensk, should appoint the ruler of Kyiv from among them and no one else. The ruler who was chosen would be the most worthy and senior of the six; he would reside in Kyiv and give control of his own city to his heir. This plan, as well conceived as it sounded (if it was even a contemporary plan), was never to be enacted. Instead, Roman's rule in Kyiv was not a long one, though it was certainly contentious.

Soon after taking control of Kyiv, Roman led an expedition against the nomadic Polovtsy of the steppe region. This campaign was even noted by the Byzantine chronicler Niketas Choniates, as it distracted the Polovtsy (known also as the Cumans and Qipchaks) from sending raiders into Byzantium.[34] This was Roman's last notable accomplishment as the Kyivan ruler; in 1203, Riurik Rostislavich mustered allies, including the Polovtsy, and attacked Kyiv.[35] Ingvar was not able to defend the city and fled, after which the city was sacked. It was said that this attack was worse than the attack of Andrei Bogoliubskii in 1169; this time, the Polovtsy (the chronicle accounts specify that they were the attackers and absolve the Rusian rulers) pillaged the churches and monasteries for all of their wealth and took many prisoners to sell into slavery. Following this attack, Riurik returned to rule Kyiv, although he did not stay in the city. The events of this year and the next are confused in the sources, but it does appear that Riurik and Roman made peace, at least briefly, and went on campaign jointly against the Polovtsy.[36] On the way home from the campaign, things seem to have changed. Roman took Riurik and his family captive. He ordered that Riurik, his wife and his daughter, who was Roman Mstislavich's own wife, should be forced to take monastic vows.[37] This was clearly a major political event and represented quite the switch from Riurik having ousted Ingvar, who was Roman's designated ruler, from Kyiv in 1203. At this time, Vsevolod 'Big Nest' intervened on behalf of his imprisoned son-in-law, Rostislav Riurikovich. To appease the powerful ruler of Vladimir-Suzdal, Roman released Rostislav and even placed him on the throne as the ruler of Kyiv, returning peace to central Rus – although Riurik, along with his wife and daughter, remained in the monastery.

Roman did not have long to enjoy this peace, however. For reasons that are not entirely clear from the sources, in 1205, he embarked on a military campaign in Poland, where he was killed.[38] The death of Roman Mstislavich brought an end to the unity of Galicia-Volhynia and to its budding status as a great power within Rus. Due to the youth of Roman's male heirs, as discussed below, there was no ability to retain the power that Roman had accumulated, although eventually, his heir Daniil would rebuild the fortunes of Galicia-Volhynia in the thirteenth century.

The Children of Roman Mstislavich

Roman and Predslava, who was the daughter of Riurik Rostislavich, had one child that we know of, Feodora, while the other children that are known of, Elena, Daniil and Vasilko, are ascribed to his second wife because of their much later dates of birth.[39] Thus, it is these four children who we will discuss here, all of whom played a role in the legacy of Roman Mstislavich and that of their family.

Feodora's marriage has already been discussed above, insofar as it related to the interactions between Galicia and Volhynia. In around 1188, after Volodimer Iaroslavich had taken the throne of Galicia from his half-brother Oleg, Roman Mstislavich arranged a marriage between his daughter Feodora and Volodimer's eldest son.[40] The entry for that year in the Hypatian Chronicle begins with Volodimer being described as a drunkard, then accuses him of taking a priest's wife for his own (as was mentioned earlier) before saying that he had two sons (presumably with the priest's wife), followed by the arranged marriage, after which Roman finds out that Volodimer took whatever woman he pleased.[41] It is an interesting sequence of events that is absolutely unlike the grand narrative of the marriage of the daughter of Vsevolod 'Big Nest' discussed in Chapter Five. Here, we see the political implications of the marriage very clearly. The chronicle entry weaves the marriage into the politics of Galicia and Roman's interest in the territory. The only other mention of Feodora and her marriage that we have is from that same entry where, after Volodimer flees to Hungary because of Roman's invasion, the people of Galicia separate her from Volodimer's entourage and she goes back to Roman.[42] Thus, it appears that her marriage did

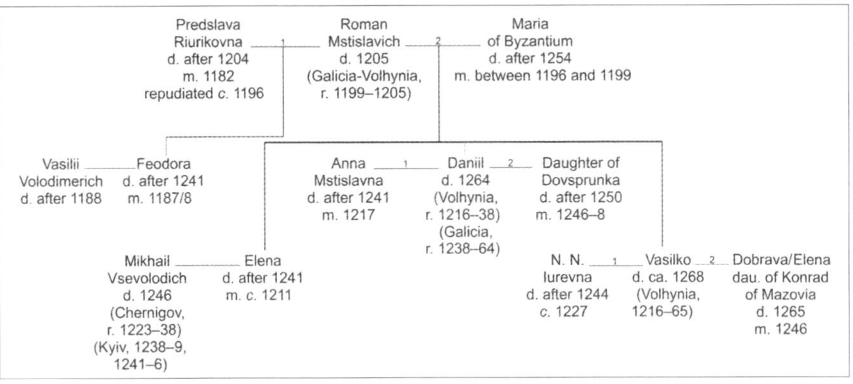

30 Roman Mstislavich, his wives and children.

not last more than a year; instead, she was returned to her father. What happened to her after that is unknown.[43]

All of Roman Mstislavich's other children were borne by his second wife, Maria; because of his marriage to her so late in his life and then his death in 1205, all these children came of marriageable age after that time. His eldest daughter with Maria is known as Elena. Scholars who have studied these individuals in depth, such as Dariusz Dąbrowski, have put the pieces together from the various sources and can tell us that she married Mikhail, the son of Vsevolod Sviatoslavich.[44] Vsevolod Sviatoslavich, of the Olgovichi, was the ruler of Chernigov and was later the ruler of Kyiv, while his son Mikhail became famous in his own right as the ruler of both places, as well as for becoming a martyr – he died for his Christian faith among the Mongols.[45] However, getting to this information is slightly more difficult. As is all too common in the medieval Rusian sources, we do not hear much about Elena directly. In 1211, the Hypatian Chronicle contains an obscure reference, saying that, 'while Vsevolod Sviatoslavich was ruling Kyiv, he had a great love for Roman's children.'[46] Martin Dimnik, who had studied the Olgovichi of Chernigov extensively, suggested that this terse reference, which is disconnected from the rest of the text, is part of a story lost to the current copy of the chronicle.[47] The next reference in the chronicle sources is much fuller and tells us that Mikhail Vsevolodovich's wife, who is unnamed, was the sister of Daniil of Galicia.[48] It is only in later sources that we learn her name, Elena, along with more about their lives.[49]

Given the paucity of sources, it is difficult to conjecture regarding the purpose of the marriage, which Dąbrowski dates to the end of 1211 or the beginning of 1212.[50] This is the same period for which the Hypatian Chronicle gives its cryptic reference to Vsevolod Sviatoslavich, the father of Mikhail, favouring the children of Roman Mstislavich. Roman, of course, had been dead for six years at this time and (as noted above) his wife and children had led a peripatetic existence in eastern Europe ever since. Daniil, the most well known of Elena's brothers, was not in a position to influence her marriage at that moment, as he was much too young, but perhaps the marriage's purpose was a way for Vsevolod Sviatoslavich, or Mikhail, to claim a tie to Galicia-Volhynia – something that Mikhail would continue to do over the next two decades.

We can speak more confidently about the life of Mikhail, the husband of Elena, who was a powerful ruler in Rus and who was able to extend his influence from Chernigov to Kyiv, in order to take Galicia,

31 Batu's invasion of the Rus land in 6745 (1237). 'Twenty-five years after the passing of Grand prince Dmitrii Vsevolod, for our sins God led the godless tsar Batu to plunder the Rus land'. *Litsevoi letopisnii svod*, vol. VI, p. 211.

and even to Novgorod. During his rule in the 1220s and '30s, he was the preeminent member of the Olgovichi and was the most powerful of the whole Volodimerovich clan in the Dnieper River Basin. In what could be considered an interesting twist, Mikhail opposed Elena's brothers, Daniil and Vasilko, numerous times when exerting his own influence in Galicia-Volhynia. It was the arrival of the Mongols that led to his fall from power, as he fled from them and their allies when leaving Kyiv.[51] In 1246, when he travelled to visit the khan, Mikhail refused to participate in sacrifices, which was a duty in the khan's court, and he was killed. His death was considered to be a martyrdom by his family and, eventually, he was declared a saint in Rus in the fifteenth century.[52]

The number and identity of the children of Mikhail and Elena are also a matter of debate. Dąbrowski states that there were only three children of whom he can be sure: Maria, Evfrosinia-Feodula and Rostislav.[53] Conversely, Dimnik argued that according to the Ermolin Chronicle the couple had the following three children, plus four more sons: 'Grand Prince Roman of Chernigov . . . Mstislav of Karachev and Zvenigorod . . . Simeon of Glukhov and Novosil' . . . Yury of Bryansk and Torusa".[54] Oddly, we actually know a good deal more about the daughters than we do about the sons.[55] Maria helped to perpetuate her father's legacy, including creating the Feast of the Miracle-Workers of Chernigov (20 September) and building a church in their honour. Feodula took the name Evfrosinia when she joined a monastery; she too became an important figure, being canonized after her death in 1250. She had helped to spread Christianity among the Mongols.

The most well known of Roman and Maria's children is Daniil. In his lifetime, he travelled through eastern Europe, engaged in conflict with other Rusian rulers and with the Mongols, and rebuilt his father's realm in Galicia-Volhynia, at least briefly. All of this began, however, with his flight to the Hungarian court of King Andrew II (r. 1205–35) along with his mother and brother. Dąbrowski has conjectured that – owing to the prevalence of royal marriages to tie families together and Andrew's use of Daniil as a subordinate ruler in Galicia – it was in Hungary that Daniil was betrothed to the daughter of Andrew II.[56] Despite this theorized engagement, no actual marriage took place and Andrew's daughters were married elsewhere. Additionally, in 1214, Andrew II and Leszek the White, a Polish ruler, agreed to marry off their own children, Koloman and Salomea, respectively, to rule Galicia-Volhynia jointly.[57] Although this did not end up ensuring political control either, the decision signalled the fact that Andrew II's intention was no longer to support Daniil's rule in the territory.

Daniil's first actual marriage occurred in 1217. Mstislav Mstislavich, of the Rostislavichi family of Smolensk, who had intermittently tried to control Galicia, was able to take control from Koloman, its Hungarian ruler.[58] Mstislav was supported by Leszek the White; the marriage between Daniil and Anna, Mstislav Mstislavich's daughter, was a way to bring peace to the territory and create a tie with the ruling line of Roman Mstislavich. This peace lasted barely a year, as Leszek the White felt betrayed by Mstislav's peace treaty with Daniil; breaking their alliance, Leszek made common cause with Andrew II, who wanted to return his son Koloman to the throne in Galicia. The two immediately began a campaign, forcing Daniil back to Volodymyr; Mstislav fled to find allies on the steppe, where his mother's people were from. It was only in 1221 that Mstislav regained Galicia, although he never passed it over to Daniil, which he supposedly apologized to him for at a later date.[59]

Daniil and Anna had numerous children who would go on to play major roles in Rusian and eastern European affairs. Their son Lev was a future ruler of Galicia, who married the daughter of King Béla IV of Hungary. Lev's brother Roman also played a role in Galicia and Volhynia and was married three times, first to a daughter of the ruler of the Polovtsy, second to Gertrude of Babenberg and third to a Rusian princess. Another son, Shvarno, was married to a daughter of Mindaugas, the ruler of Lithuania. Daniil's life was a difficult one beset by conflict, especially in his attempt to regain and hold onto his throne. However, he outlived Anna, who had borne him numerous children.[60]

Daniil's second marriage coincided with one of the more momentous events of his rule, when he was summoned to the khan's court to receive the *iarlyk* of rule. Around 1246, he married a Lithuanian princess, a niece of Mindaugas.[61] Not much is known about this marriage, or why it was arranged, but it represents the arrival on the dynastic marriage scene of the Lithuanians, an advent that would be continued and strengthened with the marriages of Daniil's own children. Daniil's connection with the Mongols would be of major importance to his life and to Galicia, throughout his reign. First, he subordinated himself to the Mongols, an act which others, such as Mikhail Vsevolodovich, his brother-in-law, had failed to do. Despite this, he also continued his alliances with both Polish and Hungarian rulers and even courted the papacy as an ally against the Mongols. In 1253, Daniil received a

32 Daniil Romanovich statue in Lviv.

crown from the papacy, along with the title of 'rex' (king). This was at least the second time that he had been described as 'rex' in the Latin sources. The first was in John of Plano Carpini's *History of the Mongols*, which recorded his participation in the Mongol world empire; this coronation by the pope was the second.[62] Daniil, however, received no tangible assistance from the papacy; thus, his actual opposition of the Mongols had mixed results. Nevertheless, Daniil is an incredibly important figure in the history of Galicia-Volhynia, and he has been considered one of the founders of Ukraine.[63]

The last son of Roman Mstislavich and Maria was Vasilko. He was briefly the ruler of Brest soon after his father's death with his mother acting as regent, and then ruled again once he and Daniil had come of age.[64] Hrushevsky notes that the brothers maintained a rare solidarity in the face of their struggles to regain their father's territory.[65] We can see this solidarity in the Hypatian Chronicle's accounts of their battles in the early thirteenth century, where they acted in concert and Vasilko moved under Daniil's direction. The interconnectedness of their lives allows us to give a brief account of Vasilko, as much of his story is the story of Daniil's rise to power.

Vasilko's first marriage occurred in around 1227 to a daughter of Iurii, who was himself the son of Vsevolod 'Big Nest' of Vladimir-Suzdal.[66]

This marriage of Volodimerovich families from opposite ends of Rus demonstrates both the interconnectedness of the entire realm and the role that the Iurevichi of Vladimir-Suzdal played throughout its history. The purpose of the marriage is not recorded; in fact, little information about this marriage is recorded in general. At that time, Vasilko was ruling in Lutsk and Peresopnytsia, while Daniil ruled in Volodymyr. In 1227, the brothers teamed up with Mstislav Mstislavich, Daniil's father-in-law, to seize control of Galicia and also defend it from Hungarian attacks. Thus, one might conjecture that Vasilko's first marriage was an attempt to gain support for these actions in the west of Rus, although this was most likely not through direct action.

Vasilko's second marriage presents us with a connection to Poland, along with a fascinating letter from the pope. Vasilko married Dobrava, the daughter of Konrad I of Mazovia. The two of them were related within the forbidden degrees of consanguinity – the closeness of blood ties in marriage – and therefore a papal dispensation was needed to make the marriage valid.[67] For much of medieval history, consanguinity included seven degrees of connection, which could be measured in different ways. The connection between Vasilko and Dobrava was particularly close, at three degrees; thus, while marriages of six, or even five, degrees of connection could be made with little comment, three degrees did require intervention. Staying in the pope's good graces was especially necessary, as Daniil was seeking papal assistance against the Mongols, which resulted in his coronation some years later.

Vasilko and Dobrava had two children, Olga and Vladimir, who was also called Ivan or Ioann.[68] There is one final complication to this marital story. The marriage of the two is known, even the bride's name is known, but we do not know anything about the death of Dobrava. Instead, the Hypatian Chronicle records *s.a.* 1264 that 'the wife of Vasilko, *velikaia kniaginia* Elena, passed away and was buried in the Church of the Holy God Mother in Volodymyr.'[69] Who is this wife, Elena? What happened to Dobrava? This question has also vexed scholars; Dąbrowski, who has studied this material copiously and is widely cited here, has solved the problem by suggesting that Elena is Dobrava.[70] Perhaps this is the case and perhaps it was a monastic name, which is not uncommon for Rusian royal women. However, it represents yet another unknown in our examination of the role of medieval women in Rus.

✠

AS ONE CAN SEE in this chapter, although the events here took place in the western part of Rus, they are intimately connected with a much wider world. There are marriages and alliances made with the Lithuanians, Poles and Hungarians at the north, west and southwestern borders; and there are similar connections internal to Rus with other members of the Volodimerovich clan. The affairs of the Romanovichi also include interactions with both the Mongols and the papacy, stretching their connections across much of western Eurasia. This is a striking difference compared to the affairs of the Iurevichi of Vladimir-Suzdal, who largely maintained a focus on their own polity and the Mongols. Their contacts with the rest of Europe were limited, in comparison with the breadth of connections demonstrated by the rulers of Galicia-Volhynia.

This chapter continues some of the themes begun in Chapter Five, including the changing position of Kyiv relative to the entirety of Rus. Much as Andrei Bogoliubskii and Vsevolod 'Big Nest' had done, Roman Mstislavich assigned Kyiv a subordinate ruler, rather than ruling it himself. Even if Tatishchev's idea of a grand plan for Roman's rule is historically accurate, it was certainly never implemented, and Kyiv's place was marginalized in the thirteenth century.

The story of Roman Mstislavich and his children has become a major pillar of the history of Ukraine, especially as narrated by Mykhailo Hrushevsky in his seminal work, *History of Ukraine-Rus'*, and its inclusion here is an attempt to demonstrate the history of the entirety of Rus rather than the history of just those places that would lead to an eventual Muscovite, and Russian, state.[71] Chapter Seven, however, will return us to Vladimir-Suzdal; we will see the growing importance of the Mongols among the Rusian elite of this and other regions, as well as the continuing rise of that power centre and its connection to Novgorod and elsewhere.

7

Alexander Nevsky and the Family of the Iaroslavichi

In the Soviet director Sergei Eisenstein's film *Alexander Nevsky* (1938), the following dialogue occurs early on, between an 'old man' and Alexander:

> *Old man*: 'The Mongols are a hard-necked people, a strong people. It won't be easy fighting them.'
> AN: 'Is there a will for the fight?'
> *Old man*: 'It's time to avenge the deaths of our forefathers.'
> AN: 'The Mongols can wait a while. We have a more dangerous enemy, an enemy who is closer and crueler. After we beat them, then we will take care of the Mongols.'
> *Old man*: 'Let it be the Germans then. You know where to start, but our patience is at its end. *Kniaz*!'[1]

This dialogue provides an answer to a question that has bedevilled those who have studied events in Rus in the mid-thirteenth century; namely, why did Alexander fight the Livonian Knights ('Germans' in the dialogue above) but co-operate with the Mongols? Eisenstein's answer was that the 'Germans' were the more immediate threat and so they had to be dealt with first. Others, however, have argued that the Mongols were the more immediate threat in that they had conquered Rus in much the same way that the Germans had conquered France in the Second World War, when leaders like Marshal Pétain, who headed the Vichy government, were collaborationists and acted as traitors to their country. Was the thirteenth-century situation more complicated than these modern-day interpretations seem to allow?

Alexander Nevsky is one of the great military heroes of Russian history. He was given the sobriquet 'Nevsky' after the Neva River, where he defeated a band of Swedes in 1240; he was also known for leading the forces of Novgorod that defeated the Livonian Knights at Lake Chud (Peipus) in 1242. Numerous streets, such as Nevsky Prospect in St Petersburg and in Petrozavodsk, where, in both, Nevsky is also the spiritual patron, have been named in his honour. The Orthodox Church has dedicated cathedrals, churches, chapels and monasteries to him. He is also the spiritual patron of the Russian diplomatic service, the Russian Army and the Russian Navy. In tsarist Russia, the Imperial Order of St Alexander Nevsky was one of the top awards that the tsar could bestow.[2] The Order was established in 1725 to honour those individuals who had defended Russia against foreign invaders. The Bolsheviks abolished it in 1917, but it was revived in 1942 as simply the Order of Alexander Nevsky and was awarded for bravery in battle. Thus, the issue of Alexander's relationship with the Mongols, who ruled over Rus for two centuries, is not just an academic one; it is a topic that is still central to Russian political culture.

From 1237 until 1240, the Mongols invaded and conquered the lands of Rus (illus. 33). That conquest had a profound impact in terms of sovereignty, taxes and tributes (which were paid to the khan of the Ulus of Jochi and subsequently to its successor states), and influenced both military and political matters. For example, all rulers in the Rus lands, no matter what their internal system for choosing a ruler, had

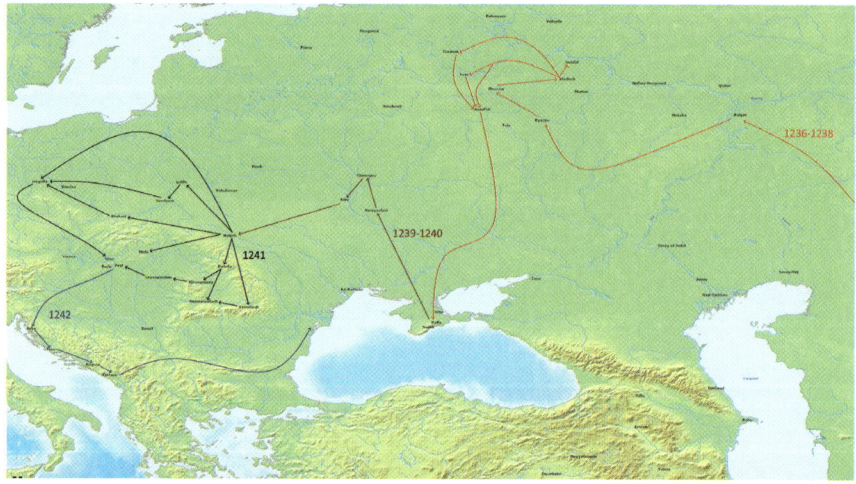

33 Batu and Subedei's conquest of eastern Europe, 1236–42.

to receive the imprimatur of the khan in the form of an *iarlyk* (patent). The effects of the Mongols' swift takeover were felt immediately. The chronicles tell us that Batu 'placed his governors and administrators everywhere, in all the Rus cities; and then he commanded all the Rus *kniazi* remaining in Rus to come to him and to bow before him'.[3] *Kniazi* and prospective *kniazi* initially had to travel to Qaraqorum, the capital of the Mongol Empire, to receive the *iarlyk* from the great khan (*qaghan*). Later on, they only had to travel to Sarai, the capital of the Ulus of Jochi (Qipchaq Khanate). John Fennell has ascertained that 'no less than nineteen visits were paid by Suzdalian princes to Baty [Batu] or his son Sartak [Sartaq]' between the years 1242 and 1252, making an average of two trips a year. Fennell also counted four visits by the Vsevolodovichi to Qaraqorum during that same time period.[4] In addition, the khan imposed a network of military governors, called *basqaq*s (Russian: *Baskaki*; Mongol: *tammači*), to rule in situ over the area. The Mongols established a resident *basqaq* in a city or land that had forcibly resisted the Mongol conquest. Whenever that city or land was subsequently pacified, or if it had not forcibly resisted the Mongols, then it was assigned a civilian governor, a *daruga*.[5] At that point, the local ruler took over the responsibilities of the military governor and acted in place of the *basqaq*.

When the Mongols invaded the land of Rus, from their perspective, the most renowned city was Kyiv. The outlying provincial capitals were the urban centres of charismatic clans, each competing with each other for power and for rule in Kyiv. These outlying capitals and clans were Vladimir-on-the-Kliazma (the Vsevolodovichi), Smolensk (the Rostislavichi), Chernigov (the Olgovichi) and Volodymyr-in-Volhynia (the Iziaslavichi).[6] The Vsevolodichi were the clan descendants of Vsevolod Iurevich (d. 1212). The Rostislavichi were the clan descendants of Rostislav Mstislavich (d. 1168), while the Olgovichi were the clan descendants of Oleg Sviatoslavich (d. 1115) and the Iziaslavichi were the clan descendants of Iziaslav Mstislavich (d. 1154). Three of these clan founders – Vsevolod, Rostislav and Iziaslav – were the grandsons of Volodimer Monomakh. The outlier from this set is Oleg, who was instead a cousin of Volodimer Monomakh. In this chapter, we will discuss the Vsevolodovichi during the first decades of Mongol rule, in particular, the Iaroslavich ruling family, of which Alexander Nevsky was a part.

Who Was the Mother of Alexander Nevsky?

The Laurentian Chronicle tells us that in 1238, 'Iaroslav Vsevolodovich sat on the throne'.[7] The throne was that of Vladimir-on-the-Kliazma, the de facto capital of the Suzdal region. Iaroslav replaced his older brother Iurii, who had been ruler of Vladimir since 1218 and who was killed by the Mongols at the Battle of the Sit River on 4 March 1238. In keeping with the system of collateral succession, Iurii had succeeded

34 The helmet of Iaroslav Vsevolodovich, found in 1808 on the site of the Battle of the Lipitsa River.

всякому делу благому был научен благочестивым своим отцом богомудрым и державным Ярославом Всеволодовичем, и святой своей матерью, боголюбивой великой княгиней Феодосией, нареченной в иночестве Ефросинией, которыми воспитан был во всяких добрых наставлениях. И вселился в сердце его страх Божий в стремлении к соблюдению заповедей Господних; ибо чтил он священнический и монашеский чин.

всякомꙋ делꙋ благꙋ наꙋчен бысть от благочестиваго си отца, богомꙋдраго и дръжавнаго Ярослава Всеволодича, и святыя своя матере, боголюбивыя великиа княгини Феодосии, иже наречена бысть во иноческом чинꙋ Єуфросиниа, от нихже воспитан бысть во всяком добром наказании. И тако вселися в сердце его страх Божий, еже соблюдати заповеди Господня и творити я во всем; бе бо повеликꙋ чтяше священнический и мнишеский чин.

35 Alexander Nevsky commemorating his parents, Iaroslav Vsevolodovich (d. 1246) and Feodosia (Euphrosina) (d. 1244). *Litsevoi letopisnyi svod*, vol. VI, p. 476.

his older brother Konstantin, who had ruled in Vladimir (1216–18), while Iaroslav was succeeded in turn by his younger brother, Sviatoslav, in 1246 (see illus. 27). Thus, the limit in the collateral system was a succession of four brothers who ruled before the succession moved on to the next generation – the Iaroslavichi (sons of Iaroslav) – when a maximum of four brothers again succeeded each other in turn.

Iaroslav was born in 1191 and, according to the chronicles, married a Polovtsian woman, whose name is not given, in 1205. She was the daughter of a chieftain named Iurii, who was the son of Konchak.[8] It has been speculated that Iurii the chieftain was a Nestorian by faith, which would have made the marriage more palatable to the Orthodox Church leaders. Reports of marriages between members of the Rus elite and the daughters of Polovtsian chieftains occur less frequently in the sources than do royal marriages to Europeans, perhaps because of the religious issue. Nonetheless, when such marriages did occur, they were probably undertaken for the same political reasons – the confirmation of an alliance. We have no record of when the marriage to Iurii's daughter ended. There is an ongoing controversy over how many wives Iaroslav Vsevolodovich actually had, and who they were. The controversy derives from an apparent contradiction in the chronicles. Some chronicles, even some of those that report this marriage to the daughter of Iurii Konchakovich, say that Iaroslav was the *ziat'* (son-in-law or brother-in-law) of Mstislav Mstislavich of the Rostislavich clan. When Mstislav and Konstantin Vsevolodovich defeated Iaroslav and his brother Iurii at the Battle of the Lipitsa River (1216), these chronicles say that Mstislav took his daughter back. This testimony, which is incorporated into 'The Tale of the Battle of the Lipitsa River', provides no name for the daughter of Mstislav who was presumably Iaroslav's wife, or whether she and Iaroslav were ever reunited.

One group of historians argues that Iaroslav married Feodosia Mstislavna in 1214 and that, despite the chronicles saying that Mstislav took his daughter back, she continued to be Iaroslav's wife because she was the mother of his children. Another group asserts that Iaroslav married a different daughter of Mstislav – that is, Rostislava, not Feodosia – in 1214, divorced her (or the marriage was dissolved) in 1216 and then married a different Feodosia, who was not Rostislava's sister (namely, Feodosia Igorevna) in 1218, who became the mother of his children. It would have to have been a different Feodosia from Feodosia Mstislavna because of the Church's prohibition against a man marrying the sister of his former wife. None of these marriages (except the one to the daughter of Iurii Konchakovich) or divorces is reported in the chronicles. The traditional view has been that Feodosia's father was Mstislav Mstislavich Udatnyi and her mother was the daughter of the Polovtsian ruler, Kotyan. Dąbrowski has disputed this view, concluding that Feodosia was the daughter of the ruler of Kyiv, Mstislav Romanovich (r. 1212–23).[9]

Whichever Feodosia it was, she and Iaroslav had twelve children that we know of – nine boys and three girls, the same number of children that his father Vsevolod 'Big Nest' had had. When Feodosia died in 1244, the chronicles tell us that her hair had been shorn when she became a nun and was given the monastic name Euphrosina (Evrosina). At that time, a person was given their monastic name according to the saint commemorated on the day on which they were tonsured, rather than taking the name of a saint whose name began with the same initial as the postulant's worldly name.[10]

Independent Towns

The wild card of territory among the ruling clans was independent towns, those that did not have a resident ruling clan or family. Clans competed for control of these towns. Independent towns were too valuable for the competing clans to give up entirely. Each of these towns has a different story to tell, but they are integral to understanding the political and economic interrelationships of the ruling families of Rus.

Kyiv was one such town that was not the resident capital of any ruling clan. It had symbolic value as the seat of the *kniaz* who was *primus inter pares*. In order to become the *kniaz* of Kyiv, one's father had to have ruled there, even if only for a short period of time. Thus, it was important for at least one member of each clan from every generation to rule in Kyiv, so that their sons would be eligible to rule. For example, let us say that a member of Clan A is serving as the Kyivan *kniaz*. His younger brother will succeed him, and so on down to the fourth brother (if there is one). In the meantime, the members of Clan B are patiently (or impatiently) waiting their turn, with their oldest member getting older by the day. If Clan A does not finish the cycle of their generation before all their cousins in Clan B have died, then Clan B is thereby excluded forever from the rulership of Kyiv. One action that Clan B can take is a coup; that is, forcibly ousting from Kyiv the existing *kniaz* from Clan A and installing one of their own members as the ruler in Kyiv. So far, so good, but what if the existing Kyivan *kniaz* is not residing in Kyiv? What if, say, he was residing in Vladimir? Would it be enough for a member of Clan B just to occupy Kyiv, or would he actually have to seek out the existing Kyivan *kniaz* in Vladimir and defeat him there? In other words, was Andrei Bogoliubskii's intention to replace Kyiv in importance with the city of Vladimir, or was he trying to make it more difficult for one of the other clans to oust him from his position as the *kniaz* of Kyiv?

As pointed out in Chapter Five, the rulership of Kyiv between 1235 and 1240 was held in turn by each of the ruling clans, as each clan had at least one member of the appropriate generation holding the position, legitimating the claim of the next generation in each clan to hold that position via the son of the person who held it. As far as our records show, no *kniaz* resided in Kyiv after 1240. Khan Batu appointed Alexander Nevsky the ruler of Kyiv in 1249, a title he retained until his death in 1263. The position of the *kniaz* of Kyiv does not seem to have passed to his brother, Iaroslav, when he took over as the ruler of Vladimir.

At some point between 1263 and 1301, Lev Daniilovich claimed the title of the *kniaz* of Kyiv. From 1301 to 1324, Kyiv was ruled by the Olgovichi. In 1324, a few years after the Battle on the Irpin River, the Grand Duke of Lithuania, Gediminas, appointed Mindaugas, who was an Olshanski. Mindaugas was descended from the family of Vseslav Briachislavich of Polotsk, who had gone into exile in Constantinople. Fëdor, most likely the younger brother of Gediminas, ruled in Kyiv from 1331 to 1362. In 1362, after the Battle of Blue Waters, Algirdas, the Grand Duke of Lithuania, retook Kyiv; it remained in Lithuanian hands until 1569, when the Union of Lublin transferred it to the administrative control of Poland.

Riazan was another independent town, the capital of the Riazan lands (with Pronsk being the second town). After the death of Iaroslav the Wise, the polity of Murom-Riazan was under the jurisdiction of the Olgovichi of Chernigov. After the sack of 1186, the rulers of Riazan pledged allegiance to Vsevolod but remained in a marriage alliance with the Olgovichi. Hostilities broke out again between the rulers of Riazan and Vsevolod. After sacking Pronsk in 1207 but sparing Riazan, Vsevolod sacked Riazan once more in 1208. According to the Laurentian Chronicle:

> Then, Grand Prince Vsevolod said that all must leave the city with their light possessions and with their other goods, and he burned the city and the suburbs . . . He moved the people, together with their wives and children, from Riazan to Vladimir, and sent them to his own towns, and he completely devastated the Riazan land.[11]

Vsevolod thus destroyed Staraia (Old) Riazan and ordered its residents to Vladimir, to populate the towns of the Suzdal region.[12]

The Vsevolodovichi also utilized marriage alliances with the ruling family of Riazan to ensure its loyalty. For example, Volodimer Konstantinovich (1214–1249), the ruler of Uglich (1218–49) married Evdokia, the daughter of Ingvar Igorevich of Riazan.

Turov was a trading centre on the Pripiat River, a tributary of the Dnieper. Pinsk was the second town in the Turov area. The town of Turov was besieged unsuccessfully for ten weeks in 1158 by the ruler of Chernigov, Iziaslav Davidovich (d. 1161, a member of the Olgovich clan). At the time, Boris, the son of Iurii Dolgorukii (who was then the *kniaz* of Kyiv), was the town's ruler. Most likely, Iziaslav saw Iurii's appointment of Boris as ruler of Turov as an attempt to lure its people and its trade revenue to the side of the Suzdal rulers. After various attempts by the *kniazi* of Vladimir, Chernigov and Galicia-Volhynia to take it over, by the fourteenth century, Turov had wound up in the hands of the Lithuanian ruler, Gediminas.

Polotsk is on the Dvina River and was another important trading town, ruled by the Briachislavichi (Briachislav Iziaslavich (d. 1044) being the grandson of Volodimer I). Thus, it was a different branch of the Volodimerovichi from that of the Iaroslavichi. Briachislav's son, Vseslav, ruled briefly in Kyiv (1068), although his father had not ruled there. However, none of his six sons succeeded to that position, so the Briachislavichi were not subsequently part of the succession system to the throne of Kyiv. Nonetheless, they managed to maintain Polotsk's independence from the ruling clans. In 1240, at the time of the Mongol conquest of Kyiv, Polotsk came under the suzerainty of the Lithuanian grand duke, Mindaugas. In 1307, Vytenis, Grand Duke of Lithuania (r. 1295–1316), formally annexed the town to Lithuania.

Pereiaslavl-Zalesskii was founded by Iurii Dolgorukii in 1152 with the idea of making it the capital of the Vladimir-Suzdal polity. It was one of the largest towns in Rus in terms of fortified territories and was a major trading area, one that was especially known for providing a type of white fish, the Pereiaslavl vendace, which is found only in nearby Lake Pleshcheevo. Alexander Nevsky was born in Pereiaslavl in 1220; his brother Andrei resided there both before his flight from and his return to Rus. Alexander's son Dmitrii also lived there while he was the ruler of Vladimir (1276–94). In 1304, Moscow and Tver fought for control of the town, with the former triumphant. Subsequent Moscow rulers granted Pereiaslavl-Zalesskii as a 'feeding' town for members of the elite, meaning that those who were assigned the town could collect taxes, duties, fees and so on from the citizens.

Novgorod was the most prominent of the non-Kyivan independent towns. The *veche* (assembly), which was made up of merchants, boyars, artisans, craftsmen and townspeople, governed the town. The archbishop was the chief executive officer, but the *veche* could invite a *kniaz* from any of the ruling clans to maintain order and defence. That meant playing off one ruling clan against another so that no one clan could gain dominance over the town. During the twelfth century, the throne of Novgorod was virtually a revolving door, as one *kniaz* replaced another, although a number of *kniazi* held the position several times. From 1200 to 1300, however, the situation changed, as successive members of the Vsevolodovich clan were rulers of Novgorod for 89 of the 100 years of that century. The Rostislavich clan, in the persons of three Mstislavichi, ruled for the other eleven years (1210–21). How that occurred is connected with how the Vsevolodichi expanded their dominance over the northeast, and that story has much to do with Iaroslav Vsevolodovich and his son, Alexander Nevsky.

Alexander's Claims to Fame

We first encounter Alexander Nevsky in the chronicles under the entry for 1228 in the Novgorod First Chronicle, which explains how Alexander and his older brother Fëdor were left in Novgorod under the supervision of two officials, while their father went to fight against Riga.[13] The next year, the two officials were forced to flee over a matter of taxation, taking Fëdor and Alexander with them.[14] In 1236, Alexander and his brother Andrei were appointed to joint rulership of Novgorod.

In 1242, when Alexander was the *kniaz* of Novgorod, he marshalled his military forces against the Livonian Knights and their allies at Lake Chud (Peipus); the Laurentian Chronicle tells us that Alexander's father, Iaroslav, 'sent his son Andrei to Great Novgorod in aid of Alexander against the Germans and defeated them beyond Pskov at the lake and [they] took many prisoners. Andrei returned to his father in honour.'[15] In this chronicle entry, the focus is on Andrei rather than on Alexander; pointedly, it mentions Andrei's returning to their father Iaroslav with honour and his sharing with Alexander the capture of prisoners. In contrast, the Suzdal Chronicle focuses on

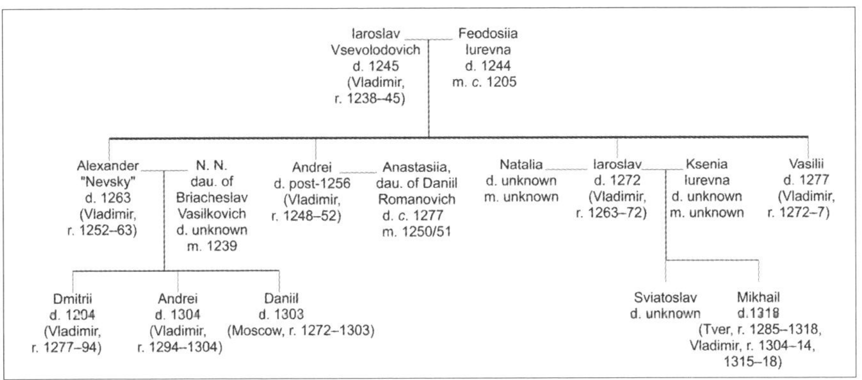

36 Iaroslav Vsevolodovich and selected family members.

Alexander and does not mention Andrei: 'Alexander Iaroslavich went with the Novgorodians against the Germans and fought with them at Lake Chud by Raven's Rock. Alexander defeated them and they chased them across the ice for 7 versts.'[16] 'The Military Tale about Alexander Nevsky' does mention Iaroslav's sending of Andrei: 'His father Iaroslav sent him help [in the form of] his younger brother Andrei, along with many brave men. *Kniaz* Alexander returned from the victory with great glory. There were a multitude of prisoners accompanying his regiment.'[17] In this tale, the focus is again on Alexander in terms of returning with 'great glory' and with prisoners. It does not mention whether Andrei returned 'with honour' to Iaroslav, but presumably he did. Why do we see these differences in the sources? We can speculate that the differences stem from either favouritism on the part of the father Iaroslav's part for the younger brother Andrei and/or a partiality on the part of the Laurentian chronicler for Andrei. A third possibility is that it might represent a subsequent interpolation. Further research should help to uncover the source of this conundrum.

The Vsevolodovichi's Dealings with the Mongol Khans

In 1243, Iaroslav journeyed to the new capital of the Ulus of Jochi at Sarai. Khan Batu, the grandson of Chinggis Khan, granted him the *iarlyk* as the ruler of Kyiv. In 1246, Iaroslav had to travel to Qaraqorum. The chronicles say that Fëdor Iarunovich slandered him to Khan Batu,[18] which is why he may have been sent for by the great khan. Iaroslav died on 20 September 1246, in Qaraqorum, ten days after the Olgovich ruler, Mikhail of Chernigov, was executed by Batu in Sarai.[19] Iaroslav was succeeded by his brother, Sviatoslav, who was the youngest son of Vsevolod. Thus, four brothers – Konstantin, Iurii, Iaroslav and Sviatoslav – served one after the other as rulers of Vladimir. Sviatoslav served as its ruler for only two years before he either stepped down or was ousted from the throne in 1248, despite the fact that he lived until 1253. The Continuation of the Patriarch of Constantinople Nikifor's Short Chronicle, which has been dated to the 1280s, and the Novgorod Fourth Chronicle say that Andrei ousted Sviatoslav from power and placed himself on the throne of Vladimir.[20] If so, and if Andrei was the eldest nephew, then we may be seeing an occurrence here of the equality of position of the fourth brother of the previous generation and the oldest brother of this generation, as described by V. O. Kliuchevskii.

As interesting as the lives of Iaroslav and Sviatoslav Vsevolodovich are, this chapter focuses instead on Iaroslav's children with Feodosia, who were the next generation of rulers of Vladimir. In particular, we will look in more detail at the four sons – Alexander, Andrei, Iaroslav and Vasilii (see illus. 36) – each of whom ruled in Vladimir.

Alexander's Non-Ruling Brothers

First, we will look at the brothers of Alexander who did not rule in Vladimir because they died prematurely. The oldest brother, Fëdor, was born in 1219. He may have been betrothed to Feodula, the daughter of Mikhail of Chernigov of the Olgovich clan, but he died at the age of thirteen before the marriage could take place.[21] A potential alliance between the Vsevolodovichi and Olgovichi was thereby thwarted. The next oldest brother who did not rule was Mikhail. He was killed at the Battle of Protva on 14 January 1248, fighting the nephews and brother of the ruler of Lithuania, Mindaugas. Two of our chronicles say that Mikhail was the ruler of Vladimir at the time, but the other chronicles make no mention of his being a *kniaz*. He was around twenty years old at the time of his death.

A third brother, Daniil, about whom we have almost no information, died in 1256. The fourth non-ruling brother, Konstantin, was sent to Qaraqorum and returned to his father (Iaroslav) in 1245 'with honour'. We do not have any evidence of whom he married, but he is supposed to have had two sons – Davyd and Vasilii. Konstantin died in 1255. Some chronicles indicate that he had another son named Afanasii, but that was also the Christian name of Iaroslav, so it is likely that they are one and the same person.

The Marriages of the Iaroslavichi

The Novgorod First Chronicle tells us that in 1239 Alexander married the daughter of Briacheslav Vasilkovich, the ruler of Polotsk and Vitebsk, in Toropets.[22] In the tomb of the Vladimir Dormition Monastery, she is referred to as the *kniaginia* Alexandra.[23] She was from a small ruling family that was not part of one of the four dominant ruling clans, but one that had connections with both the Olgovichi and Rostislavichi. In 1180, for example, Vasilko Briachislavich, the grandfather of Alexandra, helped the Olgovichi to mount a siege of Drutsk against Davyd Rostislavich; however, in 1186, Davyd helped his by-then son-in-law Vasilko to take the throne of Vitebsk.

Alexander and Alexandra had five children, but only two of their four sons succeeded to the rulership of Vladimir. Their daughter, Evdokia, married Konstantin Rostislavich, creating a link to the Rostislavichi of Smolensk. The historian Nikolai Karamzin claimed that Alexander had a second wife who was named Vasilisa or Vassa, and that she bore one child, Daniil. Karamzin made this claim on the basis that there is a second tomb in the Vladimir Dormition Monastery that is designated for 'Vassa'. Thus, it would appear that Alexander had two wives.[24] However, the claim that Vassa was a separate wife has been challenged; a counter-proposal suggests that Vassa was Alexandra's monastic name (despite the existence of two tombs) or she was the second wife of Andrei, Alexander's brother.[25] In any case, Alexander had four sons – Vasilii (d. 1271), Dmitrii (d. 1294), Andrei (d. 1304) and Daniil (d. 1303). Vasilii died before his youngest uncle – also named Vasilii – who was serving at the time as the *kniaz* of Vladimir. Dmitrii succeeded Vasilii Iaroslavich as the *kniaz* of Vladimir (1277–94), after which Andrei succeeded Dmitrii as *kniaz* (1294–1304).

Daniil of Moscow never ruled in Vladimir, predeceasing his next older brother by one year. That should have effectively eliminated Daniil's descendants from eligibility to be rulers of Vladimir, but Khan Uzbeg overrode that stipulation, meaning that the rulers of Moscow traced their heritage back to Daniil Alexandrovich. It was this genealogical connection of the founder of the Daniilovich clan to Alexander Nevsky that led to the subsequent veneration of Nevsky in the sixteenth century. He was declared a saint at a Church Council in Moscow in 1547.

Alexander's brother Andrei married Anastasia Daniilovna, the daughter of Daniil Romanovich of Galicia and of Anna Mstislavna, in 1250/51. The chronicles tell us that the wedding was performed in the town of Vladimir by Metropolitan Kirill and the Bishop of Rostov, who was also named Kirill. Dąbrowski calculated that Anastasia was born in the 1230s (no later than 1238),which would have made her between twelve and 21 when she married.[26] The marriage of her parents represented an alliance between the Rostislavich and Iziaslavich clans. Likewise, the marriage between herself and Andrei marked an alliance between the Iziaslavich and Vsevolodovich clans. Certainly, it would seem to have been more politically significant than Alexander's marriage to the daughter of Vasilko Briachislavich. Andrei and Anastasia had two children, whose names are recorded in the sources – Iurii and Mikhail – neither of whom ruled as the *kniaz* of Vladimir. Anastasia died around 1277.

The third brother, Iaroslav (1230–1272), ruled in Vladimir after Alexander from 1264 to 1272. The names of his two wives appear in the sources – Natalia (no patronymic is given) and Ksenia Iurevna. Other than their names, we have no information about them. It is assumed that Ksenia bore Iaroslav two sons, named Sviatoslav and Mikhail, and three daughters: Ksenia (wife of Iurii Lvovich of Galicia), an unnamed daughter and Sofia. We will discuss them further in the next chapter.

The fourth and final brother of that generation to rule in Vladimir was Vasilii, who was the *kniaz* from 1272 to 1277. He was married in 1268, but the name of his wife was not given, and no children were recorded.

The Iaroslavichi's Dealings with their Mongol Overlords

In 1249, according to the chronicles, Alexander and his brother Andrei went to Qaraqorum, the Mongol capital, where 'the sons of the khan' appointed Alexander as the ruler of Kyiv and Andrei, the ruler of Vladimir.[27] Historians have been puzzled by this chronicle entry. The expression 'the sons of the khan' can be explained by the fact that the Mongol khan Güyük had died in 1248 and a new khan had not yet been chosen. During this interregnum, Oghul Qaimish, the widow of Güyük, ruled as regent. Presumably, she was the one who gave the *iarlyki* to

Alexander and Andrei. One can only speculate why the chronicler did not state this fact directly but instead resorted to attributing it to the sons of the former khan. The other aspect of the appointments that has puzzled historians is that Alexander, being the oldest son, should have received the *iarlyk* to rule in Vladimir, since Kyiv was of secondary importance at the time. This puzzlement, however, is in part due to an academic acceptance of the dynastic model, in which the inheritance of power in Rus proceeded teleologically to the northeastern *kniazi* – the Vsevodolovichi (Vladimir). However, at this time, that power could have gone in any of three other possible clan directions – to the Iziaslavichi (in Volhynia and Galicia), to the Rostislavichi (in Smolensk) or to the Olgovichi (in Chernigov).

The Mongols most likely had a different perspective from modern-day historians and considered Kyiv, as *The Secret History of the Mongols* describes it, the predominant city of the 'Orusud' people.[28] The khan could have opted to bestow that power on someone from one of the other ruling clans or even on someone who was not from any of them. The question is why he opted for the Vsevolodovichi. Whereas the traditional dynastic narrative says that there was something predestined about the transfer of power to the northeast, the transfer could instead have gone to Galicia-Volhynia, Chernigov or Smolensk. Considering the Vsevolodovichi to be the clan most willing to work with them, the Mongols would naturally place the eldest eligible brother of that clan as the ruler of the most prominent city. The main city of the Vsevolodovich clan, Vladimir, went to the next oldest brother. This arrangement, however, would change three years later.

In 1252, Andrei ceased being the ruler of Vladimir and the khan appointed Alexander in his place. The various chronicles provide contradictory information about the circumstances involved. Either Andrei was ousted by the khan, or Andrei decided that he could no longer be subordinate to the Mongols. The Laurentian Chronicle and the Simeonov Chronicle, in their entries for 1252, report: 'Prince Andrei Iaroslavich thought with his boyars that it was better to flee than to serve the khan.'[29] We do not have evidence from the thirteenth century as to what Andrei was thinking or what his motivations were. Nor do we have direct evidence of any struggle for succession between Andrei and Alexander that may have occurred upon the death of their father Iaroslav or upon the ascent to the throne of Vladimir by Iaroslav's brother, Sviatoslav, in 1246. Depending on the chronicle, either Alexander went to see

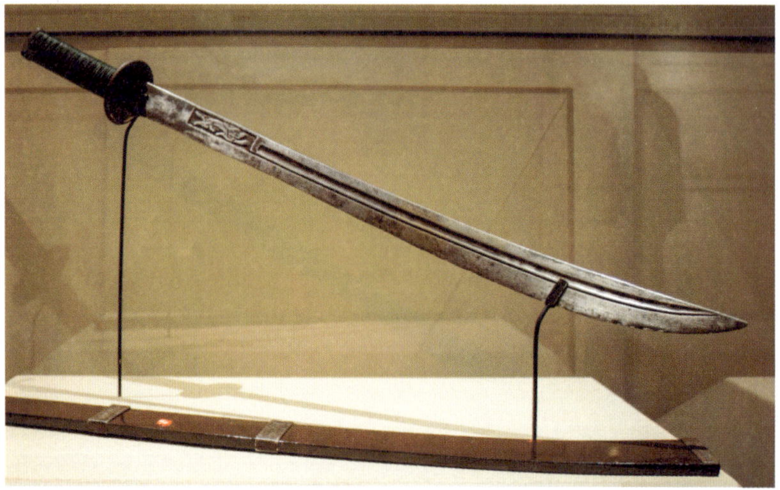

37 Mongol sabre from the 13th century, found in Iaroslavl in 2007.

Khan Batu before the campaign against his brother, or he went to see Khan Sartaq, Batu's son, or he did not go to Sarai at that time. Likewise, either Batu sent the military expedition of 1252 that ousted Andrei from the throne of Vladimir, or his son Sartaq sent it, or the two together ordered it to be sent. Either the expedition was directed against Andrei, or it was directed against the lands of Suzdal. Either Andrei fled to a place unknown, or he fled 'beyond the sea' to Sweden. Some chronicles claim that he was killed there. Despite that claim, reports of his death seem to have been greatly exaggerated because he is recorded as having returned to the Suzdal region in 1256, where he again served the Mongols.[30]

The Question of Alexander's 'Appeasement'

It has been estimated by the Russian historian Iurii Seleznev that, cumulatively speaking, Alexander Nevsky spent four and a half years of his reign at the court of the khan in Sarai.[31] Those lengthy stays, along with other circumstances and pieces of evidence, have led a number of historians to ask what exactly Alexander's role was in the khan's decision to send a military force to the Suzdal region in 1252, a decision that resulted in the ousting or fleeing of his brother Andrei. Historians have raised the question of whether Alexander, in light of his standing with the Mongols, urged Batu to oust his brother from the throne of Vladimir. Fennell summarized the arguments that asserted

Alexander was engaged in appeasing the Mongols. Given that the experiences of the Second World War were still fresh in the minds of scholars like Fennell, the sense of distaste for accommodationists in occupied Europe was strong.

Both the military tale of Alexander Nevsky and the *vita* (*zhitie*) that is devoted to his life sidestep the question with a denial:

> At that time, there was a powerful khan of the Eastern Country. That khan, hearing of the glory and courage of Alexander, sent him envoys, saying, 'Alexander, do you not know that God has submitted many nations to me? You are the only one who is not willing to submit to my power. But if you want to save your land, then come soon to me and you will see the honour of my khanate.' Having given [his proposal] due thought, Prince Alexander went to the khan. Upon seeing him, Khan Batu marvelled and said to his dignitaries: 'I was told the truth – that there is no other like this prince.' Bestowing on him honour, he let him go.[32]

By saying that Alexander had not submitted to Batu, the military tale and the *vita* can deny that the Mongols even ruled, let alone conquered Rus. Nonetheless, the formulation 'if you want to save your land, then come soon to me,' followed by Alexander's going there after 'due thought', does indicate a threat and Alexander's subsequent compliance with Batu's demand.

From the return of Alexander and Andrei from Qaraqorum in 1249 until the year 1252, the chronicles do not report any conflict among the brothers, which led Fennell to surmise that 'if indeed he [Andrei] was obliged to struggle for the retention of his throne, as was only too likely, his or later chroniclers saw to it that all traces of discord were removed from the record.'[33] Although the sources do not mention it, 'it is clear' to Fennell 'that trouble was brewing in the last three years of Andrey's reign'.[34] Fennell asserted that the motivations behind Alexander's and Andrei's actions 'can only be arrived at by deduction',[35] which he explained in the following way. The sources' portrayal of Andrei 'merely as the helpless victim of circumstances' is the result of later chroniclers 'doctor[ing], sometimes clumsily, at a later stage to justify Aleksandr's behaviour'.[36] Fennell then used what he terms 'these garbled and fictitious accounts' to ascertain 'hints of Andrey's true motives'. He speculated that Andrei's brother Iaroslav was of the same mind as Andrei, since he too fought at Pereiaslavl against the Tatars. Fennell favourably entertained Lev Gumilev's suggestion that preparations had been made between 1249 and 1252 for an armed uprising, which Alexander connived with the Khan Sartaq to suppress. None of the chronicles 'imputes to [Alexander] any blame for the defeat of his brothers' but there can be 'little doubt as to his complicity'.[37] In corroboration of this relative certainty, he quoted from the eighteenth-century history of Tatishchev, which reported that Alexander complained to Sartaq about Andrei's 'deceiving the khan, taking the grand principality from the senior prince [Alexander] and not paying in full the taxes and tributes to the khan'.[38] Thus, Alexander's return to Vladimir 'marked the end of a period of conflict of interests among the descendants of Vsevolod III and the beginning of a new era of Russia's subjugation to Tatar overlordship'.[39] It was 'the end of any form of organized resistance to the Tatars by the rulers of Russia for a long time to come' and 'the beginning of Russia's real subservience to the Golden Horde'. In other words, 'The so-called "Tatar Yoke" began not so much with Baty's [Batu's] invasion of Russia as with Aleksandr's betrayal of his brothers.'[40] The inception of Alexander's reign was 'in more ways than one a cataclysmic turning-point in the history of Russia', with his reign itself following a 'policy of appeasement'.[41]

While all this makes for dramatic reading, one must ask to what extent such conclusions are based on the source testimony or merely on the lively and creative imaginations of the historians themselves. Is one justified in dismissing the sources as 'doctored' and, if so, are only notions that may be preconceived, nationalistic and anachronistic available as alternatives? Or are there other possible ways to look at how and in what direction they were doctored? The sequence of proposed events and posited motivations that Fennell describes are possible, but there may be another explanation that is more plausible. It involves a military action by Batu that Fennell himself pointed out in 1252 to 1254, which was put into practice by Batu's *temnik* (army commander), Qurumshi.[42] Qurumshi was the nephew of Batu and undertook numerous military expeditions for him in Galicia.[43] According to the Galician-Volhynian Chronicle, this particular military action prompted Daniil Romanovich to begin fighting against the Tatars.[44] Daniil was the father-in-law of Andrei Iaroslavich, and there were attempts at this time by Pope Innocent IV to engage Daniil's support in an anti-Tatar crusade. Innocent also undertook to establish connections with the Vsevolodovichi. In a letter dated 3 May 1246, which was to be delivered by the papal legate Albert, who was the archbishop of Prussia and Livonia, the pope stated that he was pleased that the *kniaz* was prepared to accept his primacy. Historians have thought that the letter was to be delivered to Daniil of Galicia, but Church historian James Zatko argues that the intended recipient was Ivan, the brother of Iaroslav Vsevolodovich, whom Iaroslav designated to receive the letter while he travelled to Qaraqorum.[45] In January 1248, Innocent wrote to Alexander, telling him of his father Iaroslav's conversion to Catholicism, claiming that John of Plano Carpini had informed him of this event.[46] We have no evidence that Iaroslav converted to Catholicism or what he told John. Maybe he merely said that he had converted or was planning to convert (or was thinking about converting) to get the pope's help. The point here is that the pope thought that he had converted. Later that month, Innocent wrote to both Daniil of Galicia and Alexander, asking that they provide intelligence to the papacy regarding any new Mongol attack.[47] In September 1248, Innocent wrote another letter to Alexander expressing his satisfaction regarding Alexander's willingness to convert to Catholicism, saying that his legate Albert had brought the news to him. He also thanked Alexander for his efforts to raise the Catholic church in Pskov to cathedral status.[48] In 1250, after performing the marriage ceremony between Andrei Iaroslavich and Anastasia Daniilovna, Metropolitan Kirill and Bishop Kirill of Rostov went to Novgorod, ostensibly to see Alexander. This visit happened to coincide with the appearance of papal envoys in the city. Innocent was involved in efforts to form a coalition of Rus rulers, including the Vsevolodovichi of Suzdal and the Iziaslavichi of Galicia-Volhynia, against the Mongols. This coalition did not come to pass.[49]

Whether or not Iaroslav or Alexander gave any thought to recognizing the primacy of the pope, the fact of their negotiating with the papacy may have been sufficient to alarm the khan. The Mongol intelligence system was excellent, as we know from the history of their campaigns. It seems likely that Batu was aware of any conspiracy against Mongol rule. The coincident campaigns of Qurumshi in Galicia and Nevriui in Suzdal thus appear to be an attempt to head off any such conspiracy before it went too far. The Mongols were known for undertaking bifurcated military campaigns, as seen in 1242, when Batu and his general Subedei divided the Mongol army in eastern Europe to launch a simultaneous attack on the Poles and Germans at Liegnitz in the north and the Hungarians at Mohi in the south, so that neither of the opposing military forces could come to the aid of the other.

Positing such a coordinated attack and the motivation for it might also help to explain why Andrei fled to Sweden rather than to his father-in-law in Galicia. It might also help solve the mystery of why several chronicles reported that during the 1252 attack on Pereiaslavl, '[the Mongols] searched throughout the land and killed the *kniaginia* [the wife of the *kniaz*] and sent the children into captivity.'[50] A number of the chronicles specify that the *kniaginia* in question is the wife of Iaroslav. The problem with that identification is: which Iaroslav and why? Iaroslav Vsevolodovich's wife, Feodosia, died in 1244, eight years earlier, while Iaroslav's 'children' (*deti*) were already grown. Iaroslav Iaroslavich's wife in 1252 seems to be of hardly any consequence in the political scheme of things, since we do not even know to what family she belonged. Besides, this particular Iaroslav resided in Tver, not Pereiaslavl. Andrei's home seat, on the other hand, was Pereiaslavl and Andrei's wife, Anastasia Daniilovna, would have had political significance in her own right, possibly enough significance for the Mongols to go in search of her. If so, then we can posit that Anastasia Daniilovna was seen by Batu as the link in an anti-Mongol conspiracy of her father Daniil Romanovich of Galicia and her husband Andrei Iaroslavich of Suzdal.

✠

FOR THE MOST PART, the Mongol overlords in Sarai left the collateral system of succession intact among the Vsevolodovichi, yet each new ruler had to be confirmed by the khan in Sarai. Four Vsevolodovich family brothers followed each other in the succession. It is not clear whether someone ousted Sviatoslav Vsevolodovich in 1248 (the chronicles are not in agreement on this point) or if he merely decided to step down. Another four Iaroslavich family brothers followed each other in turn in the next generation. Batu (and/or Sartaq) intervened to oust Andrei Iaroslavich from being the *kniaz* of Vladimir in 1252, which may have been a result of his marriage to Anastasia, the daughter of Daniil of Galicia, whom Pope Innocent IV was trying to involve in an alliance against the Mongols. Previously Innocent had tried to enlist Andrei's father Iaroslav, as well as his other son Alexander, in an alliance with Rome. The simultaneous attack by Qurumshi on Galicia and Nevriui on Suzdal can be explained by Khan Batu's being aware of the anti-Mongol negotiations being conducted with the papacy.

While a case could be made, as Fennell did, that Alexander was a collaborationist with the Mongols and betrayed his brother Andrei, such a case is speculative because we simply do not have sufficient evidence. The interpretation given by Eisenstein, that Alexander saw 'the Germans' as the more immediate threat and that he intended to take on the Mongols later, is equally speculative. If one takes into consideration the evidence of Pope Innocent IV's letters, one could argue that both Alexander and his father Iaroslav were seeking outside help against the Mongols. In any case, the successors to Iaroslav and Alexander as rulers of the Vladimir-Suzdal polity until the fifteenth century may well have accepted Mongol rule and worked with the Mongol khans, their military commanders and administrative officials, while at the same time looking for opportunities to escape that rule.

8

Iurii Danilovich and His Family

In 1304, Iurii, the son of Daniil Aleksandrovich, asked Khan Toqta (r. 1291–1312) to declare him the *kniaz* of Vladimir and give him the *iarlyk* to rule it. This request was unusual for two reasons: first, the person who was first in line to be the *kniaz*, according to the collateral system of succession,[1] was Mikhail, the son of Iaroslav Iaroslavich; second, Iurii should not have been in the line of succession at all because his father, Daniil Aleksandrovich, had not ruled as the *kniaz* of Vladimir (see illus. 41). One's father having previously been the ruler of a particular town was one of the stipulations for the son to become the ruler of that town.[2] The result of this stipulation was that before the late fifteenth century, Rus rulers had no sense that they were part of a 'dynasty' who were destined to rule the whole of Rus. Instead, each *kniaz*, with only a few exceptions, justified his claim to rule a particular town on the basis that his father (often adding on his grandfather, brother and/or uncle) had ruled there. They did not claim that the town belonged to them, in the sense of a patrimony. Thus, a continuum of rulers of public towns was created from each individual ruler upward, rather than from a dynastic concept downward. The factor that unified the various clans was ruling in Kyiv. Members of each generation of each clan were in the line of succession to the symbolic capital of Rus. The rulers of Smolensk lost their place for a time in the sequence of succession in 1148 but rejoined it under the Rostislavichi in 1154.[3]

Iurii could not claim that his father Daniil had ruled in Vladimir because Daniil had died in 1303 while his older brother Andrei Aleksandrovich (r. 1294–1304) was still the *kniaz* of Vladimir (see illus. 36). Andrei died on 27 July 1304 but, fortunately for the family line, their grandfather, Iaroslav Vsevolodovich (r. 1238–46), had been as fecund as their great-grandfather, Vsevolod the 'Big Nest'. Four of Iaroslav's sons subsequently ruled as the *kniaz* of Vladimir: Andrei (r. 1248–52); Alexander Nevsky (r. 1252–63); Iaroslav (r. 1264–72); and Vasilii (r. 1272–6). Following Vasilii's death, the succession could have gone to Andrei's son, Iurii, as the eldest son of the first ruler of Vladimir in that generation. Instead, it went to the eldest living son of Alexander, who was the second ruler of Vladimir in that generation. That son, Dmitrii, ruled from 1277 to 1294, when his brother Andrei succeeded to the throne. When Andrei died, the next in line was Mikhail, the eldest living son of Iaroslav, who had been the third ruler of Vladimir in that older generation. Mikhail Iaroslavich, who was the ruler of Tver at the time, expected Khan Toqta to grant him the *iarlyk* to rule as the *kniaz* of Vladimir, which he did.

Iurii was probably well aware that the Mongol system of succession allowed any male of the ruling family to be chosen as successor.[4] Iurii's request to alter the system of succession in Rus set off a decades-long conflict between the rulers of Moscow and the rulers of Tver regarding ascension to the throne of Vladimir. This would not be the last time that the rulers of Moscow would want to change the system of succession.

Daniil Aleksandrovich, the Patriarch of the Clan

The decades-long conflict between the rulers of Moscow and the rulers of Tver had its origins in the 1290s, when Daniil Aleksandrovich (1261–1303), the youngest son of Alexander Nevsky, was the ruler of the former principality. The sources differ on exactly when he became the Moscow *kniaz*.[5] He was made the ruler at some point while his brother Dmitrii was the *kniaz* of Vladimir. At that time, Moscow was a relatively insignificant town. While Dmitrii was the ruler of Vladimir, Daniil supported him against his other brother, Andrei, in their conflict of the early 1280s. When his nephew Ivan (Dmitrii's son) died in 1302, to further this opposition of Andrei, who was the ruler of Vladimir at the time, Daniil took over the rule of Ivan's town, Pereiaslavl-Zalesskii.

The Rostov Cathedral commemoration book (*sinodicon*) reports that the name of Daniil's wife was Agrippina.[6] The historian Anton A. Gorskii estimated that Daniil most likely married her in the late 1270s or early 1280s.[7] He conjectured that Daniil's wife was the daughter of Lev Daniilovich of Galicia. Lev's daughter's name was also Agrippina;

Gorskii proposes that the marriage represented a dynastic connection between the Iziaslavichi of Galicia and the Vsevolodovichi of Vladimir.[8]

Daniil followed an aggressive policy as the ruler of Moscow. We are introduced to him in the chronicles in a dispute with his older brother, Andrei. Although we are not given much detail and the chronicle reports are spotty and appear under different year entries, we can surmise a scenario concerning this dispute. We must be particularly careful when making such surmises on the basis of the extant chronicles, for one simple reason. These chronicles were later redacted by subsequent scribes, who were biased in favour of the eventual winners – the Daniilovichi of Moscow. We do not have the chronicle perspective of the rulers of Riazan, Smolensk or Chernigov. Attempts to reconstruct parts of these chronicles are limited by scholars' reliance on extracting information from heavily edited Muscovite chronicles. In addition, the Galician-Volhynian Chronicle ends with the entry for 1292. However, the Novgorodian chronicles do at times present a different perspective.

Another difficulty with the use of chronicles for historical evidence is the problem of interpolations. The Nikonian and Ustiug chronicles, which were both compiled in the sixteenth century, are notorious for interpolating information that cannot be confirmed with any other source and that looks suspiciously like fabricated passages.[9] The Vladimir Chronicle from the early sixteenth century is similar to the Simeonov Chronicle, but it may also contain later interpolations and edits. The compiler of the Nikonian Chronicle did make an attempt to incorporate various chronicle traditions, including the Novgorodian and Tverian chronicles. It is possible that, in specific cases, the Nikonian Chronicle does maintain information from a non-extant fifteenth-century chronicle. The historian, therefore, must analyse each piece of information while taking into consideration the chronicle or chronicles in which that item appears, as well as the relationship of the chronicles to each other. As Soviet and Russian historian Iakov Solomonovich Lure (1921–1996) wrote: 'There still exist no established rules for the use of chronicles.'[10] As a result, many a historian has been led astray by the bias in the Moscow-edited chronicles which describe events in terms of a teleological dynastic inevitability. Basically, the story of the triumph of the Moscow *kniazi* is the only narrative available after a certain point. Nonetheless, we can reach some conclusions with a relative degree of certainty, while trying to avoid sliding down the slope of inevitability.

Pereiaslavl as a Town of Contention

After the death of Dmitrii Aleksandrovich, the ruler of Vladimir from 1277 to 1294, the rulership of Vladimir passed to his next oldest brother, Andrei. Pereiaslavl-Zalesski, however, went to Dmitrii's son Ivan. Apparently, Andrei thought that Pereiaslavl should have been given to him as the new ruler of Vladimir since Dmitrii had also ruled Pereiaslavl when he was the *kniaz* of Vladimir. While Andrei was gathering an army to take Pereiaslavl from Ivan, Andrei's younger brother Daniil (who was also Ivan's uncle) and his cousin Mikhail Iaroslavich gathered an army to oppose Andrei.[11]

Gathering an army was no simple task; at that time, rulers did not have standing armies. Generally, they relied on their brothers and other male relatives voluntarily augmenting whatever forces the ruler might have. The number of troops involved in any particular military action is almost entirely guesswork. When the chronicles do provide a number, it usually concerns a rather unusual operation, which makes it difficult to extrapolate the figure for more common operations. Nor do the chronicles tell us about the way in which the Rus troops fought. We must extract that information from other sources, such as archaeological finds and foreigners' accounts. On occasion, the chroniclers do make a distinction between, on the one hand, the 'people' (*liudi*) and, on the other, the 'warriors' (*voi*), 'troops' (*rati*) or 'forces' (*sila*) that were gathered, with the clear understanding that 'people' are not such good fighters as 'warriors', 'troops' and 'forces'. So why would the ruler of Vladimir go to all the trouble of gathering an army to take control of a town that already was within his polity? Although Iurii Dolgorukii founded Pereiaslavl-Zalesskii as the future capital of the Suzdal region, after Iurii's death, the town of Vladimir gained that distinction. Nonetheless, Pereiaslavl retained its political importance as a possible competitor to Vladimir as the capital of the Vladimir-Suzdal polity. Alexander Nevsky had been born there; his brother Andrei and his son Dmitrii had both resided there while they ruled in Vladimir. To allow Dmitrii's son Ivan to rule in Pereiaslavl meant that Ivan was a potential focal point of opposition to Andrei Aleksandrovich. Thus, Andrei had to eliminate that perceived threat to his rule.

Moscow vs the Other Towns

During the fourteenth century, the rulers of Moscow made their move for dominance over northeastern Rus within a rather unpropitious context. Three other principalities had an equal if not better chance of success than Moscow in such an endeavour. These were the principalities of Riazan, Suzdal-Nizhnii Novgorod and Tver. Each of these principalities was situated in a superior location to Moscow for profiting from trade. Each of them controlled areas along vital trade routes, which Moscow did not, and each stood in a position to put pressure on Moscow economically, in terms of restricting its outside trade: Riazan to the southeast, along the Oka and the Don; Suzdal-Nizhnii Novgorod to the east, along the Volga; and Tver to the northwest, also along the Volga and its portage routes to Great Novgorod and Velikie Luki. In addition, the Moscow *kniazi* had to deal with powerful threats, not only from the Ulus of Jochi, because the steppe only ended some 75 kilometres (47 mi.) to the south of Moscow, but from Lithuania. During the course of the fourteenth century, Lithuania had moved its borders to within 100 kilometres (62 mi.) of Moscow, to the west. Novgorod, on the far side of Tver and to the north of Lithuania, continued to represent a wealthy merchant city-state that claimed vast areas of hinterland in the northern Rus area.[12] Finally, the rulership of Kyiv, after the death of Alexander Nevsky in 1263, was in hands other than those of the Vsevolodovichi.

Congresses

Since he was opposed by his younger brother and cousin and thus could not draw upon their reserves, Andrei's forces would have been diminished. Bloodshed was avoided, however, when Khan Toqta sent his envoy Nevriui to bring the contending parties together, to settle their differences through discussion.[13] At that time, Toqta was involved in a war with another khan, Nogai, so he was eager to avoid any conflict in the Suzdal region that might necessitate drawing off his military forces. The meeting was held in Vladimir in 1297 and has, therefore, been called the Congress of Vladimir. Such a meeting of *kniazi* is sometimes referred to in the sources as a *snem*. The result of this *snem* was that, for the time being, Pereiaslavl remained in the hands of Ivan Dmitrievich. Another Congress met in Dmitrov in 1301 to discuss the distribution of polities, but the problem of who should ultimately rule Pereiaslavl remained unresolved.

The situation soon changed when Ivan Dmitrievich died in 1302. He was childless; treating it like his *otchina* (patrimony), he bequeathed Pereiaslavl to his uncle Daniil, 'who he loved more than anyone else'.[14] Daniil occupied Pereiaslavl but died himself less than a year later, in 1303. According to the Nikonian Chronicle, the people of Pereiaslavl wanted Daniil's eldest son Iurii to succeed him as ruler and would not permit him to leave the city to attend his father's funeral.[15] As a result of the aggressive policies of his father, Iurii inherited a *kniazhestvo* that was three times the size of the realm his father originally received.[16]

In addition, the taking of both Kolomna (114 kilometres (71 mi.) downstream, at the confluence of the Moskva and Oka rivers) and Mozhaisk (110 kilometres (68 mi.) upstream, where the Mozhaisk River flows into the Moskva River) ensured Moscow maintained control along its main trading artery. Kolomna was part of the Riazan *kniazhestvo*, but since 1186, when Vsevolod the 'Big Nest' replaced the Riazan *kniaz* with a Vsevolodovich occupant, it was ostensibly under the control of the ruler of Vladimir. Daniil defeated Konstantin Romanovich, the Vsevolodovich successor of the *kniaz* that Vsevolod had appointed, and incorporated Kolomna into the Moscow *kniazhestvo*. Mozhaisk first appears in our sources in 1231 under the control of the Olgovichi of Chernigov, but the town soon fell into the hands of the Rostislavichi of Smolensk. Since it lay on the main route between Smolensk and Moscow, Mozhaisk was an important outpost for the Daniilovichi. Until 1493, Mozhaisk remained under the rule of a younger brother of the *kniaz* of Moscow.

Rus Rulers at the Orda

At the time of Daniil's death, Andrei was at Sarai, the capital of the Orda (the Rusian name for a Tatar Ulus, or camp). We do not have any information concerning the topics he discussed with Khan Toqta, but we can imagine that the bringing of Pereiaslavl under Andrei's control was one of the issues. In 1304, after returning to Vladimir but before he could mount another campaign over Pereiaslavl, Andrei died. Here is where we join the story that introduced this chapter.

Both Iurii and Mikhail were well aware of the pending conflict between them, which is somewhat notable in that Iurii's father, Daniil, and Mikhail had been allies against Andrei. To bolster his claim that he should be declared ruler of Vladimir, Iurii took over possession of two-thirds of the lands comprising the Vladimir-Suzdal polity. According to the later Moscow chronicles, the boyars of Mikhail tried to stop Iurii and his retinue from reaching Sarai by laying an ambush for them along the way. They escaped the ambush, and Iurii arrived at Sarai to present his petition to Toqta.[17] However, that testimony seems to have been interpolated into the later chronicles.[18] We must be careful about accepting any information about this period that appears only in later Muscovite chronicles, especially if it depicts Mikhail in a bad light. Nonetheless, Mikhail was canonized in 1549 as a martyr to the faith because of his execution in the Orda in 1318, as happened to the Olgovich ruler, Mikhail Vsevolodovich, in 1246.

Toqta decided in favour of Mikhail, thus upholding the collateral system of succession among the Vsevolodovichi. However, Toqta's decision apparently did not prevent hostilities from ensuing between Iurii and Mikhail. Even before Toqta reached his decision, the two *kniazi* were manoeuvring for military advantage or, as the Novgorod First Chronicle put it: 'There was great commotion throughout the Suzdal region in all the towns.'[19] According to the chronicles, while Iurii was in Sarai, his younger brother Ivan was left in charge of Moscow. Ivan received reports of a plan by Tver boyars to raid Pereiaslavl; in response, he raised a military force that defeated the Tver forces. According to the Novgorod First Chronicle, 'the people of Tver sent Mikhail's lieutenants (*namestniki*) with a force' but the Novgorodians would not allow them into the city, preferring to wait until Toqta made his decision concerning who should rule Vladimir.[20] Iurii sent his younger brother, Boris, to seize Kostroma, but a Tver military force captured Boris instead.[21]

Upon his return from Sarai, bearing the *iarlyk*, Mikhail attacked and defeated the Muscovite forces. Iurii and Mikhail agreed on a temporary peace.[22] The next year, in 1306, Iurii's brothers, Boris and Alexandr, switched allegiance to Mikhail.[23] In 1307, the people of Novgorod accepted Mikhail as their ruler. In 1308, according to the Tver chronicles, Mikhail moved against Moscow again with a military force and drew up a new agreement.[24]

The Appointment of Peter as Metropolitan of Kyiv and All Rus

The year 1304 was also an eventful one for another reason. The metropolitan of Kyiv and all Rus, Maksim, died in December. Hegumen Gerontii travelled to Constantinople, presumably as Mikhail's candidate to become the new metropolitan. Iurii Daniilovich of Galicia,[25] who was married to Mikhail's sister Ksenia, sent the hegumen of the Ratsk Monastery, Peter, to Constantinople, presumably as his candidate. Patriarch Athanasios of Constantinople appointed Peter to be the metropolitan of Kyiv and all Rus in June 1307, but it was another year before Peter could travel to Vladimir. One would expect Peter to feel favourably towards Mikhail, because of the marital association between his patron, Iurii of Galicia, and Mikhail; instead, he sided with Iurii of Moscow and, in general, with Moscow over Tver, even eventually moving his residence from Vladimir to Moscow in 1325. In turn, Mikhail, with the support of Bishop Andrei of Tver, sought to unseat Peter. Bishop Andrei filed a formal complaint with Patriarch Athanasios, who sent an envoy to the Suzdal region to investigate the situation. According to the *Life of Peter* by Prokhor of Rostov and the *Life of Peter* by Metropolitan Kiprian, Peter was cleared of all charges at a council in Pereiaslavl.[26] Mikhail then wrote a letter to Athanasios's successor, Nephon, in which he accused Peter of not enforcing the prohibitions against consanguineous marriages strictly enough and of engaging in simony.[27] The opposition offered by Metropolitan Peter made it difficult for Mikhail to consolidate his power in Suzdalia. In 1311, Mikhail directed his son Dmitrii with forces 'against Nizhnii Novgorod and *kniaz* Iurii', but when Dmitrii reached Vladimir, Metropolitan Peter refused to give his blessing to the venture.[28] After three weeks, Dmitrii returned to Tver.

Khan Uzbeg

In 1313, Mikhail and Peter went to visit the new khan, Uzbeg (r. 1313–41). The previous khan, Toqta, had died the year before, on his way to visit the Suzdal region. This was the first and only time, at least so far as we have evidence, that a khan set out for northeastern Rus with anything other than a military force. What his purpose was in visiting, we do not know, and the sources do not tell us. George Vernadsky speculated that Toqta was going to abolish the *kniazhestvo* of Vladimir-Suzdal and reform the administration of the northeast so that each of the *kniazi* had to report directly to him.[29] However, there is no evidence to support such a speculation, and the Mongol khan would not need to visit a place personally to enact such a change. If Toqta was travelling to the northeast of Rus on business rather than for recreational purposes, then the visit might have been in conjunction with the Rus *kniazi* being tasked with taking over the duties of the *basqaq*s, the Tatar military governors, such as maintaining order, collecting taxes and sending the *dan* or tribute to the khan.[30]

Whatever his reason, Uzbeg allowed Peter to return to Vladimir within a short time but insisted that Mikhail stay on at his court for a year. During that time, the Novgorodians used the absence of the *velikii kniaz* to appeal to Iurii Daniilovich for his help against Mikhail's lieutenants. Iurii sent a military force to Novgorod under the command of Fëdor of Rzhev, who captured Mikhail's lieutenants. Then, a combined force of Novgorodians and Muscovites marched against a Tverian army that was led by Dmitrii, Mikhail's son. The two armies met on the opposite sides of the Volga River near Gorodets and remained there, facing each other for six weeks. When the ice started to form on the river, the two sides drew up an agreement and the armies withdrew without fighting. Iurii then travelled to Novgorod with his brother Afanasii and 'sat on its throne'.[31]

Shortly thereafter, Iurii received his own summons from Uzbeg to appear at the khan's court. Mikhail returned to the northeast with a Tatar army and defeated a Novgorodian force near Torzhok. Afterwards, Mikhail demanded that they turn over to him both Fëdor of Rzhev and Iurii's brother Afanasii, that they pay reparations of 12,000 grivnas and that they give up their armour, horses and weapons. Mikhail held Afanasii and the Novgorodian boyars in Tver until the reparations were fully paid. After payment of the reparations, the Novgorodians gathered a new army in 1316, threw out Mikhail's lieutenants and turned once more to Iurii of Moscow for leadership. Iurii, in the meantime, had spent two years at the khan's court and won his favour, married Konchaka, the khan's sister, and obtained the *iarlyk* to become the new ruler of Vladimir. Konchaka was baptized into the Rus Orthodox Church and was given the Christian name Agafia.

Travelling up the Volga with a Tatar army under the command of the khan's envoy, Kavgadyi, Iurii was able to lure away some support for Mikhail because of his having the khan's *iarlyk*. Nonetheless, Mikhail and the Tver army won the ensuing battle at Kostroma and captured Iurii's brother, Boris, and Konchaka, who died while in Tverian hands. The chronicles present differing testimonies regarding the cause of her death. The Ermolin Chronicle and the Moscow Compilation of the End of the Fifteenth Century testify that she was poisoned in Tver.[32] The Nikonian Chronicle tempers that assertion, stating that 'some say she was poisoned in Tver'.[33] The Older Redaction of the Novgorod First Chronicle testifies that 'they killed her' (*smerti predasha*) but does not specify how this was achieved,[34] while the Younger Redaction says only that she 'died' (*umorisha*).[35] The Sofia First Chronicle, however, denies outright the rumour/accusation that she was killed.[36] Conversely, the Tver chronicles do not mention the accusation at all.[37] In the meantime, Iurii travelled to Novgorod to gather a new army, but when he returned to the fray, Mikhail agreed to go to the Orda with Iurii to have the matter adjudicated by Uzbeg. Nonetheless, when Mikhail sent an 'embassy of friendship', headed by Aleksandr Markovich, to Moscow, Iurii had him killed. In Inner Eurasian societies, killing another ruler's envoys was considered a declaration of war.

38 Central Asian or Rusian Blue Orda helmet, probably *c.* 1342–57.

The *Tale Concerning the Death of Mikhail of Tver in the Orda* tells the story of the events at the court of the khan that led to the condemnation of Mikhail.[38] The *Tale* is fascinating for a number of reasons, not the least of which is that the Muscovite ruler Iurii is portrayed negatively in the text. For example, in the *Tale*, Mikhail accuses Iurii of Moscow of 'wanting to rule everywhere'. The main accusations, however, are brought by the Tatar envoy, Kavgadyi.

The historian V. A. Kuchkin, who devoted a monograph to the study of this work, concluded that it was written by Hegumen Aleksandr of the Otroch Monastery in Tver in 1319–20; that is, immediately after the events in question occurred.[39] The *Tale* appears in many chronicles and Kuchkin tells us that there is little difference among the versions.[40] According to the *Tale*, during the month and a half that Mikhail remained at the court of the khan, the Tatar envoy, Kavgadyi, made false claims about Mikhail ('uninterruptedly calumniated him to the khan'), telling him that he disobeyed the orders of the khan, that he had poisoned Iurii's wife (the khan's sister) while she was his prisoner, that he kept back some of the *dan* (the khan's tribute) that he collected, that he fought Kavgadyi and killed many of the khan's lords and Tatars, that he wanted to escape to the 'Germans' (that is, the Teutonic Knights in Livonia) with the treasury and that he sent the treasury to the pope in Rome. Uzbeg demanded that both Mikhail and Iurii should be tried, but according to the *Tale*, 'Everyone helped Iurii and put all the blame on Mikhail.' Uzbeg sentenced Mikhail to be executed but he was first kept a prisoner for almost a month. Mikhail sent his son Konstantin to appeal to the khan's wife for help, but Kavgadyi and Iurii stopped him. At this point, Kavgadyi stirred up an angry mob, which killed Mikhail. Afterwards, Iurii had the body brought back to the Suzdal region. Except for this negative portrayal of Kavgadyi, there is no denigrating of other Tatars or of the khan to be found in the *Tale*. This absence of denigration is usual in Rus works that were written before the mid-fifteenth century but even then, when reproduced in chronicles after the mid-fifteenth century, the customary practice was to add anti-Muslim slurs and disparage their actions.

As far as we can tell, there does not seem to be any attempt in later Muscovite chronicles to improve the image of Iurii that the *Tale* presents. Iurii is clearly depicted as acting in consultation with Kavgadyi. He keeps Mikhail's son Konstantin and Mikhail's boyars and servicemen as prisoners, and reluctantly returns the body of Mikhail to his widow only after Prokhor, the bishop of Rostov and Iaroslavl, has prevailed upon Aleksandr Mikhailovich to go to Iurii and agree upon the terms of peace with him as a way to recover the body.[41] To seal the deal (that is, to confirm the peace agreement), Konstantin and Iurii's daughter Sofia were married the next year in Kostroma.[42]

Iurii ruled for four years, until Uzbeg sent an envoy in 1322 to replace him as the ruler of Vladimir with his archrival, Dmitrii Mikhailovich of Tver. Exactly how and why this transfer of power came about is not clear from the chronicle accounts. Apparently, Iurii's surviving brother Ivan went to the Orda in 1320 and spent the greater part of two years there. Fennell proposes that this was when Ivan lobbied against his brother with the khan.[43] In the meantime, in the spring of 1321, Uzbeg sent an envoy, Gaianchar, to the town of Kashin in the Tver region, where he brought about 'much distress', apparently because of unpaid tributes. He ordered Iurii to march on Tver. Dmitrii and his brothers raised a military force to counter Iurii, but the bishop of Tver intervened, after which Iurii and Dmitrii signed an agreement instead of fighting. Dmitrii agreed to pay a reparation of 2,000 silver rubles, which Iurii promptly took back with him to Novgorod. Dmitrii then travelled to the Orda and obtained the *iarlyk* from Uzbeg, giving him the authority to rule in Vladimir. It is entirely open to speculation why Iurii chose to 'retire' to Novgorod with the *dan* as his pension. Iurii ruled in Novgorod for another three years until 1325, ignoring demands to appear at the khan's court. When he finally heeded the summons of Uzbeg to come to the Orda, according to the chronicles, Dmitrii was already there and hacked him to death. One year later, Dmitrii was executed by the order of Khan Uzbeg for the crime.

39 Vasilii Petrovich Vereshchagin, 'Mikhail Iaroslavich before Khan Uzbeg', 1896, from the album *History of the Russian State in the Images of Its Sovereign Rulers with a Short Explanatory Text.*

40 The murder of Iurii Daniilovich of Moscow by Dmitrii Mikhailovich of Tver in the Orda, as depicted in the *Litsevoi letopisnyi svod*, vol. VII, p. 243.

Dmitrii's brother Aleksandr received the *iarlyk* that allowed him to rule in Vladimir, while Ivan Daniilovich continued his rule in Moscow. In 1327, an uprising occurred in Tver against the khan's ambassador, Uzbeg's cousin Shevkal. The Tver chronicles testify that the uprising was a spontaneous rebellion by the people of Tver, who were outraged at Shevkal's behaviour, and that Aleksandr advised the people against doing so. However, the enraged mob trapped Shevkal and his retinue in the royal palace and burned them alive. The khan was angered by this behaviour and organized a punitive expedition against Tver, led by the Tatar commander Fëdorchuk. Uzbeg ordered Ivan Daniilovich of Moscow to join in the attack, along with Aleksandr Vasilevich of Suzdal. Uzbeg then appointed Aleksandr as the ruler of Vladimir, although his father Vasilii had never ruled the city. We know of Uzbeg's appointment of Aleksandr Vasilevich from a genealogical list of rulers in the Commission copy of the Novgorod First Chronicle.[44] However, the Moscow chronicles do not report Aleksandr's reign and give the impression that Ivan Daniilovich ruled Vladimir continuously from 1328 to 1341.

Uzbeg ordered Aleksandr Mikhailovich to come to Sarai. Aleksandr refused and instead went into exile, as Iurii Daniilovich had done in 1322. Unlike Iurii, however, he went to Pskov, Novgorod's sister city, and ruled there. Uzbeg ordered Aleksandr Vasilevich and Ivan Daniilovich to attack Aleksandr Mikhailovich in Pskov in 1329. The military expedition did not meet with success until Ivan hit upon the idea of having Metropolitan Feognost excommunicate Aleksandr Mikhailovich and the people of Pskov. In order to lift the excommunication of the Pskovians, Aleksandr Mikhailovich abdicated and then fled to Lithuania. In the meantime, Aleksandr Vasilevich of Suzdal died in 1331, at which point Uzbeg appointed Ivan Daniilovich as the ruler of Vladimir. This entire episode demonstrates the strength of the hold that the khan in Sarai had over Rus and the *kniazi*, even when one of them became recalcitrant.

Konstantin lost the rulership of Tver when Uzbeg returned the Tver *iarlyk* to Konstantin's brother, Aleksandr, in 1338, but after accusations were made against Aleksandr Mikhailovich by Ivan Daniilovich in 1339, Uzbeg again summoned Aleksandr to the Orda. The chronicle reports that Konstantin was seriously ill at that time, and Aleksandr regretted that he could not wait for his recovery. By the order of Uzbeg, Aleksandr was executed, along with his son Fëdor.

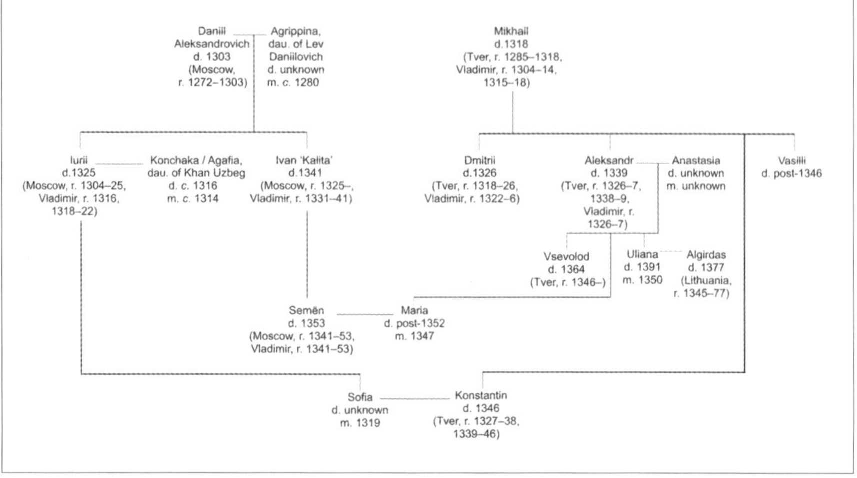

41 Iurii Daniilovich and selected family and rivals.

Konstantin Mikhailovich once again ruled Tver, but this was under the domination of Ivan Daniilovich. Ivan ordered Konstantin to remove and bring to Moscow the bell from the main Tver Church of the Transfiguration of the Saviour – the symbol of Tver's independence. There does not seem to have been any discussion regarding Konstantin's succeeding to the rulership of Vladimir in 1341, when Ivan Daniilovich died. Although Konstantin should have been the next in line, once again, the continuum of collateral succession was broken when the son of Ivan, Semën Ivanovich of Moscow was granted the *iarlyk*. Konstantin had been under the thumb of Ivan Daniilovich and he would continue in that subordinate role under Ivan's son, Semën.

In 1345, Konstantin Mikhailovich began to quarrel with Aleksandr's widow, Anastasia, and Aleksandr's son, Vsevolod, the ruler of Kholm. Konstantin began to press the Kholm district by force, capturing the boyars and royal servants. In response, Vsevolod sought help from Semën. In the same year, both Konstantin and Vsevolod went to the Orda. There, in 1346, Konstantin died and Vsevolod began to rule in Tver, with the throne bypassing his uncle, Vasilii. The collateral succession continuum was thus breached in Tver, as well as in Vladimir.

THE 'GAME OF THRONES' that Iurii Daniilovich set in motion in 1304, when he decided to challenge the legitimacy of Mikhail Iaroslavich of Tver's right to rule as the *kniaz* of Vladimir, ended with the Daniilovichi of Moscow besting the Iaroslavichi of Tver for control of the throne of Vladimir. However, as Uzbeg showed with his appointment of Aleksandr Vasilevich of Suzdal as the ruler of Vladimir from 1327 to 1331, there was nothing inevitable about the Daniilovich victory. With the breach of the continuum of collateral succession in northeastern Rus, there was no pre-existing system by which the khan could try to abide. The throne was the prize offered to the person who could be most loyal to the khan in Sarai.

In that regard, contingency played a significant role. Khan Toqta favoured Mikhail Iaroslavich of Tver as the *kniaz* of Vladimir, but Iurii Daniilovich of Moscow and Metropolitan Peter were able to undermine the trust of Toqta's successor, Uzbeg, in Mikhail. Iurii's younger brother, Ivan, in turn, undermined Uzbeg's trust in Iurii, which led to Uzbeg's choosing Mikhail's son Dmitrii to serve as the *kniaz* of Vladimir. If Dmitrii had been able to control his temper, as well as his hatred for Iurii, and had not killed him while in the khan's camp, then he could have continued as ruler of the Vladimir-Suzdal polity and would perhaps have solidified control of that position for the Tver *kniazi*. If the people of Tver had not risen up against the khan's ambassador, Shevkal, in 1327, Aleksandr Mikhailovich, who had succeeded his brother Dmitrii, might have been allowed to continue as *velikii kniaz* and would perhaps have peacefully passed on rulership of the Vladimir-Suzdal polity to his younger brothers, Konstantin and Vasilii, in turn. However, the uprising permanently eliminated the Tver *kniazi* from the favour of the khan, who chose an outsider, Aleksandr Vasilevich of Suzdal, to be the next ruler of Vladimir. By 1331, when Aleksandr Vasilevich of Suzdal died, Uzbeg seems to have overcome his distrust of the Moscow *kniazi* and appointed Ivan Daniilovich as the *kniaz* of Vladimir. From that year on, the rulership of Vladimir remained (except during the years 1359–63) in the hands of the Moscow *kniazi*. Yet, somewhat paradoxically, Tver remained independent of the ruler of Vladimir, the very position held by three Tverian *kniazi*. In 1485, Tver was absorbed into the Muscovite realm of Ivan III Vasilevich.

Another result of these events was the end of the *basqaq* system in northeastern Rus. After that system ended, the rulers of the towns in the Vladimir-Suzdal polity made more frequent trips to Sarai and remained there for extended periods. In the seven years between 1332 and 1339, the chronicles report that Ivan Daniilovich made five trips to Sarai, which prompted the historian A. N. Nasonov to remark that

'Kalita [that is, Ivan Daniilovich] spent at least half, probably more, of his reign as grand prince either at the khan's court, on his way to the khan's court, or coming from the khan's court.'[45] The chronicles report that *Kniaz* Semën travelled to Sarai at least five times between 1340 and 1350. Chronicle entries for the years 1340 and 1354 report that 'all the *kniazi* of Rus were then at the khan's court.' Rus rulers also had to leave their sons at Sarai as a guarantee of good and loyal behaviour on the part of those rulers.[46] In effect, the Moscow rulers of Vladimir had become the khan's *basqaq*s.

9

Iurii Lvovich and His Family

Galicia and Volhynia were two separate but related polities, bordered by Hungarian, Lithuanian and Polish lands to the north and west and by Kyiv to the east. Depending on the personal relationships between the respective rulers, who were part of the Iziaslavichi, the policies of the two polities often aligned and sometimes the two polities were united under one ruler. This chapter begins some twenty years after the Mongol conquest and ends in 1326, when Lithuania took over Galicia and Volhynia.

Iurii Lvovich (r. 1301–8 (or 1316)), his father Lev Daniilovich (r. 1292–1301) and his two sons Andrei and Lev (r. 1308(or 1316)–23) ruled Galicia and Volhynia for around 31 years while still being the subjects of the Tatar khan of the Ulus of Jochi. Lev Daniilovich had been the ruler of Galicia since 1264, reigning as co-ruler with his younger brother Shvarn until 1269. Shvarn married the daughter of the ruler of Lithuania, Mindaugas, in 1254/5, but no children are reported. Lev brought Volhynia under his rule in 1292 after his next-oldest brother, Mstislav, had died. Mstislav had been the ruler of Volhynia since 1288, when his cousin Volodimer had bequeathed him the polity, with the approval of Khan Töle-Buqa (r. 1287–91). Mstislav had been married since 1253 to the daughter of the Polovtsian ruler Teigak. Mstislav had two sons – Daniil and Volodimer – but rulership of the polity was transferred to Lev via the principle of lateral succession (illus. 42).

The Vsevolodovichi of the Vladimir-Suzdal polity made no claim to the rulership of Kyiv after the death of Iaroslav Iaroslavich in 1272. The Iziaslavichi of Galicia-Volhynia, the Olgovichi of Chernigov and the Rostislavichi of Smolensk were left to vie for that particular political inheritance. However, as the level of control by the khans of the Ulus

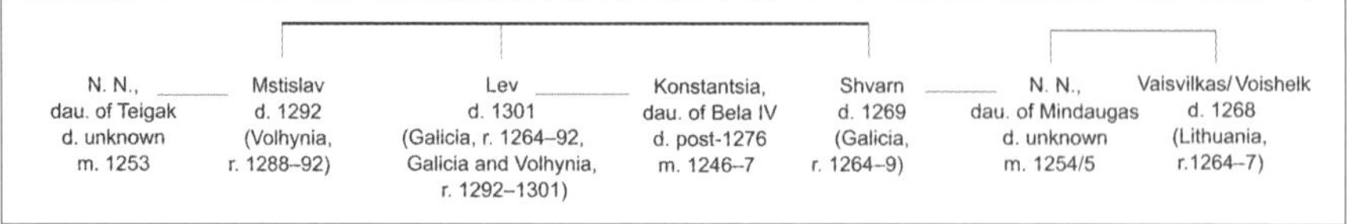

42 Lev Daniilovich and siblings.

of Jochi receded in the western reaches of the Mongol Empire, a new political player arose in the area: the Grand Duchy of Lithuania, the rulers of which moved in to claim control of Galicia, Volhynia, Polotsk and Kyiv, and ultimately all Rus.

In this chapter, we will discuss the final years of Iziaslavich rule in Galicia and Volhynia, as well as our most significant sources of information on their reign, including the quirkiness of our main source, the Galician-Volhynian Chronicle. We will also discuss the relations of the Iziaslavichi with the Olgovichi, Rostislavichi and Vsevolodovichi clans and with the khans of the Ulus of Jochi, as well as with the rulers of Poland, of Lithuania and of Hungary. One consideration to keep in mind is the assertion by the doyen of Ukrainian historians, Mykhailo Hrushevsky, who stated that the nature of the Galician-Volhynian rulers' relationship with their Mongol overlords was different from that of the Suzdal rulers.[1] We will also examine whether that assertion can be verified.

The Galician-Volhynian Chronicle as a Historical Source

The Galician-Volhynian Chronicle (hereafter the GVC) constitutes the third part of the Hypatian Codex (a manuscript book) after the PVL (until 1117) and the Kyivan Chronicle (1118–1200) have concluded. These names and divisions are somewhat arbitrary. Of the four copies of the GVC, other than the Hypatian Codex, only the Khlebnikov Codex is derived independently from the protograph (that is, the source copy) that it shares with the Hypatian Codex. The other copies are derived from the Khlebnikov Codex. Before utilizing any information from the GVC, one needs to be aware of the various theories regarding its composition. As stated before, one should avoid the uncritical acceptance of any chronicle information, treating the text as though these chronicles represent reliable testimony by objective observers. The chroniclers often had an agenda of their own and wrote their various versions to fit that agenda. In addition, a chronicler's bias can and did affect what they chose to report, mainly because they did not recognize it as bias but thought that what they wrote represented the correct view. It is possible that some of what the chronicler reports never happened, being pure inventions by the chronicler, who might have included such contrivances in the name of what they believed to be a 'higher truth'. We find this type of narrative device particularly prevalent in documents recording the lives of the saints, but it also appears elsewhere.[2]

We need to be especially careful when we have only one source reporting an event, as is the case with many of the events described in the GVC. At times, historians will resort to the statement, 'I see no reason to doubt what the source says,' but that is merely an evasion. Usually, the historian will use that answer when he or she wants to believe what the source says, but then finds no problem with saying that the same source is untrustworthy regarding something else that the historian does not want to believe. The historian is then merely expressing his or her opinion without revealing the problems with the sources because the historian wants to deny readers any basis for disagreement with what is being expressed. It is essential to provide readers with sufficient information (in the form of source testimony and differing historiographical interpretations), so that they can exercise their own judgement and not merely be told what they should think.

The traditional view has been that the GVC consists of two parts – the Galician part and the Volhynian part, respectively – each with its own perspective. The philologist Alexander N. Uzhankov asserted that the Galician part was an independent literary work; namely, a laudatory biography of *Kniaz* Daniil Romanovich of Galicia (discussed in Chapter Six).[3] The historian Andrei V. Gorovenko developed Uzhankov's idea further and suggested that the *Biography of Daniil Romanovich* had been added to the Kyivan Chronicle shortly after 1268 in the town of Volodymyr, by order of *Kniaz* Volodimer Vasilkovich.[4] The last entry in the Kyivan Chronicle is in 6708 (1199–1200), while the first entry in the GVC is dated 6709 (1200/1201), but it discusses events that other sources describe as happening in 1205. In other words, there is often a four- to five-year gap between the date when the GVC reports that an event occurred and when it occurred according to other sources.[5] One explanation for this chronological gap is that the GVC was written without year markers, in imitation of a Greek chronograph, which is usually organized around events rather than dates. The author apparently intended to fill in the appropriate years at a later date but never managed to do so. Then, a later editor added the dates but did so erroneously. Such an explanation also fits the notion that the author of the *Biography of Daniil Romanovich* did not intend the composition to be a chronicle.

Then, around 1288–90, a scribe compiled what became the Volhynian part of the GVC, but at the time it remained a separate chronicle. Finally, around the year 1300, a third scribe added the Volhynian Chronicle after the end of the Galician Chronicle (that is, the version of the *Biography of Daniil Romanovich* in chronicle form), which had already been attached to the Kyivan Chronicle. A bit convoluted, to be sure, but this timeline is helpful in understanding exactly what the GVC is. Both parts – the Galician part and the Volhynian part – could easily be considered works of early historiography that draw on primary sources, rather than being primary sources themselves.

Various views have been expressed concerning exactly when the Galician part of the GVC ends its coverage and the Volhynian part begins. Some historians place it at the year 1254,[6] others at either 1256/7 or 1260/61, 1260–63 or 1267.[7] There have also been attempts to break the GVC into more than two parts, by drawing dividing lines at the years 1238, 1246, 1263, 1269 (?) and 1289/90;[8] or at the years 1234, 1266, 1285/86, 1289 and 1292.[9] Recently, the historian Adrian Jusupovič reported that he saw four divisions in the text: first, the basic chronological framework (1201–28), which he calls 'the Kyivan Annals of the

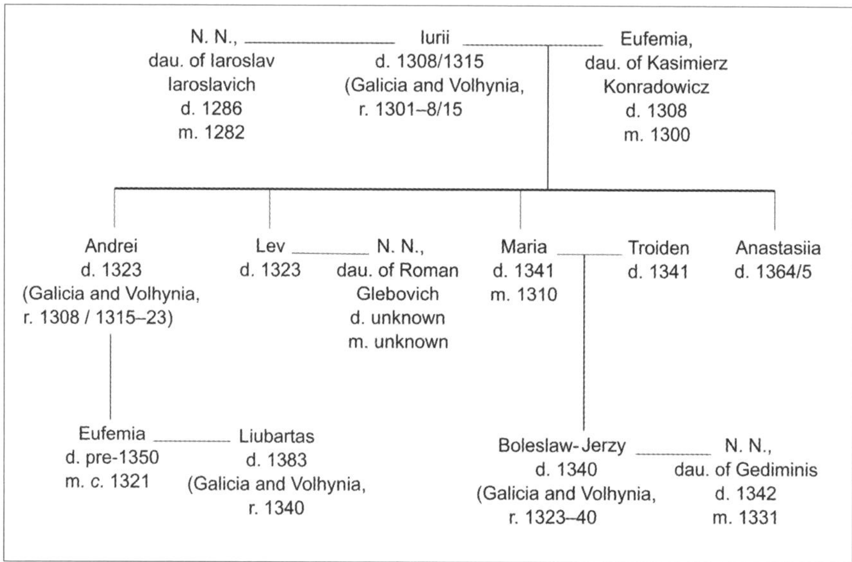

43 Iurii Lvovich and selected family members.

Rostislavich Line'; second, the Compilation (*Svod*) of Daniel (1228–44); third, a series of storylines (1245–59); and fourth, the final chronological scheme (1260–90).[10] For now, we will stay with its division into two parts – a Galician part (to 1260/61, inclusively) and a Volhynian part (from 1261/2).

The Marriages of Iurii Lvovich and His Family

The Daniilovich family of Galicia-Volhynia had diplomatic and marital connections throughout eastern Europe. Iurii's father, Lev Daniilovich, was married to Konstantsia (1237–76, or 1288 or 1302), the daughter of the Hungarian king Béla IV (see illus. 42). Lev and Konstantsia had only one son, Iurii, and two daughters – Anastasia (d. 1335) and Sviatoslava (d. 1302) – who are not shown in illustration 43. Lev's younger brother, Shvarn, was married to a daughter of the Lithuanian ruler, Mindaugas, but the marriage was without issue.[11] Iurii Lvovich was married twice: the first time, possibly, to the daughter of Iaroslav Iaroslavich, the *kniaz* of Tver and *velikii kniaz* of Vladimir;[12] the second time, he married Eufemia (*c.* 1265–1308), the daughter of Kazimierz Konradowic, Duke of Kuyawy. With his first wife, Iurii Lvovich had one child, a son named Mikhail, who died in 1286. With Eufimia, he had two sons – Andrei (d. 1323) and Lev (d. 1323) – and two daughters – Maria (*c.* 1293–1341) and Anastasia (*c.* 1306–1364/5). Andrei Iurevich had one child – Anna-Buche – but there is no indication in the sources to say whom he married. Lev Iurevich was married to the daughter of Roman Glebovich (her name is not reported in the sources). No fourteenth- or fifteenth-century source mentions their having a child, but two sixteenth-century sources – the Lithuanian-Belarusian Chronicle and the Polish chronicles of the ruler of Volhynia – tell of a son named Volodimer. Even if there was such a son, he plays no role in our story.

The Testimony of the GVC

It will be apparent from the testimony of the GVC that the chronicler of the Volhynian part of the GVC has some very definite opinions about things and is not shy about expressing them. For instance, he strongly dislikes the Tatars. Hrushevsky wrote: 'Such bitterness should not surprise us, because as a result of the savagery and generally destructive

44 Łukasz Doliński, *Prince Lev Daniilovich* (with Halich in the background), late 18th century, oil on canvas.

instincts of the Tatars, any close contact with them was very expensive for every more cultured land.'[13] The Volhynian chronicler does not feel kindly towards either Lev Daniilovich, the ruler of Galicia, or his son Iurii. He does not care much for the Poles either, but he does look favourably on Mstislav Daniilovich, the ruler of Lutsk, and Volodimer Vasilkovich, the ruler of Volhynia, as will be apparent when we investigate the evidence. We will briefly discuss eight episodes from the GVC in which Iurii plays a prominent role. The first concerns his baptism, but tells us more about Lev, his father, than about Iurii. The other seven involve, in one form or another, military campaigns and attacks on towns, whether Hungarian, Polish, Lithuanian or Volhynian. The way the chronicler describes the behaviour of Iurii in these episodes tells us much about the attitude of the chronicler towards him, if not a great deal about Iurii himself.

Events Surrounding the Baptism of Iurii Lvovich

The first appearance of Iurii Lvovich in the GVC is at his baptism, *s.a.* 6770 (1261/2). Vaišvilkas (Voishelk) was the son of the Lithuanian ruler, Mindaugas (and the brother-in-law of Shvarn, Iurii's uncle); he wanted to become a monk and went to join Daniil and Vasilko in Galicia. The chronicle does not say why he went to them, but one can presume that it was either as a courtesy, to inform them in person of his decision, or that he required their permission. Although Mindaugas had converted to Christianity, the GVC tells us that he scolded Vaišvilkas when he did eventually become a monk. In any case, while in Galicia, Vaišvilkas stood as godfather at Iurii's baptism.[14] Shortly thereafter, Vaišvilkas's mother, Morta, died; his father then took Morta's sister as his new wife. The problem was that Morta's sister was already married to Daumantas, the Duke of Nalšia; when he found out, Daumantas formed an alliance with Treniota, a nephew of Mindaugas and the ruler of Samogitia. They killed Mindaugas and two of his sons, but the third son, Vaišvilkas, survived, having just entered a monastery. He left the monastery upon hearing of his father's death and, in alliance with Shvarn, went after the assassins, killing Treniota.

In the meantime, Daumantas fled to Pskov, where he converted to Orthodox Christianity and was recognized as the ruler of that town. He married a daughter of Dmitrii Alexandrovich (Nevsky's son) since, apparently, either his previous wife was no longer living or perhaps the Church did not recognize a pagan marriage as being legitimate. Vaišvilkas ruled Lithuania until 1267, when he returned to the monastery. Before doing so, he handed over the rulership of Lithuania to Shvarn; however, Lev Daniilovich was so angry that Vaišvilkas had not divided Lithuania between Shvarn and himself that he killed Vaišvilkas, his son's godfather.

Iurii Lvovich's First Military Operation

The first military operation that Iurii Lvovich took part in, which occurred when he was no older than fifteen or sixteen, garnered mixed results. The GVC reports for *s.a.* 6785 (1276/7) that 'the godless and lawless Nogai sent his envoys – Tegichag, Kutlubug and Eshimut – with letters (*gramoty*) for Lev [Daniilovich], Mstislav [Daniilovich], and Volodimer [Vasilkovich].'[15] At the time, Nogai was an emir (although he was a Chinggisid, he did not adopt the title of *khan* until 1296/7, when battling Toqta for control of the Jochid Ulus). He governed the western part of the Ulus of Jochi. Mstislav was Lev's brother, while Volodimer was the ruler of Volhynia. The envoy's letters stated that Nogai was responding to their requests for help against Lithuanian encroachment on their territory by sending an army under his commander (*voevoda*), Mamshei. Nogai ordered the three *kniazi* to accompany Mamshei in his attack on Lithuania. Mstislav and Volodimer set out to meet Mamshei, but Lev did not go, sending his son Iurii in his stead. On the way to join the Tatar army, Iurii and his uncle, Mstislav, hatched a plot to take the town of Goroden (Hrodno) but did not inform Volodimer of their plan. When they neared Goroden, they sent their boyars and attendants to ravage the outskirts of the town, while they themselves bedded down for the night without posting sentries. The people of Goroden were forewarned of the attack and were able to kill and capture many of the boyars and attendants. Mstislav and Iurii 'were very sorry that they had caused this [setback] by their foolhardy action', while Volodimer was upset with them for undertaking this military operation without informing him. However, the next day, their attack on Goroden was going well when they decided to negotiate for the prisoners that the Gorodenians had taken the previous night. In return for agreeing not to sack the city, the three *kniazi* received their captured boyars and attendants back.

Iurii Lvovich's Second Military Operation

The next we hear of Iurii in the GVC occurs in an entry for 6788 (1279/80) regarding his father Lev's hopes of ruling the Polish land. The Polish *szlachta* (nobles) chose Leszek, the son of Kazimierz I of Kuyawy and Konstancja Śląska of Wrocław, as the *książę* (ruler) of Kraków. Lev appealed to the 'cursed, damned' Nogai again for military assistance, this time against the towns under Leszek's rule that bordered on Galicia.[16] Nogai again sent a Tatar military force to help the Rus rulers under the command of 'the cursed Konchak, Kozei and Kubatan'. The chronicler says that 'Lev and his son Iurii marched gladly in Tatar company, but Mstislav, Volodimer and Mstislav's son Daniil went because they were compelled to do so by the Tatars.' The implication is that there was a division among the Rus *kniazi* in their attitudes towards cooperation with the Mongol rulers. We saw a similar reluctance to cooperate with the Khan Uzbeg on the part of Aleksandr Mikhailovich of Tver. That reluctance led to his flight to Pskov and then Lithuania.

The combined Rus and Tatar army marched on the town of Sudomir (Sandomierz) but for some reason, they did not attack. Lev then led 'a great host of regiments' against the town of Kropiwnica (now Koprzywnica) while 'boasting greatly that he would march to Kraków'. On the way, he allowed his soldiers 'to break up to loot', at which point the defending Poles set upon them, killing 'many boyars and good servants from his regiments, as well as some of the Tatars'. Thus, the second military operation in which Iurii was involved ended in defeat and 'Lev returned with great dishonour.'[17]

Iurii Lvovich Gets Married

In the next year, *s.a.* 6789 (1280/81), the GVC tells us that Volodimer asked for Iurii's help in a campaign against Bolesław II (a son of Siemowit I, the ruler of Mazovia), to which Iurii replied:

> My uncle, I would gladly march with you myself, but I have no time. I am setting out for Suzdal, my lord, in order to get married. I am taking only a few attendants with me but behold all of my men and boyars I am delivering to you and Divine Providence. Whenever you wish, march with them.[18]

The military expedition that Iurii's troops mounted turned out well, as the combined forces captured 'Bolesław's favourite town', Gostynyn. The GVC does not report the marriage of Iurii to the daughter of Iaroslav Iaroslavich of Tver.[19] Nor does it report her death, but it does report the death of Iurii's son Mikhail as *s.a.* 6792 (1283/4 (1286/7, according to Hrushevsky; 1287/8, according to Dąbrowski)).[20]

Iurii Lvovich Does Not Accompany His Troops

The GVC, *s.a.* 6790 (1281/2, but 1285 in the chronology of Hrushevsky), tells us that 'the cursed and lawless [that is, without Christian law] Nogai' joined with Töle-Buqa to begin a military campaign against the Hungarians. He 'ordered the *kniazi* of Rus – Lev, Mstislav, Volodimer and Iurii – to march with them'.[21] Significantly, Iurii was now receiving orders directly from Nogai, along with his father (the ruler of Galicia), his great uncle (the ruler of Volhynia) and his uncle (the ruler of Lutsk). Although Volodimer could not go in person because he was ill, he sent his army with Iurii, so all of them complied with the order to march. The chronicler explains that 'at the time, the *kniazi* of Rus were Tatar subjects.'[22] This statement is also significant because it is one of the few times where a Rus source acknowledges so explicitly that the Rus *kniazi* were not ruling themselves; it is even more significant here because it comes from a chronicler who detested the Tatars, or at least certain Tatars, as evidenced by the slurs that he used when discussing Nogai and Töle-Buqa, such as 'cursed', 'damned' and 'lawless'.

After the Nogai and Töle-Buqa had finished pillaging the Hungarian lands, they returned to the Ulus of Jochi, while the Rus *kniazi* returned to their own lands.[23] The chronicler does not say that the Rus *kniazi* pillaged the Hungarian land, only that Nogai and Töle-Buqa did so. Lev had been 'dismissed' from the campaign earlier on and returned to find that Bolesław had pillaged the towns on the Volhynian side of the border. Lev contacted Volodimer to go against Bolesław and also reached out to the Lithuanians for help, but the Lithuanians did not arrive at the appointed place at the appointed time, so Lev and Volodimer had to give up on their campaign. When Iurii and Mstislav returned from the Hungarian campaign, Iurii collaborated with Volodimer to go up against Bolesław and received agreement from the Lithuanians that they would join the campaign. After they set out to meet the Lithuanians, 'Lev sent word to his son not to march alone with the Lithuanians,' because Lev had killed Vaišvilkas, back in 1262, and the Lithuanians might seek revenge by killing Iurii. As a result, Iurii did not go in person on the campaign, although he did send his army. Reading between the lines of this entry, we can see that it indicates the beginnings of the changing of the old guard. Volodimer could not go on the Hungarian campaign because he was ill, while Lev was sent back early from that campaign. Later, after the failed attempt by Lev and Volodimer to go against Bolesław with Lithuanian help, Iurii renewed his campaign as the leader of the Rus forces, but because of his father's concern about his own actions 24 years previously, Iurii did not accompany the troops.

Iurii Lvovich Is Unsuccessful Once Again

In the entry for the next year, *s.a.* 6791 (1282/3; but perhaps November 1286, according to the chronology of Hrushevsky), the beginning of the previous year's entry is repeated; however, instead of 'the cursed and lawless Nogai' ordering the Galician-Volhynian *kniazi* to accompany him, it is 'the cursed and lawless Töle-Buqa' who is ordering them. Rather than attacking Hungary, they are instead being ordered to accompany the Tatars in an attack on Poland. Again, the explanation is given that they complied because 'all the *kniazi* were Tatar subjects then.'[24] However, this time the chronicler does not mention Iurii receiving the order, only that Lev, Mstislav and Volodimer received it. Later in the entry, the chronicler does mention Iurii, but only in the context of being Lev's son. Yet, unlike in Nogai's Hungarian campaign of the year before, 'they met with no success' in Töle-Buqa's Polish campaign.[25] The chronicler of the Volhynian part of the GVC seems to take every opportunity to mention the occasions when Iurii was not successful.

Iurii Lvovich Is Described as Being Proud

In the entry for *s.a.* 6795 (1286/7), the GVC says that 'God visited His sword upon us [as instruments of] His wrath because of the increase of our sins' and that Töle-Buqa and Alqui undertook a campaign 'in great force' against the Poles, accompanied by the Rus *kniazi*: Lev, Mstislav, Volodimer, Iurii Lvovich and many others. For the third time, the chronicler explains that 'at that time the *kniazi* of Rus were Tatar subjects' but this time he adds, 'having been conquered by God's wrath'.[26] During the campaign, Volodimer became ill and returned to Volodymyr.

The GVC records several interesting exchanges of communications at this point. Volodimer, feeling that he was close to death, bequeathed all his lands to his 'brother' Mstislav, in the presence of the 'emperors' (*tsesari*), that is, Töle-Buqa and Alqui. Mstislav expressed his gratitude, but although Lev said that Volodimer did the right thing in bequeathing his lands to Mstislav, he indicated to Mstislav that after Volodimer's death he planned to demand from Mstislav what was rightfully his. Mstislav responded that if Lev had any reservations regarding the bequest, he should speak of them now, while Mstislav was in the presence of Töle-Buqa and Alqui. However, Lev was silent. In a subsequent communication to Mstislav, Volodimer said that he did not give any of his lands to Lev or Iurii because they were 'proud'.[27] Volodimer then had his will or testament drawn up, which bequeathed Volhynia to Mstislav but set aside some cities for the maintenance of his wife (her name is not given in the testament, but we know that she was Olga, the daughter of Roman Mikhailovich of the Olgovich clan of Chernigov). Volodimer made no mention in his testament of either Lev or Iurii.[28]

Iurii Lvovich Sets Out to Take Lublin

The chronicler of the Volhynian part of the GVC tells us that in early October 1288, Iurii set out to take Lublin. Konrad II, the son of Siemowit I (the ruler of Mazovia) and Pereiaslava (a daughter of Daniil Romanovich), was in the city at the time and thought that a Lithuanian army was approaching. He and his boyars fled to the tower, but when the Lubliners found out that it was Iurii approaching with a Galician army, they tried to counter their attack with a subterfuge, claiming that a much larger Polish force might be on its way. According to the chronicler, Iurii saw through their deception; however, when Iurii discovered that the Lubliners were not about to surrender their city, he set his army to pillaging the countryside. Iurii's army returned with much booty and Konrad was 'disgraced', according to the chronicler.[29] This assessment is notable since the chronicler had been critical of Iurii, as well as his father Lev, throughout the recitation but, here, it is the Polish ruler of Mazovia that he finds to be lacking in fortitude.

Iurii Lvovich Pleads for the Town of Berestia

The Volhynian chronicler tells us that later that same month (October 1288), Iurii sent an envoy to Volodimer to plead for the town of Berestia (Brest) in compensation for the towns of Belz, Cherven and Kholm that Volodimer's son Lev was taking back, towns that Lev had earlier given over to Iurii. Volodimer refused because he had already bequeathed Berestia to Mstislav; he would not go back on his promise. The implication of this response was that Iurii was asking Volodimer to do something unethical, especially since we know the true reason why Volodimer had not included either Iurii or Lev in his will in the first place – namely, their pride. Shortly thereafter, Lev sent the bishop of Peremyshl to Volodimer, tasking him with asking Volodimer to give Berestia to Lev. Volodimer turned down that request also, with the message, 'I will not give you a town, nor will you take any village from me. I will not give you [anything, because] I know your cunning.'[30] Upon the death of Volodimer, the Volhynia (*GVC*) chronicler wrote an encomium full of praise, including the statement that 'he was a great bibliophile and philosopher, the like of which there had never been in all the land, nor will there ever be after his death.'[31]

Iurii's Father, Lev, Disassociates Himself from His Son's Actions

The final episode described by the Volhynia (*GVC*) chronicler that involves Iurii occurs upon the death of Volodimer in 1289. When Mstislav was about to send his garrison troops to all the cities that had been bequeathed to him by Volodimer, he found that Iurii had already occupied Berestia, Kamenets and Belsk. The residents of Berestia had rebelled against Volodimer while he was still alive and approached Iurii, swearing on the Cross that they would hand Berestia over to Iurii when Volodimer died. Therefore, as soon as Volodimer died, Iurii went to Berestia 'and began to reign, upon the advice of his foolhardy young boyars and the rebellious inhabitants of Berestia'.[32] Mstislav's boyars told him of Iurii's actions and that they were prepared to fight Iurii's troops to get Berestia into Mstislav's hands, as Volodimer had wanted. However, Mstislav recommended patience and set about trying to resolve the issue without bloodshed. He sent envoys to both Iurii and Lev, asking whether Iurii had undertaken the occupation of Berestia on his own or if he was ordered to do so by Lev; furthermore, he

45 Seal of Iurii Lvovich.

threatened to summon the Tatars if Iurii did not leave Berestia. Mstislav wanted to know if a joint campaign of action by Mstislav's troops and the Tatar forces should be taken against Iurii alone or if it should be against both Iurii and Lev. Lev, 'greatly frightened', sent a message back to Mstislav, saying that Iurii undertook the occupation without his knowledge and that he was sending a message to Iurii, telling him to leave the town. Lev did in fact send a message to Iurii, telling him to leave Berestia and adding that if he did not do so, then Lev would join the joint Volhynian-Tatar forces against him, his own son. The chronicler then remarks that Iurii left Berestia 'in great shame', but not before he had 'pillaged his uncle's building so that not one stone remained upon another in Berestia, Kamenets and Belsk'.[33]

The Denouement

Mstislav remained the ruler of Volhynia until after 1292 (the year of his death is uncertain). Since Mstislav had no heirs, Lev Daniilovich claimed Volhynia for himself. Lev remained the ruler of Galicia and Volhynia until his death, in around 1301. When Lev died, both Galicia and Volhynia passed to Iurii, who, as nationalist historians like to mention, called himself '*Regis Rusie, Princeps Ladmerie*' (King of Rus, Prince of Volodymyr).[34] This claim to be 'king' was not all that significant, as the historian Pëtr Stefanovich has pointed out, 'since Latin neighbours of Galicia-Volhynia Rus' traditionally called the Rus' rulers by that title'.[35] Nor is there any evidence that Iurii had any negotiations with the pope over his ratification of this position, which would have implied some acceptance on Iurii's part of papal authority. On the contrary,

Iurii is credited with having an Orthodox bishop of Galicia elevated by the Patriarch of Constantinople, Athanasios, to the status of metropolitan, creating the second metropolitan for Rus. Just as the move made by Maksim, the metropolitan of Kyiv, to the town of Vladimir in 1299 enhanced the status of the rulers of the Vladimir-Suzdal polity, so too one would expect that having a metropolitan of his own appointed to Galicia would have enhanced the status of the ruler of the Galician-Volhynian polity; namely, Iurii. However, there is no mention of this in Rus sources, nor is there any indication that Iurii had anything to do with this second metropolitan. We know about this elevation to metropolitan from a Byzantine source, the *Notitia episcopatum* of Emperor Andronikos II (r. 1282–1328).[36] The potential rivalry of these two metropolitans of Rus was resolved after the death of Metropolitan Maksim of Kyiv in 1305; Peter, Iurii's nominee for the metropolitan of Galicia, was appointed instead as the metropolitan of Kyiv, thus combining the two metropolitanates back into a single metropolitanate for all Rus. Peter went first to Vladimir, then moved his residence to Moscow, thereby enhancing the status of the Moscow rulers. Under Iurii's rule, Galicia-Volhynia lost Lublin to King Wenceslas in 1302, while Hungary reacquired Transcarpathia between 1307 and 1310.[37]

In the meantime, in the 1290s, the Ulus of Jochi experienced a devastating civil war in the western steppe area (one of the most likely reasons for the metropolitan of Kyiv moving his residence to the north).[38] The conflict was between Nogai and Toqta, and ended in a defeat for Nogai, although his followers, the Manghuds, continued on in the Nogai Ordu. This also meant a diminution of Mongol power over Kyiv and Galicia-Volhynia, and an increase in Lithuanian power in those areas. After the Battle on the Irpin River (1324), the ruler of Lithuania and the khan of the Ulus of Jochi shared dominion over Kyiv, while after the Battle of Blue Waters (1362), the ruler of Lithuania took complete control of Kyiv and its surrounding area.

There is some difference in reporting in the sources as to whether Iurii died in 1308 or in 1315. At some point, his son Andrei took over as ruler, but then both he and his brother Lev died in 1323, in apparently separate incidents. According to the Lithuanian Chronicles, after concluding a treaty with the Teutonic Knights, Gediminas, the ruler of Lithuania, moved against Volhynia and captured the city of Volodymyr.[39] Andrei died defending the city. Lev then, presumably, became the new ruler of the Galician-Volhynian polity, but he fled to Dmitrii Romanovich of Briansk, who was a sworn enemy of Lithuania.[40] Gediminas next marched on Kyiv; however, at the Irpin River, 23 kilometres (4 mi.) southwest of Kyiv, he encountered a joint army led by Dmitrii of Briansk, Oleg of Pereiaslavl, Stanislav of Kyiv and Lev. During the ensuing battle, Oleg and Lev were killed; Stanislav then fled, first to Briansk and then to Riazan. Presumably, Dmitrii went back to Briansk.

Liubartas (d. 1383), also known as Demetrius of Liubar, became the ruler of a combined Galicia and Volhynia in 1340. Liubartas was the youngest son of Gediminas, the ruler of Lithuania, and the nephew of Andrei and Lev, the sons of Iurii Lvovich. Liubartas's first wife was Evfemia, who was probably the daughter of Lev II Iurevich.[41] At the time of the deaths of Andrei and Lev in 1323, Liubartas was the ruler of Lutsk and Liubar (in Volhynia). Władysław I Łokietek, who had been the king of Poland since 1320, objected to Liubartas being made ruler of a combined Galicia and Volhynia; therefore, Gediminas compromised, agreeing that it should be ruled by a grandson of Iurii Lvovich Bolesław, who also took the name Jerzy (Iurii). When Bolesław-Jerzy died in 1340, King Władysław had been dead for seven years; therefore, according to one line of argument in the historiography, Gediminas, who in the intervening years had strengthened his position vis-à-vis the Polish king, was able to appoint his son Liubartas as the ruler of a combined Galicia and Volhynia. By 1349, Kazimierz III, the king of Poland (r. 1333–70) and the brother-in-law of Bolesław-Jerzy, had taken away all the lands ruled by Liubartas except for eastern Volhynia. In 1366, Kazimierz and the Lithuanian grand duke, Algirdas (r. 1345–77), signed a treaty whereby Liubartas retained eastern Volhynia, with Lutsk as its capital, and it was acknowledged as part of the Grand Duchy of Lithuania. Kazimierz ruled over Galicia, western Volhynia and western Podolia as the crown lands of Poland. When Kazimierz died in 1370, he had fathered no sons, so his lands went to his nephew, Louis I, the king of Hungary, who ruled over the area until his death in 1382. Louis' eldest daughter, Maria, succeeded him as the ruler of Hungary until her own death in 1387. Rulership of Hungary and of the lands of Galicia, western Volhynia and western Podolia passed to Maria's sister, Jadwiga, who was also the queen of Poland. When she died in 1399, Galicia and Volhynia were absorbed into the Kingdom of Poland. Thus, within a little over 150 years, Galicia and Volhynia went from being the power base of the Iziaslavich family, some of whose members had aspirations to be the inheritors of all Rus, to being provinces of Poland.

✠

THE VOLHYNIAN-*GVC* chronicler's account of Iurii's activities begins with a 'foolhardy' attack on the town of Goroden and ends with him in shame after occupying Berestia. The only time that Iurii is represented as even mildly successful as a ruler is when he has his troops plunder the outskirts of Lublin while Konrad, the duke of Mazovia, is in the city with his boyars.

Hrushevsky referred to the destructiveness and savagery of the Mongols, saying that Galicia-Volhynia was 'more cultured'. He may have thought that he was defending the attitude of the Volhynian (*GVC*) chronicler; however, the Mongols had built the largest empire the world had known up to that point, an empire that held together for three generations. Savagery and destructiveness alone do not build and run an empire. Since Hrushevsky never seems to have made a comparison of the levels of culture of the Mongols and the Galician-Volhynians, one wonders on what basis he concluded that one was 'more cultured' than the other. Indeed, the Mongol Empire has been called 'one of the most enlightened realms the world has ever known'.[42]

While the *GVC* chronicler presents the Mongols in a negative way, using slurs as epithets, the chronicle does provide evidence that the Mongols undertook military campaigns alongside the rulers of Galicia and Volhynia. In 1277, the *GVC* says that Nogai responded to requests for help from the Rus rulers who were protesting against Lithuanian encroachment on their territory. In 1285, Nogai and Töle-Buqa undertook a campaign against the Hungarians, while in 1286, Nogai and Töle-Buqa undertook a campaign against the Poles. In each case, the Galician and Volhynian rulers accompanied them (or, in the case of the Polish campaign, sent a son as their representative, as Lev did with Iurii). Three times, the *GVC* chronicler reminded the reader that 'at that time the *kniazi* of Rus were Tatar subjects.' After the Polish campaign, Volodimer bequeathed his Volhynian holdings to Mstislav, in the presence of the Mongol rulers, and said that anyone who objected should do so while the Mongol rulers were still there. In 1289, Mstislav threatened to call in the Tatars if Iurii did not remove his troops from Berestia, Kamenets and Belsk, cities that had been bequeathed to Mstislav by Volodimer. Mstislav had apparently already sent the envoy to Töle-Buqa, because that envoy needed to be called back. Clearly, the Galician and Volhynian rulers were in close communication with their overlords, the Mongols. Even though the Volhynian (*GVC*) chronicler despised them, he could not help but provide evidence that it was the Mongols who defended Galicia and Volhynia and their rulers against threats from their Hungarian, Polish and Lithuanian neighbours. However, as a result of the weakening power of the Ulus of Jochi in the area around Kyiv and further west, the rulers of Galicia-Volhynia could no longer count on receiving support from the Mongols. Their lands were soon absorbed by their more powerful neighbours to the west and north, as we will see in Chapter Ten.

10

Uliana Alexandrovna and Her Family

Uliana Alexandrovna of Tver was born around 1325 and died in 1391. She was the daughter of Alexandr Mikhailovich of Tver and Anastasia of Galicia (who was herself the daughter of Iurii Lvovich of Galicia). Uliana's birthplace was Pskov; her father was in exile there during his disputes with the ruler of Moscow and the khan. Uliana married the ruler of Lithuania, Algirdas, around 1350. She brought to Algirdas numerous genealogical connections with both Tver and Galicia and can thereby rightly be called a nexus between Tver, Galicia and Lithuania. However, she was also the sister-in-law of Semën Ivanovich (the ruler of Moscow and of Vladimir-Suzdal), as a result of Semën marrying her older sister, Maria, in 1347 (see illus. 41). Uliana is reputed to have had sixteen children with Algirdas.

Algirdas (Olgierd) was born around 1296; at the time of his marriage to Uliana, he had already been married once – to Maria of Vitebsk, in circa 1318. The Bychovets Chronicle states: 'Then *Kniaz* Olgierd [Algirdas] took to wife *kniaginia* Uliana of Vitebsk, for whom *Kniaz* Olgierd was baptized in the Rus faith, while all the Lithuanian nobles remained pagans.'[1] The historian Raza Mažeika warned that there are several good reasons to doubt the reliability of the information in this chronicle. First, it confuses Uliana of Tver with Algirdas's first wife, Maria of Vitebsk (whom the Bychovets Chronicle calls 'Ona'). Second, the context of the quotation about Algirdas's being 'baptized in the Rus faith' needs to be understood as part of a larger narrative about a Lithuanian landowner, Peter Goštautas, who converted to Roman Catholicism and the subsequent martyrdom of fourteen Franciscan friars. Although it is not evident how the conversion of Peter Goštautas to Catholicism would necessitate or explain the conversion of Algirdas to Rus Orthodoxy, the chronicler might be trying to absolve Algirdas from any complicity with the pagans who killed the Franciscans.

It appears that Algirdas's eight children (six sons and two daughters) with his first wife had Christian names, but it is not evident whether they were raised to be Orthodox or when they received those names, whereas most of Algirdas's sixteen children (eight sons and eight daughters) with Uliana had non-Christian names and were presumably raised to be pagan. By the time Algirdas married Uliana, he was already well past fifty years old. To be sure, he may well have been a virile individual, but even if we estimate that Uliana had one child a year, that would mean that Algirdas was well into his late sixties when he fathered his last child. Of course, there are other possible explanations for how many children he had.

The Novgorod, Pskov and Voskresensk chronicles, *s.a.* 6850 (1341/2), report that when Algirdas came to the aid of Pskov against the Teutonic Knights, the people of Pskov wanted him to rule Pskov; however, this was only if he converted to Orthodoxy, which he refused to do.[2] Instead, his son Andrei converted to Orthodoxy and became the ruler of Pskov.[3] The testimony of these chronicles indicates that at the least, this one son by Maria of Vitebsk had not been raised as an Orthodox Christian.

The historian S. C. Rowell asserted that until Algirdas, the rulers of Lithuania married within the Lithuanian nobility.[4] Algirdas's marriage to the daughter of the ruler of Vitebsk occurred around 1318, but Rowell casts doubt that her name was Maria. He pointed out that the earliest reference to this marriage appears in the unreliable first redaction of the Lithuanian Chronicle, not in the more reliable hypothetical compilation (*svod*) of 1408.[5] We can, nonetheless, draw a few conclusions regarding Algirdas's choice of brides by comparing his marriage to Uliana with his first marriage.

The marriage of Uliana to Algirdas was not an isolated alliance; instead, it was part of an interconnected matrix of diplomacy and military operations that were carried out among the leaders of the major polities in Rus, including Lithuania, Tver, Moscow and the Ulus of Jochi. The Lithuanian rulers were expanding the area that they ruled while, at the same time, the ruling families of Moscow and Tver were engaged in conflict over which family would rule the Vladimir-Suzdal polity. The khan of the Ulus of Jochi determined who would rule that polity, but he was also at times in conflict with the ruler of Lithuania. At that

46 Olgerd asks to marry Uliana. 'In the same year, the Grand Duke of Lithuania Olgerd Gediminovich sent to Moscow to the Grand Duke Semën Ivanovich, asking him to give his wife's sister, that is, his sister-in-law, the daughter of Grand Duke Aleksandr Mikhailovich of Tver named Uliana. He, having consulted with his spiritual father, His Holiness Feognost, Metropolitan of Kyiv and All Rus, gave.' *Litsevoi letopisnyi svod*, vol. VIII, p. 78.

time, there were no boundaries (that is, administered borders) between polities; there were only frontiers (that is, unadministered borders, which were more like zones). This point was made by the American sinologist Owen Lattimore regarding eastern Inner Eurasia,[6] but it applies equally as well to western Inner Eurasia during this time period. As a result, the demarcation line between polities was not clear and would allow the ruler of one polity to move his military forces closer to another polity's cities, ready to attack them.

In addition to the Lithuanian rulers expanding their polity's frontiers militarily by taking control of Volhynia, Polotsk, Kyiv and Smolensk during this period, they also acquired towns and territories through marriage. Sometimes, they achieved this end by marrying into a family that ruled a town when the family had no legitimate heirs. A case in point is Algirdas himself, who married the daughter of the last independent ruler of Vitebsk, Iaroslav Vasilevich; when Iaroslav died, Algirdas incorporated Vitebsk into his own domains and made it his place of residence.

The Rise of Lithuania-Rus

The creation of a Lithuanian polity during the first half of the thirteenth century is rather a mystery. One guess is that the rulers organized the local pagan tribes. Another guess is that the tribes banded together to choose rulers to govern them, but there is no evidence to support either of these guesses. We do know that local landowners had a great deal of say over the policies of these rulers, and we might suppose that these landowners were the ones who organized protection to keep from being taken over by the Livonian Knights on one side and the Polish monarchy on the other.

The Livonian Knights and the Teutonic Knights

We need to make a slight digression here to discuss the Livonian Knights. The Catholic bishop of Riga, Albert, founded the Livonian Brothers of the Sword (*Frates Militiae Christi Livoniae*) in 1202 as a monastic-warrior community that would combat paganism in the Baltic area.[7] Pope Innocent III (r. 1198–1216) sanctioned the order in 1204. The Livonian Brothers of the Sword remained independent until the order's defeat by the Samogitians in 1236, as well as the brotherhood's quarrels with Pope Gregory IX (r. 1227–41), led to it being incorporated into the Teutonic Knights as an autonomous group, which has been called the Livonian Knights in the historiography.

The Teutonic Order was initially a German sub-organization of the Knights Hospitallers who were on the Crusades in the Levant.

Called the Order of the German House of St Mary in Jerusalem (*Ordo domus Sanctae Mariae Theutonicorum Hierosolymitanorum*), the order was transformed into a military order at Acre in 1192 after the Muslims had retaken Jerusalem in 1187. In 1211, the Teutonic Knights were transferred to Transylvania to help the king of Hungary, Andrew II, defend his kingdom against the Polovtsy. In 1225, Andrew expelled the Knights because of their allegiance to Pope Honorius III (r. 1216–27) rather than to him. In 1230, the king of Germany and Italy and the Holy Roman emperor Fredcrick II issued the Golden Bull of Rimini, which granted the Teutonic Order the right to any lands that it conquered in the Prussian Baltic. Supplied by the ruler of Mazovia, Konrad I (r. 1194–1247), the Teutonic Knights undertook a crusade to Christianize the Baltic Old Prussians and, in the process, virtually wiped them out. A decisive battle occurred in 1233, when the combined forces of the Grand Master of the Teutonic Knights, Hermann von Salza, the burgrave of Magdeburg, Duke Henry of Silesia, Konrad of Mazovia, Duke Kazimierz of Kuyawia, Duke Władysław Odonic of Greater Poland (r. 1229–34) and the dukes of Pomerania decisively defeated the Old Prussian army. The Teutonic Knights also took the area of Chełmno from Konrad I as their reward.

After incorporating the Livonian Knights, the combined Order undertook campaigns against the Polish lands, Novgorod and Pskov, and independent landholders in the Baltics. It was these independent landholders, according to one of the theories, who saw what was happening to their neighbours and to themselves at the hands of the Crusader Knights and began to band together for defence, choosing one of their own, Mindaugas, as their leader in 1236. On 17 July 1251, Pope Innocent IV ordered the bishop of Chełmno to crown Mindaugas as king of the Lithuanians. A number of these landowners came from the so-called Black Rus, a forested area along the Upper Nieman River, which had not been conquered by the Mongols. This area did not function as part of the Ulus of Jochi, so it provided a base, along with the Polotsk-Minsk land, which had also escaped being conquered, where Lithuanian rulers could organize military opposition to the Mongols. We have already discussed the attack by Nogai on Lithuania in 1277, but there had been an earlier one in 1258 that also did not resolve the Lithuanian problem, from the Mongol point of view.[8]

During the time of the creation of the Lithuanian polity, the Polish domain was divided. The Polish lands had been separated into five polities by King Bolesław III in 1138: Great Poland, Kraków, Mazovia, Sandomierz and Silesia. As we saw in Chapter Nine, none of the rulers of these polities had enough military force to fend off the Mongols. However, when Mongol power receded as the result of civil war within the Ulus of Jochi at the end of the thirteenth century, and then after the partial reunification of the Polish duchies under Władysław I Łokietek in 1320, the Polish monarchy was able to extend its control over Galicia and Volhynia.

In the meantime, after the assassination of Mindaugas in 1263 and despite attacks from the Teutonic and Livonian Knights, the Lithuanian alliance was able to begin expanding its control over Rus polities. When Gediminas came to power in 1316, he inherited a Lithuanian realm that included Lithuania Proper (*Lithuania propria*), Minsk, Navahrudak, Podlasie, Polotsk and Samogitia. Gediminas arranged marriages for his six daughters and seven sons with spouses from the main ruling families of Rus and Poland. In 1319, Gediminas allied himself with the Ulus of Jochi against the Teutonic Knights. For a time, his son Liubartas held sway over a combined Galicia and Volhynia, before the Polish king Kazimierz worked out a deal with Gediminas to put Bolesław-Jerzy in the position of ruler of the combined Galicia and Volhynia.

Algirdas, Gediminas's son and eventual successor, took Briansk, along with the bulk of Chernigov lands, during the 1350s. It is possible that he also gained control of the polity of Pereiaslavl at this time. In the meantime, with the death of Khan Berdi-Beg in 1359, the Ulus of Jochi fell into over two decades of succession struggles. Algirdas used the internal turmoil of the Ulus as an opportunity to expand Lithuanian power. After the Battle on the Irpin River in 1324, Kyiv came under dual rule, shared by the Lithuanian grand duke and the Tatar khan. This dual rule is sometimes called a 'condominium' in the historiography, whereby a representative of the Lithuanian grand duke administered the town and surrounding area, under the supervision of a Tatar military governor (*basqaq*). With the Battle of Blue Waters in 1362, this arrangement changed. We have only one description of this battle, in Maciej Stryjkowski's *Chronicle of Poland, Lithuania, Samogitia and All Ruthenia* (1582), which was written quite some time after the events so is not all that reliable. According to Stryjkowski, Algirdas's nephews, the sons of his brother Karijotas (Koriat) from Navahrudak, assisted their uncle against the opposing forces, led by three Crimean lords (*begs*).

Therefore, it clearly was not the full force of the Ulus of Jochi that they were facing. After the Battle of Blue Waters, Algirdas gained sole control of Kyiv and Eastern Podolia, thereby redirecting the tax revenue to Lithuania.

The Lithuanian Rulers' Claim to Be the Inheritors of Rus

According to the East European historian Jaroslaw Pelenski, the 'traditional scholarship' has focused on three topics regarding 'the struggles for territorial supremacy in Eastern Europe' during the fourteenth and fifteenth centuries: first, the relationship between the Vladimir-Suzdal polity and the Ulus of Jochi; second, the relationship between the rulers of Moscow and the rulers of Tver 'for hegemony in the Great Russian ethnic territory'; third, the counterposing of Lithuania to 'the Eastern Slavs', both as an outside, pagan and non-Slavic, threat and as an inside actor in the guise of 'Western Russia'.[9] In contrast, a fourth topic, the relationship between Lithuania-Rus and the Ulus of Jochi, has received little scholarly attention. In terms of viewing the history of the fourteenth century through the lens of subsequent Muscovite dynastic history, such attention to the first three topics and an absence of attention to the last topic is understandable. Yet, in the fourteenth century, a gambling person would most likely have placed their bets on either the Lithuanian rulers or Tatar khans to win these power struggles because the rulers of Vladimir-Suzdal were still vassals of the latter. In Pelenski's view,

> Muscovite bookmen and ideologists of the fifteenth and sixteenth centuries succeeded in magnifying Muscovy's role in the East European contest out of all proportion to the real developments, and in creating a myth about her protracted and farsighted 'struggle against the Tatar yoke', which has been perpetuated in Russian historiography up to the present day.[10]

Pelenski delineated 'three major interrelated conflicts' during the fourteenth century in Rus. The first conflict was between Lithuania-Rus and the Ulus of Jochi, which Pelenski sees as occurring in two phases. The first phase culminated in a Lithuanian victory at the Battle of Blue Waters in 1362; the second phase culminated in a Lithuanian defeat at the Battle of the Vorskla River in 1399.

The second conflict was between Lithuania-Rus and Moscow, a conflict in which Algirdas undertook three military campaigns against Moscow (in 1368, 1370 and 1372). Closely connected with these military campaigns was the attempt by Algirdas to have a separate metropolitan appointed for the Orthodox population of Lithuania-Rus, to escape from under the influence of the Moscow-centred metropolitan of 'Kyiv and All Rus'.

The third conflict was between Moscow and the Ulus of Jochi, where the Moscow rulers exploited quarrels within the Orda to conduct two military campaigns: the Battle of the Vozha River (1378) and the Battle at Snipes' Field (Kulikovo Pole) in 1380. We will cover this particular conflict in more detail in the next chapter, in order to concentrate in this chapter on the first two conflicts.

Along with the expansions under Vitenis (r. 1293–1316) and Gediminas (r. 1316–41) further into Rus land, there came a change in the title of the Lithuanian ruler. In 1323, Gediminas started using the title 'King of the Lithuanians and Rusians' (*Lethewinorum et Ruthenorum rex*) in his dealings with foreign rulers.[11] With this title, the Lithuanian rulers were the first to signal their challenge to the Tatar khans for control of all Rus. In contrast, the Orthodox Church metropolitan could claim his jurisdiction as 'Kyiv and all Rus' because, besides the fact that that was part of his official title, which he received from the patriarch of Constantinople, the khans did not see that jurisdictional designation as a challenge to their authority. The Mongols did not interfere with the religion of the people of Rus, as long as the Church leaders prayed for the well-being of the khans and their families. Rus was part of the Ulus of Jochi, the domain of the khan.[12] Thus, while the religious leaders could claim jurisdiction over 'all Rus', the secular leaders in Rus could not claim to rule 'all Rus'. That was the case until Algirdas used this phrase in 1358 when he formulated the goals of Lithuanian policy in the east and the south – that 'all of Rus' was to be defended by the Lithuanian rulers from the intrusions of the Tatars.[13] The timing of this declaration is significant because it comes after the death of Khan Jani-Beg (r. 1341–57), when turmoil began to engulf the Western (or White) Orda of the Ulus of Jochi. A dozen khans took the throne in rapid succession between then and 1372, when Urus Khan, who had been ruling the Eastern, or White, Orda since 1361, managed briefly to unite the two Ordas into a single khanate.

It was during this period that Algirdas succeeded in extending Lithuanian control over more of Rus: first, the still unclaimed areas around Polotsk and Minsk; second, Chernigov land, which was totally annexed by Lithuania by the 1370s; third, Novgorod-Seversk and the surrounding Severian territory (lying east of Chernigov), which was annexed by the 1360s; fourth, Kyiv and the Kyivan lands, which were completely taken over by 1363; fifth, Pereiaslavl and its surrounding land, which was taken over by 1363; sixth, large parts of Podolia, which were taken over in the early 1360s.

Lithuanian Relations with Tver

Following the events of the conflicts between the rulers of Tver and those of Moscow in the 1320s, the subsequent rulers of Tver were understandably looking for allies against Moscow. Since the rulers of Moscow were vassals of the Tatar khan, the rulers of Lithuania would understandably perceive them as potential opponents because they could be expected to defend the interests of the khan. Since the rulers of Tver were out of favour with the Tatar khan after 1327 and were presumably still enemies of the rulers of Moscow, a rapprochement between Tver and Lithuania developed, on the basis of the theory that 'the enemy of my enemy is my friend.'

The marriage of Maria Gediminaitė (the daughter of Gediminas) to Dmitrii Mikhailovich of Tver in 1320 represented the culmination of years of Tver–Lithuania diplomacy that had begun in the second half of the thirteenth century. After Khan Uzbeg executed Dmitrii for his killing of Iurii Daniilovich, Maria retired to a convent and lived for another 24 years, until 1349.[14] In the estimation of Rowell, 'it is likely that she exercised considerable political and financial influence over her Rus'ian kinsmen, if she is anything like later Lithuanian dowagers in Rus'.'[15] In the 1330s, after he was ousted from his position as the ruler of Vladimir-Suzdal, Aleksandr Mikhailovich of Tver ruled Pskov

47 The seal of Algirdas, *c*. 1366: 'Olger pechat kniazia velikogo'. M. Gumowski, 'Pieczęcie Książąt Litewskich', *Ateneum wileńskie*, VII/44 (1930), pp. 709–10.

in exile, in alliance with Gediminas.[16] In 1375, Miklausė/Maria (*c.* 1360–1405), the daughter of Algirdas's brother Kęstutis (r. 1381–2), married Ivan Mikhailovich, the future ruler of Tver (r. 1399–1425). Ivan was the son of Mikhail Aleksandrovich.

The 'crown jewel' of Lithuanian diplomacy, however, was the marriage of Algirdas to Uliana. This marriage allowed the offspring of Algirdas and Uliana to claim descent from the Vsevolodovich ruling clan. In addition, Uliana's religion gave Algirdas a certain cachet with his Eastern Orthodox subjects, as he sought to obtain a separate metropolitan for Lithuania.

The Rus Church Schism in the Fourteenth Century

One problem with the Lithuanian 'grand strategy' regarding their claim to be the inheritors of Rus was the metropolitan of Kyiv and all Rus. Except for Mindaugas (who was Catholic), all the other rulers of Lithuania before this time were probably pagan. A large percentage (no one knows how large) of their subjects were Eastern Orthodox and were administered by the metropolitan, who tended to follow anti-pagan (not to mention anti-Catholic) policies. In short, the metropolitan of Kyiv gave the Rus enemies of the Lithuanian rulers a form of leverage into the Lithuanian domain. By appointing their own metropolitan, the Lithuanian rulers could presumably cut off that outside leverage.

Now for a little lesson in Rus church politics regarding the appointment of the metropolitan. Traditionally, the Patriarch of Constantinople appointed only one metropolitan for 'Kyiv and All Rus'. With the relocation of Metropolitan Maksim to Vladimir in 1299, the rulers of Galicia and Volhynia started lobbying for a separate metropolitan for Galicia-Volhynia. A Lithuanian metropolitan may have already been appointed in 1299.[17] If so, this would merely have involved elevating the bishop of Lithuania to metropolitan status. It is unlikely that a separate metropolitanate was created because, in 1303, Patriarch Athanasios elevated the bishop of Galicia-Volhynia, Niphont, to metropolitan status at the request of the Galician ruler, Iurii Lvovich, but no separate metropolitanate of Galicia-Volhynia was established thereby. In any case, there seems to have been indecision within the Byzantine patriarchate as to whether to divide the Rus metropolitanate into two or even three parts or to keep it as one, as we will see. There was no such indecision in 1168, when the patriarch of Constantinople, Loukas Chrysoberges, rejected the request of Andrei Bogoliubskii to appoint a separate metropolitanate for the town of Vladimir.[18]

When Metropolitan Niphont died in 1305, Iurii Lvovich sent a possible successor to Constantinople – Peter, the hegumen of Rasta Monastery. Before he could be appointed, news came that Maksim, the metropolitan of Kyiv and all Rus, had died in December 1305. Mikhail Iaroslavich of Tver, the ruler of Vladimir-Suzdal, sent his own candidate, the hegumen Gerontii, to Constantinople to succeed Maksim. To be sure, the rulers of Vladimir-Suzdal preferred to have one united metropolitanate of Rus; having the metropolitan reside in their lands gave them prestige among the faithful throughout Rus. For consistency's sake, however, it would seem likely that the patriarch would appoint two metropolitans – one for Kyiv and all Rus, the other for Galicia-Volhynia. Instead, Patriarch Athanasios chose to split the difference; that is, he opted to keep the metropolitanate of Kyiv and all Rus united, as Mikhail Iaroslavich wanted, but appointed Peter to be metropolitan, as Iurii Lvovich wanted. Peter first travelled to Sarai to obtain the *iarlyk* from Khan Toqta, then dutifully took up residence in Vladimir.[19] While there, however, he tended to take political positions that were favourable to the rulers of Moscow and against the rulers of Tver. In 1325, Peter moved the residence of the metropolitan to Moscow itself, where it remained throughout subsequent centuries.

The source evidence for the metropolitans of Lithuania and of Galicia-Volhynia is convoluted for this time period and the threads are a bit knotted, so bear with us as we try to unravel them. A metropolitan of Lithuania appeared at Church councils in Constantinople in 1317, 1327 and 1329.[20] Although the name Theophilos is connected with an act of the council of 1329, there is no way to tell whether he was also the metropolitan of Lithuania who was present at the councils in 1317 and 1327. After the death of Metropolitan Peter in 1326, the see of Kyiv and all Rus remained vacant until the patriarch nominated Theognostos (Feognost), in 1328. From that time until 1329, a certain Gabriel served as the metropolitan of Galicia-Volhynia. The only evidence we have that Gabriel was metropolitan is a letter sent by the king of Poland, Kazimierz III, in 1360 to the patriarch of Constantinople. This letter lists the metropolitans of Galicia-Volhynia in sequence: Niphont, Peter, Gabriel and Fëdor.[21] We have no evidence of Gabriel's successor until 1337, when Fëdor became the metropolitan of Galicia-Volhynia and served until 1347 (when that metropolitanate was abolished). In that year, Byzantine emperor John VI Kantakouzenos (r. 1347–54) declared there should be only one metropolitanate for all of Rus.[22]

After the death of the Lithuanian metropolitan, Theophilos, around 1330, we have no evidence of a successor as metropolitan until Theodoret in 1352; however, even that evidence is suspect because Theodoret is a shadowy figure. According to the letter sent by Patriarch Philotheos Kokkinos of Constantinople to Archbishop Moisei of Novgorod in 1354, Algirdas had the Bulgarian patriarch of Tărnovo consecrate Theodoret as metropolitan two years previously. Philotheos called this 'a stupid and illegal act' that was not recognized by the patriarchate of Constantinople.[23] Theodoret resided in Kyiv and claimed to be the metropolitan of Kyiv and all Rus.[24]

In the meantime, Peter's successor as the metropolitan of Kyiv and all Rus (who was resident in Moscow), Theognostos, supported the rulers of Moscow against other rivals. The combination of the metropolitan living in Moscow and working in cooperation with the ruler there created a politico-religious juggernaut that stymied any opposition. Shortly before his death in 1353, Theognostos had his vicar, Aleksei, appointed as the bishop of Vladimir. Then, he and Semën Ivanovich, the ruler of Moscow and Vladimir-Suzdal, asked the patriarch of Constantinople, Philotheos, to favour Aleksei and promote him as Theognostos's successor. Aleksei's family were boyars from the Chernigov lands who had settled in the Moscow polity. Aleksei's godfather was Ivan Daniilovich (whom we met in Chapter Eight), who served as the ruler of Vladimir-Suzdal from 1331 to 1340. Aleksei would serve as regent during the minority of Dmitrii Ivanovich (Donskoi), until he came of age. Thus, Aleksei was intricately connected with the Moscow ruling family.

Before the appointment of Aleksei could occur, the Byzantine emperor John V Palaiologos (r. 1341–91, intermittently) ousted his co-ruler John VI Kantakouzenos and began to rule alone. The contretemps with Algirdas and the patriarch of Bulgaria was repaired, but the Byzantine Church could still not approve of the illegal appointment of Theodoret as metropolitan. Knowing that Metropolitan Aleksei would side with Moscow against Lithuania, Algirdas prevailed upon the patriarch to appoint his own candidate to the metropolitanate of Lithuania.

Here is where Uliana re-enters the picture. Algirdas's candidate was a monk named Roman, who was from a Tver boyar family and was a relative of Uliana (exactly what the relationship was, we do not know). Apparently, Algirdas enjoyed discussions with him since Roman had been spending time at the court of Algirdas. According to a later document of Patriarch Neilos in 1380, Algirdas 'had Roman consecrated . . . under the pretext that the lord Alexis was not acceptable as metropolitan in the nation that was under [Algirdas's] rule, but his real goal was to find a means, with Roman's help, of ruling Outer Rus'.[25] The speculation in the historiography is that Patriarch Philotheos may have hoped that if he appointed Roman as the metropolitan of Lithuania, his good relations with Algirdas could convince the ruler to convert to Eastern Orthodoxy, which is not an unreasonable speculation.[26]

Philotheos's predecessor as patriarch, Patriarch Kallistos, had defined the metropolitanate of Lithuania, of which Roman was in charge, as including all the territory of Lithuania and Inner Rus; in other words, it comprised all the territory over which Algirdas ruled.[27] Thus, the conflict between the rulers of Moscow and the rulers of Tver in the 1320s was renewed in the 1350s with boyars from Moscow and Tver, respectively, who had become high-ranking church prelates. This time, however, the Tver side was allied with the ruler of Lithuania, while the Moscow side continued its vassalage to the khan in Sarai. The Rogozh (Tver) Chronicle tells us that Roman (the metropolitan of Lithuania) and Aleksei (the metropolitan of Kyiv and all Rus) had quarrelled in Constantinople in 1354.[28] The two fought like cat and dog throughout their tenures in office. Roman took up residence in Kyiv and began styling himself the 'Metropolitan of Kyiv and All Rus'.[29] When Roman died in 1362, Patriarch Kallistos restored the single metropolitanate for Kyiv and all Rus, administered by Aleksei. Algirdas continued petitioning the patriarchal see for a separate metropolitan for Lithuania, but his petitions remained unsuccessful. This development was clearly a setback for Algirdas. In 1373, Patriarch Philotheos sent his favourite monk, Cyprian, as an envoy to broker an agreement between Lithuania and Moscow and to preserve the unity of the Rus metropolitan see. That diplomatic mission failed; therefore, in 1375, Philotheos temporarily re-established the metropolitanate of Lithuania and appointed Cyprian as its metropolitan. He established one condition, however: when Aleksei died (which occurred in 1378), Cyprian would be his successor and would control a reunited Rus metropolitan see. Cyprian did eventually succeed Aleksei in 1381, and the successors of Algirdas continued to petition for a separate metropolitan. In the end, other developments determined the outcome of this conflict.

Lithuanian Relations with Moscow

Algirdas's plan to snatch all of Rus away from the Ulus of Jochi was an ambitious one. It was especially ambitious because the rulers of the Vladimir-Suzdal polity were the vassals of the Tatar khans. Before the Battle of Blue Waters, Algirdas had seen the benefit of friendly relations with Moscow. The Tver Chronicle reports that in 1356, his nephew Dmitrii, the son of his brother Koriat (Mikhail), married the daughter of the ruler of Moscow, Ivan II Ivanovich (r. 1353–9).[30] One can understand why the Tver chronicler would be particularly interested in this apparent diplomatic rapprochement between Lithuania and Moscow. But he need not have worried; the accord was only temporary. Following the Battle of Blue Waters and the resultant setback for the Ulus of Jochi, Algirdas began adopting a more aggressive policy towards Moscow. If he could neutralize Moscow, then Algirdas's forces stood a better chance in a final decisive battle against the forces of the khanate.

In 1368, Algirdas led the Lithuanian forces, supported by military forces from Tver and Smolensk, in an attack on Moscow. After a three-day siege of the Kremlin, Algirdas and Dmitrii Ivanovich (Donskoi), the ruler of Moscow (r. 1359–89), reached an agreement. In return for lifting the siege, Dmitrii allowed Mikhail Aleksandrovich to return as the ruler of Tver. Dmitrii also agreed not to interfere in Mikhail's rule, as well as to turn over all the lands that Tver disputed with Moscow to Tver.

In 1370, Algirdas, again supported by forces from Smolensk and Tver, advanced to the walls of the Moscow Kremlin. The subsequent temporary truce was sealed with a marriage between Algirdas's daughter Elena and Vladimir Andreevich, the grandson of Ivan I Daniilovich (Kalita). Significantly, Elena was a daughter that Algirdas fathered with Uliana of Tver, but we have no evidence regarding what she might have thought about her daughter's marriage with a scion of the Daniilovichi of Moscow.

The third campaign, that of 1372, undid almost all the progress that Algirdas had made in the first two Moscow campaigns. Algirdas's advance guard was ambushed by Dmitrii Ivanovich and his army, who were hiding in the woods. In the subsequent agreement, although Mikhail was left in charge of Tver, he was obliged to return all the disputed lands that Dmitrii had handed over in 1368 back to Moscow. Algirdas had to agree not to intercede for Mikhail in disputes with Moscow and that any such disputes would be resolved by Dmitrii's lord, the Tatar khan. Following this setback, the alliance between Tver and Lithuania ended. Algirdas died five years later and left it up to his successors to accomplish his goals in Rus.

The Battle at Snipes' Field (Kulikovo Pole) (1380) and the Structure of the Orda

The circumstances regarding the sons of these Rus rulers accompanying Khan Toqtamish (r. 1380–95) back to the Orda were unusual, to say the least. Three years earlier, in 1380, Dmitrii of Moscow had fought the Mongol emir, Mamai, who dominated the western portion of the Ulus of Jochi. In the middle of the battle, Mamai broke off his fight with Dmitrii to face the forces of Toqtamish that were approaching from the east.

A word of explanation about the structure of the Orda might help the reader to make sense of a seemingly complex political and military set-up. When the Ulus of Jochi was established in the thirteenth century, an agreement was apparently reached by Jochi's sons whereby the Ulus was split administratively between an eastern Blue Orda (under Orda, the oldest son of Jochi (not to be confused with the term 'Orda')) and the western White Orda (under Batu, a younger son of Jochi).[31] As part of the agreement, the khan of the White Orda was pre-eminent, with the khan of the Blue Orda being subservient. In 1378, Toqtamish, with the help of the emir Timur (more popularly known as Tamerlane) (1336–1405), overthrew Timur-Malik, a son of and the second successor to his kinsman Urus as khan,[32] and ascended to the throne of the White Orda.[33] He rejected allegiance to the ruler of the Blue Orda, which by this time had seen a series of puppet khans who were appointed by the emir, Mamai. By 1380, Toqtamish had established his pre-eminence as the khan of the Blue Orda and united the two ordas under his own rule, having defeated the forces of the emir Mamai in a conflict close to the Kalka River and the coast of the Sea of Azov.

The role of Dmitrii of Moscow in this transformation has been obscured by the Rus sources and subsequent Russian historians, who insist that Dmitrii won a great victory against the Tatars. In fact, the engagement at Snipes' Field appears to have been inconclusive. Dmitrii himself left the battlefield and hid in the woods. Even the Muscovite chronicles say that Mamai left the field to raise another army, to counter the approach of Toqtamish and his army.[34] While it is plausible that

Mamai would withdraw his forces to engage in battle with Toqtamish, it is not plausible that he did so to raise another army in a relatively short period of time. The soldiers in a steppe army were not a rabble with pitchforks that one could just conscript. They were skilled horse-archer athletes, who were highly trained to operate in battle in a disciplined and organized manner. In any case, Mamai's forces were defeated by those of Toqtamish, shortly after the encounter at Snipes' Field.

The Denouement

Upon Algirdas's death in 1377, Uliana was tonsured at the Holy Spirit Women's Monastery in Vitebsk, which she is credited with founding. She was also credited with founding a monastery in Vilnius and was a patron of religious institutions throughout Lithuania.[35] She has also been given credit for the appointment of her kinsman Roman as metropolitan of Lithuania in 1354.[36] Later, in 1377, she 'endowed the Uspenskaia Church in Ozeritskaia'.[37] According to an inscription in the Spaso-Preobrazhenskii Church in Polotsk, she died on the feast of St Alexius, which falls on 17 July;[38] however, the Illustrated Chronicle Codex says that she died in the autumn. There is also differing evidence regarding where she was buried. Uliana was canonized by the Ukrainian Autocephalous Orthodox Church on 5 December 2018.[39]

As for the metropolitanate of Lithuania, it was never re-established after Cyprian became the metropolitan of Kyiv and all Rus. When Uliana's son Jogaila converted to Roman Catholicism in 1385, the Lithuanian leaders, owing to their connections with the Polish throne, were no longer in a position to request an Orthodox metropolitan for Lithuania.

Of the seven sons of Uliana and Algirdas, the eldest, Jogaila, succeeded his father as the ruler of Lithuania (1377–92); later, he ascended

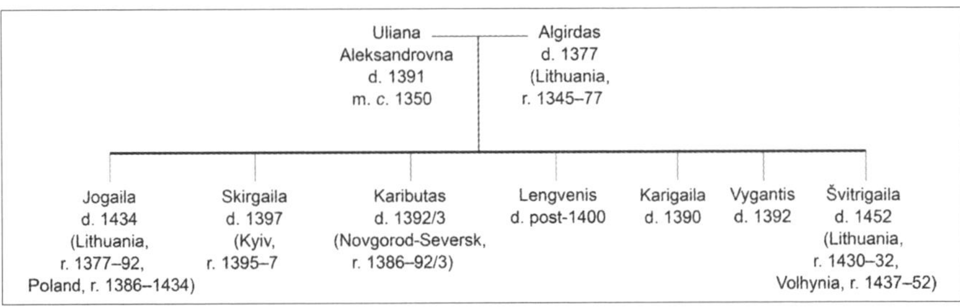

48 Uliana Aleksandrovna and her sons.

49 Uliana dies and is buried in Kyiv. 'In the same autumn, *Velikaia kniaginia* of Olgerd Gediminovich, Uliana, daughter of *Velikiĭ kniaz* Aleksandr of Tver, granddaughter of Mikhail, great-granddaughter of Iaroslav Iaroslavich, nominally named Marina, died in Lithuania, and was buried in Kyiv in the Pecherskaia Lavra'. *Litsevoi letopisnyi svod*, vol. x, p. 498.

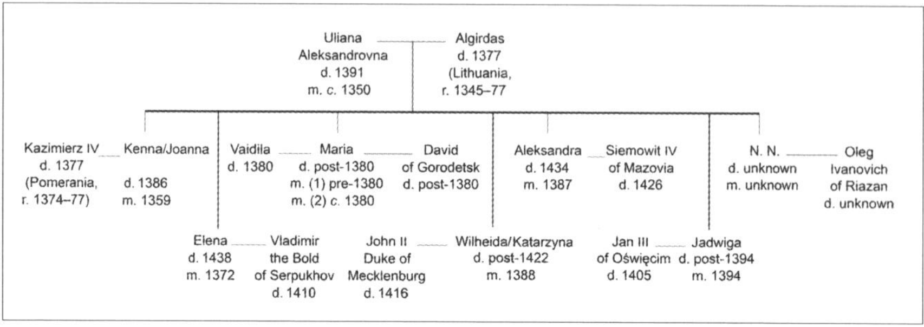

50 Uliana Aleksandrovna and her daughters.

to the throne of Poland and became king (1386–1434). The next-oldest, Skirgaila, ruled Trakai (1382–95) and then Kyiv (1395–7). The third-oldest, Kaributas, was the ruler of Novgorod-Seversk (1386–92/3). The fourth-oldest, Lengvenis, ruled Mstislavl and was the regent of Great Novgorod. The fifth-oldest son, Karigaila, ruled Mstislavl, while the next-to-youngest son, Vygantas, ruled Kernavė. The youngest son, Švitrigaila, ruled Lithuania (1430–32) and later ruled Volhynia (1437–52). A number of these sons of Algirdas and Uliana were involved in struggles for power with Kęstutis, their uncle, and, subsequently, with Kęstutis's sons (their cousins). Jogaila continued his father's policy and ambitions towards the khans of the Ulus of Jochi, as well as towards their vassals, the *kniazi* of Moscow who ruled Vladimir-Suzdal. In 1380, according to the fourteenth-century German chroniclers Johann von Posilge and Detmar of Lübeck, Jogaila and his army caught up with the army of Dmitrii Ivanovich (Donskoi) on the way back from the Battle of Snipes' Field (Kulikovo Pole) and defeated them.[40] The Muscovite-edited chronicles and tales tell a different story – here, Jogaila and the Lithuanian army arrived late for the battle but were frightened and fled back to Lithuania without a fight.

The seven daughters of Uliana and Algirdas married into the Lithuanian, Polish and Rus nobility. They wedded, respectively, Kazimierz IV, duke of Pomerania; Vladimir the Bold; Vaidila (first marriage) and David of Gorodetsk (second marriage); John II, duke of Mecklenburg-Stargard; Siemowit IV, duke of Mazovia; Jan III, duke of Oświęcim; and Oleg Ivanovich of Riazan.

As for the nephews of Algirdas who ruled Lithuania after Jogaila, they also continued his ambitious plans to take over all of Rus from the Tatar khans. After the Battle of Snipes' Field, Khan Toqtamish undertook a military expedition against Dmitrii Ivanovich of Moscow, the ruler of Vladimir-Suzdal. Why he did so is not clear and has been the subject of much speculation in the historiography. The mystery regards why he would launch an expedition against the person who was his ally in the battle against the emir Mamai only two years previously. In any case, there was no battle in 1382, possibly because there was no army that Dmitrii could gather to resist, which lends credence to the German chroniclers' claim of what happened after the Battle of Snipes' Field.[41] However, by 1391 Toqtamish was threatened by a more powerful enemy – Timur – and he sought the help of Vytautas, who had become ruler of Lithuania in 1392, but was turned down. In 1395, Timur ousted Toqtamish from power in the Ulus of Jochi and swept north towards Moscow. Toqtamish fled to Lithuania and promised Vytautas the rulership of all Rus in return for military support against Khan Temur-Qutlugh (r. 1397–9) and the emir Edigü, in a bid to regain rulership of the Orda. The combined forces of Vytautas and Toqtamish undertook three successive campaigns against Temur-Qutlugh but were decisively defeated in 1399, at the Battle of the Vorskla River, near to the place where a much later battle – the Battle of Poltava – was fought in 1709. The Lithuanian nobility suffered heavy losses, losing as much as 40 per cent of their leaders. Toqtamish fled into hiding but was killed in 1406 or 1407. This was a huge setback to the Lithuanian rulers' ambitions to rule all of Rus. At a time when the rulers of Vladimir-Suzdal were accepting the overlordship over Rus of the khan in Sarai, Algirdas and his successors were challenging that rule. One can only imagine how different the history of Rus and eastern Europe would have been if Toqtamish had won the Battle of the Vorskla River and had then honoured his promise to hand over all of Rus to Vytautas.

During the course of the next (fifteenth) century, as the result of divisions within the Orda, the Moscow rulers threw off their political vassalage to the Tatar khans. Was this the culmination of a long-term 'grand strategy' of deceiving the Tatar khans into believing that the Moscow rulers were their loyal subjects, but who were just waiting for the opportunity to escape? Were the rulers of Moscow merely cynical power-grabbers who succeeded in demonstrating to the Tatar khans that they could toady more sycophantly than any of the other rulers in Rus? Or is there another explanation? We will discuss these questions in the next chapter.

11

Vasilii Dmitrievich and His Family

The history of Vasilii Dmitrievich and his family is closely intertwined with that of the khans of the Ulus of Jochi (Orda), as well as that of the rulers of Lithuania. It was a time when the Tatar khans ruled Rus; however, the Lithuanian rulers claimed to be the true rulers of Rus and were seeking to take it away from the khans. The Daniilovichi of Moscow were subjects of the khans but had an on-again, off-again relationship with the Lithuanian rulers that ranged from open warfare (when they were fighting as vassals of the khans) to marriage alliances (when they were seeking to take an opportunity that might be offered by a change in their relationship with the khans).

Vasilii was the son of Dmitrii Ivanovich (Donskoi) and Evdokia (the daughter of Dmitrii Konstantinovich, the ruler of Suzdal and Nizhnii Novgorod) and was born on 31 December 1371. He reigned as the *velikii kniaz* of Moscow and Vladimir from 1389 until 27 February 1425. The world into which Vasilii was born was an unsettled one. His father had succeeded to the throne in 1359 as a minor at the age of nine, upon the death of Vasilii's grandfather, Ivan II Ivanovich. The metropolitan of Kyiv and all Rus, Aleksei, served as the regent. In 1360, Khan Nevruz-Beg appointed Dmitrii Konstantinovich of Suzdal as the ruler of Vladimir, presumably because Dmitrii of Moscow was a minor. Dmitrii of Suzdal was the nephew of Aleksandr Vasilevich, the last ruler of Suzdal to rule as the *velikii kniaz* of Vladimir. The Moscow chronicles, starting with the Trinity Chronicle, make the statement that 'this [appointment] was done contrary to the [rule of] fathers and grandfathers,' which Vernadsky interpreted to mean that it 'was contrary to the principle of succession from father to son'.[1] That interpretation is not completely accurate, since legitimacy in the collateral system of succession that was operative in Rus at the time required that any candidate to become the ruler of a town should be legitimized by the fact that their father had ruled in that town. This complaint made by the Muscovite chronicler was on shaky ground since the Moscow rulers, likewise, did not have the principle of legitimacy by the father's rule on their side, giving them the right to rule in Vladimir. Iurii Daniilovich and Ivan Daniilovich were appointed by the khan as rulers of Vladimir in 1318 and 1331, respectively, even though their mutual father had not ruled there (although their grandfather, Alexander Nevsky, had done so).

Around this time, the Ulus of Jochi went into a period of turmoil and 'Great Troubles', with one palace coup after another, resulting in ten different khans over eight years. This turmoil began in 1359, when Khan Berdi-Beg was overthrown by Qulpa, who then ascended to the throne. The following year, Nevruz-Beg overthrew and killed Qulpa and took the throne for himself. In 1361, Khidr, a descendent of Shiban, who was the fifth son of Jochi, overthrew and killed Nevruz. Khidr was himself overthrown and killed by his own son, Timur-Kwaja, who in turn was ousted five weeks later, possibly by the descendants of Khan Uzbeg. Two of those overthrowers divided the khanate in 1362, with Keldi-Beg ruling in Sarai and Abdullah ruling in Crimea. In the same year, a third overthrower, Bulat-Temur, established himself as emir in the middle Volga region of Bulgar. In the meantime, Murad overthrew Keldi-Beg. In the autumn of that year, the Lithuanian forces under Algirdas defeated the forces of the Crimean lords at the Battle of Blue Waters.

For some reason, Murad rescinded the *iarlyk* giving the authority to rule in Vladimir, taking it from Dmitrii of Suzdal and granting it to Dmitrii of Moscow, who was now almost thirteen years old. A problem, however, existed in the Orda; the powerful emir Mamai supported Abdullah in Crimea as khan and had him also grant the *iarlyk* to Dmitrii of Moscow.[2] Apparently, Abdullah's actions in doing so offended Murad; therefore, he rescinded the *iarlyk* from Dmitrii of Moscow and issued one to Dmitrii of Suzdal. Sending his envoy, Ilyak, with 'thirty Tatars' and Ivan, the ruler of Beloozero, to the court of Dmitrii of Suzdal, Murad had this group accompany the Suzdal forces to Vladimir to reinstate their ruler. The forces of Dmitrii of Moscow assembled and marched on Vladimir, resulting in the ousting of Dmitrii of Suzdal after twelve days back on the throne.[3] Thus, an awkward situation arose wherein the rival Orda khans had appointed different individuals to be the ruler of Vladimir. But before Khan Murad could react, he was overthrown in 1364 by Khayr-Pulad, who in turn was overthrown in 1365 by Aziz. Aziz ruled for two years before being overthrown by the Mamai-supported khan, Abdullah, in 1367. As a result, the *iarlyk* of Abdullah to Dmitrii of Moscow to rule in Vladimir thereby remained in effect.

In the meantime, back in the Vladimir-Suzdal polity, Dmitrii of Suzdal and Dmitrii of Moscow reached an agreement, according to which the former gave up his claim to the throne of Vladimir, in exchange for his daughter Evdokia's marriage to the latter. Their union resulted in the birth of Vasilii, who is the subject of this chapter.

The Young Vasilii Travels to Sarai as a Hostage

In 1383, Dmitrii of Moscow sent his eleven-year-old son Vasilii to the court of Khan Toqtamish to serve as a diplomatic hostage, guaranteeing good, loyal behaviour on Dmitrii's part, in return for the *iarlyk* giving him the authority to rule Vladimir-Suzdal.[4] Holding the sons of local rulers as hostages was a common practice of the Mongol khans to ensure their subjects' obedience. At the same time that Toqtamish required Vasilii of Moscow to accompany him back to Sarai, he also required Aleksandr (the son of Mikhail Aleksandrovich, the ruler of Tver) and Vasilii of Suzdal (the son of Dmitrii Konstantinovich of Suzdal) to do so as well. Long sojourns at the Orda allowed the sons of local Rus rulers to become familiar with the customs and methods of warfare and administration of the Ulus of Jochi. The local Rus rulers made frequent trips to the khanate in a subordinate capacity; presumably, they spent time with their sons, who were kept in Sarai by the khans throughout much of their formative years. As a result, the local rulers and their sons obtained first-hand knowledge of the administrative structures and practices of the khanate. They then applied those structures and practices to the administration of their own domains. It was only after the 1430s, when Moscow and other local Rus rulers stopped going to Sarai to pay obeisance to the Tatar khans, that Muscovite institutions began to be transformed along other lines, lines that we might, in part, call a neo-Eastern Roman Empire.[5]

Vasilii's Betrothal to Sofia

How did the son of the ruler of Moscow and Vladimir go from being a hostage of the khan to being betrothed to and eventually marrying the first cousin of the Lithuanian ruler, when that ruler, Jogaila, and his army had just crushed the army (if we accept the testimony of the German chronicles) of Vasilii's father, Dmitrii of Moscow? The way that this marriage was arranged makes for an interesting story that the chroniclers relished retelling.

The emir Timur had gathered a large empire to the east and south of Toqtamish's realm. Toqtamish fled to Timur's court after his initial failed attempt to overthrow his kinsman Urus, khan of the White Orda. In 1378, Timur aided Toqtamish's takeover of the White Orda. If Timur thought that Toqtamish would be grateful and would become a vassal khan to him, as so many khans were to Mamai, he was mistaken. While Toqtamish was undertaking military operations against his Rus vassals in 1382, Timur undertook military operations against the Azerbaijan ruler in the Caucasus. When Timur withdrew his forces from Azerbaijan, Toqtamish moved into what was presumably a region of weakened resistance and sacked the city of Tabriz during the winter of 1385–6. Toqtamish's actions did not sit well with Timur, who began to undertake military operations against Toqtamish.

While Toqtamish was occupied with Timur, Vasilii escaped from Toqtamish's Orda. The Nikonian Chronicle has two entries regarding Vasilii's escape. The first says that Vasilii escaped in the autumn of 1385, on St George's Day (which falls on 26 November).[6] The chronicle later repeats in more detail that Vasilii 'took counsel with faithful supporters' and escaped first to Podolia, then went to Petru I, the ruler of Moldavia (r. 1375–93).[7] Vasilii followed that visit by going 'secretly to the German land', where Vytautas 'recognized him' and 'kept him' (illus. 51).[8]

The Lithuania that Vasilii encountered was, like the Ulus of Jochi a few years earlier, in a state of turmoil. In this case, the 'German land' refers to the land held by the Order of Teutonic Knights, whither Vytautas had fled following his escape from Krėva Fortress, an escape facilitated by his future wife, Anna, in 1382. The Nikonian Chronicle claims that Vytautas's father, Kęstutis, was murdered.[9] Whether Kęstutis, who was 84 or 85 years old at the time, was murdered or died of natural causes is a matter of debate. What we do know is that Jogaila, the son

51 Vasilii Dmitrievich visiting his future father-in-law, Vytautas: 'And from there, hiding, he went secretly to the German land, and there he was recognized by Kniaz Vitovt Keistovich, who kept him.' *Litsevoi letopisnyi svod*, vol. X, p. 188.

of Algirdas, had both Kęstutis and Vytautas imprisoned in the Krėva Fortress and that Kęstutis died a week later. Kęstutis had worked together with his brother Algirdas, the ruler of Lithuania until the latter's death in 1377. At this point, Jogaila, Algirdas's eldest son by his second wife, Iuliana of Tver, inherited the rulership of the realm. His rule, however, was challenged by Andrei of Polotsk (*c.* 1325–1399), the oldest son of Algirdas by his first wife, Maria of Vitebsk. In 1385, Jogaila reached an agreement with the Polish lords whereby he would marry the eleven-year-old Queen Jadwiga of Poland and become king of Poland. The father of Jadwiga, Louis of Hungary, had ruled as king of Poland from 1370 until his death in 1382. The Treaty of Krėva, as the agreement was called, not only restored a male to the throne of Poland but in effect united Poland and Lithuania, although this was only provisionally. Jogaila had to agree to convert to Roman Catholicism, as well as to have his brothers and all the nobles and dignitaries of Lithuania do the same. In this last part of the agreement, Jogaila did not entirely succeed; only his brothers Skirgaila and Švitrigaila (Svidrigaila), as well as his cousin Vytautas, converted. The rest of the Lithuanian elite remained Eastern Orthodox.

This connection between Vasilii and Vytautas turned out to be a fortunate decision for both men. Vasilii could not have hoped to experience a favourable reception from Jogaila, the ruler of Lithuania, since Lithuania and Moscow were enemies. However, Vytautas harboured resentment towards his cousin Jogaila for his imprisonment, although the two later reached a temporary *modus vivendi*. Additionally, Vytautas could no doubt relate to Vasilii's escape from Toqtamish. He offered his help in exchange for Vasilii's promise to marry Vytautas's daughter Sofia when the time was right, suggesting this as a way to secure an alliance with the Vladimir polity.

Vasilii returned to Moscow on 19 January 1387, according to the Nikonian Chronicle, with 'Polish princes and lords and other Poles, as well as the senior boyars of the *velikii kniaz* [Dmitrii Donskoi] who had gone thither for him.'[10] The marriage between him and Sofia occurred four years later in 1391, on the eve of Vytautas's negotiating his ascension to the throne of Lithuania. We have no evidence of why Vytautas still agreed to the marriage of his daughter with Vasilii, a vassal of his own enemy, the khan of the Ulus of Jochi. Nor do we have much information about the young Sofia, beyond the rather catty remark by the Tver chronicler that she 'possessed the good habit of her father: she was never tired of fornication'.[11] However, she does figure prominently in a chronicle story regarding the marriage of her son, Vasilii, to Maria Iaroslavna in 1433.

In 1385, when the Polish and Lithuanian barons agreed to a personal union of their two realms, Jogaila agreed to convert to Catholicism. The historian of Poland Norman Davies sees Jogaila's decision to convert and accept the throne of Poland as being 'driven . . . by the coldest and most calculated reasons of state'.[12] Jogaila was confronted by ongoing hostilities with the Teutonic Knights on one side and with Poland on the other. Relations with his cousin Vytautas had soured in 1380, when Jogaila had agreed to a truce with the Teutonic Knights, much to Vytautas's displeasure. By agreeing to the Union of Krėva, Jogaila was able not only to end hostilities on one front but to coordinate the forces of Poland and Lithuania against the Teutonic Knights on another by installing his brother, Skirgaila, as the ruler of Lithuania. In 1389, Vytautas attempted to overthrow Skirgaila, leading to the second open conflict between Jogaila and Vytautas. In the process, Vytautas reached an agreement with the Teutonic Knights in 1389 – the same action that had upset him when Jogaila had done so in 1380. Jogaila's plan for a unified Polish-Lithuanian front against the Teutonic Knights was once more in jeopardy. Apparently, Jogaila again made a cold and calculated decision, based on considerations of state. In 1392, Jogaila and Vytautas drew up the Ostrów Agreement, by which Jogaila replaced his brother Skirgaila as the ruler of Lithuania with his cousin, Vytautas. Lithuania thus remained part of a personal union with Poland, and now, Vasilii's father-in-law was the recognized ruler of Lithuania. However, Vytautas's hold on his position was tenuous and he needed all the help he could get to keep it.

In 1399, however, Jadwiga, queen of Poland, died at the age of 24.[13] Her death abrogated the personal nature of the Union of Krėva but not the political relationship between Poland and Lithuania, which was reaffirmed by the Wilno-Radom Act of 1401.

'Of All Rus'

The Moscow rulers continued to rely on the khan in Sarai for the *iarlyk* giving them the authority to rule not only in Moscow but in Vladimir. Dmitrii Donskoi, for example, minted coins that on the obverse stated '*Velikii kniaz* Dmitrii Ivanovich', but on the reverse said in Arabic: 'Sultan Toqtamish: Long may he live.' However, change was in the air. In his will, Dmitrii had described the areas from which each of his sons was supposed to collect the tribute for the khan. After which, he wrote: 'And if God brings about a change regarding the Orda [and] my children do not have to give a payout (*vykhod*) to the Orda, then the tribute (*dan*) that each of my sons collects in his patrimonial principality shall be his.'[14] Apparently, the ruler of Vladimir being freed from vassalage to the Tatar khan was a real enough possibility that Dmitrii thought it necessary to put that contingency in his will.

We do not have exact dates for coins from the time of the reign of Vasilii, but numismatists have divided them into three time periods, depending on the wording: 1389–99, 1399–1410 and 1410–25.[15] This tripartite categorization may be useful for discussing developments during the time when Vasilii was ruling in Moscow.

For his part, shortly after ascending to the throne of Moscow following the death of his father in 1389, Vasilii began to declare himself on the obverse of coins minted in his realm as '*Velikii kniaz* Vasilii of all Rus'. Inserting the phrase 'of all Rus' with his title of '*velikii kniaz*' was clearly aspirational, if not downright cheeky. One can surmise that Vasilii was attempting to counter the claim of the Lithuanian rulers to 'all Rus'. As though to cover his bases, at least until 1399, the reverse of the coins said the same as his father's coins, again in Arabic: 'Sultan Toqtamish: Long may he live!' or 'Sultan Toqtamish: Long may his reign endure!', or 'Sultan Toqtamish Khan: Long may he live!'[16]

The presence of the names of both Vasilii and Toqtamish on the same coins raises the question of where the coins were circulating. Toqtamish's name (even if in Arabic) on coins circulating in the Vladimir-Suzdal polity indicates that Vasilii was the vassal of Toqtamish, whereas the same coins circulating in the Ulus, outside the Vladimir-Suzdal polity, might indicate the opposite. This point was made quite explicitly in a story in the Muscovite chronicles about the negotiations before the Battle of the Vorskla River in 1399, which took place between Vytautas, on one side, and Khan Timur-Qutlugh (who had replaced Toqtamish) and the emir Edigü (1352–1419) on the other.[17] According to the chronicle account, Vytautas and his army had intimidated Timur-Qutlugh, who had agreed not only to be the diplomatic 'son' to Vytautas's 'father' but to pay 'tribute and duties' (*dani i obroky*) to him every year from the entire Orda. However, when Vytautas added that he wanted all the coins of the Orda to be stamped with his own sign (*znamenie Vitovtovo*), Timur-Qutlugh asked for three days to consider this demand. When Timur-Qutlugh told Edigü of Vytautas's request, Edigü objected and said something along the lines of 'Let me talk to him.' What Edigü

52 Coin of Vasilii Dmitrievich, showing a horseman holding a falcon on the obverse and an Arabic legend on the reverse.

told Vytautas, at least according to the chronicle, was that it was appropriate for Timur-Qutlugh to be considered Vytautas's 'son' because he was younger than Vytautas but, if that was the case, Vytautas should be considered the 'son' of Edigü since Edigü was older than him. Consequently, Vytautas should give Edigü the tribute and duties (*dani i obroky*) each year from Lithuania and the Lithuanian coinage should be stamped with Edigü's Orda sign (*moemu Ordinskomu znameni*). On receiving this request, Vytautas broke off negotiations and began to prepare for battle.[18] There is no way to confirm the accuracy of this story and it does appear to be apocryphal. Direct speech, especially when reported in the chronicles, should make us immediately suspicious. What we can take from this story, however, is the importance of signifiers on coins, in terms of who was subordinate to whom.

There was a period in the 1390s, while Toqtamish was at war with Timur, when Vasilii may have felt it was safe to put 'of all Rus' on his coins. We do have other evidence that Vasilii used the term 'of all Rus' elsewhere, but that evidence is not ironclad. *The Charter to the Dvina Land of 1397* has the phrase '*velikii kniaz* Vasilii Dmitrievich of all Rus', but the only copy we have dates to around 1500,[19] which is the same time frame within which Ivan III began using 'of all Rus' regularly in his title, so we cannot entirely rule out an interpolation. Two charters – one from 1402, the other from 1419 – issued by the metropolitan, confirming church courts and their jurisdictions, have the phrase '*kniaz velikii*, Vasilii Dmitrievich of all Rus'.[20] However, none of the extant copies dates back earlier than the reign of Ivan III. In addition, one of the earliest copies (from the end of the fifteenth century) of the 1402 document does not have the phrase 'of all Rus', nor does an eighteenth-century copy in Latin of the same document. Again, we have no definitive evidence one way or the other. Yet, even if we were to conclude that the phrase 'of all Rus' was indeed in the original documents and is not an interpolation, its presence would not be determinative of Vasilii's claim to rule all of Rus. In the case of these two documents, it could simply have been a harmonization with the title of the metropolitan in the same document, whose jurisdiction was styled 'of all Rus'. In the case of the coins, the presence of the phrase 'of all Rus' could have signified that he was the one Rus ruler who was tasked with collecting the khan's tribute (*dan*) from the other Rus rulers.

Previous uses of the term 'of all Rus' by the rulers of Vladimir had been sporadic. Semën had used the term on his seal: 'Seal of *velikii kniaz*

Semën of all Rus'. Although a Certificate of Merit from *velikii kniaz* Ivan Daniilovich Kalita, sent to the Pechora falconers, includes the phrase 'of all Rus' after his name and although the document can be dated to the reign of Ivan II (r. 1328–40), the only copy of the document that we still have dates to the reign of Ivan III (r. 1462–1505), which means that, again, we cannot entirely rule out an interpolation.[21]

The scholar Thomas Noonan, who studied the coinage of Vasilii I, suggested that Vasilii's use of 'of all Rus' was a more modest conception than when it was used later by Ivan III, Vasilii III and Ivan IV. Instead, according to Noonan, 'Vasilii actually had in mind the grand principality of Vladimir, that is, the historic Suzdalia, plus the right to have one's prince in Novgorod.'[22] Thus, whoever the *velikii kniaz* of Vladimir was, he felt justified in meddling in the polities of other rulers, such as Riazan and Smolensk; however, he could not justify conquering or annexing their territory, at least not without the approval of the khan. Noonan went on to write: 'We must try to understand Vasilii's reign on its own terms and not read the sixteenth-century Muscovite version back into it.'[23] Vasilii's insertion of the phrase 'of all Rus' on his coins might be an indication that he had received Toqtamish's support to do so, but the absence of the phrase in other contexts – say, in Vasilii's last will and testament or other official documents – would seem to argue against that idea.

Toqtamish and Timur Have a Falling-Out

Toqtamish was a Chinggisid, a descendant of Chinggis Khan; Timur was not. This difference in lineage provided Toqtamish with higher status in the Turko-Mongolian world. Once Toqtamish gained control of both the Blue and White Ordas of the Jochid Ulus, he began to act as though he had enough power and authority to challenge Timur. The Caucasus continued to be an area of contention between them. Toqtamish was not acting alone; he was able to forge alliances with both the Sufi rulers of Khwarazm and the Chaghatai khan of the Moghuls. Timur undertook successful punitive expeditions against all of them over the course of four years, from 1386 to 1390.

On 18 June 1391, Timur's forces defeated Toqtamish's at the Battle of the Kondurcha River, a sub-tributary of the Volga. Vernadsky has posited a decision on Toqtamish's part at this time to support the Moscow ruler, at the expense of the rulers of the other Rus polities.

Toqtamish did so, according to Vernadsky, in order to garner support against Timur. In exchange for vowing allegiance to Toqtamish, Vasilii received the polity of Nizhnii Novgorod, as well as Gorodets, Meshchera and Tarusa. Vernadsky saw this deal as 'an important step' in the Moscow ruler's attempt to unite eastern Rus areas, 'even if it was achieved by means of dubious morality'.[24] Vernadsky's hypothesis is highly speculative because we do not have any direct evidence that Toqtamish made this calculation. One could perhaps point to what happened next in the Toqtamish–Timur war to justify this hypothesis. When the war resumed in late 1394, after Toqtamish had again moved his military forces into the Caucasus, Timur defeated Toqtamish completely and chased him and the remnants of his army up the Volga. This is in contrast to the events of 1382, when Toqtamish reached the city of Moscow and sacked it, while Timur did not. He did enter Riazan territory because Oleg Ivanovich, the ruler of Riazan, had supported Toqtamish in the most recent battle. However, that was enough to panic the inhabitants of Moscow, who became convinced that Timur planned to attack their city. The Moscow chroniclers even provided an explanation for why the expected attack never occurred – the bringing of the icon of the Mother of God from Vladimir to Moscow by Metropolitan Cyprian.[25]

When Toqtamish was ousted as the khan of the Ulus of Jochi by Edigü and Timur-Qutlugh in 1397, he fled not to Vasilii but to Vytautas, via Kyiv. Toqtamish and Vytautas reached an agreement whereby Vytautas would help Toqtamish to regain the Ulus of Jochi, in return for Vytautas gaining control of Rus.

Neither Vasilii nor Vytautas was an independent ruler. Vasilii was subordinate to the khan of the Ulus of Jochi, while Vytautas was subordinate to Jogaila, the king of Poland and Lithuania. Vasilii did not support his father-in-law in his battles against the Orda; nor does he seem to have supported Edigü and Timur-Qutlugh. Nonetheless, Vytautas attacked Moscow, which was ruled by his son-in-law, Vasilii. During the conflict, Jogaila sent a small number of troops to support Vytautas.

After Vytautas and Toqtamish lost the battle at the Vorskla River, Vasilii, if the categorization of the coins from his reign is correct, began to issue coins without the Arabic signification of the khan. The obverse reads '*Velikii kniaz* Vasilii Dmitrievich' and the reverse reads '*Velikii kniaz* Vasilii of all Rus'. One can conclude from this that Vasilii was attempting to establish independent rulership. However, in 1408, Edigü led an army against Vasilii and besieged Moscow, demanding that Vasilii agree to accept the suzerainty of the khan that Edigü designated. Vasilii's coins from around that time have a restored 'Mongol' reverse, which took various forms until the end of Vasilii's reign in 1425.[26]

Later Relations between Vasilii and Vytautas

In 1398, Vytautas attacked the Tatar forces in Crimea and built a fort there. It was at this point that Lithuania could be said to reach from sea (the Baltic) to sea (the Black Sea). However, this position of power was not to last for long; Vytautas's disastrous loss to Edigü and Temir-Qutlugh occurred the following year.

Švitrigaila, the younger brother of Skirgaila (who were both the sons of Algirdas and Iuliana), joined Vytautas and Toqtamish in the fight at the Vorskla River. Švitrigaila had been imprisoned by Jogaila from 1393 to 1396; when he was released, he visited the Prussians, Hungarians and Livonian Knights to request support to gain control of Lithuania. When these attempts failed, he reconciled temporarily with both Jogaila and Vytautas, but in 1402, he went to the Teutonic Knights to renew his attempts at gaining control of Lithuania. The next year, 1403, Pope Boniface IX forbade the Knights from attacking Lithuania, so Švitrigaila reconciled once more with Jogaila and Vytautas. From 1406 to 1408, Vytautas fought a war against Vasilii of Moscow. Švitrigaila took the opportunity of allying himself with Vasilii in July 1408, to try to take over the rulership of Lithuania. In acknowledgement, he was given the city of Vladimir and surrounding towns for his livelihood. That same year, in November, Edigü attacked Moscow; his army burned and looted the suburbs. Švitrigaila, realizing that Vasilii was not going to be of much help to him, returned to Lithuania in 1409, where Vytautas incarcerated him.

Religion and Politics

Metropolitan Aleksei had been seen to be too pro-Moscow by the patriarchate in Constantinople; thus, they began to appoint metropolitans who were neutral regarding relations between Lithuania and Moscow. The concern was that a metropolitan who was a partisan for Moscow could not effectively minister to the Orthodox congregates of Lithuania. This apprehension was difficult to counter since Aleksei had served as regent, effectively being the head of government of the Moscow-Vladimir polity while *Kniaz* Dmitrii was still a minor.

One point that Algirdas made was that Kyiv, the titular city of the Rus metropolitan, was in Algirdas's jurisdiction. The patriarch of Constantinople tended, with certain exceptions, to want the appointee to be pleasing to the local secular ruler. In order to preserve the unity of the Rus metropolitanate but to mollify the disgruntled Algirdas, Patriarch Philotheos appointed his special envoy, Cyprian, as 'Metropolitan of Kyiv, Rus, and Lithuania' in December 1375, with the stipulation that when the see became vacant (through Aleksei's death, resignation or removal), Cyprian would replace him as the metropolitan of a unified Rus diocese.

When Aleksei died in 1378, however, Dmitrii of Moscow tried to sabotage this plan to have Cyprian succeed Aleksei. He preferred half a loaf to a whole one, if the whole loaf meant accepting Cyprian. In the meantime, a palace coup in Constantinople brought a new emperor, Andronikos IV (the son of the previous emperor, John V), to the throne; he had Philotheos deposed and replaced him with Patriarch Makarios in 1376. Makarios was sympathetic to the solution of a two-metropolitanate system that Dmitrii was now proposing (Algirdas had proposed the same solution in 1355). Other exterior forces were also at play; both Venice and Genoa had an interest in the outcome of the palace coup. Venice supported John V, while Genoa supported his son, Andronikos.

In 1379, Dmitrii of Moscow sent Mikhail-Mitiai, Metropolitan Aleksei's second-in-command, to Constantinople, so that he could be consecrated as the 'Metropolitan of Great Rus', a new designation. On the way, Mitiai's entourage stopped for a time in Sarai to visit the emir Mamai, who told his khan *du jour* to issue the *iarlyk* confirming the privileges of the 'Great Rus' church. The bishop of Suzdal Dionisii, who opposed the entire plan to get Mitiai appointed as the metropolitan, decided to travel to Constantinople separately to argue against the appointment.

In the meantime, as they say, the plot thickened. Before Mitiai's group had reached Constantinople, the previous emperor, John V, ousted his usurping son and returned to the throne. He had Makarios deposed and a new patriarch, Neilos, was appointed. Just before reaching Constantinople, when he was within sight of the city, according to the *Tale concerning Mitiai* (*Povest o Mitiaia*), Mitiai died (illus. 53). The church officials who were with him at the time of his death had

Mitiai buried in Genoese-controlled Galata. Mitiai's deputy, Pimen, managed to convince Patriarch Neilos that Dmitrii had previously decided that Pimen himself should be consecrated as the metropolitan of Great Rus.[27]

Cyprian, meanwhile, considered himself the one and only metropolitan of 'Kyiv and all Rus', as Patriarch Philotheos had intended; he sent a letter to two monks (named Sergii and Feodor), saying that anyone who opposed his assumption of that dignity risked being excommunicated.[28] Dmitrii, for his part, after the events at Snipes' Field, accepted Cyprian as the legitimate metropolitan and had Pimen imprisoned when he returned to Moscow in 1381. However, after Toqtamish sacked Moscow in 1382, Dmitrii turned against Cyprian, released Pimen and acknowledged him to be the metropolitan of Great Rus.

Patriarch Neilos, according to one report, was incensed when he found out that Dmitrii had arrested Pimen; he excommunicated Dmitrii and placed the Moscow-Vladimir polity under interdict. To find a solution to the problem, Neilos had previously summoned a church council in 1380, which decided that Cyprian's position should be styled as metropolitan 'of Lithuania and Little Rus' and that Pimen's position should be that 'of Kyiv and Great Rus'. The council explicitly rejected the idea that this arrangement would establish a precedent for the continual establishment of two metropolitanates in Rus because it stated that when Cyprian died, the two sees would be combined under Pimen. However, it did not specify whether the two sees would be combined if Pimen died first. Cyprian was not happy with the decision of the council but accepted it. However, the intrigues do not end there.

Patriarch Neilos sent Bishop Dionisii of Suzdal to Moscow as his personal envoy. Dionisii, who had not been in favour of the two-metropolitanate plan in the first place, reported back to the patriarch that Metropolitan Pimen should be deposed. Neilos did so in 1384, but instead of restoring Cyprian as the only metropolitan of all Rus, he appointed Dionisii as the metropolitan of Great Rus. Dionisii was unable to accept that appointment because, on the way back from Constantinople to Moscow, he stopped in Kyiv – perhaps to meet with Cyprian – and never left. Dionisii died in Kyiv the next year. Pimen continued to plead his case that he should remain metropolitan of Great Rus and even returned to Moscow in 1388, to try to convince Dmitrii. Pimen died in 1389 upon his return to Constantinople, still unsuccessful in his attempts at regaining the metropolitan see of Great Rus.

53 The death of Michael-Mitiai: 'And they sailed on the sea, they had already crossed all the sea spaces and were already on the shores of Constantinople, they saw that near Constantinople, suddenly Mitiai became ill and died on the boat.' *Litsevoi letopisnyi svod*, vol. IX, p. 262.

When the dust of this affair settled, only Cyprian remained standing; in 1390 he was accepted by all sides, including the newly crowned Vasilii of Moscow, as the one and only metropolitan of all Rus. If all these plots and counterplots seem confusing, rest assured that they are. They are made doubly so by the contradictory misrepresentations in subsequent contemporary accounts and documents, the various authors each having their own axe to grind.

The Offspring

Vasilii and Sofia had nine children that we know about. Their oldest daughter, Anna (1393–1417), married the future basileus John (Ioannes) VIII Palaiologos (r. 1425–48), but she died before he ascended to the throne.[29] If she had lived at least until 1449, she would have been the aunt of Zoe Palaiologina, who married Ivan III in 1472; Zoe's father, Thomas, was a brother of John, Anna's husband.

The Great Sakkos of Metropolitan Photios shows Vasilii of Moscow with his wife Sofia on the front of the garment and Anna, his daughter, as the wife of Ioannes Palaiologos on the back (illus. 55). The idea was to show the marriage ties between Moscow and Lithuania on one side and those with Moscow and the Greeks on the other. Dimitri Obolensky dated the Great Sakkos to the period from 1414 to 1417, that is, just after the marriage of Anna and John in 1414 and just before the death of Anna from the plague in 1417.[30] Significantly, between the images of the two couples appear the images of three saints – the Lithuanian Christian martyrs who were killed by order of Algirdas, the father of Jogaila.

Among the other children of Vasilii and Sofia, the most prominent was Vasilii, the future ruler of Moscow and Vladimir. When his father, Vasilii I Dmitrievich, died in 1425, a dispute arose over who should succeed him. According to the principles of collateral succession that were effective in Rus until then, Iurii, the eldest brother of Vasilii I, was next in line. However, Vasilii I wanted his son to succeed him, overruling the collateral succession. Such attempts by ruling fathers to ensure

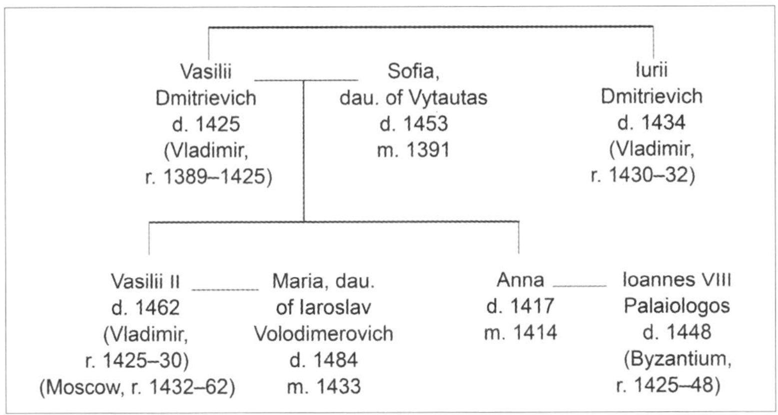

54 Vasilii Dmitrievich and his brother Iurii, and selected children of Vasilii.

that their sons succeeded them, rather than one of their brothers or cousins, had occurred before. The justification in this case, insofar as there was one, was that the previous two occurrences of succession to the throne of Moscow had been from father to eldest son. For Iurii's part, he referred to the will and testament of his father, Dmitrii Donskoi, which stated that when Dmitrii's son Vasilii died, the succession should go to 'my son who follows him', that is, the next brother in line, who at that time was Iurii.[31]

Before this, the last instance of lateral succession was in 1353, when Ivan II Ivanovich succeeded his brother, Semën Ivanovich. When Ivan II died in 1359, he had no brothers or cousins who could claim that their father had ruled in Moscow. Therefore, the succession went to his eldest son, Dmitrii. When Dmitrii died in 1389, he also had no brothers or cousins who could claim that their father ruled in Moscow. Therefore, the succession again went to his eldest son, Vasilii I Dmitrievich. Was that sufficient to establish a new principle of succession? Apparently not, because Iurii contested his nephew's claim. Thus, the matter was put to Khan Ulugh Muhammad in 1431. This problem was more significant than just the matter of who ruled in Moscow because, since 1363, the ruler of Moscow had been also the ruler of Vladimir, the ostensible capital of the Vladimir–Suzdal polity. It was still possible, however, for the khan to appoint one ruler in Moscow and another ruler in Vladimir, as Khan Nevruz-Beg had done in 1360 when he appointed Dmitrii Konstantinovich of Suzdal as the ruler of Vladimir, at a time when Dmitrii Ivanovich was recognized as the ruler in Moscow although he was still a minor.

Likewise, in 1425, Vasilii, the son of Vasilii I, was still a minor at ten years old, having been born in 1415. His mother, Sofia Vitovtna, served as regent.[32] Vytautas supported Vasilii as the ruler in Vladimir, but what happened between 1425, when Vasilii I died, and 1431, when his son Vasilii and his brother Iurii went to Sarai to have the disputed succession decided by the khan is not clear. The Muscovite sources are biased in Vasilii Vasilevich's favour, as one might expect since Vasilii won out in the dispute and became the ruler of Moscow.

Upon the death of his son-in-law Vasilii I, Vytautas transferred his support to his daughter Sofia, who was acting as regent for Vasilii's son, who was a minor. However, when Vytautas died in 1430, Sofia lost the support and protection of her father, while Vasilii Vasilevich lost the support and protection of his maternal grandfather. Iurii seized that opportunity to go to Sarai and obtain the *iarlyk* to rule in Vladimir. Here the Muscovite chronicles provide a narrative regarding what happened in Sarai. We have no way of confirming the accuracy of this narrative, but it does tell us something about the Muscovite chroniclers' understanding of events. They tell us that at first Ulugh Muhammad was inclined to side with Iurii, but a boyar, Ivan Dmitrievich Vsevolozh, persuaded the khan to choose Vasilii, using the argument that Iurii was too much in favour of the new Lithuanian leader, Švitrigaila. However, Iurii had his allies as well. 'An important lord' (according to the Muscovite chronicles), possibly a *qarachi bey*, one of the four leading lords of the khanate, who was named Shirin Tiagin, promised Iurii the polity. The name indicates a member of the Shirin clan, which is perhaps the most prominent clan of the Orda. Both Iurii and Shirin Tiagin went to spend the winter in Crimea. In the meantime, Vasilii stayed with the *daruga* (governor) of Moscow, Min-Bulat, at his residence in Sarai.

With both Iurii and Shirin Tiagin away, the boyar Ivan Dmitrievich Vsevolozh began to lobby for Vasilii. He told Min-Bulat and the other Tatar 'lords' that if they allowed the khan to choose Iurii, then Shirin Tiagin would determine what the khan did and would not listen to them. In addition, if Iurii were *velikii kniaz* and Švitrigaila, whom Iurii 'called his brother', was the ruler of Lithuania, then 'Tiagin will manipulate the khan without consulting you.' This was a fallacious argument, not mentioning that the previous ruler of Lithuania, Vytautas, was Vasilii's father-in-law. In addition, it does not follow that if the rulers of Lithuania and Moscow were friends, then Tiagin would decide what the khan should do.

When the time came for each side to present their arguments, the Nikonian Chronicle said that Vasilii based his claim to be chosen as *velikii kniaz* 'because his father and grandfather' had been *velikii kniaz*. This was the traditional formula that had been used since the eleventh century to justify a claim to a throne in Rus. Iurii, according to the Chronicle, in turn 'based his case upon the chronicles, the old charters, and the Will of his father, Dmitrii [Donskoi]'. The Chronicle neglects to mention, however, that Iurii's father and grandfather had also been *velikii kniaz*.

At this point the boyar, Vsevolozh, spoke on Vasilii's behalf, pointing out to the khan that Vasilii sought to be the *velikii kniaz* of a polity 'that is part of your ulus', which gave him the right to decide who was appointed *velikii kniaz*.[33] But Iurii, according to Vsevolozh, wanted the

55 Vasilii Dmitrievich and Sofia Vitovtna on the Great Sakkos (liturgical garment) of Metropolitan of Kyiv and All Rus Photios, 1414–17, Byzantine embroidery sewn from azure silk with gold and silver threads, trimmed with green taffeta and pearls.

rulership not on the basis of the khan's right of bestowal but on the basis of 'a charter of his dead father'. Using tactics similar to the fallacious argument that he used at the residence of Min-Bulat the previous winter, Vsevolozh argued that the khan would lose his freedom to choose who should be *velikii kniaz* if he were to heed the stipulations of Dmitrii Donskoi's will. Vsevolozh added, in a contradictory flourish, that Vasilii's father Vasilii, the previous *velikii kniaz*, had given the polity to his son. Vsevolozh explained that Vasilii's bestowal was 'in agreement with your [khan's] bestowal'. Unlike the will of Dmitrii (Donskoi), which designated 'my son who follows him', the will of Vasilii I said nothing about succession.

Again, we have no way of confirming whether Vsevolozh made these arguments or, if he did, whether they had any impact on the proceedings. However, we do know that after the khan chose Vasilii in 1432, the Moscow chronicles dropped the designation of '*velikii kniaz* of Vladimir' and began to treat Moscow as the new capital of the polity. Why, then, is Vladimir no longer considered the capital of the Vladimir-Suzdal polity? Does this change represent the genuine fact that the new capital was Moscow, or does it represent a covering-up of the fact that Iurii was still the *velikii kniaz* of Vladimir? In one sense, this change could just reflect the reality that the Moscow princes had co-opted the Vladimir-Suzdal polity as their own.

But the story does not end there. Vsevolozh, as a reward for securing the role of *velikii kniaz* for Vasilii, wanted Vasilii to marry his daughter. However, both Vasilii and his mother Sofia had chosen Maria, the daughter of Iaroslav Volodimerovich of Borovsk. Vsevolozh, the chronicles claim, saw this decision as a slight and went to Vasilii's uncle Iurii, the very one he had argued against in Sarai, advising him to take over the polity. Iurii heeded Vsevolozh's advice and immediately sent for his sons, who were at the wedding of Vasilii and Maria in Moscow. Meanwhile, at the wedding, the *namestnik* of Rostov noticed that Iurii's son Vasilii was wearing a golden belt, which he identified as the belt that had been given to Dmitrii (Donskoi) at his wedding to

56 Pavel P. Chistakov, *Velikaia kniaginia Sofia Vitovtna Grabbing the Belt from Vasilii Kosoi at the Wedding of Velikii kniaz Vasilii* II, 1861, oil on canvas.

Evdokia Dmitrievna in 1366 by Dmitrii Konstantinovich of Suzdal, as part of the dowry for his daughter.

According to the chronicle, the *tysiatskii* Vasilii had substituted another, smaller belt for the original one and gave the original to his son Mikula, who was married to Evdokia's sister Maria. For some reason, Mikula gave this belt to Vsevolozh, who in turn gave it as a dowry present to Andrei Volodimerovich when he married Vsevolozh's daughter. When Andrei died, Vsevolozh reclaimed possession of the belt and gave it to Vasilii Iurevich when the latter married his granddaughter, who was the daughter of Andrei. This is why Vasilii Iurevich was wearing the belt at the wedding. When the belt was identified, Sofia Vitovtna leapt into action and stripped him of the belt (illus. 56). So, now Iurii Dmitrievich, the uncle of the *velikii kniaz*, had two motivations to wage war against his nephew – the advice of Vsevolozh and the humiliation that his own son had endured at the hands of Sofia.

The Denouement

In 1410, the combined forces of Poland and Lithuania, under the control of Jogaila and Vytautas, dealt a devastating defeat to the Teutonic Knights at the Battle of Grunwald. Although the Knights did not lose much territory by the Treaty of Toruń (1411), their financial situation was compromised and their military strength was severely crippled. This meant a decline and eventual end to the power of the Knights in eastern Europe.

In 1411, Jalal al-Din, the son of Toqtamish, overthrew the emir Edigü and granted the right to rule Nizhnii Novgorod to local rulers, taking it away from Vasilii I. Vasilii, in turn, went to Sarai in 1412, bearing gifts for Jalal al-Din and spent several months there, but his visit seems to have had no effect on Jalal al-Din before he was assassinated. Vasilii returned to Moscow; in 1414, taking advantage of the ongoing turmoil in the Orda, he sent his brother Iurii with a military force to take back Nizhnii Novgorod.

By 1425, the prospects for Moscow being able to throw off vassalage to the khan in Sarai were still dim, while the prospects for Moscow to take over all of Rus were even dimmer. The Jochid Ulus continued to be the most powerful military and political force in the western steppe area and Central Asia after the breaking down of Timur's empire. Lithuania remained a potent military presence that could, in theory, draw upon the resources of the kingdom of Poland if needed, but the Moscow rulers had none of these advantages. In addition, the Moscow-Vladimir polity was about to devolve into a thirty-year-long, cruelly fought war of succession that debilitated the polity, both militarily and economically. However, the story of how they managed to accomplish this seemingly impossible feat of throwing off vassalage to the Tatar khans and declaring themselves the sole dynasty of Rus is the subject of the next chapter.

12

Ivan III Vasilevich and His Family

During the reign of Ivan III (1462–1505), the ruling family of Moscow became a dynasty and the Suzdal-Vladimir-Moscow polity became a state. How these two transformations occurred is quite an amazing story. Ivan III made numerous changes to the organizational structure of Muscovy, most likely being influenced by Greek refugees from Morea. He brought in Italian engineers and architects, who gave the Moscow Kremlin the look that it has today. He also limited the power that his younger brothers could wield. In many respects, he continued the policies of his father, Vasilii II, including bringing refugees from the Tatar elite into the ranks of his military leadership, thereby challenging the power and authority of the Tatar khans.

Mise-en-scene

After Vasilii II Vasilevich received the *iarlyk* to rule from Khan Ulugh Muhammad in 1432, he fought a long war of succession against his uncle Iurii Dmitrievich and Iurii's two sons, Vasilii Kosoi and Dmitrii Shemiaka. During that war, Vasilii was defeated by Iurii at a battle on the Mogza River in March 1434 and was forced to concede the rulership of the Vladimir-Suzdal polity to Iurii. Vasilii fled to Sarai to solicit help from the khan. Three months later, in June, Iurii died of natural causes and Iurii's son Vasilii claimed the right to rule. His younger brother, Dmitrii Shemiaka, disagreed and formed an alliance with Vasilii Vasilevich that ousted Vasilii Iurevich from Moscow. When Vasilii Iurevich was captured, Vasilii Vasilevich ordered that he should be blinded. This action on the part of Vasilii II alienated Dmitrii Shemiaka, who turned against his cousin.

In the meantime, Ulugh Muhammad was overthrown as khan in Sarai and took his followers with him to travel further up the Volga, where he founded a khanate at Kazan. In 1439, Ulugh Muhammad besieged Moscow; in 1445, near Suzdal, he captured Vasilii II, who had only a relatively small 1,500-man force with him. Ulugh Muhammad demanded and received a large ransom for his return. When Vasilii returned to Moscow in 1446 with a contingent of Tatar horsemen, he was captured by Dmitrii Shemiaka, who did to him what Vasilii had done to Dmitrii's older brother twelve years earlier – namely, he had him blinded. However, that did not stop Vasilii II from gathering new forces and defeating Dmitrii Shemiaka in 1447 to reclaim the throne. A truce was drawn up, but Vasilii renewed hostilities in 1450 and Shemiaka fled to Novgorod. Nineteen years earlier, in 1431, Novgorod had reached an agreement with Švitrigaila, the ruler of Lithuania, whereby Švitrigaila's nephew became the ruler of Novgorod, thus placing it outside Vasilii's authority. This agreement was in accord with the peace treaty of 1326 between Lithuania, Novgorod, Polotsk, Smolensk and the Teutonic Order. According to this peace treaty, Lithuania took on an obligation to defend Novgorod against Swedish incursion. In return, it received revenue from the Novgorodian towns that faced Swedish territory.[1] In 1389, the Lithuanian ruler of Novgorod, Lengvenis, a son of Algirdas, paid homage to the Polish King Władysław II in Sandomierz; according to some historians, this in effect made Novgorod a vassal polity of the kingdom of Poland.[2]

The Novgorodians attempted to play off one powerful neighbour against the other, by choosing who should rule them.[3] Thus, in 1470, when they felt threatened by Vasilii II's son and successor, Ivan III, the government of Novgorod chose Michael Olelkovich, a Ruthenian nobleman in the service of the Lithuanian ruler, who was a cousin of Ivan III as well as the uncle of Ivan's daughter-in-law, Elena. Ivan was following the policy that his father had begun of claiming Novgorod as the patrimony of the ruler of Moscow. Both Vasilii II and Ivan based their claim, in part, on a request by the Novgorodians in 1314 to Iurii Daniilovich of Moscow that he should rule as the *kniaz*. The idea was to protect them from the encroachment of Mikhail of Tver, who was then the ruler of Vladimir. However, in 1317, Novgorod reached a separate agreement with Mikhail. Nonetheless, Vasilii II and Ivan used the 1314 agreement, along with other fourteenth-century agreements, between the rulers of Moscow and the townsmen of Novgorod to justify their claim, disregarding the fact that the Novgorodians had made similar agreements with other rulers over time. It was part of the stipulation of the traditional collateral system of succession that the townsmen had a say in who was appointed as their *kniaz*. Ivan III was to put an end to that townsmen-approval principle for both Novgorod and Pskov.

Ivan III Keeps His Brothers at Bay

When Vasilii II eventually won out over Dmitrii Shemiaka in 1453, he appointed his own eldest son, Ivan (later to be Ivan III) as co-ruler, following the model of the Eastern Roman Empire.[4] Nonetheless, in his will, Vasilii had divided the revenue-producing towns among his five sons. Ivan received the bulk of the towns (fourteen), while the rest (twelve) were divided among Ivan's four brothers. In addition, once Ivan began to rule on his own after his father's death, he was dependent on his brothers for military support. Throughout the rest of his reign after 1462, Ivan worked to eliminate that dependency. He also continued his father's policy of requiring other Rus *kniazi* to receive their *iarlyki* from him, rather than from the khan in Sarai. In this, Ivan was aided by the khans of the Crimean Khanate, another of the khanates that succeeded the Ulus of Jochi.

Iurii, the eldest of Ivan's brothers, died intestate in September 1472, at which point Ivan seized his land. The next two brothers – Boris and Andrei the Elder – objected to this high-handedness. Ivan gave them each a town as compensation; they signed an agreement with Ivan that in return, they would be loyal to him and not have separate dealings with foreign powers. All three agreed to respect each other's lands and to allow servitors to leave their service for one of the other brothers, as they saw fit (free agency). Boris and Andrei the Elder also agreed to acknowledge the Tsarevich Daniar, a Tatar, or any Tatar tsarevich in Ivan's service as being equal to Ivan in status (that is, as 'elder brother'). For whatever reason, the youngest brother, Andrei the Younger, was not part of that agreement, but he still seems to have remained loyal to Ivan throughout.

In 1480, when Ivan and Khan Ahmed of the Orda had their stand-off across the Ugra River (illus. 57), Boris and Andrei the Elder refused to dispatch troops to help Ivan. Instead, they repaired to Velikie Luki, on the border with Lithuania, and threatened to defect. According to an isolated chronicle account, their complaints against Ivan involved

57 Stand on the Ugra, 1480. Miniature from the 16th-century Illustrated Chronicle Codex: 'And they beat many of ours with arrows and squeaks, and their arrows fell on our flanks, and never hit them and we beat them off from the shore.' *Litsevoi letopisnyi svod*, vol. XVI, p. 462.

his parsimony towards them in 1472 and again in 1479, after they had helped him capture Novgorod the previous year. Nonetheless, Andrei and Boris complained that Ivan's actions were in breach of the 1472 agreement, so they probably felt that they were no longer obligated to abide by it either. Whether Kazimierz, the Polish king and ruler of Lithuania, showed no interest in their defecting to Lithuania, as the chronicles report, or whether they were merely threatening to defect to broker a better deal with Ivan, it is difficult to tell. Whatever the truth of it, they negotiated with Ivan and continued to support him.

The next year, 1481, Andrei the Younger died and left all his possessions to Ivan. That bequest avoided any repetition of the contestations of 1472, when Iurii had died. Then, in September 1491, Ivan, according to the Nikonian Chronicle, 'renounced the pledge he had given to his brother', Andrei the Elder, and had him arrested.[5] The Ioasaf Chronicle tells us that Ivan had requested that both Andrei and Boris should send their commanders to help the Tatar khan, Mengli Giray, against the khan of the Orda, but Andrei refused.[6] Andrei died in captivity, two years later. Ivan did not arrest his other brother, Boris, but Boris died in 1494 of natural causes, to the best of our knowledge.

The Beginnings of the Establishment of a Dynasty

To create the illusion that Ivan was part of a dynasty of rulers, history had to be rewritten. In 1489, when Nicholas Poppel, ambassador of the Holy Roman emperor Maximilian, conveyed Maximilian's offer to make Ivan a king, Ivan replied rather haughtily:

> By God's Grace, we have been sovereign in our own land since the beginning, since our ancestors, and we beg God to grant us and our children to abide forever in the same state, namely, as sovereigns in our own land; and so beforehand we did not desire to be appointed by anyone, so now too do we not desire it.[7]

This statement conveniently overlooks the fact that all Rus rulers since 1240 had been appointed by the Tatar khan, and that Ivan III was the first ruler of Vladimir and Moscow not to be thus appointed, being raised to the position of co-ruler by his father in 1453. Nonetheless, it was part of the rewriting of history that the Moscow rulers and their ecclesiastical proponents were undertaking, to construct a dynastic narrative.

Ivan used the title of *tsar* sparingly and judiciously, to grant safe passage to merchants and diplomats through his realm (a function that the khan of the Orda used to exercise). It was during Ivan's reign that the construct of the Muscovite rulers being descended from Riurik (that is, inheritors of the Riurikid dynasty) came into existence, thus giving their particular family line precedence over other claimants, notably the Lithuanians, to be rulers of Rus. The entire legend was developed in three interrelated texts that were composed at the end of the fifteenth to the beginning of the sixteenth centuries – the Chudov *Tale* (*Povest*), the *Story about the Vladimir kniazi* (*Skazanie o kniaziakh Vladimirskikh*) and the *Letter* (*Poslanie*) *of Spiridon-Savva*. There is some disagreement in the historiography about their exact relationship and their dates of composition. Nonetheless, there is agreement that it was these texts and at this time that the attempt was made to connect the rulers of the Vladimir-Moscow polity with Riurik and, through Riurik, with a kinsman of Augustus Caesar named Prus, as well as to connect them with

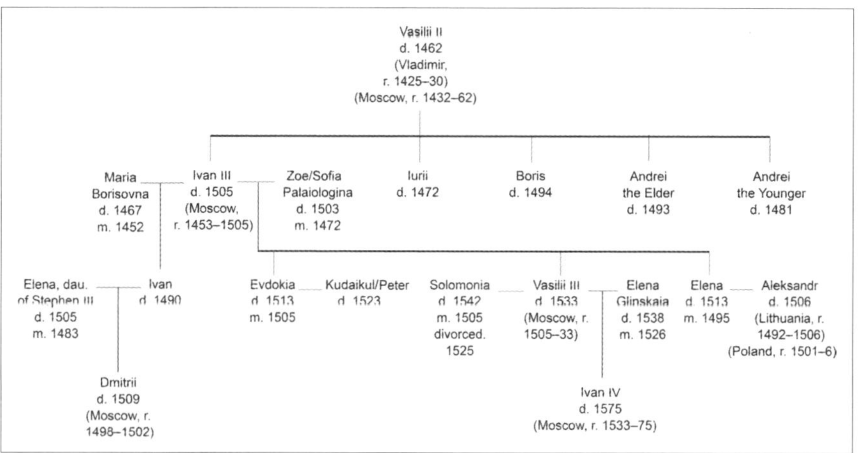

58 Selected members of Ivan Vasilievich's family.

the Byzantine emperor, Constantine IX Monomakh.[8] Thus, it was made to appear that the rulers of Moscow were, genealogically speaking, not merely the most worthy but indeed the only ruling family to form the Rus dynasty.

The Betrothal and Marriage of Ivan and Maria Borisovna

By 1447, when Boris Aleksandrovich of Tver changed his allegiance and formed an alliance with Vasilii II against Dmitrii Shemiaka, he confirmed the agreement by betrothing his daughter Maria to Vasilii's eldest son, Ivan. Vasilii, with the help of Boris, defeated Shemiaka, who fled to Novgorod, where he was poisoned in 1453. As a result of the defeat of Shemiaka, Ivan Aleksandrovich of Mozhaisk, the grandson of Dmitrii Donskoi and the father-in-law of Boris Aleksandrovich, who had gone over to support Shemiaka against Vasilii II, fled with his family to Lithuania.

Iosif Volotskii tells a story in his *Monastic Rule* concerning the events when a monk named Evfrosin returned to Savvateev Hermitage, some 4 kilometres (2½ mi.) north of the Volga, in the region of Tver. Boris sent Maria to him; at the time, she was betrothed but not yet married to Ivan. Iosif tells us that 'she was possessed of a powerful disease'.[9] The archimandrites, hegumens and boyars who accompanied her pleaded with Evfrosin to pray for her; if successful, those prayers would 'have reconciled two kingdoms'. The implication is that if she did not recover and afterwards marry the young Ivan, then the agreement

59 Forensic reconstruction by Sergei A. Nikitin of the face of Sofia Palaiologina, based on remains exhumed in December 1994 from an underground extension of the Archangel Cathedral in the Moscow Kremlin.

between her father and Ivan's father would be at an end. At first, Evfrosin refused, but when she became deathly ill, he relented and prayed for her and she recovered.

Ivan and Maria married in 1452. She was around ten years old, while Ivan was twelve. They had one child – also named Ivan – in 1458. Maria died in 1467, at the age of 24 or 25.[10] Although we cannot confirm the veracity of Iosif's story, it might indicate that Maria was not all that healthy to begin with. Without access to her medical records, we have no way of knowing whether her childhood illness was connected with her early demise.

Betrothal and Marriage to Zoë/Sofia Palaiologina

On 12 November 1472, according to the Muscovite chronicles, Zoë Palaiologina (*c.* 1455–1503, illus. 59) entered the city of Moscow with her entourage, after a long trip from Rome. She was the daughter of the last *despotes* of Morea, Thomas, and the niece of the last Byzantine emperor, Constantine XI. Shortly after her arrival in Moscow, she married Ivan. Somewhere along the line, she adopted the name Sofia. Vernadsky asserted that Metropolitan Filipp changed her name at the marriage ceremony in 1472, but he did not cite any source supporting that assertion.[11] There is a second tradition – that her name was changed in Rome. The Rus chronicles refer to her as 'Sofia' even while she is still in Rome and do not mention any name change. If the change was made in Rome, then the choice of 'Sofia' seems an odd one for the Catholics to make. 'Sofia' is not any less Greek than 'Zoë'. We do have other examples, however, of women being named Sofia in fifteenth-century Catholic domains – for example, Sofia of Bavaria Wittelsbach (1376–1425), queen of Bohemia – and in East Slavic lands, for example, Sofia Vitovtna (1371–1453), the daughter of the ruler of Lithuania; Sofia Dmitrievna, the daughter of Dmitrii Donskoi; Sofia, the wife of *velikii kniaz* Mikhail Iaroslavich of Tver and Vladimir; and Sofia, the wife of the *kniaz* Vsevolod Aleksandrovich of Khom (*s.a.* 1365). Changing the given name of a royal bride was common practice in the Middle Ages and subsequently became common in Muscovy.[12]

The Role of Morean Greeks in Moscow

The Despotate of Morea, which today is in the Peloponnese, fell to the Ottoman Turks a few years after the fall of Constantinople. Rulership of the Despotate of Morea during the fifteenth century was closely connected with the rulership of the Byzantine Empire.[13] In 1443, Constantine, the son of the Byzantine emperor Manuel II, became the despot of the Morea, and in 1449, after the death of Emperor John VIII, to whom Anna, the daughter of Vasilii I, had been married, he became emperor. In 1450, his brothers, Thomas and Demetrios, divided the Morean despotate. In 1453, Constantinople fell to the Ottoman sultan Mehmed II, and Constantine was killed. From 1458 to 1460, Thomas and Demetrios renewed the conflict with Mehmed II. In 1461, Demetrios submitted to Mehmed at Mistra. Afterwards, Thomas fled with his family to Corfu and then left his family there while he travelled to Rome, where he died in 1465. Following her father's death in that year, Zoë was brought to Rome and was made a ward of the papacy. At that time, Pope Paul II (r. 1464–71) placed her under the custodianship of the Byzantine churchman, humanist and Roman Catholic cardinal Basilios Bessarion (1403–1472). Bessarion was a supporter of the union of the Eastern Orthodox Church with the Roman Catholic Church. Pope Paul II, who also hoped to unite the Eastern and Western churches, directed Bessarion to help arrange the betrothal of Zoë to Ivan III. The Moscow chronicles testify that Cardinal Bessarion sent 'a Greek, Iurii by name' (Georgios Tarchaniotes) to Ivan III in 1469.[14] Georgios Tarchaniotes had been the chamberlain of Zoë's father in Morea.[15] Our sources provide various estimates of the numbers of Greeks and Italians in Zoë's entourage on her journey to Moscow, ranging from sixty to one hundred people.[16] These individuals were subsequently instrumental in conducting diplomatic affairs for the Muscovite government and in bringing Italian architects and engineers to Muscovy.

Until the middle of the fifteenth century, Muscovite governmental administration was similar to that of a steppe khanate, based on personal rule and allegiances.[17] By the end of the fifteenth century, the Muscovite governmental administration had already begun the transformation into a dynastic state, similar to that of other dynastic states in Afro-Eurasia. This transformation took place both in terms of governing and the physical manifestation of power and authority. The changes involved in this transformation included the beginnings of the establishment of a law code (the *Sudebnik* of 1497), setting up the means of maintaining a self-supporting military force through *pomeste* grants (1482), the creation of the symbols of dynastic rule and the conversion of that administration from a personal to a professional apparatus. In Georgios Tarchaniotes's description of the Russian military in 1486, for example, he states that Ivan III could gather between 200,000 and 300,000 horses within fifteen days from 'every city and town, as well as in each province . . . paid for by the communities, towns, and villages for the duration' while Ivan wanted to use them.[18] These transformations coincided with the influx of experienced Greek governmental personnel and it may have been the Morean Greeks who played an essential part in that transition.[19]

Greek administrators were prominent in Muscovy in the late fifteenth century. Demetrios Kabakes (Cavathis) Ralevs (Raoul), like Georgios Tarchaniotes, came from Morea via Italy and was a student of Georgios Gemistos Plethon (*c.* 1355–1452/4), a Platonist philosopher at the Morean court.[20] Demetrios accompanied Zoë/Sofia on her trip to Moscow in May 1472 and stayed there until January 1473. He later returned to Moscow as an envoy in 1474.[21] Demetrios has been described as a 'daring social and political reformer', but his brief stays may have only given him the opportunity to convey his philosophical views of governing. Subsequently, Andreas Palaiologos, the titular despot of Morea and the brother of Sofia, visited Moscow in 1480 and again in the winter of 1489/90. Andreas's daughter, Maria, went to Moscow to marry Vasilii Mikhailovich, the *kniaz* of Vereia.[22] Prominent among the Greeks who served in government positions were the representatives of four families: the Angelos-Doukas, the Lascaris, the Rhallis (Ralev, Larev) and the Tarchaniotes (Trakhaniot).[23] They would have encountered the descendants of Greeks who were already part of the government structure. The most outstanding of these was Dmitrii Vladimirovich Khovrin, who was from a Greek family that came to Moscow in 1403; he served as state treasurer (1491–1509) under both Ivan III and Vasilii III and is listed as a boyar between 1492 and 1494.[24]

According to the Muscovite chronicles, Ivan Ralev Paleolog (Johannes Ralles Palaiologos) arrived in Moscow *s.a.* 1485 'with his wife and children' (illus. 60).[25] The Rus chronicles state that he and his family came from Constantinople. His sons, Dmitrii and Manuil, became boyars and were active in Muscovite government service for over seventeen years (from 1488 to 1505), also serving as envoys to the courts of other rulers in Western Eurasia.[26] Their task on those trips was to recruit artisans, craftsmen and other specialists for Ivan III.[27] According to the information supplied by the chronicles, Dmitrii and Manuil were sent as envoys to Rome, Venice and Milan in 1488, with a report about the victory of Muscovite forces against Kazan.[28] In 1489/90, they returned to Moscow with Andreas, the brother of Sofia, as well as with Pietro Antonio Solari and his pupil, known only as 'Zamantonii', both of whom were described in the chronicles as 'masters of walls and palaces'.[29] The chronicles also tell us that they brought 'the cannon monger Jacob, along with his wife; the silver master Khristofor, with two pupils

60 The arrival of Ivan Ralev and his family in Moscow. *Litsevoi letopisnyi svod*, vol. XIII, p. 31.

from Rome; Albert the German from Lübeck; Karl with his pupil from Milan, Pietro Raika, who was a Greek from Venice; chaplain of the white monks of the Augustinian order Ivan Spasitel the organ player; as well as Leon, the Jewish doctor from Venice.'[30]

The double-headed eagle, which became the Russian state symbol, was similar to and could have been based on the Palaiologan family symbol (including a *sympilema*, or dynastic cypher, on the breast of the bird). Zoë/Sofia was entitled to its use, not because she was the niece of the last Palaiologan emperor of Constantinople, but rather because she was the daughter of the ruler of Morea. Gustave Alef, an American historian of Russia, asserted that 'the prototype for the Russian eagle is Byzantine, specifically Morean.'[31] He did not mention on what basis he made that assertion, but he hypothesized that Ivan III adopted the symbol as a counter to the Holy Roman emperor, whose insignia was also a double-headed eagle. Alef's hypothesis could be supported by the evidence of the Muscovite emblem from 1497 (illus. 61), which shows a double-headed eagle that is very similar to that of the Habsburgs (that is, showing a crown on each eagle's head). However, the double-headed eagle with a crown over each head was also the emblem of Morea. We know this from representations in the Church of St Demetrios in Mistra, where Constantine Palaiologos was crowned as the despotes in 1443.

61 Seal of Ivan III, 1497. St George and the dragon on the obverse and a crowned two-headed eagle on the reverse. Around the border of the obverse it reads: 'Иwанъ Б[о]жiею милостiю Господарь всеѧ Рꙋси Великыi кн[я]зь' (Ioan, by the grace of God, sovereign of all Rus, veliky kns). On the reverse: 'И Великы кн[я]s ·Влад[имирский] ·и Моск[овский] ·i Нов[городский] ·i Пск[овский] ·i Тве[рской] · i Уго[рский] ·и Вят[ский] ·и Пер[мский] ·и Бол[гарский]' (And veliky kns of Vlad(imir) and Mosc(ow) and Nov(gorod) and Psk(ov) and Tve(r) and Ugo(rsk) and Viat(ka) and Per(m) and Bol(gar)). A. B. Lakier, *Russkaia geral'dika* (1855).

The Tatars and the Ruler of Moscow

We have little evidence regarding what Zoë/Sofia's views might have been in general, but if we can believe the court gossip of two decades later, as reported by Sigismund von Herberstein, she did not care for the way in which her husband Ivan interacted with the Tatars:

> [Ivan] was compelled to acknowledge the sway of the Tatars, for when the Tatar ambassadors were approaching he would go forth from the city to meet them, and make them be seated while he stood to receive their addresses, a circumstance which so annoyed his Greek wife, that she would daily tell him that she had married the slave of the Tatars.[32]

To be sure, this diplomatic ceremony was reflective of the fact that the Tatar khans were Chinggisids, while the ruler of Moscow was not. The Moscow Ambassadorial Chancellery used different ceremonies when greeting the representatives of different rulers.

Tatar tsarevichi and *ulan*s were a significant part of the establishment and the expansion of the Vladimir-Moscow polity under Vasilii II and Ivan III. After Vasilii II regained the rulership of Moscow from Shemiaka in 1446, we begin to find mutual accusations that the other ruler loved the Tatars. We have a letter, dated 29 December 1447, that was sent from the council of bishops, criticizing Shemiaka. In addition to what we might expect – his refusing to defend Moscow when Ulugh Muhammad attacked it in 1439, his not going to the aid of Vasilii II in 1445 at the Battle of Suzdal, his not returning the testaments and treasury of the rulers and refusing to recognize Sadi-Ahmed as khan of the Orda – the letter also claims that Shemiaka engaged in pro-Tatar behaviours; in particular, bringing the Tatars into Rus and negotiating with the khan of Kazan without previous authorization.[33]

In contrast, according to the Novgorod Fourth Chronicle, Ivan Andreevich, the ruler of Mozhaisk and the grandson of Dmitrii Ivanovich (Donskoi), accused Vasilii II of bringing Tatars to Rus, of assigning them towns and districts as a source of revenue (*kormlenie*), of loving Tatars and their language, and of giving them 'gold, silver, and possessions'.[34] Late fifteenth-century Muscovite chronicles claim that the Devil motivated Shemiaka to make pro-Tatar charges against Vasilii II – in particular, that Vasilii had reached an agreement with Ulugh

Muhammad after his capture in 1445 that he should give Moscow and other cities to the Kazan khan, while Vasilii ensconced himself in Tver.[35] Apparently, that accusation was enough for Ivan Andreevich of Mozhaisk and Boris Aleksandrovich, the ruler of Tver, to go over to the side of Shemiaka and to justify their blinding of Vasilii, when they captured him in 1446. Such accusations of favouring the Tatars are something new in our sources for the Suzdal-Vladimir-Moscow polity. Earlier *kniazi* were vying with one another to prove how loyal they could be to the Tatar khan. This change in attitude towards their relationship with the Tatars is indicative of the development of anti-Tatar Church rhetoric in the second half of the fifteenth century.[36]

Another document, however, indicates that an additional change had already occurred concerning the Orda. In 1449, in a treaty with a Suzdal ruler, Vasilii II declared that the Suzdal *kniaz*, who was named Ivan, was 'not to have dealings with the Orda' and was 'to hand over . . . without any trickery, any old *iarlyki* . . . for Suzdal Nizhnii Novgorod, or Gorodets, or for the [Nizhnii] Novgorodian polity as a whole'. Any 'new *iarlyki* . . . that any khan might' bestow were to be surrendered to Vasilii.[37] Previously, all *kniazi* who ruled a town had received their patent (*iarlyki*) directly from the Tatar khan. By requiring the Suzdal ruler to have no dealings with the Orda and by demanding that he turn over any *iarlyki* from the khan, Vasilii II established himself as the authority over Suzdal and Nizhnii Novgorod, replacing the khan in Sarai in that respect. Only a few years later, Vasilii declared his son Ivan to be his co-ruler without bothering to obtain approval from the khan, making him the first ruler in Rus to not receive approval from the khan since 1240. However, both Vasilii II and Ivan III continued to pay tribute to the khan of the Orda until the Orda's end in 1503; after this time, the payment of *dan* (tribute) went to the khans of the successor khanates until 1699, when tribute payments to the Crimean khan were concluded.

As late as 1460, according to the Sofia Second Chronicle, the Archbishop of Novgorod Iona warned the Novgorodians not to kill Vasilii II when he was there because 'his eldest son, *Kniaz* Ivan . . . will ask for an army from the khan and march against you'.[38]

When Vasilii II returned from his captivity by Ulugh Muhammad, he brought a contingent of Tatars with him, including Ulugh Muhammad's son, Qasim. Vasilii gave Qasim the revenue-producing town of Zvenigorod for his financial support. Later, in 1452, the town of was renamed Qasim and became the capital of the Qasimov Khanate.

Zvenigorod reverted to Vasilii's ownership and was then inherited by Andrei the Elder in 1462. In the meantime, Qasim's son Daniar became the khan of Qasimov upon his father's death in 1469. Khan Daniar commanded a regiment against Novgorod in the campaigns of 1471 and 1478. He also commanded a regiment to defend Moscow from the Orda Khan Ahmed in 1472. As we have already seen in the agreement between Ivan and his brothers, Daniar was considered to be equal in status to Ivan within the Vladimir-Moscow polity. When Daniar died in 1486, Ivan commanded that Daniar's doctor, Anton, should be stabbed to death on the ice of the Moskva River.

Perhaps the most famous of these Tatars who were in the service of the Moscow ruler was the tsarevich Kudaikul/Peter. In 1487, he surrendered to the forces of Ivan III during the attack on Kazan. In 1505, Tsarevich Kudaikul converted to Christianity and took the name Peter Ibramovich; he married Evdokia, the daughter of Ivan III, and was appointed the commander of the main regiment of the Muscovite army in 1506. For the next seventeen years, Vasilii III, the son and heir of Ivan III, and Tsarevich Peter were inseparable, except when Peter commanded the defence of Moscow against the Crimean Tatar attack of 1521 (when Vasilii fled the city for safety). Their close relationship led the historian A. A. Zimin to suggest that Vasilii planned to declare Peter as his successor. Tsarevich Peter's death in 1523 may have prompted Vasilii in 1525 to divorce his wife, Solomonia, with whom he had not fathered any heirs, and to marry Elena Glinskaia the next year. He probably felt that he had to produce an heir as quickly as possible since he did not want any of his brothers to succeed him.[39] Vasilii, like his father Ivan III, had a dysfunctional relationship with his brothers.

Another Succession Crisis

In January 1483, Ivan, the son of Ivan III and Maria Borisovna, married Elena, the daughter of Stephen III, the ruler of Moldavia. The marriage confirmed an alliance between Moscow and Moldavia, which was threatened by the encroachment of the Ottoman Empire. Elena was the niece of Michael Olelkovich, who was the *kniaz* of Novgorod when Ivan III took it over. She was also the great-granddaughter of Vasilii I, making her a cousin of Ivan III's other six sons and one daughter that he shared with Sofia. Ten months later, in October 1483, Elena and Ivan had a son, Dmitrii. Seven and a half years later, in March 1490,

Ivan Ivanovich died. His doctor, Leon, who had been brought in from Venice, was executed. By this time, Sofia and Ivan III had had four sons and six daughters, and Sofia was pregnant with their fifth son, whom she delivered in October. The oldest of their sons was Vasilii, who by this time was eleven years old. Should the succession be given to the grandson or to the first son by the second marriage? According to the collateral system, the succession would have gone to Vasilii as the next in line of that generation. One question was whether the succession could be given to the grandson if his father had never actually ruled. The Daniilovichi had managed this twice before, when Iurii and Ivan became the rulers of Vladimir, in spite of the fact that their father, Daniil, had never ruled as such but their grandfather, Alexander, had. Other issues of politics and religion were also at stake.

But first, we must lay out the sequence of events. After his eldest son died in 1490, Ivan apparently made no decision for seven years regarding who should be appointed as his successor; eventually, in late 1497, he chose his grandson, Dmitrii. When it became known that Dmitrii was to be co-ruler, Vasilii, Ivan's oldest son with Sofia, was implicated in a plot to overthrow his father and set up a centre of resistance in the Vologda and Beloozero area. He was arrested, and six of the conspirators were executed by beheading on the frozen Moskva River, on 27 December 1497.[40] Sofia was in disgrace because 'women were coming to her with herbs.'[41] The concern may have been that some of those herbs were being used to make poisons. In February 1498, Ivan had Dmitrii crowned as co-ruler of 'Vladimir, Moscow, and All Rus', in a Byzantine-based ceremony. During the ceremony, gold and silver coins were poured over the head of Dmitrii because of a misunderstanding (one that was, perhaps, intentional) regarding the Byzantine rituals. In the original ceremony, coins were thrown into the crowd as largesse, which the crowd could keep, but in Dmitrii's ceremony, the government could keep the coins after the ceremony was over.[42]

In January 1499, without any forewarning, Ivan arrested three members of the Boyar Council – Ivan Iurevich Patrikeev (a grandson of Vasilii I) and two of his sons, Vasilii Kosoi and Ivan Mynin – as well as their brother-in-law, Semën Ivanovich Riapolovskii.[43] All four men were sentenced to death. Riapolovskii was executed by beheading on the frozen Moskva in February. As the result of the intervention of Metropolitan Simon, the Patrikeevs were instead tonsured as monks.[44] Ivan Iurevich was tonsured at the Trinity St Sergius Monastery, while his son Vasilii was tonsured at the Kirillo-Beloozersk Monastery and took the monastic name of Vassian. In April, another boyar, Vasilii Vasilevich Romodanovskii, was arrested, but he was apparently released shortly afterwards; he is reported to have commanded a regiment in a campaign in September 1501. Whether the arrests of these boyars had anything to do with the succession issues or, as has been suggested, whether they had not followed Ivan's instructions in terms of negotiating with Lithuania (or even whether the arrest of Romodanovskii in April was related to the earlier arrests in January), we have no evidence. The *Stepennaia kniga* (Book of Degrees), written sixty years later, states that from that time onwards, Ivan was suspicious of Elena and Dmitrii, though this could be merely a conjecture on the part of the author. We do know that when Vasilii III became the ruler in his own right, he brought Vassian to court, where he acted as an adviser to Vasilii, but that could also have been an entirely separate occurrence, just as his approving the conversion of the Muslim Tsarevich Kudaikul to the Christian Peter Ibramovich and the marriage of Peter to his sister in 1506 were separate from the succession issues.

We must expect that the Moscow chronicles were scrubbed of all anti-Vasilii details, but one extant unofficial chronicle does report that at some point *s.a.* 7008 (September 1499–August 1500), Vasilii left the court and went to Viazma. The location of Viazma may be significant because, like Velikie Luki (where Andrei the Elder and Boris has fled in 1480), it was on the frontier with Lithuania. If this flight by Vasilii did occur (assuming that the chronicler had not merely confused the earlier proposed flight to Vologda and Beloozero), then, instead of being angered, Ivan welcomed Vasilii back like the prodigal son. He granted him rule of Novgorod and Pskov, which were presumably still held by Dmitrii. The Pskovians objected to being put under the governorship of Vasilii and petitioned Ivan to rescind the appointment. But Ivan is reported to have responded, 'Am I not free to choose between my grandson and my children? To whomsoever I please I will grant the right to rule.'[45] This response by Ivan marked the end of one of the principles of the old succession system, wherein the townsmen had some say over who ruled them.

Then, in April 1502, Ivan changed his mind about whom he would appoint as his successor. He ousted Dmitrii from co-rulership and placed his mother, Elena, under *opala* (in disgrace). A few days later, Ivan replaced Dmitrii with Vasilii as his co-ruler.[46] However, no new crowning ceremony appears in our sources. What prompted Ivan's action at this time is not specifically known. Elena's father, Stephen III of Moldavia, complained to Mengli Giray, the khan of Crimea, who then asked Ivan about his actions. Ivan replied that Dmitrii 'became rude' to him.[47] However, we also have the statement, for what it is worth, of Sigismund von Herberstein some twenty years later that, on his deathbed, Ivan changed his mind again and wanted Dmitrii to succeed him.[48]

These events have lent themselves to diverse historiographical interpretations.[49] A possible connection might be that Iosif Volotskii managed to convince Ivan that Dmitrii and his mother Elena had adopted Judaism, or some form of Judaistic heresy, as he states in his letter to Mitrofan.[50] That statement more or less correlates with the timeline of Ivan's turning against Dmitrii.

The Archbishop of Novgorod, Gennadii, and the hegumen of the Volokolamsk Monastery, Iosif, had been conducting a campaign against what they considered to be heresy within the Rus Church. According to Iosif's history of the matter, a Jew named Skharia originated the heresy. He had come from Lithuania with Michael Olelkovich when he became the *kniaz* of Novgorod in 1470 and converted two Russian Orthodox priests, Aleksei and Denis. Then, according to Iosif, a group of Jews from Lithuania went to Novgorod and converted more Christians to Judaism. Ivan III met Aleksei and Denis when he was in Novgorod in 1480 and brought them back to Moscow. Iosif asserted that a number of prominent Muscovites, including the state secretary, Fëdor Kuritsyn, and Archimandrite Zosima of the Simonov Monastery were taken in by the heretics. Nonetheless, in Iosif's account, Aleksei was able to persuade Ivan III to appoint Zosima as metropolitan in September 1490.[51] Iosif's account, however, is highly tendentious and does not correlate with other evidence, including that presented by his co-heretic hunter, Archbishop Gennadii.

In 1487, Gennadii, the recently appointed archbishop of Novgorod, reported the presence of a number of heretics in Novgorod. Three of them fled to Moscow, seeking amnesty, but they were captured and sentenced by a council in 1488, which ordered them to be flogged. Gennadii does not, however, focus on their being Jewish or on any Judaizing behaviour. Instead, he says that 'they dignify the Jewish faith.'[52] In the end, we cannot be sure what the heretics professed; we have only the word of their accusers, who were not engaging in a genuine polemic but only in a prosecution. We can, however, closely analyse the accusations that were made regarding heresy and see if we can account for those accusations in the religious beliefs of the time. The most likely connection is with the Hussites of Bohemia, who were followers of Jan Hus, whose views were condemned by the Catholic Church.

The connection between the Hussites (as influenced by the English churchman John Wycliffe) and the Rus heretics, however, can be ascertained with regard to six characteristics: (1) an objection to the worldliness of the clergy; (2) an emphasis on the Bible as the authority; (3) the rejection of indulgences; (4) questioning the theology of the Eucharist; (5) criticizing monastic temporal possessions; and (6) the theology of the Eucharist.[53] One can detect elements of similarity between their beliefs and the development of proto-Protestant thought. There was also a possible mechanism for the transfer of Hussite belief to Muscovy. Fëdor Kuritsyn, whom Iosif Volotskii accused of being a heretic, had been in Hungary and Moldavia from 1482 to 1484 on a diplomatic mission, part of which was to arrange the marriage of Elena and Ivan Ivanovich. He was there at a time when Hussites were prevalent in Hungary and had fled to Moldavia to escape persecution.[54] Kuritsyn was a state secretary and played a prominent part in the foreign policy of Muscovy. If he was the mechanism for bringing Hussite ideas to Moscow, that does not preclude a parallel transfer of Hussite ideas to Novgorod.

The fact that Elena, Kuritsyn, Zosima and Ivan III were open to the ideas professed by those accused of heresy by Gennadii and Iosif may help to explain, at least in part, the extraordinary sequence of events comprising the succession crisis.

Marriage Politics

Until 1505, members of the ruling family married the sons and daughters of boyars, the appanage *kniazi*, and foreigners. The major foreign marriage during the reign of Ivan III was that of his daughter Elena to the ruler of Lithuania, Alexander, in 1495 (illus. 63). There were negotiations with two separate envoys from the German emperor, Frederick III, involving five different potential foreign husbands for Elena before they settled on Alexander.[55] Ivan insisted that Elena be allowed to remain Orthodox while married to Alexander, who was a Roman Catholic. Alexander promised not to try to convert Elena to Catholicism, but

62 Alexander I of Poland with his wife Elena of Moscow, daughter of Ivan III, ruler of Vladimir and Moscow and Sophia Palaiologina.

the Muscovite sources say that he did make such attempts. Furthermore, it appears somewhat naive of the Muscovite court to think that Alexander would follow any part of the Orthodox wedding ceremony, such as taking the ritual bath the morning after the ceremony or donning the Muscovite groom's garb, but this is what the inventory indicates.[56] It may have been the difficulties and expenses encountered with this particular marriage, according to the American historian of Russia Russell Martin, that led the Muscovites to reconsider the utility of foreign marriage in foreign policy.[57] After 1505, all royal Muscovite marriages until 1710 were either internal or with spouses who already had established connections in Moscow (be it personal or familial). One reason for this practice is the refusal to allow the marriage of anyone in the royal family to someone who was not of the Eastern Orthodox faith. None can be considered a true foreign diplomatic match.[58] Although the Muscovites did continue to try to arrange foreign matches during that time, all attempts foundered on Muscovite and foreign intransigence over the religious issue. Martin contends that, as a result, the Moscow rulers began to marry women from the lower nobility so as to not upset the political balance among the powerful boyar families. To make sure that the right marriage partner was found, bride shows were established to test the suitability of various candidates at the court.[59]

In the summer of 1503, Ivan suffered a stroke that debilitated him until his death two years later, in October 1505. The Moscow government and military that he left behind were very different from those that he inherited from his father. The area that Moscow controlled had almost tripled in size between 1462 and 1505, as a result of the annexation of the polities of Iaroslavl (1471), Perm (1472), Rostov (1473), Tver (1485) and Viatka (1489), but mostly by the annexation of Novgorod and its northern lands, all the way to the White Sea (1478). The Moscow rulers could now lay claim to being the rulers of Rus, since Ivan and his father Vasilii had eliminated any vassalage to the Tatar khans (except for the payment of a nominal tribute).

With the presence of a number of Morean Greeks who were prominent in the Muscovite government of Ivan III and, given his marriage to Zoë/Sofia and the adoption of a state symbol that was similar to that of Morea, it would appear that the Muscovite polity's transformation from a steppe khanate-type government to a dynastic state was at least informed by those who had played a part in the Morean despotate. Muscovy was now a state with institutions, administrative procedures and record-keeping, along with many layers of governance. The ideologues of the regime were well on their way to constructing a dynastic narrative that stretched back over six hundred years, linking the ruling family to an obscure Viking adventurer named Riurik and even beyond, to a mythical kinsman of Augustus Caesar named Prus. By moulding this dynastic past, the success of the Daniilovichi in positioning themselves to claim rulership of all Rus was no longer the result of the concomitance of individual events and exigencies (not to mention many dead ends) but could instead be presented as a God-ordained teleological inevitability.

Epilogue: The Family Lines Continue . . .

Our claim throughout this book has been that approaching Rus history in terms of the ruling families and their competition for power is a better and more accurate path of study than approaching that history through the lens of a single dynasty. The observant reader may have noticed that we have been using the term Volodimerovichi to describe a corporate entity, in the sense that all towns within Rus in the eleventh and twelfth centuries were ruled by the descendants of Volodimer I. Furthermore, the participants of the conferences that were held to self-regulate the succession – such as those in Liubech (1097) and Uvetichi (1100) – were descendants of Volodimer I. Finally, although there is no direct evidence that the rulers of Rus towns identified themselves as the descendants of Volodimer I, at least not before the fifteenth century, one could extrapolate from their actions that they had some sense of being part of a larger corporate entity, just as we can extrapolate from their actions with regard to succession to the rulership of towns that they had some sense of and tried to abide by a collateral system of succession, down to the fourth brother. Nonetheless, we want to make it clear that we are not using the term 'Volodimerovichi' in the sense of a dynasty or as a substitute for 'Riurikid', but merely to distinguish them from those who were not descended from Volodimer I. One may well ask, why not?

There are at least two issues here, probably more, but two will do for now. One is how the rulers viewed themselves; the other is whether their actions conform, whether cognizant or not, to a larger corporate entity. An added layer of consideration is that we are dealing mostly with sources written by clergy, who tended to have their own take on things. In other words, we have little evidence from the rulers or members of the ruling elite themselves, except as reported by the monastic writers. To what extent did these writers accurately represent the thoughts and opinions of the rulers or ruling elite? Did the rulers share the beliefs attributed to them in the monastic writings, or were they written to maintain the prestige of the Church? Perhaps significantly, the monastic writers used the pagan names of the rulers – Iaroslav, Iziaslav, Sviatopolk and so forth – rather than their Christian names – Iurii, Dmitrii and Mikhail, respectively – until the late twelfth century. We cannot be sure of the significance of that choice.

So, to put it in concrete terms, did those who met at Liubech in 1097 and Uvetichi in 1100 see themselves as Riurikids? Probably not. One could also suppose that they saw themselves as Sviatoslavichi (descendants of the father of Volodimer I) or as Igorevichi (descendants of Sviatoslav's father). It might help if we could figure out how the participants at Liubech (1097) and Uvetichi (1100) were chosen or why other Volodimerovichi or Iaroslavichi were not present. At both conferences, the rulers of Kyiv, Chernigov and Pereiaslavl – Sviatopolk Iziaslavich, Volodimer Monomakh and Oleg Sviatoslavich, respectively – were present. The PVL mentions that three other individuals were also there – David Igorevich, Vasilko Rostislavich and David Sviatoslavich (the brother of Oleg). At Uvetichi, the PVL mentions one other individual, besides the 'big three', who participated – David Sviatoslavich – as well as David Igorevich, whom they had come to judge. Would they have seen themselves as Volodimerovichi (in the sense of being descendants of Volodimer I)? Possibly, but they might have considered the question irrelevant.

As far as we can tell from the evidence, being a descendant of Volodimer I did not enter into their justification for being the ruler of a town or for attending a conference on succession, or even as self-identification. In addition, the reputation of Volodimer, as Francis Butler has documented, was not as exalted in the eleventh and twelfth centuries as it is today.[1] Initially, according to Butler, Volodimer was 'portrayed both as the transformer of Rus' and as a ruler who had perpetuated the successful political and military policies of his ancestors'. Then came a 'waning of interest in him' which seems to have correlated with 'a waning in the glory of Kiev itself'. He attributed to 'dynastic, rather than civic, pride' the raising of 'interest to a new peak in sixteenth-century Muscovy, where Vladimir was perceived and portrayed as the "root" of the Muscovite dynasty'.[2] Butler's research should be a warning to us not to assume that the descendants of Volodimer viewed him in the same light that we do.

The Rus rulers could have seen themselves as Iaroslavichi (in the sense of being descendants of Iaroslav the Wise). Danish historian and Slavist John Lind has written about the 'brotherhood' of the Iaroslavichi in the context of what exactly constituted 'Rus' and when it began.[3] The earliest appearance of the term *Rus* in the PVL is as a land. In the first lines of the PVL, the author says that he wants to show the reader how 'the Rus land' (*Russkaia zemlia*) came into being.[4] The second appearance, however, refers to a people, the Rus, as part of the lot of Japheth.[5] The entry for *s.a.* 6360 (851/2) also refers to 'the Rus land' during the reign of the ruler of the Eastern Roman Empire, Mikhail (842–67), when the Rus land was being referred to within the context of the attack on Constantinople by the Rus, as described in the Greek chronicle of George Hamartolos. The next appearance, however, of 'Rus' is as a people before there was a Rus land. One could define the Rus land as the jurisdictional area of the metropolitan of Kyiv and all Rus, while another way to define it is as the land inhabited by the Rus people.[6] A third way defines it as the area governed by the Rus rulers. How did the Rus themselves or the Rus rulers define it?

Henryk Paszkiewicz documented forty examples wherein the Novgorod First, Kyivan, Laurentian and Galician-Volhynian chronicles sometimes distinguish when someone is travelling from a local town, such as Novgorod, Smolensk, Murom, Riazan, Rostov, or Polotsk to Rus. Not all these examples demonstrate the attitude that Paszkiewicz thought they represented. Citing chronicle entries can also be contentious since chronicles exist in layers of text edits, redactions and scribal errors, rather like archaeological strata. Sometimes, a wording from a later stratum 'falls' (is interpolated) into an earlier stratum and must be distinguished from that earlier stratum. Paszkiewicz also thought that the chronicles demonstrated that Rus only signified the local areas administered by three cities – Kyiv, Chernigov and Pereiaslavl. This does seem to be what the chronicles indicate to be the case after about 1130, but there continue to be instances after 1130 when they refer to Rus as a larger entity.

Paszkiewicz pointed out similar changes in wording for other local towns. He asserted that Galicia and Volhynia were not part of Rus, beginning in 1018, but the evidence provided for the 1018 date does not support his contention.[7] Nor does his citation for the date 1097.[8]

Entries beginning in 1145 do, however, support the contention that Galicia and Volhynia were not part of Rus in a political sense,[9] although it still remained so for the purposes of the metropolitanate of Rus. Chronicle entries beginning in 1146 support the contention that the Vladimir–Suzdal polity was not part of Rus.[10] Chronicle entries beginning in 1147 support the contention that the towns of Riazan and Murom were not considered part of Rus.[11] Paszkiewicz also cited chronicle entries reporting Smolensk and Polotsk as being outside Rus.[12]

Nonetheless, Charles Halperin has explained that there is no contradiction here: as 'the Kievan dynasty expanded in the eleventh and twelfth centuries, newly acquired regions were "incorporated" into the Russian Land, until eventually the patrimony of the Riurikids encompassed all of East Slavdom' while '[a]t the same time the Russian Land retained its earlier meaning of the Kievan triangle'.[13] Halperin sees the split between 'the two geographical meanings' of 'Rus land', referring to the Kyiv-Chernigov-Pereiaslavl triangle, with 'all of East Slavdom', which he terms 'the myth of the Russian Land', being held coincidentally, this division having occurred as a result of the Mongol conquest and continuing 'for roughly a century after' it.[14]

As for Galicia and Volhynia, Halperin remarked that the GVC 'essentially does not use the term the Russian Land except in one suggestive entry'. That entry occurs *s.a.* 1250, wherein 'the chronicler excoriates Daniil Romanovich of Galich for paying tribute to the Mongols . . . since he "ruled the Russian Land, Kyiv and Vladimir [in Volhynia] and Galich . . . (and his) father was tsar in the Russian Land".' As pointed out in Chapter Nine, this statement by the chronicler can be considered aspirational rather than representing the reality on the ground.

Some historians initially tried to use this 'small Rus' concept to argue that the term 'Rus' was a southern term, in that it initially designated just the three provinces of Kyiv, Chernigov and Pereiaslavl, and that it later expanded from there.[15] To be sure, the rulers of Kyiv expanded their control from Kyiv to a huge swath of territory, but the evidence to support this contention of nomenclature is meagre and ambiguous at best. The Greek–Rus treaties, as reported in the PVL *s.a.* 912 and 945, seem to undercut this contention, as the agents and merchants from the Rus are designated as receiving monthly payments, 'first from Kyiv, then from Chernigov and Pereiaslavl and the other cities [*I prochii gradi*]'.[16] What exactly is being referred to by 'and the other cities' is fodder for much debate – whether it refers to cities outside the Kyiv-Chernigov-Pereiaslavl triangle, such as Smolensk, or within it, such as Liubech, or to both. The weight of other evidence, however, implies that it refers to the area outside the triangle. The PVL itself and the *Annals Bertiniani*, for example, testify to the ninth-century Rus people being Scandinavians, not those from the south.[17]

By the twelfth century, the chronology of the evidence indicates a reverse transformation – that is, from a 'large Rus' to a 'small Rus'. Lind, basing his conclusions on the Novgorod First Chronicle, sided with Paszkiewicz in arguing that the transformation occurred in the twelfth, not the thirteenth century.[18] Lind's point is that if, for example, we have evidence that for a hundred years or so people are said to travel 'from Dayton to Cleveland' (which are both in Ohio), and the accounts begin to change to saying that people travel 'from Dayton to Ohio' when referencing the same journey, then we are justified in concluding that Dayton is no longer part of Ohio. The evidence is not that unambiguous, however; we continue to find examples in the Novgorod First Chronicle describing someone as travelling from Novgorod to Kyiv during this time, which is equivalent in our example of travelling from Dayton to Cleveland. So, why go to all that trouble to distinguish Kyiv, Chernigov and Pereiaslavl as being in Rus and Novgorod, Smolensk, Murom, Riazan, Suzdal, Galicia-Volhynia and so forth as not being in Rus?

Lind goes on to write: 'In Vladimir-Suzdal, the picture is much the same.' In 1152, we find the first example of Iurii Dolgorukii going to 'Rus' to move against Iziaslav, the ruler of Kyiv. Lind finds it not 'coincidental that "Rus"is used precisely now', whereas for the chronicle entries during the previous four years (1147–51), the designation 'Rus' is not mentioned once regarding similar campaigns by Iurii against Iziaslav.[19] Lind proposes that this change was related to the system of succession of Kyiv. For example, when Iurii Dolgorukii renewed the struggle in 1152, he no longer saw himself as being part of the collateral system of succession to the rulership of Kyiv and did not recognize the authority of the ruler of Kyiv as the senior *kniaz*: 'He, and his principality, were outside Rus', that is, outside the Kyivan body politic.'[20]

Lind saw no indication in Iaroslav's 'Testament' of 1054 of a 'future procedure of succession'; it merely placed his sons in certain cities in 'a descending order of importance according to age'.[21] The 'Testament', through its 'fervent admonitions to live in peace, brotherly love, mutual support and due respect to the oldest', created a 'brotherhood' among the Iaroslavichi of Rus. It took nine years and the deaths of his two brothers for Volodimer I to attain undisputed power, while it took 21 years and ten dead brothers, as well as the imprisonment of one brother, for Iaroslav to do so; the extremes of 'internecine warfare', according to Lind, 'were later avoided through the consensus of a sufficient number of princes to a dynastic ideology which, as reflected in the PVL, stress rule through a triumvirate within the brotherhood of the Jaroslavids'.[22] That 'brotherhood' and the succession system to the rulership of Kyiv broke apart in the twelfth century, especially in the 1150s, according to Lind, when the rulers of the Vladimir-Suzdal polity removed themselves from the system.

We think that Lind is on the right track, but we do not entirely agree with him. In fact, the succession system did not break apart at that time, although that is what happened to what Lind terms the 'brotherhood of Rus'. That is, the rulers of Vladimir-Suzdal and other outer polities no longer recognized the authority of the 'triumvirs' – the rulers of Kyiv, Chernigov and Pereiaslavl – to regulate succession and other political matters. The 'non-Rus' rulers of Rus regulated such matters within their own polities. Nonetheless, they still remained in the system of succession, with someone from their own clan in each generation ruling in Kyiv. As discussed in Chapter Five, between 1235 and 1240, at least one member of each of the major ruling houses – the Olgovich, Igorevich, Rostislavich and Vsevolodovich – served as the ruler of Kyiv. In fact, it was by means of the Vsevolodovich member Iaroslav (Alexander Nevsky's father) that Alexander could then lay claim to becoming the *kniaz* of Kyiv. With the death of Alexander Nevsky in 1263, the Vladimir-Suzdal rulers withdrew entirely from that system since no subsequent Vladimir-Suzdal ruler claimed to be the *kniaz* of Kyiv, at least not until the end of the fifteenth century. It was the turn of the Lithuanian rulers to make that claim.

✠

THE PVL AND NOVGOROD First Chronicle present a narration in which the Rus rulers of Kyiv expanded their kingdom outwards until the eleventh century, under Iaroslav the Wise. The kingdom encompassed an area that included Chernigov, Pereiaslavl, Novgorod, Smolensk, Suzdal, Rostov, Murom, Riazan, Vladimir and Galicia. Then, during the course of the twelfth century, all of the ruling families of these polities, except for those in Chernigov and Pereiaslavl, broke away from the succession system requiring that each of them have at least one member of each generation rule in Kyiv. It was only in the late fourteenth century that the rulers of Moscow began to try to reconstitute what Halperin calls 'the myth of the Rus land'. Significantly, this only happened after the rulers of Lithuania had begun to try to create such a narrative for themselves and was perhaps in response to their attempt. At first, the Moscow rulers did not meet with success, for it took another hundred years, until the end of the fifteenth century and in the person of Ivan III, that 'the myth' was fully reconstituted. Joined to that reconstituted myth of the Rus land was another equally powerful myth, that of the Riurikid dynasty, of which the Moscow ruling family was the sole embodiment. That myth was more fully developed in the later sixteenth century, in such works as the *Stepennaia kniga*; by the twentieth century, it was fully ensconced in modern Russian history textbooks, with their genealogical charts showing the rulers of Rus stretching from Kyiv to Muscovy in a single, unbroken line.

When Fëdor, the son and successor of Ivan IV, died in 1598, reality reared its formidable head. The traditional explanation of the end to that particular dynastic line is that because Fëdor died childless, the Riurikid dynasty ended with him. The coronation ceremony record for Ivan IV in 1547 had declared as much, when it reports Metropolitan Makarii as saying that the custom of olden times was for Rus rulers to bestow the rulership on 'their firstborn sons' (*synovom svoim prvym*).[23] As we have seen in this book, firstborn sons only succeeded their fathers directly in rare and specific circumstances. In any case, although Fëdor was a third-born son, he had no sons himself. Therefore, so the explanation goes, it was necessary to pick someone to be tsar who was not a Riurikid, namely, Boris Godunov. Then, when that choice was not a success, leading as it did to the Time of Troubles, a new dynasty, the Romanovs, was chosen in 1613.

Yet, in 1598, in 1613 and even today, there are those who claim to be 'Riurikids', the descendants of Riurik. The Russian historian Karamzin asked, over two hundred years ago, why one of these Riurikids was not chosen.[24] In 1606, the Assembly of the Land had chosen one of them, Vasilii Shuiskii, to be the tsar. Although he could and did claim the same line of descent from Riurik as the sixteenth-century Moscow rulers, he is not considered to be part of the Riurikid dynasty.[25] When he was deposed in 1610, another 'Riurikid' was not chosen.

There were plenty of competent individuals who could claim descent from Riurik, but the 'dynasty' was not upheld. Other elites would resort to wives, cousins, distant relatives and so on, to maintain the dynastic line (for example, the Romanovs in the eighteenth century), but the Muscovite elite did not. If the claim was that Boris Godunov was a 'Riurikid' by fiat, being the son-in-law of Ivan IV, then why do we not say that the Riurikid dynasty ended with him, or with Vasilii Shuiskii?

One possible answer is that by that time, the Muscovite ruling class had instituted a new mechanism of determining succession; namely, choosing a successor through the Assembly of the Land (also known as the Zemskii sobor), which was established under Ivan IV. This Assembly was made up of the boyars, prelates, members of the gentry and sometimes even the merchants and townsmen.[26] The Assembly system gave the ruling elite great flexibility in choosing successors to the previous ruler because it could choose the next ruler on the basis of the competence of that person, rather than merely a bloodline. Every Russian ruler from Fëdor to Peter was chosen by the Assembly of the Land. Nonetheless, the fiction that there was a Riurikid dynasty had to be maintained, with the childless last 'Riurikid' being given as the explanation for its demise.

Remarkably, the sources of the time provide no objective justification for this organizational process of choosing rulers. For example, the tales of the Time of Troubles, as Daniel Rowland has pointed out, attributed the decision by the Assembly of the Land, who appointed Mikhail Romanov as the tsar in 1613, to God's having already chosen Mikhail for the role while he was still in his mother's womb.[27]

It was the prevailing notion in Muscovite political thought that God worked through the people (the 'strong in Israel') to choose the tsar.[28] The voice of 'the people' was the voice of God (*vox Dei, vox populi*), while 'the people' were represented by the Assembly of the Land. Ruling charisma had been bestowed on a new family, the Romanovs, and the myth of a new dynasty needed to be created. The notion of this being a God-ordained dynasty made it easier for the populace to accept the new ruling family, and the seeming inevitability of Mikhail's appointment simplified and tidied up an otherwise quite complex and messy history, albeit making it less accurate.

GLOSSARY

basqaq	military governor appointed by Mongol-Tatar khans
beg/bek/bey	a title of Turko-Mongol origin, meaning clan chief or military commander
calendar	until 1700, the Russian state used the Anno mundi (years since the creation of the world) calendar, which was derived from that of the Eastern Roman Empire. In that calendar the creation of the world occurred on 1 September 5509 BC, a date calculated according to both the Julian and Gregorian calendars
Chinggisid	direct descendant of Chinggis Khan. This genealogical descent bestowed ruling charisma on the descendant. That is, a Chinggisid could be chosen to be the khan, while a non-Chinggisid could not
clan	a group of interrelated families, descended from a common ancestor
consanguinity	blood relationships between individuals. Consanguinity was regulated in the medieval period by the Church, which prohibited marriages within certain degrees of familial relationships. The goal of this prohibition was to prevent marriages with close kin
dan	a tribute paid by Rus rulers to their Mongol-Tatar overlords, collected in the form of a tax from the local populace
daruga	a civilian governor appointed by Mongol-Tatar khans
Eastern Roman Empire (Byzantium)	a continuation of the Roman Empire, whose western part collapsed in the fifth century. Its capital was Constantinople and it survived until 1453, when the Ottoman Turks captured the city
epithets	nicknames for rulers such as 'the Wise' and 'Big Nest' are later, probably nineteenth-century, historiographical inventions, and thus anachronistic. Nonetheless, we use them here to distinguish the various Iaroslavs, Vsevolods and so forth from each other, supplementing the use of patronymics

Eurasia	we are using the term to mean all of Europe and Asia combined. What we are calling 'Inner Eurasia' is the area that the geographer Halford Mackinder describes as 'the Heartland', which he initially defined as that area drained by the following rivers: the Ob, Enisei, Lena, Volga, Oxus (Syr Darya), Jaxartes (Amu Darya), Don, Dnieper, the middle and lower Danube (which drain into the Black Sea), and the Oder, Vistula and Neva rivers, as well as the streams of Finland and Sweden (which drain into the Baltic Sea). To this definition, LeDonne added the mountain chains, including the Carpathians, Caucasus, Dinaric Alps, Taurus, Zagros, Himalaya and Stanovoi that divide Inner Eurasia from Outer Eurasia
family	we are using the term 'family' as an expanded nuclear family. So, a husband and wife and their children and their children's spouses, sometimes extending to grandchildren of the original husband and wife
iarlyk **(pl.** ***iarlyki*****)**	'Tatar term meaning a charter of the khan . . . granting privileges and immunities' (*Dictionary of Russian Historical Terms from the Eleventh Century to 1917*, comp. Sergei G. Pushkarev, ed. George Vernadsky and Ralph T. Fisher Jr (New Haven, CT, 1970), p. 30)
khan (also qan)	the ruler of a khanate. After the Mongol conquest, the khan had to be a descendant of Chinggis Khan. A qagan was an emperor (that is, a khan of khans)
Kiev/Kyiv	we have chosen to follow the modern spelling for the city, while keeping the historic spelling for Chernigov and other cities
kniaginia	the wife or daughter of a *kniaz*. Accordingly this could be translated as princess or queen, depending on one's translation of *kniaz*, as well as the relationship of the *kniaginia* to the *kniaz*
kniaz **(pl.** ***kniazi*****)**	in early Rus, only a ruler could be called a *kniaz*. The traditional way to translate *kniaz* is 'prince', but a *kniaz* from tenth- to fourteenth-century Rus was a ruler, sometimes equivalent to a king in medieval Europe. However, by the fifteenth century, members of the elite who were not rulers of anything were also called *kniazi*. We use 'ruler' when we can and keep *kniaz* otherwise

kniazhestvo	the area ruled over by a *kniaz*
namestnik (pl. *namestniki*)	'local administrators and judges appointed by the . . . [rulers] for the major towns and adjacent territories' (*Dictionary of Russian Historical Terms,* p. 66)
ordu (Russ. orda)	'A Mongolian and Turkic term referring to the camp of a prince or general. It also served as the root of the English word "horde"' (Timothy May, *The Mongol Art of War: Chinggis Khan and the Mongol Military System* (Yardley, 2007), p. 150)
patronymics	patronymics may be confusing to someone who is not used to using them, but they are essential for distinguishing between the various Iaroslavs, Vasiliis and Andreis. Once one understands how patronymics are formed, then they become easier to understand. A patronymic is made up of two parts for a male, the name of the father and the suffix -ovich. In early Rus written sources, the -ov- was not present for elite names (such as ruling families) although still present for non-elite and foreign names. Thus, Iaroslav Volodimerich indicates Iaroslav, the son of Volodimer (note: the spelling Volodimir also occurs in our sources, so the form could also be Volodimirich). So, just as Johnson means 'son of John' and Ericson means 'son of Eric', one can think of the suffix -son playing the same role as -(ov)ich. Around the fourteenth century, the sources begin to add the -ov for elite names. For a female, the patronymic is formed from the name of the father and the suffix -ovna. Thus, Uliana Alexandrovna = Uliana, daughter of Alexander
polity	a political entity. This is a purposefully generic term that allows scholars to talk about kingdoms, empires, khanates and so on in one sentence without needing to engage with specific terminological differences
posadnik	the mayor, or sometimes translated as governor, of a town in Rus. We know about these individuals specifically from the Novgorod Chronicle, where they are first recorded in entries from the early twelfth century relating not just to Novgorod but Pskov and Ladoga
s.a. = *sub anno* (under the year)	we have used this abbreviation for chronicle entries. Given the Anno mundi dating of the

	chroniclers, most entries fall between 1 September of one year and 31 August of the next year. Thus, the entry for 6609 is equivalent to 1 September 1100 to 31 August 1101
snem	a council of *kniazi*
tsarevich	the son of a tsar or khan
tysiatski	literally, the commander of 1,000 troops, although the term is often used more generally in the Rusian sources to signifiy a military commander
Ulus of Jochi (or Juchi)	The term 'Golden Horde' is anachronistic and misleading, for a number of reasons. It was never 'golden' in the sense of the central Eurasian directional-colour system. The term 'horde' was meant as a translation of orda, which is the term that appears in the Rus sources. However, 'horde' has unfortunate connotations for the anglophone reader, signifying a disorganized swarm. A more accurate rendition of orda would be Order, as in the Teutonic Order. The phrase 'Qipchaq Khanate' is better in that it describes more accurately the nature of the polity and the placement of it, that is, in the desht-i-Qipchaq (the Polovtsian Steppe). Even more accurate is the name 'Ulus of Jochi', in that *ulus* means area and *Jochi* refers to the son of Chinggis Khan. Pushkarev's dictionary defines *ulus* as: 'In a broad sense, realm or domain of a Tatar sovereign. In a narrow sense, a Tatar settlement . . .' (*Dictionary of Russian Historical Terms*, p. 168). The Ulus of Jochi was internally divided into the blue (western) and white (eastern) ordas
veche	a town meeting
vita (zhitie)	literally, a 'life', the name typically used to refer to the recorded lives of the saints. These *vitae* (in Latin) or *zhitie* (in East Slavic) were used to commemorate the saint and remember their life. The *vitae* often followed formulaic models
voevoda	a generic term for a military leader in Rus
Volodymyr-in-Volhynia	we have chosen the modern spelling for this city, in part to avoid confusion with Vladimir Zalesskii (literally, 'beyond the forest'; that is, in Suzdal lands)

REFERENCES

Introduction: The Problem with Dynasty

1 *The Merriam-Webster Dictionary*, s.v. 'Dynasty'. Other dictionaries provide similar definitions.
2 Natalia Nowakowska, 'What's in a Word? The Etymology and Historiography of Dynasty – Renaissance Europe and Beyond', *Global Intellectual History*, 7 August 2020, 10.1080/23801883.2020.1796233.
3 *Oxford English Dictionary*, s.v. 'Dynasty'.
4 We have chosen to render the latter's name in the popular way as Alexander Nevsky, rather than the transliterated Aleksandr Nevskii.
5 Donald Ostrowski, 'Systems of Succession in Rus' and Steppe Societies', *Ruthenica*, IX (2012), pp. 31–3; Donald Ostrowski, 'Was there a Riurikid Dynasty in Early Rus'?', *Canadian–American Slavic Studies*, LII (2018), pp. 33–5.
6 David McCullough, *Brave Companions: Portraits in History* (New York, 1992), p. 214.
7 According to the historian S. V. Zagraevskii, the town of Bogoliubovo received its name from Andrei's sobriquet and not vice versa, as the *Zhitie Andreia Bogoliubskogo* contends. S. V. Zagraevskii, 'K voprosu o proiskhozhdenii prozvishcha kniazia Andreia Bogoliubskogo i nazvaniia goroda Bogoliubova', in *Materialy XVIII mezhdunarodnoi kraevedcheskoi konferentsii (19 April 2013)*, ed. A. K. Tikhonov, M. A. Barashev, I. V. Mishina and M. I. Novikova (Vladimir, 2014), pp. 9–16.

1 What Is the Kingdom of Rus?

1 John Haywood, *Historical Atlas of the Medieval World, AD 600–1492* (New York, 2000).
2 Hrushevsky's *History of Ukraine-Rus'* has been translated into English in the twenty-first century by the Canadian Institute of Ukrainian Studies. See www.ualberta.ca, accessed 15 October 2022.
3 These have also been translated into English, though one hundred years earlier than Hrushevsky. For volume I see V. O. Kliuchevskii, *A History of Russia*, trans. C. J. Hogarth (London, 1911), vol. I.
4 'Putin: "Kiev is the Mother of All Russian Cities"', www.washingtonpost.com, accessed 5 March 2021. One can see also his 2021 essay 'On the Historical Unity of Russians and Ukrainians', which expresses his view of the historical situation, at https://en.wikipedia.org, accessed 7 May 2022.
5 There are multiple versions of the PVL, but the most authoritative was created by Donald Ostrowski and can be found in *The Povest' vremennykh let: An Interlineâr Collation and Paradosis*, comp. and

ed. Donald Ostrowski, with David Birnbaum and Horace G. Lunt (Cambridge, MA, 2003) (hereafter *PVL: An Interlinear Collation*). It is accessible in a searchable digital version at http://pvl.obdurodon.org/pvl.html. An English translation was also produced: *The Russian Primary Chronicle: Laurentian Text*, trans. and ed. Samuel Hazzard Cross and Olgerd P. Sherbowitz-Wetzor (Cambridge, MA, 1953) (hereafter RPC). *PVL: An Interlinear Collation*, col. 19, lines 7–8 (*s.a.* 6367 = 858/9). RPC, p. 59.

6 *The Annals of St-Bertin* (Ninth-Century Histories, vol. I), trans. and ed. Janet L. Nelson (Manchester, 1991), p. 44.

7 For a further discussion of this evidence, see Marika Mägi, *The Viking Eastern Baltic* (Leeds, 2019).

8 Donald Ostrowski, 'The Return of the Rhos: Patria, Chacanus, and the *Annales Bertiniani s.a.* 839', *Canadian–American Slavic Studies*, LII (2018), pp. 300–302.

9 *PVL: An Interlinear Collation*, col. 19, lines 14–16 (*s.a.* 6370 = 861/2). RPC, p. 59.

10 Regarding Rus and comparisons to early modern stories, see Norman Ingham and Christian Raffensperger, 'Rurik and the First Rurikids', *American Genealogist*, LXXXII/1 (2007), pp. 1–13 (part 1); LXXXII/2 (2007), pp. 111–19 (part 2); while for medieval Ireland, see Clare Downham, 'The Historical Importance of Viking-Age Waterford', *Journal of Celtic Studies*, IV (2004), pp. 81–2.

11 Simon Franklin and Jonathan Shepard, *The Emergence of Rus, 750–1200* (New York, 1996), p. 47 and elsewhere.

12 *PVL: An Interlinear Collation*, col. 22, lines 18–21 (*s.a.* 6387 = 878/9); RPC, p. 60.

13 *PVL: An Interlinear Collation*, col. 21, line 3–col. 21, line 6 (*s.a.* 6370 = 861/2); RPC, p. 60.

14 *PVL: An Interlinear Collation*, col. 23, lines 15–16 (*s.a.* 6390 = 881/2); RPC, p. 61.

15 *PVL: An Interlinear Collation*, col. 23, lines 16–17 (*s.a.* 6390 = 881/2); RPC, p. 61.

16 *PVL: An Interlinear Collation*, col. 23, line 23 (*s.a.* 6390 = 881/2); RPC, p. 61.

17 *PVL: An Interlinear Collation*, col. 23, lines 23–5 (*s.a.* 6390 = 881/2); RPC, p. 61.

18 *PVL: An Interlinear Collation*, col. 32, lines 27 (*s.a.* 907, 912).

19 For an analysis of this and other treaties, see Frank Edward Wozniak Jr, 'The Nature of Byzantine Foreign Policy toward Kievan Russia in the First Half of the Tenth Century: A Reassessment', PhD dissertation, Stanford University, 1973.

20 *PVL: An Interlinear Collation*, col. 29, lines 13–15 (*s.a.* 6411 = 902/3); RPC, p. 64.

21 According to https://history.stackexchange.com, the oldest woman to give birth in the Middle Ages was Eleanor of Aquitaine: 'In 1166, Eleanor of Aquitaine, wife of Henry II of England, gave birth to the future King John when she was at least 42 years old (it is more likely she was 43 or 44). Eleanor of Castile, wife of Edward I of England, also gave birth to a future king, Edward II, when she was either 41 or

42.' In response five on the same site, someone mentions several other medieval women who gave birth in their forties. Olga would beat that record by at least ten years. (The PVL (58.6) says that Sviatoslav was a child (be bo detesk), *s.a.* 946.) Igor would have been in his mid-sixties, at least, at the time of Sviatoslav's birth.

22 PVL: *An Interlinear Collation*, col. 64, lines 22–4 (*s.a.* 6472 = 963/4); RPC, p. 84.

23 PVL: *An Interlinear Collation*, col. 44, line 27–col. 45, line 6 (*s.a.* 6449 = 940/41); RPC, p. 72.

24 PVL: *An Interlinear Collation*, col. 46, line 20–col. 47, line 16 (*s.a.* 6453 = 944/5); RPC, pp. 73–74.

25 PVL: *An Interlinear Collation*, col. 60, lines 25–6 (*s.a.* 6463 = 954/5).

26 *Constantine Porphyrogennetos: The Book of Ceremonies*, trans. Ann Moffatt and Maxeme Tall (Leiden, 2012), book II, chap. 15, pp. 594–8.

27 Ibid., p. 594.

28 John Skylitzes, *A Synopsis of Byzantine History, 811–1057*, trans. John Wortley (Cambridge, 2010), chap. 11, sec. 6.

29 This embassy is dated to 959 in Continuator Reginionis. *Fontes ad historiam aevi Saxonici illustrandam: Widukindi res gestae Saxonicae. Adalberti continuato Reginonis. Liudprandi opera*, ed. Albert von Bauer and Reinhold Rau (Darmstadt, 2002), p. 214.

30 For more on this issue and the relevant religious politics, see Christian Raffensperger, *Reimagining Europe: Kievan Rus' in the Medieval World* (Cambridge, MA, 2012), pp. 156–8, and Chapter Five more broadly.

31 Continuator Reginionis, p. 216.

32 This subject is covered exceptionally fully by A. V. Nazarenko in *Drevniaia Rus' na mezhdunarodnykh putiakh: Mezhdistsiplinarnye ocherki kul'turnykh, torgovykh, politicheskikh sviazei IX–XII vekov* (Moscow, 2001), chap. 5.

33 PVL: *An Interlinear Collation*, col. 65, lines 6–11 (*s.a.* 6473 = 964/5); RPC, p. 84.

34 George Vernadsky, *Kievan Russia*, pb. edn. (New Haven, CT, 1973), p. 44. This was not the end of the Rusian campaigns against the Khazars, however. Vernadsky notes, following Islamic sources, that Rusian forces, who were not led by Sviatoslav, continued the campaign against Khazaria in 968, sacking the capital of Itil (ibid., p. 46).

35 Anthony Kaldellis, *Streams of Gold, Rivers of Blood: The Rise and Fall of Byzantium, 955 AD to the First Crusade* (Oxford, 2017), pp. 62, 68–74. Kaldellis notes, however, that there is no evidence that the Byzantines masterminded any of the opposition to Sviatoslav.

36 PVL: *An Interlinear Collation*, col. 67, lines 20–27 (*s.a.* 6477 = 968/9); RPC, p. 86.

37 Vernadsky also raises the possibility that it was the Bulgars who had contacted the Pechenegs about Sviatoslav's return. Vernadsky, *Kievan Russia*, p. 47.

38 PVL: *An Interlinear Collation*, col. 69, lines 8–22 (*s.a.* 6478 = 969/70); RPC, p. 87. For more on the Volodimer-Dobrynia relationship, see Christian Raffensperger, 'Shared (Hi)Stories: Vladimir of Rus' and Harald Fairhair of Norway', *Russian Review*, LXVIII/4 (2009), pp. 569–82.

39 PVL: *An Interlinear Collation*, col. 79, lines 11–15 (*s.a.* 6488 = 979/80); RPC, p. 93.
40 For more information on Slavic pre-Christian religion, see *Sources of Slavic Pre-Christian Religion*, ed. Juan Antonio Álvarez-Pedrosa (Leiden, 2021).
41 Maria Gimbutas, 'Ancient Slavic Religion: A Synopsis', in *To Honor Roman Jakobsen: Essays on the Occasion of his Seventieth Birthday, 11 October 1966*, 3 vols (Mouton, 1967), vol. I, pp. 738–59.
42 Donald Ostrowski, 'The Account of Volodimer's Conversion in the *Povest' vremennykh let*: A Chiasmus of Stories', *Harvard Ukrainian Studies*, XXVIII/1–4 (2006), pp. 567–80.
43 PVL: *An Interlinear Collation*, col. 84, line 17–col. 106, line 14 (*s.a.* 6494 = 985/6); RPC, pp. 96–110.
44 PVL: *An Interlinear Collation*, col. 106, line 15–col. 107, line 6 (*s.a.* 6495 = 986/7); RPC, p. 110.
45 PVL: *An Interlinear Collation*, col. 108, lines 12–13 (*s.a.* 6495 = 986/7); RPC, p. 111.
46 PVL: *An Interlinear Collation*, col. 109, lines 1–3 (*s.a.* 6496 = 987/8); RPC, p. 111.
47 PVL: *An Interlinear Collation*, col. 121, line 24–col. 122, line 3 (*s.a.* 6499 = 990/91); RPC, p. 121. For another view of the baptism of Rus, see Andrzej Poppe, 'The Political Background to the Baptism of Rus': Byzantine-Russian Relations between 986–989', in *The Rise of Christian Russia* (London, 1982), pp. 197–244.
48 PVL: *An Interlinear Collation*, col. 111, lines 24–6 (*s.a.* 6496 = 987/8); RPC, p. 113.
49 For an account of this rebellion, see Kaldellis, *Streams of Gold, Rivers of Blood*, pp. 94–102.
50 Michael Psellus, *Fourteen Byzantine Rulers: The Chronographia of Michael Psellus*, trans. E.R.A. Sewter (New York, 1966), book I, chaps 14–15.
51 PVL: *An Interlinear Collation*, col. 80, lines 2–6 (*s.a.* 6488 = 979/80), col. 121, lines 6–11 (*s.a.* 6496 = 987/8); RPC, pp. 94, 119.
52 Thietmar of Merseburg, *Chronica*, ed. J. M. Lappenberg, in *Monumenta Germaniae Historica*, ed. George Pertz, vol. III (Hanover, 1839, reprinted Leipzig, 1925), book VII, chap. 52; for the English, see *Ottonian Germany: The 'Chronicon' of Thietmar of Merseburg*, trans. David A. Warner (Manchester, 2001), book VII, chap. 72.
53 PVL: *An Interlinear Collation*, col. 121, lines 9–11 (*s.a.* 6498 = 987/8); RPC, p. 119.
54 Valerie A. Kivelson and Ronald Grigor Suny, *Russia's Empires* (Oxford, 2017).
55 Nikolai Trubetskoi [I. R.], *Nasledie Chingiskhana. Vzgliad na russkuiu istoriiu ne s Zapada, a s Vostka* (Berlin, 1925); George Vernadsky, *The Mongols and Russia* (New Haven, CT, 1953); and Lev Gumilev, *Drevniaia Rus' I velikaia step* (Moscow, 1989). Note that this school of historical study is not to be confused with the Eurasia political movement.
56 David Christian, 'Inner Eurasia as a Unit of World History', *Journal of World History*, V/2 (1994), pp. 173–211; David Christian, *A History of*

Russia, Central Asia and Mongolia, vol. I: *Inner Eurasia from Prehistory to the Mongol Empire* (Malden, MA, 1998); John P. LeDonne, 'The Geopolitical Context of Russian Foreign Policy, 1700–1917', *Acta Slavica Iaponica*, XII (1994), pp. 1–23; John P. LeDonne, *The Russian Empire and the World 1700–1917: The Geopolitics of Expansion and Containment* (Oxford, 1997); Donald Ostrowski, *Russia in the Early Modern World: The Continuity of Change* (Lanham, MD, 2022).

57 For example, Samuel Hazzard Cross, 'Yaroslav the Wise in Norse Tradition', *Speculum*, IV/2 (April 1929), pp. 177–97.

58 Christian Raffensperger, *Reimagining Europe: Kievan Rus' in the Medieval World* (Cambridge, MA, 2012); Yulia Mikhailova, *Property, Power, and Authority in Rus and Latin Europe, ca. 1000–1236* (Leeds, 2018); Talia Zajac, 'Remembrance and Erasure of Objects Belonging to Rus′ Princesses in Medieval Western Sources: The Cases of Anastasia Iaroslavna's "Saber of Charlemagne" and Anna Iaroslavna's Red Gem', in *Moving Women, Moving Objects, 400–1500*, ed. Tracy Chapman Hamilton and Mariah Proctor-Tiffany (Leiden, 2019), pp. 33–58.

2 Rule and Succession among the Volodimerovich Clan

1 This section is built upon Donald Ostrowski's article on the subject: Donald Ostrowski, 'Was There a Riurikid Dynasty in Early Rus′?', *Canadian–American Slavic Studies*, LII (2018), pp. 30–49. Because of its heavy reliance on this article, and the shared authorship of that article and the current book, citations to the article beyond this one will be omitted.

2 For the first mention of this theory, see *Historia Brittonum*, ed. Theodore Mommsen, book II, accessed online at www.thelatinlibrary.com/histbrit.html, 15 October 2022.

3 Isidore of Seville, *Etymologies*, book IX, line 102, accessed online at https://penelope.uchicago.edu, 15 October 2022.

4 Saxo Grammaticus, *The History of the Danes: Books I–IX*, trans. Peter Fisher, ed. Hilda Ellis Davidson (Cambridge, 1996), book I.

5 Ibid., Preface.

6 Jan Długosz (1415–1480), *Historiae Polonicae*, libri XII (1711).

7 *Polnoe sobranie russkikh letopisei* (PSRL), 43 vols (St Petersburg/Petrograd/Leningrad and Moscow, 1841–2007), vol. XXXII (1975), pp. 15, 16, 30, 34, 128, 129, 134.

8 Note that neither the Palemon myth nor the Prus myth involve any connection with Constantinople, thus disregarding the Eastern Roman Empire completely.

9 As noted, there is a wide literature in the field of anthropology on this topic, but one could begin with the following to familiarize oneself. David Parkin, *Kinship: An Introduction to the Basic Concepts* (New York, 1997); and *New Directions in Anthropological Kinship*, ed. Linda Stone (New York, 2000).

10 Karl Schmid, 'Zur Problematik von Familie, Sippe und Geschlect, Haus und Dynastie beim mittelalterlichen Adel', *Zeitschrift für die Geschichte des Oberrheins*, CV (1957), pp. 1–62; Georges Duby,

'Structures de parenté et noblesse dans la France du Nord aux XIe et XIIe siècles', in *Hommes et structures du moyen âge: Recueil d'articles* (Paris, 1973), pp. 267–85.

11 Constance B. Bouchard, 'Family Structure and Family Consciousness among the Aristocracy in the Ninth to Eleventh Centuries', *Francia*, XIV (1986), p. 640.

12 Alexander Callander Murray, *Germanic Kinship Structure: Studies in Law and Society in Antiquity and the Early Middle Ages* (Toronto, 1983).

13 Christian Raffensperger has added to this discussion with ideas of kinship webs and situational kinship networks, which we can see in action in some of what is discussed in this book, but it does not necessarily need definition here. See *Conflict, Bargaining, and Kinship Networks in Medieval Eastern Europe* (Lanham, MD, 2018) for more information.

14 Donald Ostrowski, 'Systems of Succession in Rus' and Steppe Societies', *Ruthenica*, IX (2012), pp. 47–8, 58; Ostrowski, 'Was There a Riurikid Dynasty?', pp. 33–5.

15 *Das Metropolitan Ilarion Lobrede auf Vladimir den Heligen und Glaubensbekenntnis*, ed. Ludolf Müller (Wiesbaden, 1962), p. 100.

16 A. A. Zimin, 'Pamiat' i pokhvala Iakova mnikha i Zhitie kniaziaVladimira po drevneishemu spisku', *Kratkie soobshcheniia Instituta slavianovedeniia*, XXXVII (1963), p. 67. 'Memorial and Encomium for Prince Volodimer of Rus', in *The Hagiography of Kievan Rus*, trans. Paul Hollingsworth (Cambridge, MA, 1992), p. 175.

17 *PSRL*, vol. II (1908), cols 383–4. Lisa Heinrich, 'The Kyivan Chronicle: A Translation and Commentary', PhD dissertation, Vanderbilt University, 1977, p. 115.

18 *PSRL*, vol. II (1908), col. 709. 'Kyivan Chronicle', p. 490.

19 Butler makes the point that the cult of Volodimer was established relatively late in the history. Francis Butler, *Enlightener of Rus': The Image of Vladimir Sviatoslavich across the Centuries* (Bloomington, IN, 2002).

20 *PSRL*, vol. II (1908), pp. 1–2.

21 *PSRL*, vol. III (2000), pp. 465–6. The Archaeographic Commission manuscript is the earliest version of the Younger Redaction of the Novgorod I Chronicle. The only copy of the Older Redaction of the Novgorod I Chronicle is the Synodal manuscript, which dates to the thirteenth century, but it is incomplete, lacking the beginning part of the chronicle. One could speculate that the lost beginning of the Synodal copy had an earlier version of the fifteenth-century genealogy, but such a speculation would be complete supposition.

22 Zimin, 'Pamiat i pokhvala Iakova mnikha i Zhitie kniazia Vladimira po drevneishemu spisku', p. 72; 'Memorial and Encomium for Prince Volodimer of Rus''', p. 176. See Hollingsworth, 'Introduction', in *The Hagiography of Kievan Rus*, pp. lxxxv–lxxxvi.

23 *PSRL*, vol. XI (1897), p. 108.

24 *The Letter of Spiridon-Savva* was published by R. P. Dmitrieva, in *Skazanie o kniaziakh vladimirskikh* (Moscow and Leningrad, 1955), pp. 159–70.

25 *The Tale about the Vladimir Princes* was published by R. P. Dmitrieva, in *Skazanie o kniaziakh vladimirskikh*, pp. 171–81. For a discussion of hypotheses concerning the complex of texts connected with the *Tale*, see Donald Ostrowski, *Muscovy and the Mongols: Cross-Cultural Influences on the Steppe Frontier* (Cambridge, 1998), pp. 171–5.
26 Sigismund Freiherr von Herberstein, *Notes upon Russia*, trans. and ed. R. H. Major, 2 vols (London, 1851), vol. I, p. 9.
27 Nancy Shields Kollmann, 'The Cap of Monomakh', in *Picturing Russia: Explorations in Visual Culture*, ed. Valerie Kivelson and Joan Neuberger (New Haven, CT, 2008), pp. 38–41.
28 Michael S. Flier, 'The Throne of Monomakh: Ivan the Terrible and the Architectonics of Destiny', in *Architectures of Russian Identity: 1500 to the Present*, ed. James Cracraft and Daniel Rowland (Ithaca, NY, 2003), pp. 21–33, 216–18.
29 David Hackett Fischer, *Historians' Fallacies: Toward a Logic of Historical Thought* (New York, 1970), p. 209.
30 Ibid., p. 135.

3 Iaroslav the Wise, Ingigerd and Their Family

1 Thietmar of Merseburg, *Chronica*, book VII, chap. 72.
2 For a listing of wives and named children, see Christian Raffensperger, *Ties of Kinship: Genealogy and Dynastic Marriage in Kyivan Rus'* (Cambridge, MA, 2016), pp. 180–81, table 1.
3 The court drama is evocatively reconstructed in the historical portrait written by Susana Torres Prieto, 'Anna Porphyrogenita, Byzantine Princess and Queen of the Rus'', in *Portraits of Medieval Eastern Europe*, ed. Donald Ostrowski and Christian Raffensperger (New York, 2018), pp. 159–65.
4 PVL: *Interlinear Collation*, col. 130, line 9–col. 130, line 11 (*s.a.* 1014); RPC, p. 124.
5 For an English translation of this law code, see *Medieval Russian Laws*, trans. George Vernadsky (New York, 1947).
6 There is debate about the parentage of Sviatopolk. Some people suggest that he was the son of Iaropolk, Volodimer's brother; others suggest that he was the eldest son of Volodimer. For more on the two opinions, see Raffensperger, *Ties of Kinship*, pp. 19–21; Simon Franklin and Jonathan Shepard, *The Emergence of Rus, 750–1200* (New York, 1996), pp. 184–93.
7 See below for a further discussion of one pair of those sons – the subsequently sainted Boris and Gleb.
8 In approximately 1009, Sviatopolk had married a daughter of Bolesław, most likely as part of a larger political arrangement between Rus and its western neighbour. The Boleslavna had brought with her a bishop to act as her confessor, as well as to help Christianize Rus, but before long, Volodimer had imprisoned Sviatopolk, his wife and the priest, as he believed they had planned a revolt against him. *Ottonian Germany: The 'Chronicon' of Thietmar of Merseburg*, book IV, chap. 58; book I, chap. 72.

9 *Ottonian Germany: The 'Chronicon' of Thietmar of Merseburg*, book VIII, chap. 33.

10 The PVL (*s.a.* 1018) records that Sviatopolk ordered that all of the Poles found in the city of Kyiv be killed; thus, Bolesław fled. PVL: *Interlinear Collation*, col. 143, lines 27–8; RPC, p. 132. Conversely, the *Gesta Principum Polonorum* records that Bolesław missed his son so much that he desired to leave Rus. A middle ground between these two extreme positions seems most likely. *Gesta Principum Polonorum: The Deeds of the Princes of the Poles*, trans. and ed. Paul W. Knoll and Frank Schaer (New York, 2003), pp. 42–3.

11 PVL: *Interlinear Collation*, col. 146, lines 8–9 (*s.a.* 1019); RPC, p. 134.

12 PVL: *Interlinear Collation*, col. 147, lines 17–23; col. 148, line 5–col. 149, line 19, *s.a.* 1023, 1024, 1026. RPC, pp. 134–6.

13 All of this information is recorded in Snorri Sturluson, *Heimskringla: History of the Kings of Norway*, trans. Lee M. Hollander (Austin, TX, 1964), pp. 342–3.

14 Ibid., pp. 429–31.

15 For more information on these marriages, along with an analysis of them, see Raffensperger, *Ties of Kinship*, pp. 25–8 (for Iaroslav and Ingigerd), pp. 41–5 (for Harald and Elisabeth).

16 *Morkinskinna: The Earliest Icelandic Chronicle of the Norwegian Kings, 1030–1157*, trans. Theodore M. Andersson and Kari Ellen Gade (Ithaca, NY, 2000), p. 89. Interestingly, Iaroslav's appellation of 'the Wise' seems to be a much later addition.

17 There is much, much more about the Golden Age of Rus than can be covered here. For a fuller treatment, see Franklin and Shepard, *The Emergence of Rus*, pp. 208–44.

18 *Ottonian Germany: The 'Chronicon' of Thietmar of Merseburg*, book VIII, chap. 32.

19 PVL: *An Interlinear Collation*, col. 151, lines 24–5 (*s.a.* 1037); RPC, p. 137.

20 J. Brutzkus, 'Trade with Eastern Europe, 800–1200', *Economic History Review*, XIII/1–2 (1943), pp. 31–41.

21 Norman Golb and Omeljan Pritsak, *Khazarian Hebrew Documents of the Tenth Century* (Ithaca, NY, 1982).

22 Elena Boeck, 'Simulating the Hippodrome: The Performance of Power in Kiev's St Sophia', *Art Bulletin*, XCI/3 (2009), pp. 283–301.

23 PVL: *An Interlinear Collation*, col. 155, lines 26–8 (*s.a.* 1051); RPC, p. 139.

24 Ilarion, 'Sermon on Law and Grace', in *Sermons and Rhetoric of Kievan Rus'*, trans. Simon Franklin (Cambridge, MA, 1991), pp. 3–30.

25 Norman W. Ingham, 'The Martyred Prince and the Question of Slavic Cultural Continuity in the Early Middle Ages', in *Medieval Russian Culture*, ed. Henrik Birnbaum and Michael S. Flier (Berkeley, CA, 1984), pp. 31–53.

26 'Lesson concerning the Life and Murder of the Blessed Passion-Sufferers Boris and Gleb', in *The Hagiography of Kievan Rus'*, pp. 3–32.

27 PVL: *An Interlinear Collation*, col. 152, lines 1–3 (*s.a.* 1037); RPC, p. 137. The forthcoming Harvard Ukrainian Research Institute English translation of the PVL by Horace G. Lunt notes multiple complications with this section of the chronicle.

28 Simon Franklin, *Writing, Society and Culture in Early Rus', c. 950–1300* (Cambridge, 2002), p. 23.
29 PVL: *An Interlinear Collation*, col. 48, lines 9–15 (*s.a.* 945); RPC, p. 74.
30 *Medieval Russian Laws*, pp. 34, 46.
31 There is a wonderful repository of the birch bark documents online at gramoty.ru.
32 This idea is examined much more with regard to Rus in Raffensperger, *Reimagining Europe*, pp. 47–70.
33 This marriage and its sources are noted fully in Raffensperger, *Ties of Kinship*, pp. 48–52. For more on Anna, see Wladimir V. Bogomoletz, 'Anna of Kiev: An Enigmatic Capetian Queen of the Eleventh Century: A Reassessment of Biographical Sources', *French History*, XIX (2005), pp. 299–323.
34 Jean Dunbabin, 'What's in a Name? Philip, King of France', *Speculum*, LXVIII/4 (October 1993), pp. 949–68.
35 *Recueil des actes de Philippe I-er, roi de France (1059–1108)*, ed. Maurice Prou (Paris, 1908), doc. no. 6.
36 Ibid., no. 16.
37 For the sources and information on this marriage, see Raffensperger, *Ties of Kinship*, pp. 33–6.
38 For the sources and information on this marriage, see ibid., pp. 28–32.
39 Iziaslav's flight and travels are detailed in Christian Raffensperger, 'Iziaslav Iaroslavich's Excellent Adventure: Constructing Kinship to Gain and Regain Power in Eleventh-Century Europe', *Medieval Prosopography*, XXX (2015), pp. 1–30.
40 A full discussion of this attack is conducted in Jonathan Shepard, 'Why Did the Russians Attack Byzantium in 1043?', *Byzantinisch-Neugriechische Jahrbücher*, XXII (1985), pp. 147–212.
41 PVL: *An Interlinear Collation*, col. 160, lines 29–31 (*s.a.* 1053); RPC, p. 142. For the sources and information on this marriage, see Raffensperger, *Ties of Kinship*, pp. 52–5.
42 One can see the name 'Monomakh' on a seal from the period, recorded in *Aktovye pechati drevnei rusi X-XV vv.*, vol. I of III: *Pechati X–nachala XIII v.*, ed. V. L. Ianin (Moscow, 1970), table 3, no. 25. It is also possible that we see a record of Volodimer's mother, Vsevolod's wife, in no. 23.
43 For a discussion of the onomastics of this example, see Raffensperger, *Reimagining Europe*, p. 108.
44 PVL: *An Interlinear Collation*, col. 161, lines 3–5 (*s.a.* 1054); RPC, p. 142.
45 PVL: *An Interlinear Collation*, col. 161, lines 13–17 (*s.a.* 1054); RPC, p. 142.
46 PVL: *An Interlinear Collation*, col. 161, lines 21–3 (*s.a.* 1054); RPC, pp. 142–3.

4 Mstislav/Harald Volodimerich and His Family

1 PVL: *An Interlinear Collation*, col. 199, line 12b (*s.a.* 1076). This information appears only in the Hypatian branch, and thus may be a later interpolation.
2 For a wider discussion of these individuals, see Christian Raffensperger, 'Runaway Rulers: Marriage, Power, and Building a Wider Medieval

Europe', *Royal Studies Journal*, VIII/2 (2021), pp. 55–75.

3 This marriage is discussed in more detail in Christian Raffensperger, *Ties of Kinship: Genealogy and Dynastic Marriage in Kyivan Rus'* (Cambridge, MA, 2016), pp. 62–3.

4 A. F. Litvina and F. B. Uspenskii, *Vybor imeni u russkikh kniazei v X–XVI vv.: Dinasticheskaia istoriia skvoz' prizmu antroponimiki* (Moscow, 2006), p. 26.

5 Snorri Sturluson, *Heimskringla: History of the Kings of Norway*, trans. Lee M. Hollander (Austin, TX, 1964), p. 790.

6 PVL: *An Interlinear Collation*, col. 229, lines 12–18 (*s.a.* 1095); RPC, p. 181.

7 This is conjectural, based upon his later possession of Chernigov. See Raffensperger, *Ties of Kingship*, p. 273.

8 Omeljan Pritsak, 'Introduction', in *The Old Rus' Kyivan and Galician-Volhynian Chronicles: The Ostroz'kyj (Xlebnikov) and četvertyns'kyj (Pogodin) codices* (Cambridge, MA, 1990), p. xx.

9 PSRL, vol. II (1908), col. 275 (*s.a.* 1113).

10 It is possible that this was a consequence of the Volodimerovichi meetings that were held in Liubech and Uvetichi, recorded in the PVL under the years 1097 and 1100, respectively.

11 PSRL, vol. II (1908), col. 284 (*s.a.* 1117).

12 Ibid.

13 PSRL, vol. I/2 (1928), cols 293–5 (*s.a.* 1125).

14 PSRL, vol. I/2 (1928), col. 295 (*s.a.* 1125); PSRL, vol. II (1908), col. 289 (*s.a.* 1126); 'Kyivan Chronicle', p. 8.

15 This marriage is discussed in more detail in Raffensperger, *Ties of Kinship*, pp. 85–7.

16 Adam of Bremen, *The History of the Archbishops of Hamburg-Bremen*, trans. Francis J. Tschan (New York, 2002), book III, schol. 84 (85, 86).

17 Snorri Sturluson, *Heimskringla*, p. 790; 'Wilhelmi Abbatis Genealogia Regum Danorum', in *Scriptores minores historiae danicae medii ævi*, ed. M.C.L. Getz, 2 vols (Copenhagen, 1917), vol. I, p. 182.

18 PSRL, vol. III (2000), pp. 21, 205 (*s.a.* 1122); *The Chronicle of Novgorod, 1016–1471*, trans. Robert Michell and Nevill Forbes (London, 1914), p. 10.

19 Of course, it is possible that there are many such marriages and our lack of source material simply makes it impossible for us to know about them.

20 See Henrik Birnbaum, *Lord Novgorod the Great: Essays in the History and Culture of a Medieval City-State, Part One: The Historical Background* (Columbus, OH, 1981), pp. 45–7, for some of the main moments in the creation of an independent Novgorod (per Birnbaum). An excellent, revisionist history of the *veche* can be found in Jonas Granberg, *Veche in the Chronicles of Medieval Rus: A Study of Functions and Terminology* (Gothenburg, 2004).

21 Janet Martin, *Medieval Russia, 980–1584*, 2nd edn (Cambridge, 2007), p. 280.

22 For Mstislav's death, see PSRL, vol. I/2 (1928), col. 301 (*s.a.* 1132); PSRL, vol. II (1908), col. 294 (*s.a.* 1133); 'Kyivan Chronicle', p. 14.

23 PVL: *An Interlinear Collation*, col. 240, line 23–col. 256, line 3. The *Testament of Monomakh* appears only in the Laurentian copy of the PVL and not in any of the other primary witnesses, which has led the editor of the PVL: *An Interlinear Collation* to conclude that it was a later interpolation. The *Testament* has been translated and is included in RPC, pp. 206–15.
24 M. P. Alekseev, 'Anglo-saksonskaia parallel' k Poucheniu Vladimira Monomakha', *Trudy Otdela drevnerusskoi literatury*, II (1935), pp. 39–80.
25 Simon Franklin and Jonathan Shepard, *The Emergence of Rus, 750–1200* (New York, 1996), pp. 313–15.
26 RPC, p. 206. Pages 206–10 are much more religious in content than the rest of the text.
27 Ibid., p. 210.
28 Ibid., p. 211.
29 The most comprehensive and accurate edition is *The Povest' vremennykh let: An Interlinear Collation and Paradosis*, compiled and edited by Donald Ostrowski, with David Birnbaum as assistant editor and Horace G. Lunt as senior consultant (Cambridge, MA, 2003). It is also accessible in a searchable digital version at http://pvl.obdurodon.org/pvl.html.
30 V. N. Rusinov, 'Letopisnye stat'i 1051–1117 gg. v sviazi s problemoi avtorstva i redaktsii "Povesti vremennykh let"', *Vestnik Nizhegorodskogo universiteta im. N. I. Lobachevskogo. Seriia istoriia, politilogiia, mezhdunarodnye otnosheniia*, I/2 (2003), pp. 123–38; cf. Donald Ostrowski, 'The Debate over the Authorship of the Rus' Primary Chronicle: Compilations, Redactions, and Urtexts', in *Historiography and Identity*, vol. V: *The Emergence of New Peoples and Polities in Europe, 1000–1300*, ed. Walter Pohl, Francescro Borri and Veronika Wieser (Turnhout, 2022).
31 Franklin and Shepard note that 'Between 1128 and 1161 the Polovtsy intervened to support Oleg's descendants on approximately fifteen occasions.' *The Emergence of Rus*, p. 327.
32 Martin Dimnik has attempted to shift this perception with his dynasty of Chernigov duology, which favours the Sviatoslavichi. Martin Dimnik, *The Dynasty of Chernigov, 1054–1146* (Toronto, 1994); Martin Dimnik, *The Dynasty of Chernigov, 1146–1246* (Cambridge, 2003).
33 All of these marriages are discussed in much greater detail in Raffensperger, *Ties of Kinship*, pp. 81–5.
34 PSRL, vol. II (1908), col. 308 (*s.a.* 1141); 'Kyivan Chronicle', p. 29.
35 These machinations are narrated in more detail in Christian Raffensperger, *Conflict, Bargaining, and Kinship Networks in Medieval Eastern Europe* (Lanham, MD, 2018), pp. 113–28.
36 *Medieval Russian Laws*, trans. George Vernadsky (New York, 1947), article 53.
37 Ibid., articles 56–62.
38 Ibid., articles 63–6, 110–21.
39 Ibid., articles 71–3, 75–7.
40 Ibid., articles 80–87.
41 Ibid., article 88.

42 Ibid., articles 91, 93.
43 Ibid., article 106.
44 Simon Franklin, *Writing, Society and Culture in Early Rus', c. 950–1300* (Cambridge, 2002), p. 23.
45 This is clear in the source material for Raffensperger, *Ties of Kinship*.
46 Consanguineous marriages are those within a restricted limit of blood lines. For more information, see Raffensperger, *Reimagining Europe*, pp. 58–60.
47 PSRL, vol. III (2000), pp. 21, 205; *Chronicle of Novgorod*, 10 (*s.a.* 6631 = 1123). For more on this marriage, see Raffensperger, *Ties of Kinship*, pp. 122–3.
48 PSRL, vol. III (2000), pp. 24, 209 (*s.a.* 1136); *Chronicle of Novgorod*, p. 14.
49 PSRL, vol. I/2 (1927), col. 341 (*s.a.* 1154).
50 PSRL, vol. III (2000), pp. 27, 213 (*s.a.* 1143); *Chronicle of Novgorod*, p. 18. For more on this marriage, see Raffensperger, *Ties of Kinship*, pp. 130–31.
51 This marriage is discussed in more detail ibid., pp. 106–7.
52 These marriages are discussed in more detail ibid., pp. 112–18; and idem, 'Dynastic Marriage in Action: How Two Rusian Princesses Changed Scandinavia', in *Imenoslov: Istoriia iazyka. Istoriia kul'tury*, ed. F. B. Uspenskij (Moscow, 2010), pp. 193–205.
53 We are indebted for this theory to F. B. Uspenskii and A. F. Litvina, who first proposed it in Litvina and Uspenskii, *Vybor imeni u russkikh kniazei v X–XVI vv.*, p. 247 n. 26.
54 Saxo Grammaticus, *Danorum Regum Heroumque Historia: Books X–XVI*, vol. I: *Books X, XI, XII and XIII*, trans. and ed. Eric Christiansen (Oxford, 1980), book XIII, p. 110.
55 Raffensperger, 'Dynastic Marriage in Action', pp. 193–205.
56 It should come as no surprise that both Malfrid and Ingeborg named their firstborn daughters after their own mother. It simply reinforces our understanding of the importance of natal families.
57 Raffensperger, 'Dynastic Marriage in Action'.
58 Raffensperger, *Conflict, Bargaining, and Kinship Networks*; see the multiple examples included there.

5 Vsevolod 'Big Nest' Iurevich and His Family

1 Natalia Polonska-Vasylenko, *Two Conceptions of the History of Ukraine and Russia*, ed. Wolodymyr Mykula (London, 1968), pp. 30–37.
2 PVL: *An Interlinear Collation*, col. 20, line 14; col. 147, line 24 (*s.a.* 907, 1024). RPC, pp. 60, 134.
3 PSRL, vol. II (1908), cols 517–21 (*s.a.* 1162).
4 See the English translation in the 'Kyivan Chronicle', p. 263.
5 Interestingly, the twelfth-century writer John Kinnamos records a later version of the Danubian land grant, circa 1165: 'At the same time Vladislav, one of the principal persons in Rusia, came as a refugee to the Romans with his children and his wife and all his forces, and a property along the Danube was granted to him. Previously the emperor had given it to the refugee Vasilika the son of George, who had the principal place among the chieftains in Russia.' John Kinnamos, *Deeds*

of John and Manuel Comnenus, trans. Charles M. Brand (New York, 1976), p. 178.

6 Janet Martin, *Medieval Russia, 980–1584*, 2nd edn (Cambridge, 2007), p. 126.

7 Simon Franklin and Jonathan Shepard, *The Emergence of Rus, 750–1200* (New York, 1996), p. 350.

8 PSRL, vol. II (1908), col. 567 (*s.a.* 1174); 'Kyivan Chronicle', p. 324.

9 PSRL, vol. II (1908), col. 570 (*s.a.* 1174); 'Kyivan Chronicle', p. 326.

10 PSRL, vol. II (1908), col. 578 (*s.a.* 1174); 'Kyivan Chronicle', p. 335.

11 PSRL, vol. II (1908), cols 586–89 (*s.a.* 1175); 'Kyivan Chronicle', pp. 346–50. Michael S. Flier, 'The Murder of Andrej Bogoljubskij in Word and Image', in *Philology Broad and Deep: In Memoriam Horace Gray Lunt*, ed. Michael S. Flier, David J. Birnbaum and Cynthia M. Vakareliyska (Bloomington, IN, 2014), pp. 103–18; and Michael S. Flier, 'Murder Most Foul: Picturing the Death of Andrei Bogoliubskii', in *Seeing Muscovy Anew: Politics – Institutions – Culture, in Honor of Nancy Shields Kollmann*, ed. Michael S. Flier, Valerie Kivelson, Erika Monahan and Daniel Rowland (Bloomington, IN, 2017), pp. 143–57.

12 However, it is important to note that there were people there, whether returned or still there, when the Mongols arrived just a few decades later.

13 Nicolas de Baumgarten, 'Généalogies et mariages Occidentaux des Rurikides Russes du X-e au XIII-e siècle', *Orientalia Christiana*, IX/25 (1927), table X.

14 Hyptian Chronicle, *s.a.* 1176. PSRL, vol. II (1908), col. 602; 'Kyivan Chronicle', p. 365.

15 For Iurii's rule in Novgorod, see *Novgorodskaia pervaia letopis' starshego I mladshego izvodov*, *s.a.* 1172, 1175. PSRL, vol. III (2000), pp. 34, 222–3; *Chronicle of Novgorod*, pp. 27, 28.

16 Donald Rayfield, *Edge of Empires: A History of Georgia* (London, 2012), p. 109.

17 Lois Huneycutt, 'Tamar of Georgia (1184–1213) and the Language of Female Power', in *A Companion to Global Queenship*, ed. Elena Woodacre (Leeds, 2018), p. 30.

18 For the whole hypothesis, see Litvina and Uspenskii, *Vybor imeni u russkikh kniazei v X–XVI vv.*, pp. 374–81.

19 PSRL, 10 (1885), 60 (*s.a.* 1209); *The Nikonian Chronicle*, ed. Serge A. Zenkovsky, trans. Serge A. Zenkovsky and Betty Jean Zenkovsky, 5 vols (Princeton, NJ, 1984–9), vol. II, p. 242.

20 V. N. Tatishchev, *Istoriia Rossiiskaia*, 7 vols (Moscow, 1964), vol. III, p. 182 (*s.a.* 1209). For a critique of Tatishchev as a source, see Oleksii Tolochko, '*Istoriia Rossiiskaia*' *Vasiliia Tatishcheva: Istochniki i izvestiia* (Kyiv, 2005).

21 Upon Andrei Bogoliubskii's death, the Hypatian Chronicle records a glowing, and lengthy, account of the construction of this and other churches by Andrei. PSRL, vol. II (1908), cols 580–83 (*s.a.* 1175); 'Kyivan Chronicle', pp. 339–42.

22 Arthur Voyce, *The Art and Architecture of Medieval Russia* (Norman, OK, 1967), p. 120.

23 Samuel Hazzard Cross, *Medieval Russian Churches*, ed. Kenneth John Conant (Cambridge, MA, 1949), pp. 53–4.

24 Laurentian Chronicle, *s.a.* 1200; *PSRL*, vol. I/2 (1927), col. 415.

25 Laurentian Chronicle, *s.a.* 1206; *PSRL*, vol. I/2 (1927), col. 424. For more information about this monastery, see Talia Zajac, 'The Social-Political Roles of the Princess in Kyivan Rus, ca. 945–1240', in *A Companion to Global Queenship*, ed. Woodacre, pp. 139–40.

26 *PSRL*, vol. IX (1862), pp. 223–9; Andrzej Poppe, 'Leontios, Abbot of Patmos, Candidate for the Metropolitan See of Rus'', in *Christian Russia in the Making* (Aldershot and Burlington, VT, 2007), pp. 1–13.

27 Novgorod Chronicle, *s.a.* 1204. *PSRL*, vol. III (2000), pp. 46–9, 240–46; *Chronicle of Novgorod*, pp. 43–8.

28 Novgorod Chronicle, *s.a.* 1234. *PSRL*, vol. III (2000), pp. 61, 264; *Chronicle of Novgorod*, pp. 63–4.

29 'Tale of the Destruction of Riazan', in *Medieval Russia's Epics, Chronicles, and Tales*, revised and enlarged edn, ed. and trans. Serge A. Zenkovsky (New York, 1974), p. 202.

30 Martin, *Medieval Russia*, p. 176.

31 Ibid., p. 164.

32 Laurentian Chronicle, *s.a.* 1194, 1196, 1198; *PSRL*, vol. I/2 (1927), cols 411, 412, 414.

33 Laurentian Chronicle, *s.a.* 1186; *PSRL*, vol. I/2 (1927), cols 396–7.

34 Voskresenskaia Chronicle, *s.a.* 1196; *PSRL*, vol. VII (1856), p. 103. Dąbrowski discusses this marriage in more detail, but it is important to note that if Konstantin was born in 1186, he would have only been nine at the time of the marriage. Dariush Dombrovskii, *Genealogiia Mstislavichei: pervye pokoleniia (do nachala XIV v.)* (St Petersburg, 2015), p. 538, n. 2388.

35 For an acknowledgement of Vsevolod's place as the eldest, see the statements in the Hypatian Chronicle, *PSRL*, vol. II (1908), col. 683 (*s.a.* 1195); 'Kyivan Chronicle', p. 460.

36 *PSRL*, vol. VII (1856), p. 117; *PSRL*, vol. XXV (1949), p. 108; *PSRL*, vol. X (1885), p. 63; *Nikonian Chronicle*, vol. II, pp. 246–7. Janet Martin notes that Vsevolod knew that Konstantin preferred his position as ruler of Rostov and thus appointed Iurii as his heir. Martin, *Medieval Russia*, p. 112. The story of Vsevolod's asking Konstantin to come to him three times as he was dying may be problematic. The story appears only in later chronicles, such as the Voskresenskaia, the Compilation of the End of the Fifteenth Century and the *Nikonian Chronicle*. It does not appear in the Laurentian Chronicle, which absence Fennell explained as being the result of the fact that 'at the time [the Laurentian Chronicle] was devoted almost entirely to Konstantin's interest'. John Fennell, *The Crisis of Medieval Russia, 1200–1304* (London, 1983), p. 46. But there might be another explanation; namely, it might have been made up by a later chronicler to explain why Iurii, not Konstantin, succeeded Vsevolod.

37 *PSRL*, vol. I/2 (1927), col. 407 (*s.a.* 1189); *PSRL*, vol. II (1908), col. 658 (*s.a.* 1187); 'Kyivan Chronicle', pp. 429–30.

38 *PSRL*, vol. II (1908), col. 658 (*s.a.* 1187); 'Kyivan Chronicle', p. 430.

39 Ibid.
40 Barbara H. Rosenwein, *Generations of Feeling: A History of Emotions, 600–1700* (Cambridge, 2015).
41 PSRL, vol. I/2 (1927), col. 408 (*s.a.* 1189).
42 This episode is discussed in some detail in Martin Dimnik, *The Dynasty of Chernigov, 1146–1246* (Cambridge, 2003), pp. 267–70.
43 PSRL, vol. I/2 (1927), col. 435 (*s.a.* 1211).
44 Ibid., cols 442–4 (*s.a.* 1218).
45 Ibid., col. 426 (*s.a.* 1205).
46 Ibid., col. 465 (*s.a.* 1237).
47 Ibid., col. 408 (*s.a.* 1190).
48 PSRL, vol. II (1908), col. 674 (*s.a.* 1192); 'Kyivan Chronicle', p. 450.
49 Donald Ostrowski, '"Dressing a Wolf in Sheep's Clothing": Toward Understanding the Composition of the *Life of Alexander Nevskii*', in *Centers and Peripheries in the Christian East: Papers from the Second Biennial Conference of the Association for the Study of Eastern Christian History and Culture*, ed. Eugene Clay, Russell Martin and Barbara Skinner, *Russian History*, XL (2013), pp. 57, 65; 'Tale of the Life and Courage of the Pious and Great Prince Alexander [Nevsky]', in *Medieval Russia's Epics, Chronicles, and Tales*, p. 226, where Zenkovsky translates her name as 'Theodosia'.
50 PSRL, vol. I/2 (1927), col. 426; PSRL, vol. VII (1856), p. 112; PSRL, vol. X (1885), p. 50.
51 PSRL, vol. III (2000), pp. 56, 257 (*s.a.* 1216); *Chronicle of Novgorod*, p. 57.
52 Fennell, *Crisis*, p. 36.
53 PSRL, vol. III (2000), pp. 74, 285; *Chronicle of Novgorod*, pp. 80–81.
54 Fennell, *Crisis*, p. 74.
55 Laurentian Chronicle, *s.a.* 1238; PSRL, vol. I/2 (1927), col. 467.

6 Roman Mstislavich and His Family

1 PVL: *An Interlinear Collation*, col. 121, line 15 (*s.a.* 6496 = 987/8); col. 161, line 18 (*s.a.* 6562 = 1053/4); and col. 162, lines 21–2 (*s.*a. 6565 = 1056/7); RPC, pp. 119, 142 and 143. For a full account of the history of Volhynia see Mykhailo Hrushevsky, *History of Ukraine-Rus'*, vol. II: *The Eleventh to Thirteenth Centuries*, trans. Ian Press, ed. Christian Raffensperger and Frank E. Sysyn, with the translation and editorial assistance of Tania Plawuszczak-Stech (Edmonton and Toronto, 2020), chap. 6. Although dated in some places, Hrushevsky's treatment of the history of the region, based on the chronicle accounts, is excellent. For a modern analysis of the regions that were combined, see A. V. Maiorov, *Galitsko-Volynskaia Rus': Ocherki sotsial'no-politicheskikh otnoshenii v domongol'skii period* (St Petersburg, 2001).
2 For a full account of the history of Galicia, see Hrushevsky, *History of Ukraine-Rus'*, vol. II, chap. 7.
3 Janet Martin, *Medieval Russia, 980–1584*, 2nd edn (Cambridge, 2007), p. 107.
4 Christian Raffensperger, *Conflict, Bargaining, and Kinship Networks in Medieval Eastern Europe* (Lanham, MD, 2018), pp. 117–20.

5 Initially, the throne passed to Iziaslav's brother, Sviatopolk, and then back to Iziaslav when he was expelled from Kyiv, then to someone else, but eventually it came to Iziaslav's son, Mstislav.
6 Martin, *Medieval Russia*, pp. 107, 123.
7 These events are recorded under the year 1169 (6677) in the Hypatian Chronicle, which is two years off from the timeline presented in other chronicles at this point. It is likely to have happened because the chronicle was created without dates and they were only added later, circa 1300. PSRL, vol. II (1908), cols 532–4; 'Kyivan Chronicle', pp. 279–82. For the dating issue, see Hrushevsky, *History of Ukraine-Rus'*, vol. II, chap. 3, p. 20, n. 49.
8 Hypatian Chronicle, PSRL, vol. II (1908), cols 535–7 (*s.a.* 6679 = 1170/71). 'Kyivan Chronicle', pp. 294–5. Despite Andrei Bogoliubskii's military leadership, the political instigation against Mstislav was begun by Volodimer Mstislavich.
9 The Novgorod First Chronicle records Roman's ousting, following a note about the high prices of food. PSRL, vol. III (1950), pp. 33, 221–2 (*s.a.* 6678 = 1169/70); *Chronicle of Novgorod*, p. 27.
10 PSRL, vol. II (1908), col. 559 (*s.a.* 6680 = 1171/2); 'Kyivan Chronicle', p. 313; PSRL, vol. I/2 (1927), col. 362 (*s.a.* 6678 = 1169/70).
11 PSRL, vol. I/2 (1927), col. 362 (*s.a.* 6678 = 1169/70); Hypatian Chronicle, *s.a.* 1173. PSRL, vol. II (1908), cols 561–2; 'Kyivan Chronicle', p. 316. Interestingly, the Hypatian Chronicle records that Roman left Novgorod because of his father's death. The Hypatian Chronicle says he heard of his father's death 'while travelling' [*iskhodiashcha*], while the Novgorod Chronicle is the source for his being forced out. PSRL, vol. III (1950), pp. 33, 221 (*s.a.* 6677); *Chronicle of Novgorod*, pp. 26–7.
12 Simon Franklin and Jonathan Shepard, *The Emergence of Rus, 750–1200* (New York, 1996), p. 349.
13 Dariush Dombrovskii, *Genealogiia Mstislavichei: pervye pokoleniia (do nachala* XIV *v.* (St Petersburg, 2015), p. 266, n. 1125.
14 Dombrovskii, *Genealogiia Mstislavichei*, table 5d, pp. 268–73. Andrzej Poppe suggested, following H. Grala, that she was Maria Kamatera, niece of the Byzantine nobleman Andronikos, one of Emperor Manuel Komnenos's closest advisors. Poppe, 'Leontios, Abbot of Patmos', pp. 7–8, p. 8, n. 20.
15 Márta Font and Gábor Barabás, *Coloman: King of Galicia and Duke of Slavonia (1208–1241): Medieval Central Europe and Hungarian Power* (Leeds, 2019), pp. 12–14. Hrushevsky, however, suggests that she had kinship ties with Leszek the White. Mykhailo Hrushevsky, *History of Ukraine-Rus'*, vol. III: *To the Year 1340*, trans. Bohdan Strumiński, ed. Robert Romanchuk with Uliana Pasicznyk and Marta Horban-Carynnyk (Toronto, 2016), p. 17.
16 Font and Barabás, *Coloman: King of Galicia and Duke of Slavonia*, p. 14.
17 Ibid., pp. 15–16. In fact, we see that Andrew II, after this time, adds 'king of Galicia and Volhynia' to his title.
18 Font and Barabás, *Coloman: King of Galicia and Duke of Slavonia*, pp. 16–18. These episodes are narrated in more detail in Hrushevsky, *History of Ukraine-Rus'*, vol. III, pp. 17–26.

19 PSRL, vol. II (1908), cols 656–7 (*s.a.* 6695 = 1186/7); 'Kyivan Chronicle', pp. 427–9.
20 PSRL, vol. II (1908), cols 659–60 (*s.a.* 6696 = 1187/8); 'Kyivan Chronicle', p. 432.
21 PSRL, vol. II (1908), cols 660–61 (*s.a.* 6696 = 1187/8); 'Kyivan Chronicle', p. 433.
22 PSRL, vol. II (1908), cols 661, 662 (*s.a.* 6697 = 1187/8); 'Kyivan Chronicle', pp. 434, 435.
23 PSRL, vol. II (1908), col. 661 (*s.a.* 6697 = 1187/8); 'Kyivan Chronicle', p. 434.
24 PSRL, vol. II (1908), col. 662 (*s.a.* 6698 = 1188/9); 'Kyivan Chronicle', p. 435.
25 PSRL, vol. II (1908), cols. 662–3 (*s.a.* 6698 = 1188/9); 'Kyivan Chronicle', pp. 435–6.
26 PSRL, vol. II (1908), col. 666 (*s.a.* 6698 = 1189/90); 'Kyivan Chronicle', pp. 439–40.
27 PSRL, vol. II (1908), cols 666–7 (*s.a.* 6698 = 1189/90); 'Kyivan Chronicle', pp. 440–41.
28 Hrushevsky, *History of Ukraine-Rus'*, vol. II, chap. 3, p. 51.
29 PSRL, vol. I/2 (1927), col. 417 (*s.a.* 6710 = 1201/2).
30 Hrushevsky, *History of Ukraine-Rus'*, vol. II, chap. 7, p. 47.
31 PSRL, vol. I/2 (1927), col. 417 (*s.a.* 6710 = 1201/2).
32 PSRL, vol. II (1908), col. 715 (*s.a.* 6709 = 1200/1201); *The Galician-Volynian Chronicle* (hereafter GVC), trans. George A. Perfecky (Munich, 1973), p. 17.
33 Tatishchev, *Istoriia Rossiiskaia*, vol. III (*s.a.* 1203), p. 169.
34 Niketas Choniates, *O City of Byzantium, Annals of Niketas Choniates*, trans. Harry J. Magoulias (Detroit, MI, 1984), chap. 522. Niketas Choniates also refers to Roman as the ruler of Galicia, rather than the ruler of Kyiv, in accord with Ingvar being placed in Kyiv. See also the Laurentian Chronicle, PSRL, vol. I/2 (1927), col. 417 (*s.a.* 6710 = 1201/2). For a full list of the names given to, or used by, the Polovtsy see Omeljan Pritsak, 'The Polovcians and Rus'', *Archivum Eurasiae medii aevi*, II (1982), pp. 321–80.
35 PSRL, vol. III (1950), 45, 240 (*s.a.* 6611 = 1202/3); *Chronicle of Novgorod*, p. 43. PSRL, vol. I/2 (1927), col. 417 (*s.a.* 6710 = 1201/2).
36 PSRL, vol. III (1950), p. 240 (*s.a.* 6611 = 1202/3); *Chronicle of Novgorod*, p. 43; PSRL, vol. I/2 (1927), col. 420 (*s.a.* 6713 = 1204/5). For a discussion of the chronological issues, see Hrushevsky, *History of Ukraine-Rus'*, vol. II, chap. 3, p. 56, n. 139.
37 PSRL, vol. III (1950), pp. 45, 240 (*s.a.* 6611 = 1202/3); *Chronicle of Novgorod*, p. 43; PSRL, vol. I/2 (1927), col. 417 (*s.a.* 6710 = 1201/2).
38 PSRL, vol. I/2 (1927), cols 425–6 (*s.a.* 6713 = 1205/6).
39 Dombrovskii, *Genealogiia Mstislavichei*, table 5b.
40 PSRL, vol. II (1908), cols 659–60 (*s.a.* 6696 = 1197/8); 'Kyivan Chronicle', p. 432.
41 Ibid.
42 PSRL, vol. II (1908), col. 660 (*s.a.* 6696 = 1187/8); 'Kyivan Chronicle', p. 433.

43 However, Dąbrowski suggests that she may have joined a religious order. *Genealogiia Mstislavichei*, pp. 302–4.
44 Dombrovskii, *Genealogiia Mstislavichei*, pp. 304–8.
45 For a full-length study of Mikhail, see Martin Dimnik, *Mikhail, Prince of Chernigov and Grand Prince of Kyiv, 1224–1246* (Toronto, 1981).
46 *PSRL*, vol. II (1908), col. 729 (*s.a.* 6719 = 1210/11); *GVC*, p. 23; Dimnik, *The Dynasty of Chernigov, 1146–1246*, p. 269.
47 Dimnik, *The Dynasty of Chernigov, 1146–1246*, p. 270.
48 *PSRL*, vol. II (1908), cols 782–3 (*s.a.* 6746 = 1237/8); *GVC*, p. 47.
49 Dombrovskii, *Genealogiia Mstislavichei*, p. 305.
50 Ibid., p. 307.
51 *PSRL*, vol. II (1908), col. 782 (*s.a.* 6746 = 1237/8); *GVC*, p. 47.
52 Dombrovskii, *Genealogiia Mstislavichei*, p. 308.
53 Ibid.
54 Dimnik, *The Dynasty of Chernigov, 1146–1246*, p. 81.
55 The information provided regarding the children of Elena and Mikhail comes ibid., pp. 375–80.
56 Dombrovskii, *Genealogiia Mstislavichei*, pp. 321–4.
57 Font and Barabás, *Coloman: King of Galicia and Duke of Slavonia*, pp. 21–3.
58 For Koloman's rule in Galicia, see Font and Barabás, *Coloman: King of Galicia and Duke of Slavonia*.
59 *PSRL*, vol. II (1908), col. 752 (*s.a.* 6735 = 1226/7); *GVC*, p. 33.
60 For more on these marriages, see Dombrovskii, *Genealogiia Mstislavichei*, table 5d.
61 Ibid., p. 324.
62 This reference to Daniil as 'rex' appears only in Chapter Nine of *Ystoria Mongalorum*. There is a theory that all of Chapter Nine is a later addition to the text, written by someone other than John of Plano Carpini. See Donald Ostrowski, 'Second-Redaction Additions in Carpini's *Ystoria Mongalorum*', *Harvard Ukrainian Studies*, XIV/3–4 (December 1990), pp. 548–9.
63 For instance, he founded the city of Lviv, named after his son Lev, where there is an equestrian statue of him; the airport is also named after him.
64 Hrushevsky, *History of Ukraine-Rus'*, vol. III, pp. 18, 33.
65 Ibid., p. 33.
66 Dombrovskii, *Genealogiia Mstislavichei*, table 5d, pp. 329–30.
67 Ibid., p. 330. For more on consanguinity, see Constance B. Bouchard, 'Consanguinity and Noble Marriages in the Tenth and Eleventh Centuries', *Speculum*, LVI/2 (1981), pp. 268–87.
68 Dombrovskii, *Genealogiia Mstislavichei*, p. 331.
69 *PSRL*, vol. II (1908), col. 863 (*s.a.* 6773 = 1273/4); *GVC*, p. 84.
70 Dombrovskii, *Genealogiia Mstislavichei*, pp. 330–31.
71 For a brief analysis of the historiography of this attempt to demonstrate the history of the entirety of Rus, see Christian Raffensperger, 'Mykhailo Hrushevsky and the Construction of the Medieval History of Rus'', *Harvard Ukrainian Studies*, XXXVIII/1–2 (2021), pp. 71–86.

7 Alexander Nevsky and the Family of the Iaroslavichi

1 Sergei M. Eisenstein and Dmitrii Vasilev, dir., *Aleksandr Nevskii* (Moscow, 1938).
2 In *Anna Karenina* (part 5, chapter 26), Leo Tolstoy describes it as the third highest award in Russia at the time, after the Order of Saint Andrew and the Order of Saint Vladimir.
3 *The Nikonian Chronicle*, ed. Serge A. Zenkovsky, trans. Serge A. Zenkovsky and Betty Jean Zenkovsky, 5 vols (Princeton, NJ, 1984–9), vol. III, p. 17.
4 John Fennell, *The Crisis of Medieval Russia, 1200–1304* (London, 1983), p. 99.
5 Donald Ostrowski, *Muscovy and the Mongols: Cross-Cultural Influences on the Steppe Frontier* (Cambridge, 1998), pp. 37–43; idem, 'The Tamma and the Dual-Administrative Structure of the Mongol Empire', *Bulletin of the School of Oriental and African Studies*, LXI (1998), pp. 262–77.
6 Martin Dimnik, *Mikhail, Prince of Chernigov and Grand Prince of Kyiv, 1224–1246* (Toronto, 1981), pp. 158–61, tables 2–5.
7 PSRL, vol. I/2 (1927), col. 467.
8 Ibid., col. 426; PSRL, vol. VII (1856), p. 112; PSRL, vol. X (1885), p. 50. As is the case too often in our sources, a woman is identified only either by whose daughter she is or by whose wife she is, not by her name.
9 Dariush Dombrovskii, *Genealogiia Mstislavichei: pervye pokoleniia (do nachala XIV v.)* (St Petersburg, 2015), pp. 555–8. Dąbrowski's conclusion has been challenged by A. V. Gorovenko, 'Blesk i nishcheta genealogii', *Valla*, II/3 (2016), pp. 125–7.
10 *Nikonian Chronicle*, vol. III, p. 14.
11 PSRL, vol. I/2 (1927), col. 434 (*s.a.* 6716 = 1207/8); PSRL, vol. XXV (1949), p. 107 (*s.a.* 6716 = 1207/8); *Nikonian Chronicle*, vol. II, p. 241.
12 New Riazan was built 64 kilometres (40 mi.) north of the old town.
13 PSRL, vol. III (2000), pp. 67, 272; *Chronicle of Novgorod*, p. 71. At the time, Alexander was seven years old and his brother was nine.
14 PSRL, vol. III (2000), pp. 67, 273; *Chronicle of Novgorod*, p. 72.
15 PSRL, vol. I/2 (1927), col. 470 (*s.a.* 6750 = 1241/2).
16 PSRL, vol. I/3 (1928), col. 523 (*s.a.* 6750 = 1241/2).
17 *The Military Tale about Alexander Nevsky* (reconstruction) in Donald Ostrowski, '"Dressing a Wolf in Sheep's Clothing": Toward Understanding the Composition of the *Life of Alexander Nevskii*', in *Centers and Peripheries in the Christian East: Papers from the Second Biennial Conference of the Association for the Study of Eastern Christian History and Culture*, ed. Eugene Clay, Russell Martin and Barbara Skinner, *Russian History*, XL (2013), p. 66.
18 PSRL, vol. X (1885), p. 131. Fëdor's father, Iarun, was a military commander under Mstislav Mstislavich Udatnyi, a member of the rival Iziaslavich ruling clan. GVC, p. 25. Iarun had fought against Iaroslav and his brother Iurii at the Battle of Lipitsa. PSRL, vol. III (2000), pp. 55, 255 (*s.a.* 6724 = 1215/6); *Chronicle of Novgorod*, p. 56.
19 According to Chapter Nine of the *Ystoria Mongalorum*, Iaroslav became ill after dining with the qagan's mother and died seven days later,

leading people to think that she had poisoned him. Chapter Nine, however, was most likely a second-edition addition to the text and was written by someone other than John of Plano Carpini. Ostrowski, 'Second-Redaction Additions in Carpini's *Ystoria Monaglorum*', *Harvard Ukrainian Studies*, XIV/3–4 (December 1990), p. 549.

20 'Nikifora patriarkha Tsesariagrada letopisets' v'skore', in M. N. Tikhomirov, 'Zabytye i neizvestnye proizvedeniia russkoi pis'mennosti', *Arkheograficheskii ezhegodnik za 1960 g.* (Moscow, 1962), p. 239 (fol. 575). Nikifor's Chronicle adds: 'for 5 years'. PSRL, vol. IV (1915), p. 229. The Abbreviated Chronicle Compilation of 1497 and the *Nikonian Chronicle* claim that Mikhail Iaroslavich overthrew Sviatoslav, then was killed by the Lithuanians, *s.a.* 1248. PSRL, vol. XXVIII , p. 57; PSRL, vol. X (1885), pp. 136–7; *Nikonian Chronicle*, vol. III, p. 27.

21 This supposition is based on the *Vita of Efrosinia* (Efrosinia being the monastic name of Feodula), which states that she had been engaged to marry a '*kniaz* of Suzdal', but the *kniaz* died before the marriage could take place. According to Dimnik, the name 'Mina Ivanovich' is associated with this *kniaz*, but Mina Ivanovich was not a *kniaz* (Dimnik, *Mikhail, Prince of Chernigov*, p. 23, n. 23), so the guess is that Fëdor Iaroslavich was the intended *kniaz*.

22 PSRL, vol. III (2000), pp. 77, 289; *Chronicle of Novgorod*, p. 84; PSRL, vol. X (1885), p. 114; *Nikonian Chronicle*, vol. II, p. 318.

23 Aleksei Iu. Karpov, *Velikii kniaz' Aleksandr Nevskii* (Moscow, 2010), p. 89.

24 Nikolai M. Karamzin, *Istoriia gosudarstva rossiiskogo*, 12 vols, 5th edn (St Petersburg, 1842), vol. IV, col. 58.

25 Karpov, *Velikii kniaz' Aleksandr Nevskii*, p. 89.

26 Dombrovskii, *Genealogiia Mstislavichei*, pp. 379–81.

27 PSRL, vol. I/2 (1927), col. 471.

28 'The Secret History of the Mongols', trans. Igor de Rachewiltz, *Papers on Far Eastern History*, XXXI (1985), p. 31.

29 PSRL, vol. I/2 (1927), col. 473; PSRL, vol. XVIII (1913), p. 70. The *Nikonian Chronicle*, whose compiler was apparently aware of this speech in early chronicles, changed the focus from a specific political decision not to serve Batu to a general religious decision not to serve 'the Tatars': 'O Lord, why do we quarrel among ourselves and lead the Tatars against one another! It would be better for me to flee to a foreign land than to be friends with, and serve, the Tatars.' Although Batu was not Muslim, the Rus Church, during the fifteenth and sixteenth centuries, was promoting the idea that a 'Russian' was someone who accepted Christianity under the aegis of the head of the Rus Church and, by that time, being Tatar was equated with being Muslim.

30 PSRL, vol. I/2 (1927), col. 474; PSRL, vol. XVIII (1913), p. 71.

31 Iurii Seleznev, *Russkie kniazi pri dvore khanov Zolotoi Ordy* (Moscow, 2019), p. 119.

32 *Military Tale*, p. 67.

33 Fennell, *Crisis*, p. 107.

34 Ibid.

35 Ibid.

36 Ibid.

37 Ibid., p. 108.
38 Ibid.
39 Ibid.
40 Ibid.
41 Ibid., p. 109.
42 Rashid al-Din tells us that Qurumshi was the third son of Orda (the grandson of Chinggis Khan), that he had no sons and the names of his wives are not known. Rashid al-Din (Rashududdin Fazlullah), *Jami'u't-Tawarikh: Compendium of Chronicles. A History of the Mongols*, trans. and annot. W. M. Thackston (Cambridge, MA, 1999), p. 351.
43 PSRL, vol. II (1908), col. 829; GVC, p. 68.
44 PSRL, vol. II (1908), col. 838; GVC, p. 73.
45 James J. Zatko, 'The Union of Suzdal' 1222–1252', *Journal of Ecclesiastical History*, VIII/1 (April 1957), pp. 41–3. For the letter, see *Acta Innocentii PP. IV, 1243–1254*, ed. Theodosius T. Haluščynskyj and Meletius M. Wojnar, Pontificia Commissio ad Redigendum Codicem Iuris Canonici Orientalis, Fonte,. 3rd series, vol. IV/1 (Vatican City, 1962), pp. 66–7, no. 26a.
46 *Acta Innocentii PP. IV, 1243–1254*, pp. 110–11, no. 59. Rochcau expressed scepticism that Iaroslav would have confessed obedience to the Roman Catholic Church. Georges Rochcau, 'Innocent IV devant le péril tatar: ses lettres à Daniel de Galicie et à Alexandre Nevsky', *Istina*, VI (1959), pp. 178–9.
47 *Acta Innocentii PP. IV, 1243–1254*, p. 108, no. 57; p. 112, no. 59.
48 *Acta Innocentii PP. IV, 1243–1254*, p. 117, no. 65.
49 See Peter Jackson, *The Mongols and the West, 1221–1410*, 1st edn (Harlow, 2005), pp. 92–7; 2nd edn (Oxford, 2015), pp. 97–102.
50 PSRL, vol. I/2 (1927), p. 473; PSRL, vol. XVIII (1913), p. 70; PSRL, vol. XXIII (1910), p. 84; PSRL, vol. XXVIII (1963), p. 57; PSRL, vol. XXV (1949), pp. 141–2; PSRL, vol. XXVIII (1963), p. 216; PSRL, vol. XV (1922), pp. 396–7.

8 Iurii Danilovich and His Family

1 Kliuchevskii called the reckoning of one's status within a clan '*mestnichestvo* arithmetic', but he acknowledged that the system preceded *mestnichestvo* and was used to determine who was next in line in succession in the early Rus polities. In Kliuchevskii's description: 'The first place belonged to the oldest brother, the house master, the *bolshak*, and the two places after him were his two younger brothers, the fourth place, his oldest son. If the *bolshak* had a third brother, he was not able to sit either higher or lower than the oldest nephew, to whom he was equal.' V. O. Kliuchevskii, *Kurs Russkoi istorii. Sochineniia v vos'mi tomakh* (Moscow, 1956–9), vol. II: pp. 147–8. Kliuchevskii speculated that this equality was due to the oldest son of the oldest brother's being born about the same time as the fourth oldest brother. That may be so, but in the two cases we have from the thirteenth century of at least four brothers surviving to succeed to the throne of Vladimir (the case of the Vsevolodovichi in 1246 and the case of the Iaroslavichi in 1271), the fourth brother in each case, Sviatoslav and Vasilii, took precedence

over their respective eldest nephews, Alexander Iaroslavich and Dmitrii Aleksandrovich.

2 Donald Ostrowski, 'Systems of Succession in Rus' and Steppe Societies', *Ruthenica*, IX (2012), p. 58.

3 Ibid., p. 42.

4 Fletcher termed this system 'tanistry', based on a Gaelic term used to describe the clan system of succession in medieval Scotland and Ireland. Joseph Fletcher, 'The Mongols: Ecological and Social Perspectives', *Harvard Journal of Asiatic Studies*, XLVI/1 (1986), p. 17.

5 We can dismiss the testimony of the *Stepennaia kniga* that it was his father Alexander Nevsky who gave the right to rule to him; that would mean that Daniil was at most two years old when he was made *kniaz* of Moscow by 1263, the year of Alexander's death. The Moscow Compilation of the End of the Fifteenth Century obliquely testifies *s.a.* 1282 that he was the ruler of Moscow by that date. PSRL, vol. XXV (1949), p. 154. The Supraslskaia Chronicle asserts that upon his death in 1303, he had been ruler of Moscow for eleven years, which would place his assuming the title in 1292. PSRL, vol. XVII (1907), p. 27. Tikhomirov proposed that the '11' was a copyist's error for '21', which would then bring it into conformity with the testimony of the Moscow Compilation. M. N. Tikhomirov, *Drevnaia Moskva (XII–XV vv.)* (Moscow, 1947), p. 23.

6 S. B. Konev, 'Sinodikologiia. Chast' II: Rostovskii sobornyi sinodik', *Istoricheskaia genealogiia* (Ekaterinburg), 6 (1995), p. 95. Baumgarten says that we do not know her name, but he did not know of the Rostov Sinodicon.

7 A. A. Gorskii, 'O dinasticheskikh sviaziakh pervykh Moskovskikh kniazei', *Drevniaia Rus'. Voprosy medievistiki*, no. 4 (74) (2018), pp. 42–51.

8 Gorskii, 'O dinasticheskikh sviaziakh', p. 51.

9 Iakov S. Lure asserted that, insofar as is possible, one should use the Rogozh, Simeonov and Trinity Chronicles for information about the fourteenth century (to 1390) and the 'unofficial' chronicles (the Simeonov, Nikanor, Vologda-Perm and Ermolin) for the fifteenth century (to the 1470s). Ia. S. Lure, *Dve istorii Rusi XV veka. Rannie i pozdnie, nezavisimye i ofitsial'nye letopisi ob obrazovanii Moskovskogo gosudarstva* (St Petersburg, 1994), pp. 13–18.

10 Iakov S. Lure, 'Fifteenth-Century Chronicles as a Source for the History of the Formation of the Muscovite State', in *Medieval Russian Culture*, ed. Michael S. Flier and Daniel Rowland, 2 vols (Berkeley, CA, 1994), vol. II, pp. 48–9.

11 PSRL, vol. I/2 (1927), col. 484; PSRL, vol. I/3 (1928), col. 528.

12 Donald Ostrowski, 'Military Mobilization by the Muscovite Grand Princes (1313–1533)', in *The Military and Society in Russia, 1450–1917*, ed. Eric Lohr and Marshall Poe (Leiden, 2002), pp. 19–40.

13 PSRL, vol. X (1885), p. 171 (*s.a.* 6804); *The Nikonian Chronicle*, 5 vols, ed. Serge A. Zenkovsky, trans. Serge A. Zenkovsky and Betty Jean Zenkovsky (Princeton, NJ, 1984–9), vol. III, p. 85; PSRL, vol. XVIII (1913), p. 83 (*s.a.* 6805); PSRL, vol. XXV (1949), p. 158 (*s.a.* 6804). Some chronicles report that Ivan went to the Orda to seek the khan's help.

14 PSRL, vol. X (1885), p. 174 (*s.a.* 6810); *Nikonian Chronicle*, vol. III, p. 90.

15 PSRL, vol. X (1885), p. 174 (*s.a.* 6811); *Nikonian Chronicle*, vol. III, p. 91.

16 L. V. Cherepnin, *Obrazovanie russkogo tsentralizovannogo gosudarstva v XIV–XV vekakh* (Moscow, 1960), p. 460.

17 PSRL, vol. X (1885), p. 175 (*s.a.* 6812 = 1303/4); *Nikonian Chronicle*, vol. III, p. 92; PSRL, vol. XXIII (1910), p. 96; PSRL, vol. XXV (1949), p. 393.

18 Fennell cited the story about the ambush as being in an earlier Muscovite Chronicle, the Trinity Chronicle, which is thought to reflect the compilation of 1409, but Priselkov's reconstruction of the Trinity Chronicle (it was destroyed in the fire of 1812) does not allow such a conclusion. M. D. Priselkov, *Troitskaia letopis'. Rekonstruktsiia teksta* (Moscow-Leningrad, 1950), p. 352 (*s.a.* 6813); PSRL, vol. XVIII (1913), p. 86 (*s.a.* 6813).

19 PSRL, vol. III (1950), pp. 92, 332 (*s.a.* 6812); *Chronicle of Novgorod*, p. 116.

20 PSRL, vol. III (1950), pp. 92, 332 (*s.a.* 6812); *Chronicle of Novgorod*, p. 116; PSRL, vol. VI/1 (2000), col. 368 (*s.a.* 6812).

21 PSRL, vol. XXIII (1910), p. 96; PSRL, vol. XXV (1949), p. 393 (*s.a.* 6812); PSRL, vol. X (1885), p. 175 (*s.a.* 6812); *Nikonian Chronicle*, vol. III, p. 92; PSRL, vol. XVIII (1913), pp. 86 (*s.a.* 6813); Priselkov, *Troitskaia letopis'*, p. 352 (*s.a.* 6813).

22 PSRL, vol. XVIII (1913), p. 86 (*s.a.* 6814); PSRL, vol. X (1885), p. 176 (*s.a.* 6812); *Nikonian Chronicle*, vol. III, p. 93.

23 PSRL, vol. XXIII (1910), p. 96; PSRL, vol. XXV (1949), p. 393; PSRL, vol. X (1885), p. 176 (*s.a.* 6813); *Nikonian Chronicle*, vol. III, p. 94; PSRL, vol. XVIII (1913), p. 86 (*s.a.* 6815).

24 PSRL, vol. XV (1863), col. 407 (*s.a.* 6816); PSRL, vol. XV (1922), col. 35 (*s.a.* 6816); PSRL, vol. XXIII (1910), p. 97.

25 Not to be confused with Iurii Daniilovich of Moscow.

26 Mitropolit Makarii (Bulgakov), *Istoriia russkoi tserkvi* (St Petersburg, 1866), vol. VI/1, p. 310; and B. S. Angelov, *Iz starata Bŭlgarska, Russka i Srbska literatura* (Sofia, 1958), pp. 170–71.

27 We know what was in Mikhail's letter from an extant reply from Nephon in Slavonic translation. *Pamiatniki drevne-russkogo kanonicheskogo prava: pamiatniki XI–XV v.*, in *Russkaia istoricheskaia biblioteka (RIB)*, 2nd edn (1908), vol. VI, pp. 148–50.

28 PSRL, vol. X (1885), p. 177 (*s.a.* 6819); *Nikonian Chronicle*, vol. III, pp. 96–7.

29 George Vernadsky, *The Mongols and Russia* (New Haven, CT, 1953), p. 195.

30 See Donald Ostrowski, 'The Tamma and the Dual-Administrative Structure of the Mongol Empire', *Bulletin of the School of Oriental and African Studies*, LXI (1998), pp. 262–77.

31 PSRL, vol. III (1950), pp. 94, 335 (*s.a.* 6822); *Chronicle of Novgorod*, p. 119.

32 PSRL, vol. XXIII (1910), p. 98; PSRL, vol. XXV (1949), p. 161 (*s.a.* 6825).

33 PSRL, vol. X (1885), p. 181 (*s.a.* 6825).

34 PSRL, vol. III (1950), p. 96 (*s.a.* 6826); *Chronicle of Novgorod*, p. 121.

35 PSRL, vol. III (1950), p. 338 (*s.a.* 6826).

36 PSRL, vol. V (1851), p. 207; PSRL, vol. V/1 (2000), col. 375.

37 PSRL, vol. XV/1 (1965), col. 38; PSRL, vol. XV/2 (1965), col. 410.

38 Not to be confused with the *Tale of Mikhail Aleksandrovich*, another fourteenth-century ruler of Tver.
39 V. A. Kuchkin, *Povesti o Mikhaile Tverskom* (Moscow, 1974).
40 PSRL, vol. V (1851), pp. 207–15; PSRL, vol. V/I (2000), cols 375–96; PSRL, vol. VII (1856), pp. 188–97 (*s.a.* 6826); PSRL, vol. X (1885), pp. 182–6 (*s.a.* 6827); PSRL, vol. XV (1922), cols. 38–41 (*s.a.* 6826); PSRL, vol. XXI (1908), pp. 333–42; PSRL, vol. XXIII (1910), pp. 98–101; PSRL, vol. XXIV (1921), pp. 108–14 (*s.a.* 6826); PSRL, vol. XXV (1949), pp. 161–6 (*s.a.* 6826); PSRL, vol. XXVI (1959), pp. 99–107 (*s.a.* 6827); PSRL, vol. XXVII (1962), pp. 56–61; PSRL, vol. XXVIII (1963), pp. 65–7, 225–7; and so forth. Kuchkin, *Povesti o Mikhaile Tverskom*, pp. 75–155.
41 PSRL, vol. X (1885), p. 186 (*s.a.* 6828); *Nikonian Chronicle*, vol. III, p. 111.
42 PSRL, vol. XV (1922), col. 41 (*s.a.* 6828); PSRL, vol. XV (1863), cols 413–14 (*s.a.* 6828).
43 John Fennell, *The Emergence of Moscow, 1304–1359* (Berkeley, CA, 1968), p. 92.
44 PSRL, vol. III (2000), p. 469. Not much is known about Vasilii, Aleksandr's father. No chronicle, with one exception, testifies to his patronymic. Some historians, nonetheless, posit that he was the son of Andrei Iaroslavich, which has led historians to speculate which Iaroslav was Andrei's father. The *Nikonian Chronicle* gives him the patronymic Mikhailovich, and Kuchkin accepted this, proposing that Vasilii was the grandson of Iurii Andreevich, with Mikhail Iurevich being his father.
45 A. N. Nasonov, *Mongoly i Rus' (Istoriia tatarskoi politiki na Rusi)* (Moscow and Leningrad, 1940), p. 110. 'Kalita', meaning 'moneybags', was a sobriquet added later by historians to distinguish this Ivan from other Ivans of the time.
46 Donald Ostrowski, 'The Mongol Origins of Muscovite Political Institutions', *Slavic Review*, XLIX/4 (1990), pp. 528–9.

9 Iurii Lvovich and His Family

1 Mikhailo Hrushevsky, *Istoriia Ukrainy-Rusy*, vol. III: *do Roku 1340*, 8 vols, 2nd edn (Lviv, 1905–13), p. 103.
2 In a recent interview, the film director Werner Herzog used a similar justification for modifying facts in his documentaries: 'But you see, there's nothing wrong with modifying facts, for digging into a much deeper truth.' Quoted in Mark Zastrow, 'Human + Nature according to Werner Herzog', *Discover: Science That Matters* (May 2021), p. 47. Such an approach is unscientific because no one can verify the truthfulness of conclusions that are based on a modification of the evidence.
3 A. N. Uzhankov, '"Letopitsa Daniila Galitskogo". Redaktsii, vremia sozdaniia', *Germenevtika drevnerusskoi literatury*, I (1989), pp. 248–83.
4 A. V. Gorovenko, *Mech Romana Galitskogo. Kniaz Roman Mstislavich v istorii, epose i legendakh* (St Petersburg, 2011), pp. 209–37: 'K voprosy ob etapakh formirovaniia sovremennoi struktury Ipatevskogo letopisi.'
5 We follow the corrected chronology of Hrushevsky, which he based on a comparison with Rus chronicles and European sources that mention the same events. Mykhailo Hrushevsky, 'Khronologiia podii

Halytsko-Volynskoi litopysy', *Zapysky Naukovoho Tovarystva imeni Shevchenka*, XVI/3 (Lviv, 1901), pp. 1–72. See also O. V. Romanova, 'O khronologii Galitsko-Volynskoi letopis XIII v. po Ipatevskomy spisku', in *Proshloe Novgorod i Novgorodskoi zemli. Materialy konferentsii 11–13 noiabria 1997 goda* (Novgorod, 1997).

6 Hrushevsky, 'Khronologyia'; cf. idem, *Istorija Ukrainy-Rusy*, vol. III.

7 L. V. Cherepnin, 'Letopisets Daniila Galitskogo', *Istoricheskie zapiski*, XII (1941), pp. 228–53; D. S. Likhachev, *Russkie letopisi i ikh kul'turno-istoricheskoe znachenie* (Moscow–Leningrad, 1947), p. 256; D. Tschizewskij, 'Zum Stil der Galizisch-Volynischen Chronik', *Südostforschungen*, XII (1953), pp. 88, 99; A. S. Orlov, *Drevniaia russkaia literatura XI–XVI vv.* (Moscow–Leningrad, 1937), p. 119.

8 V. T. Pashuto, *Ocherki po istorii Galitsko-Volynskoi Rusi* (Moscow, 1950), pp. 21–133. Eremin critiqued Pashuto's method and results. I. P. Eremin, 'Volynskaja letopis 1289–1290 gg.', *Trudy Otdela drevnerusskoi literatury*, XIII (1957), pp. 102–17.

9 A. I. Hensorskyi, 'Redaktsiji Halycko-Volynskoho litopysu', *Doslidžennja z movy to literatury* (Kyiv, 1957), pp. 68–72.

10 Adrian Jusupovič, *Kronika halicko-wołyńska (Kronika Romanowiczów) w latopisarskiej kolekcji historycznej* (Cracow and Warsaw, 2019); *The Chronicle of Halych-Volhynia and Historical Collections in Medieval Rus'* (Leiden, 2022).

11 Dariush Dombrovskii, *Genealogiia Mstislavichei: pervye pokoleniia (do nachala XIV v.)* (St Petersburg, 2015), p. 398.

12 Thus far, I have found no source for this assertion.

13 Hrushevsky, *Istoriia Ukrainy-Rusy*, vol. III, p. 103.

14 PSRL, vol. II (1908), col. 859; GVC, p. 82.

15 PSRL, vol. II (1908), col. 876; GVC, p. 90.

16 PSRL, vol. II (1908), col. 881; GVC, p. 92.

17 PSRL, vol. II (1908), col. 882; GVC, p. 92.

18 PSRL, vol. II (1908), cols 883–4; GVC, p. 93.

19 Karamzin reports the marriage between Iurii and the daughter of Iaroslav Iaroslavich of Tver, but he does not provide his source. Karamzin, *Istoriia gosudarstva rossiiskogo*, vol. IV, col. 92.

20 PSRL, vol. II (1908), col. 895; GVC, p. 98. Hrushevsky, 'Khronologyia'; Dariusz Dąbrowski, *Kronika halicko-wołyńska. Kronika Romanowiczów* (Cracow and Warsaw, 2017), p. 242, n. 1624.

21 PSRL, vol. II (1908), col. 888; GVC, p. 95.

22 Ibid.

23 PSRL, vol. II (1908), col. 890; GVC, p. 96.

24 PSRL, vol. II (1908), col. 892; GVC, p. 96.

25 PSRL, vol. II (1908), col. 893; GVC, p. 97.

26 PSRL, vol. II (1908), col. 897; GVC, p. 99.

27 PSRL, vol. II (1908), col. 900; GVC, p. 100.

28 PSRL, vol. II (1908), cols 903–4; GVC, pp. 101–2.

29 PSRL, vol. II (1908), cols 910–11; GVC, pp. 104–5.

30 PSRL, vol. II (1908), col. 913; GVC, p. 106.

31 PSRL, vol. II (1908), col. 913; GVC, p. 106.

32 PSRL, vol. II (1908), col. 928; GVC, p. 113.

33 PSRL, vol. II (1908), col. 931; GVC, p. 114. This formulation that 'not one stone remained upon another' is biblical (Mark 13:2 and Matthew 24:2).
34 See, for example, Ivan Krypiakevych, *Halytsko-Volynske kniazivstvo* (Kyiv, 1984), p. 115; Leontii V. Voitovych, *Halytsko-Volynski etiudy* (Bila Tserkva, 2011), pp. 319–20.
35 Pëtr Stefanovich, 'Politicheskoe razvitie Galitsko-Volynskoi Rusi v 1240–1340 gg. i otnosheniia s Ordoi', *Rossiiskaia istoriia*, IV (2019), p. 128.
36 Heinrich von Gelzer, *Ungedruckte und ungenügend veröffentlichte Texte der Notitiae episcopatum ein Beitrag zur byzantinischen Kirchen- und verwaltungsgeschichte* (Munich, 1901) p. 599. The metropolitanate of Galicia was listed as no. 81 on the list of all the metropolitanates of the Eastern Church, whereas the metropolitanate of Kyiv was listed as no. 71.
37 Leontii V. Voitovych, 'Iurii Lvovych i ioho polityka', in *Halychyna ta Volyn u dobu serednovichchia, do 800-richchia z dnia narodzhenna Danyla Halytskoho* (Lviv, 2001), p. 75.
38 Donald Ostrowski, 'Why Did the Metropolitan Move from Kiev to Vladimir in the Thirteenth Century?', in *Christianity and the Eastern Slavs*, vol. I: *Slavic Cultures in the Middle Ages*, ed. Boris Gasparov and Olga Raevsky-Hughes, *California Slavic Studies*, vol. XVI (Berkeley, CA, 1993), pp. 83–101.
39 PSRL, vol. XXXV (1980), pp. 152–3. Cf. Hrushevsky, *Istoriia Ukrainy-Rusy*, vol. III, p. 190.
40 The Lithuanian Chronicles call him Roman and say that he is the brother-in-law of Lev. Cf. S. C. Rowell, *Lithuania Ascending: A Pagan Empire within East-Central Europe, 1295–1345* (Cambridge, 1994), pp. 97, 307–8.
41 Hrushevsky, *Istoriia Ukrainy-Rusy*, vol. III, p. 94.
42 Craig Benjamin, 'The Mongol Empire', www.thegreatcourses.com, accessed 15 October 2022.

10 Uliana Alexandrovna and Her Family

1 PSRL, vol. XVII (1907), col. 498.
2 PSRL, vol. V (2003), p. 19; PSRL, vol. IV (1848), pp. 56, 188; PSRL, vol. VII (1856), p. 208; PSRL, vol. IV/1 (1915), p. 274; PSRL, vol. IV/2 (1917), p. 258.
3 The *Nikonian Chronicle* has an interpolation wherein Algirdas claims 'I have already been baptized and I am Christian.' PSRL, vol. X (1885), p. 215; *The Nikonian Chronicle*, ed. Serge A. Zenkovsky, trans. Serge A. Zenkovsky and Betty Jean Zenkovsky, 5 vols (Princeton, NJ, 1984–9), vol. III, p. 152. But this statement does not appear in the earlier chronicles and may have been an attempt by the editor of *The Nikonian Chronicle* to square the fact that Algirdas was the husband of Uliana and since she was Orthodox, so too must he have been. In the context of the story, it does not make sense, because if both the father and the mother were baptized, then why was the son not baptized before that?
4 S. C. Rowell, *Lithuania Ascending: A Pagan Empire within East-Central Europe, 1295–1345* (Cambridge, 1994), p. 87.
5 Ibid., p. 88, n. 27; PSRL, vol. XXXV (1980), p. 115.

6 Owen Lattimore, *Inner Asian Frontiers of China* (New York, 1940), pp. 238–9.
7 Bishop Albert's activities are recorded in the contemporary chronicle of Henry of Livonia. Henricus Lettus, *The Chronicle of Henry of Livonia*, trans. James A. Brundage (New York, 2003). For an overview of the Baltic situation at the time, see Eric Christiansen, *The Northern Crusades*, 2nd edn (London, 1997). See also William Urban, *The Last Years of the Teutonic Knights: Lithuania, Poland and the Teutonic Order* (Barnsley, 2019).
8 PSRL, vol. III (2000), pp. 82, 310 (*s.a.* 6766 = 1257/8); *Chronicle of Novgorod*, p. 96.
9 Jaroslaw Pelenski, 'The Contest between Lithuania-Rus' and the Golden Horde in the Fourteenth Century for Supremacy over Eastern Europe', *Archiwum Eurasiae Medii Aevi*, II (1982), pp. 300–320 (pp. 304–5).
10 Ibid., pp. 304–5.
11 *Skarbiec diplomatów papiezkich, cesarskich, królewskich, książęcych; uchwał narodowych, postanowień różynych władz i urzędów posługujących do krytycznego wyjaśnenia dziejów Litwy, Rusi Litewskiéj i ościennych im krajów*, 2 vols, ed. Ignacy Daniłowicz (Wilno, 1860–62), vol. I, p. 153, no. 297), p. 154 (nos. 298 and 299), p. 155 (no. 300), p. 159 (no. 308) and so on; and *Russisch-livländische Urkunden*, ed. K. E. Nepiersky (St Petersburg, 1868), pp. 30–32 and 49–50.
12 Charles Halperin, 'Tsarev ulus: Russia in the Golden Horde', *Cahiers du monde russe et soviétique*, XXIII/2 (1982), pp. 257–63.
13 'Item postulabant, quod ordo locaretur ad solitudines inter Tartaros et Rutenos ad defendendum eos ab impugnacione Tartarorum et quod nihil iuris ordo sibi reservaret apud Rutenos, sed omnis Russia ad Letwinos deberet simpliciter pertinere; et dicebant: 'Si postulata consequi poterimus, voluntatem Caesaris faciemus".' This declaration is preserved in the Chronicle of Hermann von Wartberge, a member of the Livonian Order. *Scriptores rerum Prussicarum*, ed. Theodor Hirsch, Max Töppen and Ernst Strehlke, 5 vols (Leipzig, 1861–74), vol. II, p. 80.
14 PSRL, vol. X (1885), p. 190 (*s.a.* 6834 = 1325/6), p. 221 (*s.a.* 6857 = 1348/9); *Nikonian Chronicle*, vol. III, pp. 119, 163.
15 Rowell, *Lithuania Ascending*, pp. 89–90.
16 John Fennell, The *Emergence of Moscow, 1304–1359* (Berkeley, CA, 1968), pp. 134–5.
17 Michał Giedroyć, 'The Arrival of Christianity in Lithuania: Between Rome and Byzantium, 1281–1341', *Oxford Slavonic Papers*, XX (1987), pp. 15–17, based his argument on an error in a Notitia memorandum. Senyk accepted Giedroyć's interpretation, but Rowell rejected it and proposed a date that fell between 1315 and 1317 instead. Sophia Senyk, *A History of the Church in Ukraine*, vol. II: *1300 to the Union of Brest* (Rome, 2011), p. 25; Rowell, *Lithuania Ascending*, pp. 155–8.
18 PSRL, vol. IX (1862), pp. 223–9.
19 Meyendorff explained that the Rusians 'considered their conquerors as having taken the place of the Christian emperor ("tsar") of Constantinople, by virtue of a decree of divine Providence. The

acceptance of the khan's power was basically a Christian idea.' John Meyendorff, *Byzantium and the Rise of Russia* (Cambridge, 1980), p. 69.

20 *Das Register des Patriarchats von Konstantinopel*, ed. Herbert Hunger and Otto Kresten (Vienna, 1981), vol. I, pp. 334 (1317), 542 (1327); 554 (1329).

21 *Acta patriarchatus constantinopolitani (APC)*, 2 vols, ed. Francis Miklosich and Joseph Müller (Vienna, 1860–62), vol. I, p. 577; *RIB*, VI (supplement), col. 125. Kazimierz was considering Peter to be the metropolitan of Galicia-Volhynia and of Kyiv and all Rus at the same time because to acknowledge that he was metropolitan of only Kyiv and all Rus would be to give up on the idea that there was a Galician-Volhynian metropolitanate.

22 *APC*, vol. I, pp. 261–71; *Jus graeco-romanum*, ed. K. E. Zachariae von Lingenthal, 4 vols (Leipzig, 1856–65), vol. III, pp. 700–703.

23 *APC*, vol. I, pp. 352–3.

24 John Meyendorff, 'Alexis and Roman: A Study in Byzantine-Russian Relations (1352–1354)', *Byzantinoslavica*, XXVIII/2 (1967), pp. 281–2; cf. Senyk, *History of the Church in Ukraine*, vol. II, pp. 47, 48.

25 *APC*, vol. II, pp. 12–13. 'Outer Rus' in this context was all the rest of Rus that was not part of 'Inner Rus', that is, Galicia-Volhynia.

26 Gregoras even tells us that Algirdas had promised as much if Roman was chosen metropolitan. Gregoras, *Byzantina historia*, ed. Ludwig Shopen and Immanuel Bekker, 3 vols (Bonn, 1829–55), vol. II, p. 518 (book XXVI, § 34).

27 *APC*, vol. I, p. 426; *RIB*, VI (Supplement), col. 77. The relationship between Kallistos and Philotheos seems to be an interesting one. Kallistos stepped down as patriarch in 1353 because he refused to crown John VI's son as co-emperor with his father. Then, when John VI abdicated two years later, Kallistos was restored to the patriarchal throne. Philotheos seems to have been close to him because he succeeded Kallistos after the latter died in 1363.

28 *PSRL*, vol. XV/1 (1922), col. 63 (*s.a.* 6862 = 1353/4). Meyendorff, *Byzantium and the Rise of Russia*, pp. 168–70; John Fennell, *A History of the Russian Church to 1448* (London, 1995), pp. 140–42.

29 *APC*, vol. I, p. 428; *RIB*, VI (Supplement), col. 77.

30 *PSRL*, vol. XV/1 (1922), col. 65 (*s.a.* 6864 = 1355/6); *PSRL*, vol. X (1885), p. 228 (*s.a.* 6864 = 1355/6); *Nikonian Chronicle*, p. 178.

31 White for west and blue for east coincides with the Turko-Mongol colour-directional system of the time; see Timothy May, 'Color Symbolism in the Turko-Mongolian World', in *The Use of Color in History, Politics, and Art*, ed. Sungshin Kim (Dahlonega, GA, 2016), p. 61. It also corresponds with the Rus sources' terminology for the two parts of the Orda. Persian sources reverse these two directional colours, which can lead to confusion.

32 According to Barthold, it is not clear whether Urus was Toqtamish's uncle or a more distant relation. W. Barthold, 'Toktamish', in *Encyclopedia of Islam*, 9 vols, 1st edn (Leiden, 1913–36), vol. VIII, p. 850.

33 Sharaf ad-Din Ali Yazdi, *The History of Timur-Bec: Known by the Name of Tamerlain the Great, Emperor of the Moguls and Tartars: being an historical*

journal of his conquests in Asia and Europe, 2 vols (London, 1723) vol. I, pp. 178–86.

34 PSRL, vol. XV/1 (1922), col. 141; PSRL, vol. XVIII (1913), p. 131; *Skazanie i povesti o Kulikovskoi bitve*, ed. L. A. Dmitriev and O. P. Likhacheva (Leningrad, 1982), p. 15. PSRL, vol. VI/1 (2000), col. 470; PSRL, vol. IV/1 (1915), p. 320; PSRL, vol. IV/2 (1925), p. 325; PSRL, vol. VIII (1859), p. 39; *Skazanie i povesti*, p. 24.

35 Rowell, *Lithuania Ascending*, p. 298.

36 Ibid.

37 *Akty, otnosiashchiesia k istorii Zapadnoi Rossii*, vol. I: *1340–1506*, ed. I. Grigorovich, 5 vols (St Petersburg, 1846), p. 21, no. 5; Rowell, *Lithuania Ascending*, p. 180, n. 134.

38 Inna L. Kalechits, 'Istoricheskie lichnosti v graffiti Polotskoi Spaso-Preobrazhenskoi tserkvi', www.youtube.com, accessed 7 November 2022.

39 Evgenii Nikolskii, 'O kanonizatsii sviatoi blagovernoi velikoi kniagini Iulianii Aleksandrovny Tverskoi i Litovskoi', *#muzeemaniia*, 6 December 2018, https://muzeemania.ru.

40 *Scriptores rerum Prussicarum*, vol. III, pp. 114–15.

41 Ostrowski, *Muscovy and the Mongols*, pp. 155–6.

11 Vasilii Dmitrievich and His Family

1 *Troitskaia letopis'*, p. 377; PSRL, vol. X (1885), p. 231 (*s.a.* 6868 = 1359/60); *The Nikonian Chronicle*, ed. Serge A. Zenkovsky, trans. Serge A. Zenkovsky and Betty Jean Zenkovsky, 5 vols (Princeton, NJ, 1984–9), vol. III, p. 185; George Vernadsky, *The Mongols and Russia* (New Haven, CT, 1953), p. 250. Zenkovsky interpreted it to mean that the tradition was that 'the Grand Principality of Valdimir [*sic*] was in the hands of the Prince of Moscow, sometimes of Tver', and very rarely in the hands of other princes', which is not entirely accurate either. The first Moscow *kniaz* to rule in Vladimir was Iurii Daniilovich in 1318, a little over forty years earlier, which means that it was a rather short 'tradition'.

2 Mamai was an emir, not a khan, but nevertheless was one of the most powerful individuals in the Orda and helped to make and define the policy for its rulers.

3 PSRL, vol. XI (1897), p. 2; *Nikonian Chronicle*, vol. III, p. 191.

4 PSRL, vol. VI/1 (2000), col. 483 (*s.a.* 6891 = 1382/3); PSRL, vol. XV/1 (1922), col. 148; PSRL, vol. XVIII (1913), p. 134; PSRL, vol. XXV (1949), p. 211. Vernadsky, *The Mongols and Russia*, p. 268. See L. V. Cherepnin, *Obrazovanie russkogo tsentralizovannogo gosudarstva v XIV–XV vekakh* (Moscow, 1960), p. 649, n. 5.

5 Donald Ostrowski, 'The Mongol Origins of Muscovite Political Institutions', *Slavic Review*, XLIX/4 (1990), pp. 525–42 (p. 525).

6 PSRL, vol. XI (1897), p. 86 (*s.a.* 6894 = 1385/6); *Nikonian Chronicle*, vol. IV, pp. 21–2; PSRL, vol. XXV (1949), p. 213.

7 PSRL, vol. XI (1897), p. 90 (*s.a.* 6894 = 1385/6); *Nikonian Chronicle*, vol. IV, p. 26. Later in the entry for the same year (6894), the *Nikonian Chronicle* says that Vasilii Dmitrievich of Suzdal, the grandson of

Konstantin, escaped from the Orda but was recaptured. When he returned, Toqtamish had him tortured. We do not have independent confirmation of the torture, nor do we have any indication of what it comprised, but we can assume that Toqtamish was not pleased with his hostages escaping.

8 PSRL, vol. XI (1897), p. 90 (*s.a.* 6894 = 1385/6); *Nikonian Chronicle*, vol. IV, pp. 26–7.

9 PSRL, vol. XI (1897), p. 90 (*s.a.* 6894 = 1385/6); *Nikonian Chronicle*, vol. IV, p. 27.

10 PSRL, vol. XI (1897), p. 91. *Nikonian Chronicle*, vol. IV, p. 27. Meyendorff says that Vasilii remained in Kyiv from 1385 through 1387, when Metropolitan Cyprian brokered the agreement between Vytautas and Vasilii, who only returned to Moscow in 1388. John Meyendorff, *Byzantium and the Rise of Russia* (Cambridge, 1980), p. 244. Meyendorff cites I. V. Grekov, *Vostochnaia Evropa i upadok Zolotoi Ordy (na rubezhe XIV–XV vv.)* (Moscow, 1975), pp. 189–95, to support this interpretation.

11 PSRL, 15 (1863), col. 445 (*s.a.* 6898 = 1389/90).

12 Norman Davies, *God's Playground: A History of Poland*, 2 vols, vol. I: *The Origins to 1795* (New York, 1982), p. 116.

13 She may have hated the Polish and Lithuanian barons for forcing her to marry Jogaila, as Davies states, but it is unlikely that she expressed gratitude to God for the victory of the Tatars at the Vorskla River over the forces of Poland and Lithuania for 'humbling their pride'. Davies, *God's Playground*, vol. I, p. 118. That battle occurred on 12 August 1399, which was almost a month after she had died (17 July).

14 'Second Testament of Dmitriy Donskoy', in *The Testaments of the Grand Princes of Moscow*, trans. and ed. Robert Craig Howes (Ithaca, NY, 1967), pp. 215–16.

15 See A.V. Chernetsov, *Types on Russian Coins of the XIV and XV Centuries: An Iconographic Study*, trans. H. Bartlett Wells (Oxford, 1983).

16 Thomas Noonan, 'Forging a National Identity: Monetary Politics during the Reign of Vasilii I (1389–1425)', in *Culture and Identity in Muscovy, 1359–1584*, ed. Ann M. Kleimola and Gail D. Lenhoff (Moscow, 1997), pp. 495, 501–3.

17 Edigü, like Mamai and Timur before him, was not a Chinggisid and therefore could not be a khan, but like them he was powerful enough to puppetize the khan.

18 PSRL, vol. XI (1897), pp. 173–4; *Nikonian Chronicle*, vol. IV, pp. 117–18.

19 Rossiiskaia publichnaia biblioteka (RPB), O.IV.14, fols 14–16.

20 *Drevnerusskie kniazheskie ustavy XI–XV vv.*, ed. Ia. N. Shchapov (Moscow, 1976), pp. 183–5.

21 *Akty sotsialno-ekonomicheskoi istorii Severo-Vostochnoi Rusi kontsa XIV–nachala XVI v.*, ed. B. D. Grekov and L. V. Cherpnin, 3 vols (Moscow–Leningrad, 1952–64), vol. III, p. 15, no. 2.

22 Noonan, 'Forging a National Identity', p. 498.

23 Ibid.

24 Vernadsky, *The Mongols and Russia*, p. 274.

25 PSRL, vol. XI (1897), pp. 159–61; *Nikonian Chronicle*, vol. IV, pp. 96–100; PSRL, vol. XXV (1949), pp. 223–5.

26 Noonan, 'Monetary Politics', p. 503.

27 Meyendorff is sceptical of the claim in the *Tale concerning Mitiai* that Pimen was able to bamboozle Neilos with faked letters. Meyendorff, *Byzantium and Russia*, p. 219. He thinks it was a fictitious story to exonerate Neilos, Emperor Ioannes V and Dmitrii of Moscow of any wrongdoing.

28 *RIB*, VI (1908), col. 186.

29 *PSRL*, vol. XI (1885), p. 153 (*s.a.* 6900 = 1391/2), *PSRL*, vol. XI (1885), p. 217 (*s.a.* 6919 = 1410/1).

30 Dimitri Obolensky, 'Some Notes Concerning a Byzantine Portrait of John VIII Palaeologus', *Eastern Churches Review*, IV/2 (1972), pp. 141–6.

31 *Testaments of the Grand Princes*, p. 215.

32 The *Stepennaia kniga* has Sofia telling 'all the boyars and officials and functionaries and bureaucrats, that they were to be loyal to her son'. *PSRL*, vol. XXI/2 (1913), p. 458. However, that could be merely a conjecture on the part of the author of the *SK*, some 140 years later.

33 *Nikonian Chronicle*, vol. V, p. 24.

12 Ivan III Vasilevich and His Family

1 V. L. Ianin, 'Medieval Novgorod', in *The Cambridge History of Russia*, vol. I: *From Early Rus' to 1689*, ed. Maureen Perrie (Cambridge, 2006), pp. 201–2.

2 Katarzyna Krupa, 'Książęta Litewscy w Nowogrodzie Wielkim do 1430 roku', *Kwartalnik Historyczny*, C/1 (1993), p. 37.

3 Kazan played the same game in the sixteenth century, playing off the Crimean Khanate against Moscow, with the same result – Moscow won the game. Donald Ostrowski, 'Ruling Class Structures of the Kazan' Khanate', in *The Turks*, ed. Hasan Celâl Güzel, C. Cem Oğuz, and Osman Karatay, 6 vols (Ankara, 2002), vol. II: *Middle Ages*, pp. 841–7. Cf. the similar strategy of the Zaporozhian Cossacks in the seventeenth century, between Moscow and Poland.

4 Ivan was the second son of Vasilii and Maria, who was the daughter of Iaroslav Vladimirovich, the ruler of Serpukhov, Borovsk and Maloiaroslav.

5 *PSRL*, vol. XII (1901), p. 231 (*s.a.* 7000 = 1491/2); *The Nikonian Chronicle*, ed. Serge A. Zenkovsky, trans. Serge A. Zenkovsky and Betty Jean Zenkovsky, 5 vols (Princeton, NJ, 1984–9), p. 233.

6 *Ioasafskaia letopis*, ed. A. A. Zimin (Moscow, 1957), p. 129.

7 *Pamiatniki diplomaticheskikh snoshenii drevnei Rossii s derzhavami inostrannymi* (*PDS*), 10 vols (St Petersburg, 1851–71): V Tip. II Otdeleniia Sobstvennoi E. I. V. kantseliarii.

8 For a discussion of these interrelated texts, their dates and interrelationship, see Donald Ostrowski, *Muscovy and the Mongols: Cross-Cultural Influences on the Steppe Frontier* (Cambridge, 1998), pp. 171–6.

9 *The Monastic Rule of Iosif Volotsky*, ed. and trans. David M. Goldfrank, 2nd edn (Kalamazoo, MI, 2000), p. 235.

10 The Ioasaf Chronicle (*Ioasafskaia letopis*, p. 54) and the Tolstoi VII (Golitsyn) copy of the *Nikonian Chronicle* (*PSRL*, vol. XII, p. 117) place Maria's death *s.a.* 1465 (6973). The other copies of the *Nikonian*

Chronicle place her death *s.a.* 1467 (6975) (PSRL, vol. XII, p. 116). Zimin places her death in April 1465 (A. A. Zimin, *Formirovanie boiarskoi aristokratii v Rossii. Vo vtoroi polovine XV–pervoi treti XVI v.* (Moscow, 1988), p. 106). Fennell places her death in 1467 (J. L. I. Fennell, *Ivan the Great of Moscow* [London, 1961], p. 316).

11 George Vernadsky, *Russia at the Dawn of the Modern Age* (New Haven, CT, 1959), p. 21.

12 Russell E. Martin, *A Bride for the Tsar: Bride-Shows and Marriage Politics in Early Modern Russia* (DeKalb, IL, 2012), pp. 90–92.

13 On Morea from 1407 to 1460, see Nevra Necipoğlu, *Byzantium between the Ottomans and the Latins: Politics and Society in the Late Empire* (Cambridge, 2009), pp. 259–84.

14 PSRL, vol. XII (1901), p. 120 (6977); PSRL, vol. XXVI (1959), p. 225.

15 Gino Barbieri, *Milano e Moscow nella politica del Rinascimento. Storia delle relazioni diplomatiche tra la Russia e il Ducato di Milano nell' epoca sforzesca* (Bari, 1957), pp. 46–7.

16 *Die Chroniken der fränkischenschen Städte. Nürnberg*, 5 vols (Leipzig, 1862–74), vol. IV, pp. 330–31 and vol. V , pp. 468–9; Joannes Martynov, *Annus Ecclesiasticus Greco-Slavicus* (Brussels, 1863), p. 134; PSRL, vol. XI (1897), p. 147: 'the legate Antonio [Cardinal Bonumbre] was sent to her as the Pope's envoy, and with them were many Romans, and the envoy of the princess was Dmitrii Manuilovich with many Greeks, and many other Greeks who served her accompanied her.'

17 See, for example, Donald Ostrowski, 'Muscovite Adaptation of Steppe Political Institutions: A Reply to Halperin's Objections', *Kritika: Explorations in Russian and Eurasian History*, I (2000), pp. 267–304.

18 Robert M. Croskey and E. C. Ronquist, 'George Trakhaniot's Description of Russia in 1486', *Russian History/Historie Russe*, XVII/1 (1990), p. 63.

19 Ostrowski, *Muscovy and the Mongols*, p. 17, cf. p. 83.

20 Necipoğlu, *Bzyantium between the Ottomans and the Latins*, pp. 274–6. Cf. S[terios N.] Fassoulakis [Phassoulakes], *The Byzantine Family of Raoul-Ral(l)es* (Athens, 1973), pp. 83–5. The traditional date for Plethon's death is 1452 but, recently, the date 1454 has been argued for. See John Monfasani, 'Pletho's Date of Death and the Burning of His *Laws*', *Byzantinische Zeitschrift*, XCVIII/2 (2006), pp. 459–63.

21 PSRL, vol. XXV (1949), pp. 300, 305.

22 Later, Vasilii and Maria fled to Lithuania over the matter of some jewels that they received from Sofia as part of Maria's dowry.

23 For a discussion of the members of these families in Muscovy, see Robert Croskey, 'Byzantine Greeks in Late Fifteenth- and Early Sixteenth-Century Russia', in *The Byzantine Legacy in Eastern Europe*, ed. Lowell Clucas (Boulder, CO, 1988), pp. 35–56.

24 *Sbornik Imperatorskogo Russkogo istoricheskogo obshchestva* (SIRIO), XXXV (1882), p. 75, no. 18, and XXXV (1882), p. 114, no. 24; *Pamiatniki diplomaticheskikh snoshenii drevnei Rossii s derzhavami inostrannymi*, 10 vols (St Petersburg, 1851–71), vol. I: *Snosheniia s gosudarstvami evropeiskimi*, col. 82 (1491); *Razriadnaia kniga, 1475–1598 gg.*, comp. V. I. Buganov, ed. M. N. Tikhomirov (Moscow, 1966), p. 44 (1511).

25 PSRL, vol. XII (1901), p. 216 (6993), p. 222 (6998); PSRL, vol. XXVII (1962), p. 287.
26 PSRL, vol. XII (1901), p. 219 (6996: Dmitrii and Manuel sent to Rome, Venice and Milan), p. 222 (6998), p. 236 (7001), p. 238 (7002), p. 249 (7007), p. 258 (7013).
27 Croskey, 'Byzantine Greeks', p. 39.
28 PSRL, vol. XXVII (1962), p. 288.
29 PSRL, vol. XII (1901), p. 222 (Shumilov); PSRL, vol. XVIII (1913), pp. 272–3; PSRL, vol. XXIV (1921), p. 206; PSRL, vol. XXVIII (1963), p. 154.
30 PSRL, vol. XII (1901), p. 222 (Shumilov); PSRL, vol. XVIII (1913), pp. 272–3; PSRL, vol. XXIV (1921), p. 206; PSRL, vol. XXVIII (1963), p. 154. Leon was subsequently beheaded when he failed to cure Ivan Ivanovich, the heir to the throne.
31 Gustav Alef, 'The Adoption of the Muscovite Two-Headed Eagle: A Discordant View', *Speculum: A Journal of Mediaeval Studies*, XLI/1 (1966), p. 14, repr. in Gustave Alef, *Rulers and Nobles in Fifteenth-Century Muscovy* (London, 1983), item 9.
32 Herberstein, *Notes upon Russia*, vol. I, p. 25.
33 AI, vol. I, no. 40, pp. 75–83.
34 PSRL, vol. VIII (1859), p. 115; PSRL, vol. XVIII (1913), p. 196; PSRL, vol. XXV (1949), p. 263; cf. PSRL, vol. XXXIII (1977), pp. 51–2.
35 PSRL, vol. IV/1.2 (1925), p. 443; cf. PSRL, vol. XII (1901), pp. 66–8, 72; PSRL, vol. XVI (1889), p. 189. *Nikonian Chronicle*, vol. V, pp. 77–8.
36 Ostrowski, *Muscovy and the Mongols*, pp. 139–43.
37 *Dukhovnye i dogovornye gramoty velikikh i udel'nykh kniazei XIV–XVI vv.* (DDG), ed. L. V. Cherepnin (Moscow and Leningrad, 1950), no. 52, p. 156.
38 PSRL, vol. VI/2 (1853), col. 131.
39 Donald Ostrowski, 'The Extraordinary Career of Tsarevich Kudai Kul/Peter in the Context of Relations between Muscovy and Kazan'', in *States, Societies, Cultures: East and West: Essays in Honor of Jaroslaw Pelenski*, ed. Janusz Duzinkiewicz, Myroslav Popovych, Vladyslav Verstiuk and Natalia Yakovenko (New York, 2004), pp. 697–719.
40 PSRL, vol. VI/2 (2001), col. 352.
41 PSRL, vol. XII (1901), p. 263. Cf. PSRL, vol. VIII (1859), p. 243; and PSRL, vol. XII (1901), p. 246.
42 Ostrowski, *Muscovy and the Mongols*, pp. 186–7 fn. 104.
43 PSRL, vol. VIII (1859), p. 236.
44 PSRL, vol. XII (1901), p. 264. M. N. Tikhomirov, 'Iz "Vladimirskogo letopistsa"', *Istoricheskie zapiski*, XV (1945), p. 291.
45 PSRL, vol. V [1940] (2003), pp. 83–4; *Pskovskie letopisi*, 2 vols, ed. A. N. Nasonov (Moscow, 1941–55), vol. I, pp. 83–4.
46 PSRL, vol. VIII (1859), p. 242.
47 Vernadsky, *Russia at the Dawn*, p. 130.
48 Herberstein, *Notes upon Russia*, vol. I, p. 21.
49 Fennell provides brief summaries of the various interpretations. J.L.I. Fennell, *Ivan the Great of Moscow* (London, 1961), pp. 355–61.

50 'Poslanie Arkhimandritu Mitrofanu Andronnikovikomu', in *Poslanie Iosifa Volotskogo*, ed. A. A. Zimin and Ia. S. Lur'e (Moscow and Leningrad, 1959), p. 176.
51 Iosif, *Prosvetitel'*, Introduction.
52 'Fevral' 1488 g. Gramoty velikogo kniazia Ivana III i mitropolita Gerontiia arkhiepiskopu Gennadiiu Novgorodskomu', in N. A. Kazakova and Ia. S. Lur'e, *Antifeodal'nye ereticheskie dvizheniia na Rusi XIV–nachala XVI veka (AfED)* (Moscow and Leningrad, 1955), p. 314.
53 For an analytical comparison of what we can discern about the Rus heretics' beliefs from their accusers and the beliefs of the Hussites, see Ostrowski, *Russia in the Early Modern World: The Continuity of Change* (Lanham, MD, 2022), pp. 329–33.
54 *AfED*, p. 148; *PDS*, vol. I, col. 161.
55 Russell E. Martin, *The Tsar's Happy Occasion: Ritual and Dynasty in the Weddings of Russia's Rulers, 1495–1745* (Ithaca, NY, 2021), pp. 103–11.
56 Russell E. Martin, 'Gifts for the Bride: Dowries, Diplomacy, and Marriage Politics in Muscovy', *Journal of Medieval and Early Modern Studies*, XXXVIII/1 (2008), p. 125.
57 Martin, 'Gifts for the Bride', p. 129.
58 A possible exception might be the marriage of Kuchenyi, the daughter of Temriuk, a Kabardian ruler, to Ivan IV in 1561. However, she converted to Russian Orthodoxy before the marriage, as had Kudaikul before his marriage to the sister of Vasilii III in 1505.
59 Martin, *A Bride for the Tsar*.

Epilogue: The Family Lines Continue . . .

1 Francis Butler, *Enlightener of Rus': The Image of Vladimir Sviatoslavich across the Centuries* (Bloomington, IN, 2002), p. 157.
2 Ibid.
3 John Lind, 'The "Brotherhood of Rus": A Pseudo-Problem Concerning the Origin of "Rus'"', *Slavica Othiniensia*, V (1982), pp. 66–81.
4 *PVL: Interlinear Collation*, col. 0, line 3–col. 0, line 4.
5 *PVL: Interlinear Collation*, col. 4, line 3 and col. 4, line 12.
6 An example of this definition is Michell and Forbes, who define *Russkaia zemlia* (Rus land) as 'usually used to denote all the Slavonic inhabitants of Great, Little and West Russia and the country occupied by them'. (See Michell and Forbes in the *Chronicle of Novgorod, 1016–1471*, trans. Robert Michell and Nevill Forbes (London, 1914), p. 233). Defining the geographical limits of Rus by the areas where the Rus people lived is a modern, nationalistic concept that has been used as a justification to carve off pieces of other countries, such as Russia did in 2014, justifying the annexation of Crimea by claiming that Russians lived there, or as Hitler did in 1938, justifying the annexation of the Sudeten mountain area of Czechoslovakia by claiming that Germans lived there.
7 *PVL: An Interlinear Collation*, col. 143, lines 1–3; *RPC*, p. 132.
8 *PVL: An Interlinear Collation*, col. 269, lines 20–23; *RPC*, p. 195.
9 For example, the Novgorod I Chronicle states: 'The whole land of Rus marched against Galicia' (1145). *PSRL*, vol. III (2000), pp. 27, 213;

Chronicle of Novgorod, p. 18. The Kyivan Chronicle states: 'Sviatoslav [Vsevolodovich] gave Galich to Riurik [Rostislavich], and wished [to keep] all the Rus land around Kyiv for himself' (1189). PSRL, vol. II (1908), col. 663. 'Kyivan Chronicle', p. 436. The Kyivan Chronicle states: 'Sviatoslav sent to Riurik [in Volhynia] and said to him: ". . . But go now into Rus; guard your land." Riurik . . . went into Rus with all his troops' (1193). PSRL, vol. II (1908), col. 678. 'Kyivan Chronicle', p. 455. The Laurentian Chronicle states: 'Roman having gathered the troops of Galicia and Volodymyr, invaded the Rus land' (1202). PSRL, vol. I/2 (1927), col. 417. The Galician-Volhynian Chronicle states: 'Daniil [of Galicia] captured the town of Torchesk, belonging to the Rus land' (1231). PSRL, vol. II (1908), col. 766 *s.a.* 6739 = 1231 (1232/3). GVC, p. 40. However, the GVC begins with a statement referring to Roman Mstislavich as 'the unforgettable autocrat of all Rus' *s.a.* 6709 = 1201 (1205), PSRL, vol. II (1908), col. 715; GVC, p. 17, but that would probably be a phrase from a later redactor; that is, an interpolation into an earlier annalistic layer.

10 The Kyivan Chronicle states: 'Sviatoslav weeping sent to Iurii in Suzdal saying, ". . . Go to the Rus Land, to Kyiv"' (1146). PSRL, vol. II (1908), col. 329; 'Kyivan Chronicle', p. 53. According to the Kyivan Chronicle: 'Iurii . . . said, "Neither I nor my children have any part in the Rus land"' (1149). PSRL, vol. II (1908), col. 374; 'Kyivan Chronicle', p. 104. The Laurentian Chronicle states: 'Iurii went forth with the men of Rostov, Suzdal, and Riazan . . . to Rus' (1152). PSRL, vol. I/2 (1927), col. 338. Cf. PSRL vol. I/2 (1927), col. 341. The Laurentian Chronicle states: 'This winter . . . Iurii . . . went forth . . . to Rus . . . and went himself to Kyiv' (1154). PSRL, vol. I/2 (1927), col. 344. The Laurentian Chronicle states: 'the Bishop [of Rostov] Nestor went forth [from Rostov] to Rus' (1156). PSRL, vol. I/2 (1927), col. 347. The Laurentian Chronicle states that Mikhail Iurevich left Vladimir 'and went forth to Rus' (1175). PSRL, vol. I/2 (1927), col. 373. The *Nikonian Chronicle* changed the text to read 'to Chernigov' rather than 'to Rus''. PSRL, vol. IX (1862), p. 253; *Nikonian Chronicle*, 5 vols, ed. Serge A. Zenkovsky, trans. Serge A. Zenkovsky and Betty Jean Zenkovsky (Princeton, NJ, 1984–9), vol. II, p. 164. The Novgorod I Chronicle states: '*Kniaz* Sviatoslav Vsevolodovich . . . went forth from Rus to Suzdal in force' (1180). PSRL, vol. III (2000), pp. 36, 226; *Chronicle of Novgorod*, p. 30. The Laurentian Chronicle states that Sviatoslav 'returned again to Rus and *Kniaz* Vsevolod to Vladimir' (1181). PSRL, vol. I/2 (1927), col. 388. The Kyivan Chronicle states: '*Kniaz* Riurik sent *Kniaz* Gleb . . . to Vsevolod, to Suzdal for Verkhuslava [as wife] for Rastislav . . . , and Vsevolod . . . gave his daughter Verkhuslava .. and sent her to Rus' (1187). PSRL, vol. II (1908), col. 658; 'Kyivan Chronicle', pp. 429–30.

11 When Sviatoslav Vsevolodovich was at Nerinsk in the Riazan Land with his men, 'a youth fled there from Rus . . .' (1147). PSRL, vol. II (1908), col. 341; 'Kyivan Chronicle', p. 68. 'Volodimer, hearing that his son-in-law Iurii [after gathering troops in Riazan] was going into Rus, went from Galich to Kyiv' (1152). PSRL, vol. II (1908), col. 455; 'Kyivan Chronicle', p. 189. The men of Rostov and Suzdal assembled

in Vladimir and decided that their envoys 'should go to Rus to ask for a kniaz . . . ' (1175). *PSRL*, vol. I/2 (1927), col. 372.

12 Henryk Paszkiewicz, *The Origin of Russia* (London, 1954), pp. 7–10: Smolensk is outside Rus: when Rastislav arrived from Smolensk to Kyiv he was greeted 'by all of Rus' (1154); 'Go to Smolensk . . . I order you not to stay in the Rus land' (1174); 'David sent his son Constantine [from Smolensk] to Rus' (1197). Polotsk is outside Rus: 'Mstislav, ruler of Kyiv, summoned the ruler of Polotsk to Rus' (1140).

13 Charles J. Halperin, 'The Concept of the Russian Land from the Ninth to the Fourteenth Centuries', *Russian History*, II/1 (1975), p. 30.

14 Ibid., p. 33. In a later article, Halperin changed the phrase to 'Myth of the Rus Land'. Charles J. Halperin, 'The Concept of the Russkaia Zemlia and Medieval National Consciousness from the Tenth to the Fifteenth Centuries', *Nationalities Papers*, VIII/1 (1980), pp. 75–86.

15 V. V. Mavrodin, *Proiskhozhdenie russkogo naroda* (Leningrad, 1978), pp. 148–69; M. N. Tikhomirov, 'Proiskhozdenie nazvanii "Rus'" i 'Russkaia zemlia"', in his *Russkoe letopisanie* (Moscow, 1979), pp. 22–45.

16 *PVL: Interlinear Collation*, col. 31, lines 25–6; col. 49, lines 1–3; *RPC*, pp. 64 and 74.

17 *PVL: Interlinear Collation*, col. 19, lines 20–24 and col. 20, lines 8–9; *RPC*, p. 59. *The Annals of St-Bertin* (Ninth-Century Histories, vol. I), trans. Janet L. Nelson (Manchester, 1991), p. 44.

18 Lind cited the Novgorod I Chronicle, where it says that in 1117 Mstislav went to 'Kyiv' not to 'Rus', and in 1118 he brought the boyars of Novgorod to 'Kyiv' not to 'Rus'. *PSRL*, vol. III (2000), pp. 20–21, 204–5; *Chronicle of Novgorod*, pp. 9, 10. Similarly, in 1126, *Kniaz* Vsevolod went to 'Kyiv', and in 1129 'Daniil came from Kyiv to be *posadnik* in Novgorod'. *PSRL*, vol. III (2000), pp. 22, 206; *Chronicle of Novgorod*, p. 11. Lind, 'Brotherhood of Rus'', p. 70. In 1139, 'the men of Novgorod sent to Kyiv for Sviatoslav Olgovich'. *PSRL*, vol. III (2000), pp. 25, 211; *Chronicle of Novgorod*, p. 16. In 1141, 'they came from Vsevolod from Kyiv for his brother Sviatoslav to take him to Kyiv'. *PSRL*, vol. III (2000), pp. 26, 211; *Chronicle of Novgorod*, p. 16. Already in the entry for 1132 we begin to see the change in designation from 'Kyiv' 'Chernigov', and 'Pereiaslavl' to 'Rus': 'Vsevolod left Novgorod to go "into Rus, to Pereiaslavl"'. *PSRL*, vol. III (2000), pp. 22, 207; *Chronicle of Novgorod*, p. 12.; Lind, 'Brotherhood of Rus'', p. 69. In 1135, the Novgorod First Chronicle reports that Archbishop Niphont of Novgorod 'went into Rus and found the men of Kyiv and the men of Chernigov ranged against each other'. *PSRL*, vol. III (2000), pp. 23–4, 208; *Chronicle of Novgorod*, p. 14. In 1142 he and other Novgorodians are not allowed to leave 'Rus' to return to Novgorod. *PSRL*, vol. III (2000), pp. 26, 212; *Chronicle of Novgorod*, p. 16. In 1146 Vsevolod Olgovich, ruler of Kyiv, 'died in Rus'. *PSRL*, vol. III (2000), pp. 27, 213; *Chronicle of Novgorod*, p. 19. Lind, 'Brotherhood of Rus'', p. 70.

19 Lind, 'Brotherhood of Rus'', pp. 70–71.

20 Ibid., p. 71.

21 Ibid., p. 72.

22 Ibid., p. 73.

23 *Dopolnenie k Aktam istoricheskim* (DAI), 12 vols (St Petersburg, 1846–72), vol. I, p. 44, no. 39: 'Chin venchaniia na tsarstvo tsaria Ioanna Vasilevica', 16 January 1547.
24 Karamzin, *Istoriia gosudarstva Rossiiskogo*, vol. X, cols 131–2.
25 Vasilii declared himself 'tsar and grand prince over the Russian state, which God did grant to our forebear Riurik, who was [descended] from the Roman Caesar'. *Sobranie gosudarstvennykh gramot i dogovorov khraniashchikhsia v gosudarstvennoi kollegii inostrannykh del (SGGD)*, 5 vols (Moscow, 1813–94), vol. II, p. 299. Translation from Isaiah Gruber, *Orthodox Russia in Crisis: Church and Nation in the Time of Troubles* (DeKalb, IL, 2012), p. 44. For a discussion of this point, see ibid., pp. 44–5.
26 Donald Ostrowski, 'The Assembly of the Land (Zemskii sobor) as a Representative Institution', in *Modernizing Muscovy: Reform and Social Change in Seventeenth-Century Russia*, ed. Jarmo Kotilaine and Marshall Poe (London, 2004), pp. 117–18.
27 Daniel Rowland, 'The Problem of Advice in Muscovite Tales about the Time of Troubles', *Russian History*, VI/2 (1979), pp. 259–83 (p. 276).
28 See Daniel Rowland, 'Towards an Understanding of the Political Ideas in Ivan Timofeyev's *Vremennik*', *Slavonic and East European Review*, LXII/3 (July 1984), p. 396. Cf. Gruber, *Orthodox Russia in Crisis*, pp. 75–96.

BIBLIOGRAPHY

The following bibliography has been divided into sources and studies.

Sources

Acta Innocentii PP. IV *(1243–1254)*, ed. Theodosius T. Haluščynskyj and Meletius M. Wojnar, Pontificia Commissio ad Redigendum Codicem Iuris Canonici Orientalis, Fontes, 3rd series, IV/I (Vatican City, 1962)

Acta patriarchatus constantinopolitani, ed. Francis Miklosich and Joseph Müller, 2 vols (Vienna, 1860–62)

Adam of Bremen, *The History of the Archbishops of Hamburg-Bremen*, trans. Francis J. Tschan (New York, 2002)

Aktovye pechati drevnei rusi X–XV *vv.*, vol. I: *Pechati* X*–nachala* XIII *v.*, ed. V. L. Ianin (Moscow, 1970)

Akty, otnosiashchiesia k istorii Zapadnoi Rossii, vol. I: *1340–1506*, ed. I. Grigorovich, 5 vols (St Petersburg, 1846)

Akty sotsialno-ekonomicheskoi istorii Severo-Vostochnoi Rusi kontsa XIV*–nachala* XVI *v.*, ed. B. D. Grekov and L. V. Cherepnin, 3 vols (Moscow–Leningrad, 1952–64)

The Annals of St-Bertin, vol. I: *Ninth-Century Histories*, trans. Janet L. Nelson (Manchester, 1991)

Barbieri, Gino, *Milano e Moscow nella politica del Rinascimento. Storia delle relazioni diplomatiche tra la Russia e il Ducato di Milano nell' epoca sforzesca* (Bari, 1957)

The Chronicle of Novgorod, 1016–1471, trans. Robert Michell and Nevill Forbes (London, 1914)

Chroniken der fränkischenschen Städte, Die, Nürnberg, 5 vols (Leipzig, 1862–74)

Constantine Porphyrogennetos: The Book of Ceremonies, trans. Ann Moffatt and Maxeme Tall (Leiden, 2012)

Długosz, Jan, *Historiae Polonicae*. Libri XII (1711)

Drevnerusskie kniazheskie ustavy XI–XV *vv.*, ed. Ia. N. Shchapov (Moscow, 1976)

Fontes ad historiam aevi Saxonici illustrandam: Widukindi res gestae Saxonicae; Adalberti continuato Reginonis; Liudprandi opera, ed. Albert von Bauer and Reinhold Rau (Darmstadt, 2002)

The Galician-Volhynian Chronicle, trans. George A. Perfecky (Munich, 1973)

Gelzer, Heinrich von, *Ungedruckte und ungenügend veröffentlichte Texte der Notitiae episcopatum ein Beitrag zur byzantinischen Kirchen- und verwaltungsgeschichte* (Munich, 1901)

Gesta Principum Polonorum: The Deeds of the Princes of the Poles, trans. and ed. Paul W. Knoll and Frank Schaer (New York, 2003)

Gregoras, *Byzantina Historia*, 3 vols, ed. Ludwig Shopen and Immanuel Bekker (Bonn, 1829–55)

The Hagiography of Kievan Rus, trans. Paul Hollingsworth (Cambridge, MA, 1992)

Heinrich, Lisa, 'The Kyivan Chronicle: A Translation and Commentary', PhD dissertation, Vanderbilt University, 1977

Henricus Lettus, *The Chronicle of Henry of Livonia*, trans. James A. Brundage (New York, 2003)

Herberstein, Sigismund Freiherr von, *Notes upon Russia*, 2 vols, trans. and ed. R. H. Major (London, 1851)

Historia Brittonum, ed. Theodore Mommsen, book 2, accessed online at www.thelatinlibrary.com/histbrit.html, 15 October 2022

Ioasafskaia letopis, ed. A. A. Zimin (Moscow, 1957)

Isidore of Seville, *Etymologies*, book 9, line 102, accessed online at https://penelope.uchicago.edu, 15 October 2022

Jus graeco-romanum, ed. K. E. Zachariae von Lingenthal, 4 vols (Leipzig, 1856–65)

Kinnamos, John, *Deeds of John and Manuel Comnenus*, trans. Charles M. Brand (New York, 1976)

Martynov, Joannes, *Annus Ecclesiasticus Greco-Slavicus* (Brussels, 1863)

Medieval Russia's Epics, Chronicles, and Tales, revised and expanded edn, ed. and trans. Serge A. Zenkovsky (New York, 1974)

Medieval Russian Laws, trans. George Vernadsky (New York, 1947)

Metropolitan Ilarion Lobrede auf Vladimir den Heligen und Glaubensbekenntnis, Das, ed. Ludolf Müller (Wiesbaden, 1962)

Morkinskinna: The Earliest Icelandic Chronicle of the Norwegian Kings, 1030–1157, trans. Theodore M. Andersson and Kari Ellen Gade (Ithaca, NY, 2000)

Niketas Choniates, *O City of Byzantium, Annals of Niketas Choniates*, trans. Harry J. Magoulias (Detroit, MI, 1984)

The Nikonian Chronicle, 5 vols, ed. Serge A. Zenkovsky, trans. Serge A. Zenkovsky and Betty Jean Zenkovsky (Princeton, NJ, 1984–9)

Ottonian Germany: The 'Chronicon' of Thietmar of Merseburg, trans. David A. Warner (Manchester, 2001)

Pamiatniki diplomaticheskikh snoshenii drevnei Rossii s derzhavami inostrannymi, 10 vols (St Petersburg, 1851–71)

Pamiatniki drevne-russkogo kanonicheskogo prava: pamiatniki XI–XV *v.*, in *Russkaia istoricheskaia biblioteka*, VI (1908)

Polnoe sobranie russkikh letopisei (PSRL), 43 vols (St Petersburg/Petrograd/Leningrad and Moscow, 1841–2007)

Poslanie Iosifa Volotskogo, ed. A. A. Zimin and Ia. S. Lure (Moscow and Leningrad, 1959)

The Povest' vremennykh let: An Interlinear Collation and Paradosis, comp. and ed. Donald Ostrowski with David Birnbaum and Horace G. Lunt (Cambridge, MA, 2003), available online at http://pvl.obdurodon.org/pvl.html

Psellos, Michael, *Fourteen Byzantine Rulers: The Chronographia of Michael Psellus*, trans. E.R.A. Sewter (New York, 1966)

Pskovskie letopisi, ed. A. N. Nasonov, 2 vols (Moscow, 1941–55)

Rashid al-Din (Rashududdin Fazlullah), *Jami'u't-Tawarikh: Compendium of Chronicles. A History of the Mongols*, trans. and annotated by W. M. Thackston (Cambridge, MA, 1999)

Razriadnaia kniga, 1475–1598 gg., comp. V. I. Buganov, ed. M. N. Tikhomirov (Moscow, 1966)

Recueil des actes de Philippe I-er, roi de France (1059–1108), ed. Maurice Prou (Paris, 1908)

Register des Patriarchats von Konstantinopel, Das, ed. Herbert Hunger and Otto Kresten (Vienna, 1981)

The Russian Primary Chronicle: Laurentian Text, trans. and ed. Samuel Hazzard Cross and Olgerd P. Sherbowitz-Wetzor (Cambridge, MA, 1953)

Russisch-livländische Urkunden, ed. K. E. Nepiersky (St Petersburg, 1868)

Saxo Grammaticus, *The History of the Danes: Books I–IX*, trans. Peter Fisher, ed. Hilda Ellis Davidson (Cambridge, 1996)

—, *Danorum Regum Heroumque Historia: Books X–XVI*, vol. I: *Books X, XI, XII and XIII*, trans. and ed. Eric Christiansen, 3 vols (Oxford, 1980–81)

Sbornik Imperatorskogo Russkogo istoricheskogo obshchestva (SIRIO), 148 vols (St Petersburg, 1867–1916)

Scriptores Rerum Prussicarum, ed. Theodor Hirsch, Max Töppen and Ernst Strehlke, 5 vols (Leipzig, 1861–74)

'Secret History of the Mongols, The', trans. Igor de Rachewiltz, *Papers on Far Eastern History*, 31 (1985), pp. 21–93

Sermons and Rhetoric of Kievan Rus', trans. Simon Franklin (Cambridge, MA, 1991)

Skarbiec diplomatów papiezkich, cesarskich, królewskich, książęcych; uchwał narodowych, postanowień różynych władz i urzędów posługujących do krytycznego wyjaśnenia dziejów Litwy, Rusi Litewskiéj i ościennych im krajów, ed. Ignacy Daniłowicz, 2 vols (Wilno, 1860–62)

Skazanie i povesti o Kulikovskoi bitve, ed. L. A. Dmitriev and O. P. Likhacheva (Leningrad, 1982)

Skylitzes, John, *A Synopsis of Byzantine History, 811–1057*, trans. John Wortley (Cambridge, 2010)

Snorri Sturluson, *Heimskringla: History of the Kings of Norway*, trans. Lee M. Hollander (Austin, TX, 1964)

Sobranie gosudarstvennykh gramot i dogovorov khraniashchikhsia v gosudarstvennoi kollegii inostrannykh del (SGGD), 5 vols (Moscow, 1813–94)

Sources of Slavic Pre-Christian Religion, ed. Juan Antonio Álvarez-Pedrosa (Leiden, 2021)

The Testaments of the Grand Princes of Moscow, trans. and ed. Robert Craig Howes (Ithaca, NY, 1967)

Thietmar of Merseburg, *Chronica*, ed. J. M. Lappenberg, in *Monumenta Germaniae Historica* [1839], ed. George Pertz (Leipzig, 1925), vol. III

'Wilhelmi Abbatis Genealogia Regum Danorum', in *Scriptores minores historiae danicae medii ævi*, ed. M.C.L. Getz, 2 vols (Copenhagen, 1917), vol. I

Studies

Alef, Gustav, 'The Adoption of the Muscovite Two-Headed Eagle: A Discordant View', *Speculum: A Journal of Mediaeval Studies*, XXXXI/1 (1966), pp. 11–21, reprinted in Gustave Alef, *Rulers and Nobles in Fifteenth-Century Muscovy* (London, 1983), item 9

Alekseev, M. P., 'Anglo-saksonskaia parallel' k Poucheniu Vladimira Monomakha', *Trudy Otdela drevnerusskoi literatury*, II (1935), pp. 39–80
Angelov, B. S., *Iz starata Bŭlgarska, Russka i Srbska literature* (Sofia, 1958)
Barthold, W., 'Toktamish', in *Encyclopedia of Islam*, ed. M. Th. Houtsma, T. W. Arnold, R. Basset and R. Hartmann, 9 vols (Leiden, 1913–36)
Baumgarten, N. de., 'Généalogies et mariages Occidentaux des Rurikides Russes du X-e au XIII-e siècle,' *Orientalia Christiana*, IX/25 (1927), pp. 5–95
Birnbaum, Henrik, *Lord Novgorod the Great: Essays in the History and Culture of a Medieval City-State*, Part One: *The Historical Background* (Columbus, OH, 1981)
Boeck, Elena, 'Simulating the Hippodrome: The Performance of Power in Kiev's St Sophia', *Art Bulletin*, XCI/3 (2009), pp. 283–301
Bogomoletz, Wladimir V., 'Anna of Kiev: An Enigmatic Capetian Queen of the Eleventh Century: A Reassessment of Biographical Sources', *French History*, XIX (2005), pp. 299–323
Bouchard, Constance B., 'Consanguinity and Noble Marriages in the Tenth and Eleventh Centuries', *Speculum*, LVI/2 (1981), pp. 268–87
—, 'Family Structure and Family Consciousness among the Aristocracy in the Ninth to Eleventh Centuries', *Francia*, XIV (1986), pp. 639–58
Brutzkus, J., 'Trade with Eastern Europe, 800–1200', *Economic History Review*, XIII/1–2 (1943), pp. 31–41
Butler, Francis, *Enlightener of Rus': The Image of Vladimir Sviatoslavich across the Centuries* (Bloomington, IN, 2002)
Cherepnin, L. V., 'Letopisets Daniila Galitskogo', *Istoricheskie zapiski*, 12 (1941), pp. 228–53
—, *Obrazovanie russkogo tsentralizovannogo gosudarstva v XIV–XV vekakh* (Moscow, 1960)
Chernetsov, A. V., *Types on Russian Coins of the XIV and XV Centuries: An Iconographic Study*, trans. H. Bartlett Wells (Oxford, 1983)
Christian, David, 'Inner Eurasia as a Unit in World History', *Journal of World History*, V/2 (1994), pp. 173–211
—, *A History of Russia, Central Asia and Mongolia*, vol. I: *Inner Eurasia from Prehistory to the Mongol Empire* (Malden, MA, 1998)
Christiansen, Eric, *The Northern Crusades*, 2nd edn (London, 1997)
Croskey, Robert, 'Byzantine Greeks in Late Fifteenth- and Early Sixteenth-Century Russia', in *The Byzantine Legacy in Eastern Europe*, ed. Lowell Clucas (Boulder, CO, 1988), pp. 35–56
Croskey, Robert M., and E. C. Ronquist, 'George Trakhaniot's Description of Russia in 1486', *Russian History/Historie Russe*, XVII/1 (1990), pp. 55–64
Cross, Samuel Hazzard, 'Yaroslav the Wise in Norse Tradition', *Speculum*, IV/2 (April 1929), pp. 177–97
—, *Medieval Russian Churches*, ed. Kenneth John Conant (Cambridge, MA, 1949)
Dąbrowski, Dariusz, *Kronika halicko-wołyńska. Kronika Romanowiczów* (Cracow and Warsaw, 2017)
Davies, Norman, *God's Playground: A History of Poland*, 2 vols (New York, 1982)

Dictionary of Russian Historical Terms from the Eleventh Century to 1917, comp. Sergei G. Pushkarev, ed. George Vernadsky and Ralph T. Fisher Jr (New Haven, CT, 1970)
Dimnik, Martin, *Mikhail, Prince of Chernigov and Grand Prince of Kyiv, 1224–1246* (Toronto, 1981)
—, *The Dynasty of Chernigov, 1054–1146* (Toronto, 1994)
—, *The Dynasty of Chernigov, 1146–1246* (Cambridge, 2003)
Dmitrieva, R. P., *Skazanie o kniaziakh vladimirskikh* (Moscow–Leningrad, 1955)
Dombrovskii [Dąbrowski], Dariush [Dariusz], *Genealogiia Mstislavichei: pervye pokoleniia (do nachala XIV v.)* (St Petersburg, 2015)
Downham, Clare, 'The Historical Importance of Viking-Age Waterford', *Journal of Celtic Studies*, IV (2004), pp. 71–96
Duby, Georges. 'Structures de parenté et noblesse dans la France du Nord aux XIe et XIIe siècles', in *Hommes et structures du moyen âge: Recueil d'articles* (Paris, 1973), pp. 267–85
Dunbabin, Jean, 'What's in a Name? Philip, King of France', *Speculum*, LXVIII/4 (October 1993), pp. 949–68
Eisenstein, Sergei M., and Dmitrii Vasilev, dir., *Aleksandr Nevskii* (Moscow, 1938)
Eremin, I. P., 'Volynskaja letopis 1289–1290 gg.', *Trudy Otdela drevnerusskoi literatury*, XIII (1957), pp. 102–17
Fassoulakis [Phassoulakes], S[terios N.], *The Byzantine Family of Raoul-Ral(l)es* (Athens, 1973)
Fennell, J.L.I. [John], *Ivan the Great of Moscow* (London, 1961)
Fennell, John, *The Emergence of Moscow, 1304–1359* (Berkeley, CA, 1968)
—, *The Crisis of Medieval Russia, 1200–1304* (London, 1983)
—, *A History of the Russian Church to 1448* (London, 1995)
Fischer, David Hackett, *Historians' Fallacies: Toward a Logic of Historical Thought* (New York, 1970)
Fletcher, Joseph, 'The Mongols: Ecological and Social Perspectives', *Harvard Journal of Asiatic Studies*, XLVI/1 (1986), pp. 11–50
Flier, Michael S., 'The Throne of Monomakh: Ivan the Terrible and the Architectonics of Destiny', in *Architectures of Russian Identity: 1500 to the Present*, ed. James Cracraft and Daniel Rowland (Ithaca, NY, 2003), pp. 21–33
—, 'The Murder of Andrej Bogoljubskij in Word and Image,' in *Philology Broad and Deep: In Memoriam Horace Gray Lunt*, ed. Michael S. Flier, David J. Birnbaum and Cynthia M. Vakareliyska (Bloomington, IN, 2014), pp. 103–18
—, 'Murder Most Foul: Picturing the Death of Andrei Bogoliubskii,' in *Seeing Muscovy Anew: Politics – Institutions – Culture in Honor of Nancy Shields Kollmann*, ed. Michael S. Flier, Valerie Kivelson, Erika Monahan and Daniel Rowland, pp. 143–57 (Bloomington, IN, 2017)
Font, Márta, and Gábor Barabás, *Coloman: King of Galicia and Duke of Slavonia (1208–1241): Medieval Central Europe and Hungarian Power* (Leeds, 2019)
Franklin, Simon, *Writing, Society and Culture in Early Rus', c. 950–1300* (Cambridge, 2002)

Franklin, Simon, and Jonathan Shepard, *The Emergence of Rus, 750–1200* (New York, 1996)
Giedroyć, Michał, 'The Arrival of Christianity in Lithuania: Between Rome and Byzantium, 1281–1341', *Oxford Slavonic Papers*, XX (1987), pp. 15–17
Gimbutas, Maria, 'Ancient Slavic Religion: A Synopsis', in *To Honor Roman Jakobsen: Essays on the Occasion of his Seventieth Birthday, 11 October 1966*, vol I: *738–59*, 3 vols (Mouton, 1967)
Golb, Norman, and Omeljan Pritsak, *Khazarian Hebrew Documents of the Tenth Century* (Ithaca, NY, 1982)
Gorovenko, A. V., *Mech Romana Galitskogo. Kniaz Roman Mstislavich v istorii, epose i legendakh* (St Petersburg, 2011)
—, 'Blesk i nishcheta genealogii', *Valla*, II/3 (2016), pp. 125–7
Gorskii, A. A., 'O dinasticheskikh sviaziakh pervykh Moskovskikh kniazei', *Drevniaia Rus'. Voprosy medievistiki*, no. 4(74) (2018), pp. 42–51
Granberg, Jonas, *Veche in the Chronicles of Medieval Rus: A Study of Functions and Terminology* (Gothenburg, 2004)
Gruber, Isaiah, *Orthodox Russia in Crisis: Church and Nation in the Time of Troubles* (DeKalb, IL, 2012)
Gumilev, Lev, *Drevniaia Rus i velikaia step* (Moscow, 1989)
Halperin, Charles J., 'The Concept of the Russian Land from the Ninth to the Fourteenth Centuries', *Russian History*, II/1 (1975), pp. 29–38
—, 'The Concept of the Russkaia Zemlia and Medieval National Consciousness from the Tenth to the Fifteenth Centuries', *Nationalities Papers*, VIII/1 (1980), pp. 75–86
—, 'Tsarev ulus: Russia in the Golden Horde,' *Cahiers du monde russe et soviétique*, XXIII/2 (1982), pp. 257–63
Haywood, John, *Historical Atlas of the Medieval World, AD 600–1492* (New York, 2000)
Hensorskyi, A. I., 'Redaktsii Halytsko-Volynskoho litopysu', *Doslidžennja z movy to literatury* (Kyiv, 1957), pp. 68–72
Hrushevsky, Mykhailo, 'Khronologiia podii Halytsko-Volynskoi litopysy', *Zapysky Naukovoho Tovarystva imeni Shevchenka*, XVI/3 (Lvov, 1901), pp. 1–72
—, *Istoriia Ukrainy-Rusy*, vol. III: *do Roku 1340*, 8 vols, 2nd edn (Lviv, 1905–13)
—, *History of Ukraine-Rus'*, vol. II: *The Eleventh to Thirteenth Centuries*, trans. Ian Press, ed. Christian Raffensperger and Frank E. Sysyn, with the translation and editorial assistance of Tania Plawuszczak-Stech (Edmonton and Toronto, 2020)
—, *History of Ukraine-Rus'*, vol. III: *To the Year 1340*, trans. Bohdan Strumiński, ed. Robert Romanchuk, with Uliana Pasicznyk and Marta Horban-Carynnyk (Toronto, 2016)
Huneycutt, Lois, 'Tamar of Georgia (1184–1213) and the Language of Female Power', in *A Companion to Global Queenship*, ed. Elena Woodacre (Leeds, 2018), pp. 27–38
Ianin, V. L., 'Medieval Novgorod', in *The Cambridge History of Russia*, vol. I: *From Early Rus' to 1689*, ed. Maureen Perrie (Cambridge, 2006), pp. 188–210

Ingham, Norman W., 'The Martyred Prince and the Question of Slavic Cultural Continuity in the Early Middle Ages', in *Medieval Russian Culture*, ed. Henrik Birnbaum and Michael S. Flier (Berkeley, CA, 1984), pp. 31–53

Ingham, Norman, and Christian Raffensperger, 'Rurik and the First Rurikids', *American Genealogist*, LXXXII/1 (2007), pp. 1–13 (part 1); LXXXII/2 (2007), pp. 111–19 (part 2)

Jackson, Peter, *The Mongols and the West, 1221–1410*, 2nd edn (Oxford, 2015)

Jusupovič, Adrian, *Kronika halicko-wołyńska (Kronika Romanowiczów) w latopisarskiej kolekcji historycznej* (Cracow–Warsaw, 2019)

Kaldellis, Anthony, *Streams of Gold, Rivers of Blood: The Rise and Fall of Byzantium, 955 AD to the First Crusade* (Oxford, 2017)

Kalechits, Inna L., 'Istoricheskie lichnosti v graffiti Polotskoi Spaso-Preobrazhenskoi tserkvi', www.youtube.com, accessed 7 November 2022

Karamzin, Nikolai M., *Istoriia gosudarstva rossiiskogo*, 12 vols, 5th edn (St Petersburg, 1842)

Karpov, Aleksei Iu., *Velikii kniaz' Aleksandr Nevskii* (Moscow, 2010)

Kazakova N. A., and Ia. S. Lur'e, *Antifeodal'nye ereticheskie dvizheniia na Rusi XIV–nachala XVI veka (AfED)* (Moscow and Leningrad, 1955)

Kivelson, Valerie A., and Ronald Grigor Suny, *Russia's Empire* (Oxford 2017)

Kliuchevskii, V. O., *A History of Russia*, trans. C. J. Hogarth, 5 vols (London, 1911), vol. I

—, *Kurs Russkoi istorii. Sochineniia v vos'mi tomakh* (Moscow, 1956–9)

Kollmann, Nancy Shields, 'The Cap of Monomakh', in *Picturing Russia: Explorations in Visual Culture*, ed. Valerie Kivelson and Joan Neuberger (New Haven, CT, 2008), pp. 38–41

Krupa, Katarzyna, 'Książęta Litewscy w Nowogrodzie Wielkim do 1430 roku', *Kwartalnik Historyczny*, C/1 (1993), pp. 29–46

Krypiakevych, Ivan, *Halytsko-Volynske kniazivstvo* (Kyiv, 1984)

Konev, S. B., 'Sinodikologiia. Chast' II: Rostovskii sobornyi sinodik', *Istoricheskaia genealogiia* (Ekaterinburg), 6 (1995), pp. 7–15

Kuchkin, V. A., *Povesti o Mikhaile Tverskom* (Moscow, 1974)

Lattimore, Owen, *Inner Asian Frontiers of China* (New York, 1940)

LeDonne, John P., 'The Geopolitical Context of Russian Foreign Policy, 1700–1917', *Acta Slavica Iaponica*, XII (1994), pp. 1–23

—, *The Russian Empire and the World, 1700–1917: The Geopolitics of Expansion and Containment* (Oxford, 1997)

Likhachev, D. S., *Russkie letopisi i ikh kul'turno-istoricheskoe znachenie* (Moscow–Leningrad, 1947)

Lind, John, 'The "Brotherhood of Rus": A Pseudo-Problem Concerning the Origin of "Rus"', *Slavica Othiniensia*, V (1982), pp. 66–81

Litvina, A. F., and F. B. Uspenskii, *Vybor imeni u russkikh kniazei v X–XVI vv. Dinasticheskaia istoriia skvoz' prizmu antroponimiki* (Moscow, 2006)

Lure, Ia. S., *Dve istorii Rusi XV veka. Rannie i pozdnie, nezavisimye i ofitsial'nye letopisi ob obrazovanii Moskovskogo gosudarstva* (St Petersburg, 1994)

—, 'Fifteenth-Century Chronicles as a Source for the History of the Formation of the Muscovite State', in *Medieval Russian Culture*,

ed. Michael S. Flier and Daniel Rowland, 2 vols (Berkeley, CA, 1994), vol. II, pp. 47–56
McCullough, David, *Brave Companions: Portraits in History* (New York, 1992)
Mägi, Marika, *The Viking Eastern Baltic* (Leeds, 2019)
Maiorov, A. V., *Galitsko-Volynskaia Rus': Ocherki sotsial'no-politicheskikh otnoshenii v domongol'skii period* (St Petersburg, 2001)
Makarii (Bulgakov), Mitropolit, *Istoriia russkoi tserkvi*, 12 vols (St Petersburg, 1857–83)
Martin, Janet, *Medieval Russia, 980–1584*, 2nd edn (Cambridge, 2007)
Martin, Russell E., 'Gifts for the Bride: Dowries, Diplomacy, and Marriage Politics in Muscovy', *Journal of Medieval and Early Modern Studies*, XXXVIII/1 (2008), pp. 119–45
—, *A Bride for the Tsar: Bride-Shows and Marriage Politics in Early Modern Russia* (DeKalb, IL, 2012)
—, *The Tsar's Happy Occasion: Ritual and Dynasty in the Weddings of Russia's Rulers, 1495–1745* (Ithaca, NY, 2021)
Mavrodin, V. V., *Proiskhozhdenie russkogo naroda* (Leningrad, 1978)
May, Timothy, *The Mongol Art of War: Chinggis Khan and the Mongol Military System* (Yardley, 2007)
—, 'Color Symbolism in the Turko-Mongolian World', in *The Use of Color in History, Politics, and Art*, ed. Sungshin Kim (Dahlonega, GA, 2016), pp. 51–77
Meyendorff, John, 'Alexis and Roman: A Study in Byzantine-Russian Relations (1352–1354)', *Byzantinoslavica*, XXVIII/2 (1967), pp. 278–88
—, *Byzantium and the Rise of Russia* (Cambridge, 1980)
Mikhailova, Yulia, *Property, Power, and Authority in Rus and Latin Europe, ca. 1000–1236* (Leeds, 2018)
Monfasani, John, 'Pletho's Date of Death and the Burning of His Laws', *Byzantinische Zeitschrift*, XCVIII/2 (2006), pp. 459–63
Murray, Alexander Callander, *Germanic Kinship Structure: Studies in Law and Society in Antiquity and the Early Middle Ages* (Toronto, 1983)
Nazarenko, A. V., *Drevniaia Rus' na mezhdunarodnykh putiakh: Mezhdistsiplinarnye ocherki kul'turnykh, torgovykh, politicheskikh sviazei IX–XII vekov* (Moscow, 2001)
Necipoğlu, Nevra, *Byzantium between the Ottomans and the Latins: Politics and Society in the Late Empire* (Cambridge, 2009)
New Directions in Anthropological Kinship, ed. Linda Stone (New York, 2000)
Nikolskii, Evgenii, 'O kanonizatsii sviatoi blagovernoi velikoi kniagini Iulianii Aleksandrovny Tverskoi i Litovskoi', *#muzeemaniia*, 6 December 2018, https://muzeemania.ru
Noonan, Thomas, 'Forging a National Identity: Monetary Politics during the Reign of Vasilii I (1389–1425)', in *Culture and Identity in Muscovy, 1359–1584*, ed. Ann M. Kleimola and Gail D. Lenhoff (Moscow, 1997), pp. 495–529
Nowakowska, Natalia, 'What's in a Word? The Etymology and Historiography of Dynasty – Renaissance Europe and Beyond', *Global Intellectual History*, VII/3 (7 August 2020), pp. 453–74

Obolensky, Dimitri, 'Some Notes Concerning a Byzantine Portrait of John VIII Palaeologus', *Eastern Churches Review*, IV/2 (1972), pp. 141–6

Orlov, A. S., *Drevniaia russkaia literatura* XI–XVI *vv.* (Moscow–Leningrad, 1937)

Ostrowski, Donald, 'Second-Redaction Additions in Carpini's *Ystoria Mongalorum*', *Harvard Ukrainian Studies*, XIV/3–4 (December 1990), pp. 522–50

—, 'The Mongol Origins of Muscovite Political Institutions', *Slavic Review*, XLIX/4 (1990), pp. 525–42

—, 'Why Did the Metropolitan Move from Kiev to Vladimir in the Thirteenth Century?', in *Christianity and the Eastern Slavs*, vol. I: *Slavic Cultures in the Middle Ages*, ed. Boris Gasparov and Olga Raevsky-Hughes, *California Slavic Studies*, vol. XVI (Berkeley, CA, 1993), pp. 83–101.

—, 'The Tamma and the Dual-Administrative Structure of the Mongol Empire', *Bulletin of the School of Oriental and African Studies*, LXI (1998), pp. 262–77

—, *Muscovy and the Mongols: Cross-Cultural Influences on the Steppe Frontier* (Cambridge, 1998)

—, 'Muscovite Adaptation of Steppe Political Institutions A Reply to Halperin's Objections', *Kritika: Explorations in Russian and Eurasian History*, I (2000), pp. 267–304

—, 'Military Mobilization by the Muscovite Grand Princes (1313–1533)', in *The Military and Society in Russia, 1450–1917*, ed. Eric Lohr and Marshall Poe (Leiden, 2002), pp. 19–40

—, 'Ruling Class Structures of the Kazan' Khanate', in *The Turks*, ed. Hasan Celâl Güzel, C. Cem Oğuz and Osman Karatay, 6 vols (Ankara, 2002), vol. II, pp. 841–7

—, 'The Assembly of the Land (Zemskii sobor) as a Representative Institution', in *Modernizing Muscovy: Reform and Social Change in Seventeenth-Century Russia*, ed. Jarmo Kotilaine and Marshall Poe (London, 2004), pp. 117–42

—, 'The Extraordinary Career of Tsarevich Kudai Kul/Peter in the Context of Relations between Muscovy and Kazan', in *States, Societies, Cultures: East and West: Essays in Honor of Jaroslaw Pelenski*, ed. Janusz Duzinkiewicz, Myroslav Popovych, Vladyslav Verstiuk and Natalia Yakovenko (New York, 2004), pp. 697–719

—, 'The Account of Volodimer's Conversion in the *Povest' vremennykh let*: A Chiasmus of Stories', *Harvard Ukrainian Studies*, XXVIII/1–4 (2010), pp. 567–80

—, 'Systems of Succession in Rus' and Steppe Societies,' *Ruthenica*, IX (2012), pp. 29–58

—, '"Dressing a Wolf in Sheep's Clothing": Toward Understanding the Composition of the *Life of Alexander Nevskii*', in *Centers and Peripheries in the Christian East: Papers from the Second Biennial Conference of the Association for the Study of Eastern Christian History and Culture*, ed. Eugene Clay, Russell Martin and Barbara Skinner, *Russian History*, XL (2013), pp. 41–67

—, 'The Return of the Rhos: Patria, Chacanus, and the *Annales Bertiniani* s.a. 839', *Canadian–American Slavic Studies*, LII (2018), pp. 290–311
—, 'Was There a Riurikid Dynasty in Early Rus'?', *Canadian–American Slavic Studies*, LII (2018), pp. 30–49
—, *Russia in the Early Modern World: The Continuity of Change* (Lanham, MD, 2022)
—, 'The Debate over the Authorship of the Rus' Primary Chronicle: Compilations, Redactions, and Urtexts', in *Identity*, vol. V: *The Emergence of New Peoples and Polities in Europe, 1000–1300*, ed. Walter Pohl, Francescro Borri and Veronika Wieser (Turnhout, 2022).
Parkin, David, *Kinship: An Introduction to the Basic Concepts* (New York, 1997)
Pashuto, V. T., *Ocherki po istorii Galitsko-Volynskoi Rusi* (Moscow, 1950)
Paszkiewicz, Henryk, *The Origin of Russia* (London, 1954)
Pelenski, Jaroslaw, 'The Contest between Lithuania-Rus' and the Golden Horde in the Fourteenth Century for Supremacy over Eastern Europe', *Archiwum Eurasiae Medii Aevi*, 2 (1982), pp. 303–20
Polonska-Vasylenko, Natalia, *Two Conceptions of the History of Ukraine and Russia*, ed. Wolodymyr Mykula (London, 1968)
Poppe, Andrzej, 'The Political Background to the Baptism of Rus': Byzantine-Russian Relations between 986–89', in *The Rise of Christian Russia* (London, 1982), pp. 197–244
—, 'Leontios, Abbot of Patmos, Candidate for the Metropolitan See of Rus'', in *Christian Russia in the Making* (Aldershot and Burlington, VT, 2007), pp. 1–13
Priselkov, M. D., *Troitskaia letopis'. Rekonstruktsiia teksta* (Moscow–Leningrad, 1950)
Pritsak, Omeljan, 'The Polovcians and Rus'', *Archivum Eurasiae medii aevi*, II (1982), pp. 321–80
—, 'Introduction', in *The Old Rus' Kyivan and Galician-Volhynian Chronicles: The Ostroz'kyj (Xlebnikov) and četvertyns'kyj (Pogodin) codices* (Cambridge, MA, 1990), pp. xv–xxxvii
Raffensperger, Christian, 'Shared (Hi)Stories: Vladimir of Rus' and Harald Fairhair of Norway', *Russian Review*, LXVIII/4 (2009), pp. 569–82
—, 'Dynastic Marriage in Action: How Two Rusian Princesses Changed Scandinavia', in *Imenoslov: Istoriia iazyka. Istoriia kul'tury*, ed. F. B. Uspenskij (Moscow, 2010), pp. 193–205
—, *Reimagining Europe: Kievan Rus' in the Medieval World* (Cambridge, MA, 2012)
—, 'Iziaslav Iaroslavich's Excellent Adventure: Constructing Kinship to Gain and Regain Power in Eleventh-Century Europe', *Medieval Prosopography*, XXX (2015), pp. 1–30
—, *Ties of Kinship: Genealogy and Dynastic Marriage in Kyivan Rus'* (Cambridge, MA, 2016)
—, *Conflict, Bargaining, and Kinship Networks in Medieval Eastern Europe* (Lanham, MD, 2018)
—, 'Mykhailo Hrushevsky and the Construction of the Medieval History of Rus'', *Harvard Ukrainian Studies*, XXXVIII/1–2 (2021), pp. 71–86

—, 'Runaway Rulers: Marriage, Power, and Building a Wider Medieval Europe', *Royal Studies Journal*, VIII/2 (2021), pp. 55–75

Rayfield, Donald, *Edge of Empires: A History of Georgia* (London, 2012)

Rochcau, Georges, 'Innocent IV devant le péril tatar: ses lettres à Daniel de Galicie et à Alexandre Nevsky', *Istina*, VI (1959), pp. 167–86

Romanova, O. V., 'O khronologii Galitsko-Volynskoi letopis XIII v. po Ipatevskomy spisku', in *Proshloe Novgorod i Novgorodskoi zemli. Materialy konferentsii 11–13 noiabria 1997 goda* (Novgorod, 1997)

Rosenwein, Barbara H., *Generations of Feeling: A History of Emotions, 600–1700* (Cambridge, 2015)

Rowell, S. C., *Lithuania Ascending: A Pagan Empire within East-Central Europe, 1295–1345* (Cambridge, 1994)

Rowland, Daniel, 'The Problem of Advice in Muscovite Tales about the Time of Troubles', *Russian History*, VI/2 (1979), pp. 359–83

—, 'Towards an Understanding of the Political Ideas in Ivan Timofeyev's *Vremennik*', *Slavonic and East European Review*, LXII/3 (July 1984), pp. 371–99

Rusinov, V. N., 'Letopisnye stat'i 1051–1117 gg. v sviazi s problemoi avtorstva i redaktsii "Povesti vremennykh let"', *Vestnik Nizhegorodskogo universiteta im. N. I. Lobachevskogo. Seriia istoriia, politilogiia, mezhdunarodnye otnosheniia*, I/2 (2003), pp. 123–38

Schmid, Karl, 'Zur Problematik von Familie, Sippe und Geschlect, Haus und Dynastie beim mittelalterlichen Adel', *Zeitschrift für die Geschichte des Oberrheins*, CV (1957), pp. 1–62

Seleznev, Iurii, *Russkie kniazi pri dvore khanov Zolotoi Ordy* (Moscow, 2019)

Senyk, Sophia, *A History of the Church in Ukraine*, vol. II: *1300 to the Union of Brest* (Rome, 2011)

Shepard, Jonathan, 'Why Did the Russians Attack Byzantium in 1043?', *Byzantinisch-Neugriechische Jahrbücher*, ed. Nikos A. Bees, vol. XXII (Athens, 1985), pp. 147–212

Stefanovich, Petr, 'Politicheskoe razvitie Galitsko-Volynskoi Rusi v 1240–1340 gg. i otnosheniia s Ordoi', *Rossiiskaia istoriia*, IV (2019), pp. 116–34

Tatishchev, V. N., *Istoriia Rossiiskaia*, 7 vols (Moscow, 1964)

Tikhomirov, M. N., 'Iz "Vladimirskogo letopistsa"', *Istoricheskie zapiski*, XV (1945), pp. 278–300

—, *Drevnaia Moskva (XII–XV vv.)* (Moscow, 1947)

—, 'Zabytye i neizvestnye proizvedeniia russkoi pis'mennosti,' *Arkheograficheskii ezhegodnik za 1960 g.* (Moscow, 1962), pp. 234–43

—, *Russkoe letopisanie* (Moscow, 1979)

Tolochko, Oleksii, *'Istoriia Rossiiskaia' Vasiliia Tatishcheva: Istochniki i izvestiia* (Kyiv, 2005)

Torres Prieto, Susana, 'Anna Porphyrogenita, Byzantine Princess and Queen of the Rus'', in *Portraits of Medieval Eastern Europe*, ed. Donald Ostrowski and Christian Raffensperger (New York, 2018), pp. 159–65

Trubetskoi [I. R.], Nikolai, *Nasledie Chingiskhana. Vzgliad na russkuiu istoriiu ne s Zapada, a s Vostka* (Berlin, 1925)

Tschizewskij, D., 'Zum Stil der Galizisch-Volynischen Chronik', *Südostforschungen*, XII (1953), pp. 79–109

Urban, William, *The Last Years of the Teutonic Knights: Lithuania, Poland and the Teutonic Order* (Barnsley, 2019)
Uzhankov, A. N., '"Letopitsa Daniila Galitskogo". Redaktsii, vremia sozdaniia', *Germenevtika drevnerusskoi literatury*, I (1989), pp. 248–83
Vernadsky, George, *The Mongols and Russia* (New Haven, CT, 1953)
—, *Russia at the Dawn of the Modern Age* (New Haven, CT, 1959)
—, *Kievan Russia*, 2nd edn (New Haven, CT, 1976)
Voitovych, Leontii V., 'Iurii Lvovych i ioho polityka', in *Halychyna ta Volyn u dobu serednovichchia, do 800-richchia z dnia narodzhenna Danyla Halytskoho* (Lviv, 2001)
—, *Halytsko-Volynski etiudy* (Bila Tserkva, 2011)
Voyce, Arthur, *The Art and Architecture of Medieval Russia* (Norman, 1967)
Worth, Dean S., 'A Problem of Dating in the Galician-Volhynian Chronicle', in *On the Structure and History of Russian: Selected Essays* (Munich, 1977), pp. 221–36
Wozniak, Frank Edward Jr, 'The Nature of Byzantine Foreign Policy toward Kievan Russia in the First Half of the Tenth Century: A Reassessment', PhD dissertation, Stanford University, 1973
Yazdi, Sharaf ad-Din Ali, *The History of Timur-Bec: Known by the Name of Tamerlain the Great, Emperor of the Moguls and Tartars: being an historical journal of his conquests in Asia and Europe*, 2 vols (London, 1723)
Zagraevskii, S. V., 'K voprosu o proiskhozhdenii prozvishcha kniazia Andreia Bogoliubskogo i nazvaniia goroda Bogoliubova', in *Materialy XVIII mezhdunarodnoi kraevedcheskoi konferentsii (19 April 2013)*, ed. A. K. Tikhonov, M. A. Barashev, I. V. Mishina and M. I. Novikova (Vladimir, 2014), pp. 9–16
Zajac, Talia, 'The Social-Political Roles of the Princess in Kyivan Rus, *c.* 945–1240', in *A Companion to Global Queenship*, ed. Elena Woodacre, pp. 125–46 (Leeds, 2018)
—, 'Remembrance and Erasure of Objects Belonging to Rus' Princesses in Medieval Western Sources: The Cases of Anastasia Iaroslavna's "Saber of Charlemagne" and Anna Iaroslavna's Red Gem', in *Moving Women, Moving Objects (400–1500)*, ed. Tracy Chapman Hamilton and Mariah Proctor-Tiffany (Leiden, 2019), pp. 33–58
Zastrow, Mark, 'Human + Nature according to Werner Herzog', *Discover: Science That Matters*, XLII/3 (May 2021), pp. 44–9.
Zatko, James J., 'The Union of Suzdal, 1222–1252', *Journal of Ecclesiastical History*, VIII/1 (April 1957), pp. 33–52
Zimin, A. A., 'Pamiat' i pokhvala Iakova mnikha i Zhitie kniazia Vladimira po drevneishemu spisku', *Kratkie soobshcheniia Instituta slavianovedeniia*, XXXVII (1963), pp. 13–22
—, *Formirovanie boiarskoi aristokratii v Rossii. Vo vtoroi polovine XV–pervoi treti XVI v.* (Moscow, 1988)

ACKNOWLEDGEMENTS

Acknowledgements typically consist of giving thanks, and there are plenty of people to whom I offer my gratitude. I would like to thank Michael Leaman for reaching out and beginning the process that led to this book, as well as for his supportive encouragement throughout.

I would like to give special thanks to my co-author Donald Ostrowski. Without him, this book would not have been written. I am incredibly grateful for his encouragement, support and willingness to take on large amounts of work to make this book a reality. While vast troves of citations did not make it into the finished book due to space constraints, I want to thank David Miller and David Das, in particular, whose generosity endowed me with numerous books to which I would otherwise not have had easy access. The presence of their books in my library made it so much easier for me to find the information I needed for the writing of this book. Similarly, my excellent colleagues, who are scattered throughout Europe, sent copies of books or articles for this and other publications. Dariusz Dąbrowski's work on genealogy is an excellent example of such generosity, and it has come in most handy.

Work on this book was largely conducted during my sabbatical from Wittenberg University, and so due thanks must go to the university for granting me that sabbatical, as well as to the members of the History Department for agreeing to do without me for a semester. I would also like to acknowledge the National Humanities Center, where I was made an Archie K. Davis Fellow in spring 2022.

This book entered production during Vladimir Putin's horrific invasion of Ukraine in spring 2022. Colleagues whose books we have read and cited, whom we know and consider friends, who have contributed to this volume and to our scholarship in manifold ways, are now in a warzone, fighting for their lives and the future of their country. The ramifications of this war are unfolding around the world; it has also had a tremendous impact on the scholarship of the period explored in this book. Vladimir Putin cares about history; he believes that Rus is Russia and that this gives him the right to invade the modern nation of Ukraine. Such a misguided use of history makes our task, the task of all historians, even more important in these troubled times. Rus, as this book aims to show, is solely Rus. It is not Russia, but neither is it Ukraine or Belarus. The ruling families of Rus are the ancestors of the modern nation-states of Ukraine, Belarus and Russia, and are not the sole property of any of these three.

C. R.

First and foremost, I must acknowledge Chris Raffensperger's willingness to take me on as a co-author in this project. The entire conceptualization was Chris's. He had already written the complete book proposal and had submitted it when he allowed me to come on board so that I could focus on a few areas in which I claim to have some expertise.

We also need to thank the Harvard Ukrainian Research Institute for allowing us to give a presentation at a HURI seminar of our yet-unwritten work on 24 March 2021, and to thank those who helped make the talk a success: Megan Duncan Smith, Kristina Conroy and Michael Flier.

In addition, I need to express my personal gratitude to several individuals who read parts or all of the manuscript and provided valuable commentary: David Goldfrank, Charles Halperin, Ian Mladjov and Russell Martin. Thank you.

Finally, I concur completely with the sense of outrage that Chris expresses about the delusional misuse of history to justify the stupid, barbaric and destructive invasion of an independent country. It was especially disheartening to receive news updates while we were studying the evidence and bibliographic sources of that history and to see how this evidence has been willingly ignored for crass, political reasons.

D. O.

PHOTO ACKNOWLEDGEMENTS

The authors and publishers wish to thank the relevant organizations and individuals listed below for authorizing reproduction of their work.

Alamy: 55 (Archive Collection), 59 (Album), 62 (Heritage Image Partnership); authors: 8, 9, 16, 21, 27, 30, 36, 41, 42, 43, 48, 50, 54, 58; M. Gumowski, 'Pieczecie Ksiazat Litewskich', *Ateneum wileńskie*, VII/44 (1930), pp. 709–10: 47; Samuel Hazzard Cross, *Medieval Russian Churches*, ed. Kenneth John Conant (Cambridge, MA, 1949): 25; courtesy of V. L. Ianin: 7, 10, 11, 17, 19; Maria Lavrenchenko: 23; www.ma-shops.com/wallinmynt: 52; Metropolitan Museum of Art, New York: 12 (Gift of J. Pierpont Morgan, 1917), 38 (Purchase, Arthur Ochs Sulzberger Gift, by exchange, 2007); Béla Nagy: 4; public domain: 7, 8, 9, 15, 24, 26, 28, 31, 34, 35, 40, 44, 45, 46, 49, 51, 53, 56, 57, 60, 61; Karen Swain/NC Museum of Natural Sciences: 37; © Trustees of the British Museum: 13, 18, 20, 22; Vasilii Petrovich Vereshchagin: 39 (public domain); Myroslav Voloshchuk: 29, 32; Wikimedia Commons: 6 (Vash Alex kun/public domain), 14 (George Chernilevsky/public domain), 33 (Qiushufang/CC BY-SA 4.0); Yale University Art Gallery: 5.

INDEX

Illustration numbers are indicated in *italics*